CHOOSING A COLLEGE PRESIDENT

A SPECIAL REPORT

Choosing a College President
OPPORTUNITIES AND CONSTRAINTS

JUDITH BLOCK McLAUGHLIN AND DAVID RIESMAN

WITH A FOREWORD BY
ERNEST L. BOYER

THE CARNEGIE FOUNDATION
FOR THE ADVANCEMENT OF TEACHING

5 IVY LANE, PRINCETON, NEW JERSEY 08540

Library of Congress Cataloging-in-Publication Data

McLaughlin, Judith Block, 1948–
    Choosing a college president : opportunities and constraints / Judith Block McLaughlin
and David Riesman ; with a foreword by Ernest L. Boyer.
        p.   cm.
    Includes bibliographical references and index.
    ISBN 0-931050-40-5
    1. College presidents—United States—Selection and appointment.
2. College presidents—United States—Selection and appointment—Case studies.
I. Riesman, David, 1909–   . II. Title.
LB2341.M365   1990
378.1'11—dc20   90-47689

Copies are available from the
PRINCETON UNIVERSITY PRESS
3175 Princeton Pike
Lawrenceville, New Jersey 08648

To Ted McLaughlin and Evelyn Riesman

CONTENTS

ACKNOWLEDGMENTS

THIS BOOK had its origins in 1980, somewhere over New England, in a conversation on an airplane flight from Toronto to Boston. The two of us had just attended a meeting of the National Academy of Education. Judith McLaughlin was then serving as executive director of this association; David Riesman was one of the Academy's founding members. A doctoral student at the Harvard Graduate School of Education, Judith McLaughlin was writing her dissertation on the subject of confidentiality and disclosure in the presidential search, a topic in which David Riesman had long been interested.

This chance discovery of our mutual interest in the search process for college and university presidents led to a collaboration on research and writing that has lasted more than ten years. And this volume is in every sense a collaborative effort. The discussion chapters in particular have been rewritten and revised so many times that no paragraph remains which is of one authorship only. *Choosing a College President* is a blend of our data, analyses, and writing, and the book has grown out of this synthesis of our individual contributions.

But, while this book began with a conversation between two people, it is the out-growth of conversations with many, many others. During our ten years of studying searches, we have spoken and corresponded with literally hundreds of people, whose accounts of their experiences have furthered our understanding of the dynamics of the presidential search and the larger issues of leadership and governance. In this Acknowledgments section, we want to thank all of these people, without whose generosity in sharing their experiences and insights this book could not have come into being.

From the beginning of our joint research, we agreed on the crucial question of confidentiality, not only as a topic of inquiry in higher education and in the wider society, but also as a mandate to ourselves in proceeding with our inquiry. We promised informants to keep confidential what we learned from them, scrupulously checking with individuals before we cited them concerning something they had told us. Correspondingly, we cannot acknowledge here by name the wonderfully cooperative trustees, faculty members, administrators, students, and journalists who helped us to understand the search processes in which they were participants or observers. In many cases, these people spent several hours in interviews with one or both of us, and then additional time reviewing early drafts of our stories about their searches. Similarly, we will not name here individually the countless candidates for presidential positions with whom we have spoken, both those who were successful and those who were not (and many of the latter became, eventually, one of the former), with whom we have spoken, but we are much indebted to them for their candor, reflections, and time.

Early in our work together, we discovered what today can be called the consultant industry, that is, those individuals whose line of work involves advising boards of trustees and search committees on the search and selection process. As we came to know some of the more observant search consultants, we found them to be valuable resources to aid our own understanding of the search process. Ruth Weintraub, the doyenne of search consultants in higher education, opened her files in her New York office to us when we were preparing our account of the Winthrop College search, which she and her staff assisted. Frederic Ness, Ronald Stead, Shirley Chater, Christine Young, and their associates in the Academic Search Consultation Service have been particularly helpful to us over the years in thinking aloud about the issues of searching and the use of consultants in this endeavor. We have learned much from long conversations with Nancy Archer-Martin, Kenneth Langstaff, Millington McCoy, William Bowen, William Tipping, Raymond Klemmer, Ira Krinsky, Richard Lancaster, Maria Perez, Charles Neff, Charles Fisher, and John Isaacson, all alike in their willingness to share with us the stories of their consultations and in their desire to think aloud about how to improve the practice of searching for leadership. We are grateful to Stephen Garrison, Harry Marmion, Charles Nelson, and John Synodinos for their thoughtful reviews of our chapter drafts on the use of consultants in the presidential search process.

A few search committee chairs deserve special mention for their contributions to our work. Terry Peterson, chair of the Winthrop College search whose story is told in Chapter VIII, and Mary Sue McElveen, chair of the Winthrop board of trustees at the time of that search, hosted Judith McLaughlin in South Carolina. They gave her permission to proceed with interviewing members of the search committee, helped her to make arrangements for these conversations, and read and reread drafts of the Winthrop case. Ralph O'Connor, chair of the Rice search process, was generous in helping us understand the Rice University search. Robert Aller, co-chair of the Antioch College board of trustees and co-chair of the Antioch search committee, helped us understand the way he was able to navigate in order to maintain confidentiality, despite Antioch's long tradition of participatory governance. Judith Eissner, Skidmore's board chair, shared with us her experiences with the Skidmore search, illustrating the way in which a search consultant can be of great assistance in the final stages of the search process, especially in the negotiations with the prospective incumbent. Ellis Verink, chair of the 1983 University of Florida advisory committee, spoke at length with Judith McLaughlin about searching in the sunshine, describing in detail the work he and his committee had done.

Our understanding of the Florida story has also been aided greatly by exchanges with Barbara Newell, former chancellor of the Florida system of higher education, and Ulric Haynes, Jr., who shared with us his study of the impact of the Florida sunshine proceedings in the search for a new president for Florida International University in 1987. Both of us enjoyed many long telephone conversations with Jack Wheat, education writer for the *Gainesville Sun*, and we learned a great deal from his considerable knowledge about and thoughtful perceptions of the state of higher education in Florida. J. Wayne Reitz, president emeritus of the University of Florida, kept us apprised of legislative efforts to remove college and university presidential searches from the mandates of Florida's open meeting law, a cause in which he has been indefatigable. To Seymour and Gertrude Block, Judith McLaughlin's parents, both at the University of Florida, we owe special thanks for their keeping us regularly supplied with newspaper stories about developments in Florida searches, serving as our Florida clipping service.

Many other individuals have stimulated our thinking about the issues treated in this book and helped us find support for our work. We would be remiss if we did not mention here Anne Alexander, Robert Birnbaum, Ernest Boyer, Richard Chait, William E. (Bud) Davis, Nicholas Farnham, Thomas North Gilmore, Vartan Gregorian, Gregory Jackson, Clark Kerr, Virginia Lester, Arthur Levine, Ralph Lundgren, Michael Maccoby, Martin Meyerson, Robert Payton, and Robert Scott. We also owe thanks to Stephen J. Trachtenberg, who seems somehow to read almost everything that appears in the media concerning higher education, and has relayed to us many items of interest.

Special thanks is owed to four people who read and commented upon a complete draft of this manuscript. Because we are great admirers of their writing on higher education, we sought advice on ours from Marian Gade, Zelda Gamson, Joseph Kauffman, and Martin Trow, and their criticisms and suggestions substantially strengthened this volume.

Extra special thanks goes to Verne Stadtman, the editor of this volume. Verne's advice on matters large and small, from treatment of major issues to detailed line editing, was immensely important in earlier and later drafts of the manuscript. We also wish to acknowledge the editorial assistance of Jan Hempel at The Carnegie Foundation for the Advancement of Teaching, of Patricia Marks who works with Carnegie, the logistical help of Linda Snook and Margaret Caragannopoulous, and the Department of Sociology of Harvard University.

This book took shape over many years, the result of hundreds of pages of interview notes, and thousands of pages of chapter drafts. All of these were typed by Martha Fuller, whose support—editorial, clerical, logistical, and moral—has been enormously important to both of us. We have learned much from her throughout the course of our work.

Our work was made possible by the financial assistance of many foundations and individuals. These include the Association of Governing Boards of Colleges and Universities, the AT&T Foundation, the Bullitt Foundation, the Ella Lyman Cabot Trust, Douglas Carmichael, the Carnegie Corporation, the Carnegie Foundation for the Advancement of

Teaching, Lewis A. Dexter, the Christian A. Johnson Endeavor Foundation, the Exxon Educational Foundation, the Ford Foundation, the Harman Foundation, the Institute for Educational Affairs, the Lilly Endowment, the Markle Foundation, the Mellon Foundation, and the Spencer Foundation. Additionally, we are grateful for the support of TIAA-CREF.

JUDITH BLOCK MCLAUGHLIN
DAVID RIESMAN
Cambridge, Massachusetts
July, 1990

FOREWORD

by Ernest L. Boyer

WHEN THE TIME COMES for a college or university to pick a new president, what role should the various campus constituencies play? How can the committee charged with this responsibility ensure broader participation while completing a successful search? What lessons lie in the experiences of the past?

Choosing a College President: Opportunities and Constraints is a timely and important book that sheds much light on what was once the most dimly lit hall of academe. We could not ask for wiser or more knowledgeable guides on this subject. Judith Block McLaughlin is currently educational chair for the Harvard Seminar for New Presidents, lecturer at the Harvard Graduate School of Education, and research associate in Harvard's Department of Sociology. She has worked closely with David Riesman to explore the limits and possibilities of the modern presidential search and has published numerous articles on this subject in professional journals, as well as articles on higher education governance.

David Riesman is an eminent sociologist whose lifetime of research and reflection on the American experience gives him a uniquely valuable vision of the broad issues underlying the details of academic life. His areas of study have included the sociology of higher education, intra- and interinstitutional competition and cooperation, and problems of financing and organizing higher education.

This book reveals the drama of the search, which begins at hundreds of campuses each year as presidents retire, accept other positions, or, less frequently, are asked to move on. The authors present rich case studies allowing the reader to join those conducting the presidential search and watch the participants improvise their roles, encounter disappointment, court catastrophe, and frequently celebrate success.

McLaughlin and Riesman remind us just how much an individual can shape a committee task that is inherently complicated and frustrating. Few colleges have worked out procedures in advance, so committees often start from scratch, with little institutional memory about how to organize themselves, how to select the groups to be represented, screen candidates, and choose the finalists to be invited to the campus.

One of McLaughlin's and Riesman's most important points is that a successful search must begin with—or quickly develop—a clear idea of the particular kind of leadership required. At various times in its history, the authors show, an institution may need a builder or a consolidator, an innovator or an interpreter, a navigator—or even a savior.

Right up front, then, the authors answer the most essential question: "Do leaders matter?"

McLaughlin and Riesman reject the popular conclusion that the power of the university presidency has all but disappeared, that presidents can't truly make a difference. They maintain that "there is a significant number of presidents who do change the course of the colleges and universities they head." At the same time, the authors acknowledge that the successes of presidents are "most visible at the margins, at those institutions enjoying flush times and those whose very survival is precarious."

This was not always so. In the early days, the mind of the American college was preeminently the mind of its president. Selected for an unlimited term, the president ordinarily served as the executive agent of the board of trustees. At the same time, he was the principal teacher of the college. In those days, many young tutors were inexperienced and "only the president could stand before the governing body as a mature man of learning."[1]

America's first colleges were small, easily managed, uncomplicated organizations. Consider that in 1850 the University of Michigan was one of the largest institutions in the nation; yet it had only twenty faculty members. Two decades later, the nation's colleges and universities still had, on average, about ten faculty members and ninety students.[2]

[1] Frederick Rudolph, *The American College and University: A History* (New York: Vintage Books, 1962), p. 165.
[2] Calculated from U.S. Bureau of the Census, *Historical Statistics of the United States, Colonial*

Gradually campuses became larger and more complex. By 1910, the number of students had quadrupled, and at some institutions—Michigan and Harvard, for example—enrollment soared to more than five thousand. Increasingly, administrative duties were delegated and assignments made more formal. First, librarians were hired, then registrars. Deans became common in the 1890s and, at about the same time, a few of the larger universities appointed their first vice-president.[3]

Arthur Twining Hadley, president of Yale from 1899 to 1921, observed a fascinating shift in the presidential role of his immediate predecessors. When Hadley visited Noah Porter, president of Yale from 1871 to 1886, he found him "reading Kant in his study." Later, he observed president Timothy Dwight, Porter's successor, "examining balance sheets in his office."[4]

With the rise of the modern university, the nation's most distinguished institutions of higher learning were led by a generation of builders. William Rainey Harper, David Starr Jordan, and Daniel Coit Gilman, through a rare combination of energy and intellect, determinedly—sometimes autocratically—directed the destinies of their institutions.

Following World War II, the dramatic expansion of American higher education was accompanied by an equally dramatic growth in administration. A veritable army of new specialists was hired—financial aid officers, computer-center directors, grant administrators, to name a few. The added layers, while essential, diluted the force of leadership as presidents became increasingly isolated from both academic and social functions on the campus.

Driven by the mandates of expansion, presidential attention has, in recent years, focused almost singlemindedly on the financial aspects of the institution. The modern president has become preoccupied with external constituencies—legislators, alumni, and donors—and presidents who get large legislative appropriations or complete big fund drives are hailed as "distinguished leaders."

Times to 1970. Bicentennial Edition, Part 1 (Washington, D.C.: 1975), pp. 382–385. Also J. Victor Baldridge *et al.*, *Policy Making and Effective Leadership* (San Francisco: Jossey-Bass, 1978), p. 253.

[3] Ibid.

[4] John L. Brubacher and Willis Rudy, *Higher Education in Transition: A History of American Colleges and Universities, 1636–1976* (New York: Harper & Row, 1976), pp. 365–366.

Academic concerns, once at the very heart of the president's role, have been delegated, almost entirely, to the dean or provost. Indeed, at many institutions, the chief academic officer is known as "the inside man," and that is where *educational* leadership is lodged. The president, in turn, is left with "outside" functions, which often are rather derisively referred to as the "Rotarian" aspects of campus life.

Given this dramatic shift in the nature of presidential leadership, how should search committees proceed? What experiences and special skills does the presidency now require?

For a brief period, committees flirted with the prospect of choosing businessmen because hard-nosed financial management was needed. More recently, a background in fund-raising is judged an asset—and such experience occasionally proves decisive when presidential candidates are screened.

While budgeting and courting donors are crucial, I'm convinced that a larger, more inspired vision of the presidency is required, and, in the coming decades, a vigorous educational and moral leadership will be needed to strengthen the spirit of community on campus, give a clear sense of direction to the enterprise, and bring personal integrity and creativity to the task.

Specifically, the president must become a more highly regarded *academic* leader and participate more actively—with the provost and the faculty—in key decisions. The president also should be viewed, once again, as the administrator concerned deeply about students, as well as about the overall quality of campus life.

At the same time, responsibility for fund-raising, which has become a large and highly specialized task, must be assigned increasingly to development officers, who should be held accountable for completion of the job. The president should keep a close eye on fund-raising, but this duty should not be all-consuming. What we imagine is a president who coordinates all efforts, not one who assumes responsibility for a single function.

The presidency, in its fullest, richest sense, must be reclaimed, and Judith Block McLaughlin and David Riesman have greatly clarified how to accomplish this objective. In *Choosing a College President*, the authors

xviii

make clear that the presidential search goes far beyond procedures. It is, they say, a crucial step in shaping the destiny of an institution.

As search committees use the tools described so clearly in this report, they will be empowered to choose presidents who are not only managerially well prepared, but also have the courage and vision to truly lead.

INTRODUCTION

SOME THREE TO FOUR HUNDRED presidential successions occur every year in America's two thousand baccalaureate-granting institutions. In some of these transitions, the outgoing president has enjoyed a long tenure and the institution is gearing up for a search for the first time in many years. More often these days, however, with the average tenure of college and university presidents at seven years,[1] trustees, administrators, and faculty members remember all too well the vicissitudes of the past search. In some cases, the trustees are determined to do this search better than the last one; in others, the board is satisfied with the previous experience and hopes to repeat the success. But just as no two colleges or universities are alike, no two presidential searches are the same, not even at the same institution. Each college or university has its own unique history of presidents and changes of leadership, of faculty involvement or inertia, of student participation or apathy, of alumni loyal to the point of hoarseness or indifferent to the point of somnolence. Some searches begin in strife and end in cohesiveness; some begin in confidentiality and end in damaging publicity; some searches are routine, but in many, the human drama follows no single script, and neither the process nor the outcome is routine. The particular blend of board authority and constituent participation, of campus cohesiveness or internal strife, of confidentiality and publicity, varies greatly from institution to institution and from search to search within the same institution.

This book examines searches for college and university presidents in all their variety and intricacy. We describe the practices and problems we have found as we have studied searches in widely varying locales, noting common patterns and concerns and the significant differences that reflect the particular contexts in which the search occurs. We analyze the issues

---

[1] Clark Kerr and Marian L. Gade, *The Many Lives of Academic Presidents: Time, Place and Character* (Washington, D.C.: AGB, 1986), p. 21.

and the dilemmas of the search process, in order to understand better the process of leadership transition in American higher education and the changing dynamics and political resonances of contemporary academic life. In many, if not most, searches, the exit of one president and the choice of another provides an opening in which assumptions about shared values are challenged and divergent moralities compete—moralities extant in the wider polity and culture. Hence, the search for a president serves as a microcosm of institutional politics and pressures. Like a projective test such as the Rorschach, searches reveal the internal complexities, the pathologies, and the strengths of a college or university. At times, the pathologies that become evident during the search are latent in the institution, whereas at other times the need for a search grows out of dissatisfaction with current leadership among influential faculty members, board members, and, more rarely today, student activists.

THE CHANGING SEARCH PROCESS

Transitions in the leadership of American colleges and universities share features with executive selection in both corporate and political life. In corporations large and small, the transition from one chief executive officer to another is generally a private affair, planned in advance of the actual changing of the guard. The president moves up and out to become chairman of the board, and a previously identified vice-president or chief operating officer becomes president. In instances where there is no heir-apparent, executive recruiting firms typically handle the search, identifying a small number of prospects for consideration by the exiting president and the executive committee of the board of directors. In the past, such searches have usually been brief, a matter of a few months. Most of them still are. In some very large corporations, however, traditional successions have been disrupted either by takeover battles launched by outsiders or by defensive maneuvers by management to limit the prospects for takeover. In the arenas where leveraged buyouts can occur, managements cannot so securely pass leadership from one person to another, to be noticed only in the financial pages.

If most corporate transitions receive little publicity, executive transitions in the American polity, which occur at electoral intervals, are always publicized. Rarely is there an heir apparent—whether a vice-president or lieutenant governor or, even more rarely, the wife of a deceased official— to succeed to the top position. In the American constitutional system of primaries and winner-take-all elections, candidates are chosen in intra-party coalitions, and then the determination of which candidates will become "finalists" is made in primary elections.

In an earlier day, the choice of political "finalists" to run against each other in the general election was made by party regulars and bosses, who, in a sense, were serving as the "trustees" of the prospects of their party. Their choice was made not only on the basis of which candidate had the most support from the regulars, the insiders, the stalwarts, but also reflected the outcome of sometimes acrimonious judgments as to which candidate would best vanquish an opponent from the other party.[2] Today, however, professional politicians, especially in the Democratic Party, no longer control party conventions. The indirect rule of party leaders has given way to more majoritarian patterns.[3] The result has been that the more plebiscitary the process of selecting candidates for political office, the more likely it is that each political party will end up with a candidate who can appeal to an activist and readily mobilized minority within the party, without much reference to the person's ability to win the general election.

Just as the political process of candidate selection has become more plebiscitary in recent years, the process of presidential selection in American higher education has moved farther away from the corporate mode and closer to the political mode of executive selection. In an earlier day, the selection of the college or university president was understood to be the exclusive prerogative of the institution's board of trustees. Faculty members or others connected with an institution might be consulted, but the

[2] Occasionally, as with the Democrats' nomination of William Jennings Bryan in 1896 pursuant to his impassioned "Cross of Gold" address, the national party could be swayed toward a candidate who had only a problematic chance for election, or the whole procedure could be disrupted, as when Theodore Roosevelt and his Bull Moose Party broke away from the Republican regulars, handing the election of 1912 to Woodrow Wilson. (The Goldwater candidacy of 1964 had some of this same quality.) But in the common run of political affairs, at the state level as well as nationally, the person chosen to run in the general election was not invariably the candidate that any one group of trustees would have preferred if their party had reasonably complete control of the state or the country, but was the least unacceptable person who, it was believed, could triumph in the general election.

[3] For further discussion, see Mona Harrington's analysis of majoritarian, localist, and functional political cultures in the United States in *The Dream of Deliverance in American Politics* (New York: Alfred A. Knopf, 1986).

selection itself took place quietly and privately, and was announced only afterward to the campus and community.[4] Today, in contrast, the search process at many public and private institutions more closely resembles a political contest. To be sure, academic protocol dictates that candidates for college and university presidencies do not campaign actively but wait to be "drafted" for the position, and, hence, those interested in a presidential opening typically do not apply for the job, but let it be known to colleagues that they would like to be nominated.[5] In one search we studied, a member of the search committee commented to us that she virtually disregarded any candidates who directly applied for the position, believing that if they did not understand the mores of academic searches at this level well enough to arrange to be nominated, then they also might not know the necessary social and academic requirements of a presidency. Many members of search committees fear those who seem overly ambitious or desirous of power, seeming to agree with Harold Stoke, who remarked in his 1959 classic on the presidency, "Those who enjoy exercising power shouldn't have it, and those who should exercise it are not likely to enjoy it."[6] Other search committee members, however, especially faculty members and students, have told us they like it when someone appears eager for the job. But even though candidates typically do not compete openly for the college or university presidency, the struggle among multiple constituencies for control of the process of selection has come more and more to resemble the political arena beyond the institution. Faculty factions compete with each other and with trustees for hegemony; students, alumni, administrators, nonprofessional staff, and advocacy groups inside and outside of the college or university demand representation on the

[4] This is not to say that the search process of an earlier day was necessarily simple or without controversy. We learned, however, only considerably after the fact (generally in presidential memoirs or biographies) of the conflicts and intrigues of the presidential selection. Henry Wriston's autobiography, *Academic Procession: Reflections of a College President* (New York: Columbia University Press, 1959), revealed the story of the selection of the president at Wesleyan long after the main actors had passed from the scene. James Bryant Conant's *My Several Lives: Memoirs of a Social Inventor* (New York: Harper and Row, 1970) tells the story of his own selection as successor to Abbott Lawrence Lowell, remarkable because of Lowell's fierce objection to Conant, who had criticized the whole Lowell outlook on Harvard, including the House Plan and its tutors.

[5] Presidential searches in community colleges differ in this regard. In this sector of American higher education, it is considered perfectly acceptable to put oneself forward directly as a candidate. Community college searches differ in other respects as well from four-year college and university searches, and are a universe we do not directly discuss in this book.

[6] Stoke, *The American College President* (New York: Harper and Brothers, 1959), p. 20.

search committee and participation in campus forums with those candidates whom the search committee has identified as finalists. If there has been controversy, some may interpret a transition in leadership as a chance to "throw the rascals out;" some alumni will see the search as an opportunity to restore the idyllic campus frozen in memory, while other alumni, along with others inside and outside, may seize the chance to make a statement that the institution is forward-looking, liberal and even risk-prone rather than staid. The search process can offer opportunities for veto groups to attempt to disrupt prospects for a consensual choice. Commonly, the nature and extent of the change a transition can bring may be overestimated, but that reality does not prevent the search process from becoming, both in public and private institutions, a clamorous and public spectacle.

When one compares a contemporary search with those that preceded it in the same institution, the changes in the process become fully apparent. Consider, for example, the process of presidential succession at "Abbott College," the private liberal arts college whose search for a fourteenth president we describe in Chapter II. Thirty-five years ago, when the twelfth president of "Abbott College" was chosen, several influential members of the board of trustees discussed among themselves who would be well suited for the presidency. When they arrived at a name they found mutually agreeable, they approached this man one night as he was having dinner at one of New York's more prestigious private clubs and offered him the position. Intrigued by the invitation, he was quickly persuaded to accept the presidency, and his appointment to the position was announced to the campus the next day. The faculty at "Abbott College" seemed reasonably satisfied with the selection. Had they not been, however, it would not have occurred to them to do more than grumble, for they accepted the premise that the selection of the college's chief executive officer was the exclusive prerogative of the board of trustees.

In 1969, when this president was ready to step down from office and a search committee of trustees was constituted to identify a successor, a new step was added to the selection process. The trustee search commitee asked the faculty to nominate prospective candidates for the presidency. This was the first time ever that Abbott faculty members had been asked to suggest names. Pleased by this new recognition, the faculty did not press to become more involved in the presidential succession.

While the Abbott College faculty still acknowledged the authority of the trustees to select the president of the college, other college and university faculties in 1969 were far less willing to do so. During the 1960s and 1970s, many colleges and universities—not only the protest-prone campuses—were being transformed. Thanks, first, to the GI Bill of Rights and then to the presence of the baby-boom generation who had reached college age, colleges and universities expanded greatly, and many more professors were needed to teach these large student bodies. Correspondingly, faculty members found that they possessed new leverage. Faculty bargaining power grew, in part reflected in unionization, and in much greater part reflected in rearrangements of campus governance that gave considerable, and in most matters exclusive, power over academic matters to the faculty.[7] All manner of new governance arrangements sprang up, such as the college council at Carleton College, which includes trustees, the president and vice-presidents and dean, elected faculty members, and elected students. The search committee, already a familiar device in selecting faculty members, increasingly became another form of shared governance, even at the presidential level.

By the end of the 1960s, a new sort of "revolution" was getting under way, particularly in the more selective "university colleges" of the west and east coasts. This so-called student revolution often had the rhetorical and sometimes even the tactical and physical support of ardent faculty members. Civil rights activists and anti-war protesters brought issues of student power into the struggles for campus hegemony. The temporal juxtaposition of the increasing leverage of faculty and the visibility of student revolts had the consequence of developing a norm in which not only faculty members were included on presidential search committees, but one or more students as well.[8]

[7] In their book, *The Academic Revolution* (Garden City, New York: Doubleday and Company, 1968), Jencks and Riesman identify the rise of the faculty as the principal power in college and university life, triumphing not only in the eminent but also in many less visible institutions over the former power of trustees, clerical orders, and state governmental authorities.

[8] To reread in 1988 the criteria developed by the Harvard Corporation for a president to be chosen to succeed Nathan Pusey in 1971 is startling. It was not to be a participatory search in terms of creating a search committee that would include members beyond the governing boards. However, Francis Burr, senior fellow of the Corporation, was to consult extensively with faculty members and with students,

Consequently, in 1984, when the Abbott trustees prepared to search for the college's fourteenth president, they realized that all-trustee searches were an anachronism at Abbott College, as at practically every other college or university on the landscape of American higher education. The faculty would have to be involved in some manner if the search were to be seen as legitimate. After consulting with leaders of the faculty, the Abbott College trustees assembled a fourteen-member search committee which included seven trustees, five faculty members chosen by the faculty, and two students chosen by the student government. No longer was the determination of the presidency to be made over dinner at an all-male New York club. No longer were the candidates all white males, either. The slate of finalists was seen by students and faculty as making a political statement about changes that had taken place and were desired in the image and ethos of the college.

Throughout the course of the Abbott College search, the faculty members and the trustee members of the search committee struggled with the question of how much confidentiality and disclosure were desirable. Faculty members were willing to keep the names of candidates secret until a slate of finalists was chosen, but they wanted a promise from the trustees that these finalists would be invited to the campus to meet in open forums with the entire faculty. Many of the trustees on the search committee believed that confidentiality should be maintained until the full board had made its selection, in other words, that no one except for the members of the search committee and the board should ever know the identities of any candidates other than the new president. The faculty members' insistence on open forums was especially strong because of their fear that the board of trustees would pursue a "corporate" succession strategy and choose the acting president, a man with a background in finance and not in academic life.[9] The faculty wanted, instead, to pursue a course that was more polit-

---

and for months he did so. Perhaps of greater significance was the emphasis of the criteria on finding a president who could and would relate to and be concerned with Harvard College undergraduates. That emphasis was reflected in the selection of Derek Bok, not an alumnus of the college but of Harvard Law School, which he was then serving as dean, and who in the times of turmoil had shown sympathy for students. Students themselves did not influence the outcome, but faculty members in the core Faculty of Arts and Sciences did so by insisting to Francis Burr that their faculty was so polarized that no one should be chosen from inside, a way of negating the selection of provost and professor of economics John Dunlop, who otherwise would have been a serious prospect.

[9] It has become standard practice to choose as an acting president someone who has declared that he or she is not a candidate. Otherwise, many outsiders and some insiders would be unwilling to become

ical in nature, to give the full faculty a chance to express their preferences and perhaps even to exercise a veto with regard to the finalists.

SALIENT ISSUES FOR SEARCHES

Many of the tensions evident in the "Abbott College" search—the degree of responsibility delegated to the search committee versus direct participation by campus constituents; the struggles over confidentiality versus disclosure; and the issues related to affirmative action—are reflected in varying degree in all of the five cases presented in this book. Given their salience in American life, it would be surprising if this were not the case. Questions concerning how the search committee will be constituted, which constituents should be represented with membership on the search committee, and how these representatives should be determined often embroil a campus in controversy at the very outset of the search process. In Chapter III we discuss the tasks required at the start of the search: the formation of the search committee, the role of committee members and the committee chair, and the attempt to establish criteria by which candidates will be evaluated. As we have already suggested, these decisions are not a matter of standard operating procedure, but on many college and university campuses today they quickly become rallying points for symbolic crusades, as well as for the more covert forms of campus politics.

Similarly, the question of confidentiality versus publicity is often one of the most important and controversial issues of the search process. In the Abbott College search, the trustee chair of the search committee reluctantly agreed to faculty demands that the five finalists chosen by the search committee come to the campus for open forums and, in anticipation of these events, the search committee distributed on campus names and brief biographical sketches of the finalists. However, when this information was printed in the metropolitan newspaper, the trustees were furious. They had not anticipated that the names would be disclosed beyond the borders of the college, and they also felt embarrassed about the awkwardness it caused for several of the candidates at their home milieux.

---

candidates themselves. It can happen, however, that acting presidents who have, quite without disingenuousness, accepted the position as temporary come in fact to like it and, upsetting what had been planned, to become candidates. If they then succeed to the presidency, their legitimacy may be somewhat flawed, though much depends on the attractiveness of the outside candidates.

In the search for a president of "Southern State University," the flagship state university[10] whose search we present in disguised form in Chapter IV, the search process and several candidates suffered as a result of repeated leaks to the press. The instructions to the search committee and assurances made to candidates were that the search would remain confidential until its final stages, when the most serious prospects would be brought to the campus. Some viable prospects withdrew when leaks made their candidacies public, and the career of one of these was crippled when his home institution, judging his candidacy to be disloyal, forced his immediate resignation.

In Chapter V, we discuss conflicts over privacy and publicity in the search process and in American society more generally. The typically American antagonism to secrets and to privacy is manifest today in state and national "government in the sunshine" and "open meeting and open records" laws. Often these sunshine laws exist alongside laws and constitutional provisions protecting the individual's right to privacy.[11] In some states, the college and university presidential search process is interpreted as a personnel matter, exempted in many states by law or judicial decision. For example, the University of Montana in Missoula was permitted to conduct its presidential evaluation in secret, despite the *Daily Missoulian*'s challenge to "closed doors," because the court, weighing the value of privacy over that of publicity, gave priority to the former.[12] Increasingly, however, the press has succeeded in forcing searches in state institutions into the public arena. In Chapter VI, we present an account of the 1983 search at the University of Florida in the glare of Florida's open meeting and open records laws. These laws stipulate that all considerations of what sort of person an institution needs, all that is said or written about all candidates, and all deliberations and votes of the search committee must be open to the public and the media. Our case study of the 1983 University

[10] The naval metaphor, "flagship," refers to a state's leading public university, which may sometimes also be its land-grant university. This is the case with such well-known flagships as the Universities of Illinois, Minnesota, and Massachusetts, and Ohio State University. In a few states, California in particular, the state college system has grown in size and prominence, so that the "flagship" designation means less than it once did.

[11] E.g., the Fourth Amendment in the federal Bill of Rights, which inhibits "searches and seizures." The Fifth Amendment in a way protects privacy also, preventing "search and seizure" of what the person might be forced to say under threat of punishment for perjury if the person lies.

[12] *The Missoulian* vs. *Board of Regents of Higher Education*, 207 Mont. 513 (No. 82-269, submitted Oct. 31, 1983, decided Jan. 23, 1984, 675 P.2d 962).

of Florida search and our discussion in Chapter VII of sunshine searches elsewhere document the problems and the ironies of the public search. Although the Florida law and other laws resembling it elsewhere are often defended on the ground that disclosure of proceedings helps educate the public, the presence of the media inhibited candid discussions of the direction the University of Florida might take and led to pro forma consideration of candidates. Although conducting a search in the sunshine is often seen as assurance that the process is "aboveboard," when the University of Florida process produced Marshall Criser, an undergraduate and law school alumnus of the University of Florida, a former chairman of the Florida Board of Regents, and a well-known Palm Beach lawyer and real estate developer, many people in and out of Florida concluded that this outcome had been decided in advance and was corrupt.

In contrast to the University of Florida search is our account in Chapter X of the 1984 Rice University search for a president to succeed physicist Norman Hackerman. In this search, issues of trust and confidentiality were very much at stake. The search process began in mutual suspicion of faculty vis-à-vis trustees, a legacy of the previous presidential search conducted fifteen years earlier, and ended in magnanimity, with this happy conclusion in large measure due to the committee's extensive confidential discussion of what Rice might need in the way of leadership and confidential deliberations concerning prospects for the presidency.

When we began our collaboration in 1980, the use of professional search consultants in the higher education search process was rare. Now their use is widespread, and the number of search firms and individual search consultants eager to tap this new market has risen concomitantly. This very efflorescence has created its own set of problems. Some are logistical, as individual consultants have to balance the claims of competing institutions for which they are simultaneously working; other concerns are ethical, for example whether the standard practice among the leading corporate search firms—to delay for two years turning to a former client in search of an executive for another client—implies that individuals who would like to move may be denied the opportunity by the restraints on the particular search firm. For many searches today, whether to use a consultant, which consultant to employ, and what to expect in the way of assistance are salient questions. We have chosen one of our case studies to illustrate how one search consultant worked with a search committee. In Chapter VIII, we describe the 1985–1986 search for a president at Winthrop College, a state college in Rock Hill, South Carolina. After talking with consultants from two firms, the Winthrop search committee employed the search services of the Academy for Educational Development. The consultant, Ruth Weintraub, helped the search committee identify prospects for the presidency, conducted background checks on leading candidates, and persuaded the search committee of the wisdom of bringing three finalists for campus visits.

Other search consultants strongly oppose bringing finalists to the campus, fearing the breaches of confidentiality that generally occur, and urge the search committee and the board of trustees to settle on a single person as the preferred candidate, and only bring this person to the campus. In Chapter IX we examine the different approaches consultants take to their tasks, the hazards if they do too much and the equally significant, often unrecognized hazards if they do too little in the course of a search. We believe, for example, that the search consultant can be of particular help at the end of the search in acting as a go-between in the negotiations with the prospective incumbent. The search consultant can assist the candidate and the board chairman with working out the details of the terms of employment, helping the board chairman and the board appreciate that a more secure president is a more effective one.

One common use of consultants is for guidance vis-à-vis what may be the requirements of affirmative action, a topic on which college and university lawyers (as well as campus affirmative action officers) are often consulted. We shall see dramatized in the "Abbott College" search how strong were the moral and political, as distinct from the juridical requirements of affirmative action. The same pressures manifest themselves in other searches as well. Probably the most visible manifestation of the awareness of the need to seek capable women and minorities for the presidency is the national advertising of vacancies. No longer is it likely that a president, or almost any major administrative officer, will be appointed without at least the appearance of a "national search," and the classified section of the *Chronicle of Higher Education* has swelled in size as a result.

Today, most searches are national in coverage, even if localist in their final choice. Advertisements of positions and letters sent to prospective nominators of candidates ordinarily contain the exhortation that minority males and women are actively sought. In some searches, this language is simply the prevailing piety, and there is no serious intention of selecting a women, a black, or a hispanic as president. These search committees care more about the statement they are making when they include women and "candidates of color" on their short-list of finalists, than they do about the candidates themselves who, have been used in this fashion, are understandably reluctant to enter future searches where they are uncertain as to their real standing. There are many searches, however, in which they are not tokens, but are part of an effort to find "the best person" for the presidency and to give the institution some real choices. Few searches today have a plethora of really outstanding candidates, and many of the most thoughtfully planned and carefully pursued searches even at institutions both affluent and promising may ultimately discover only a single candidate who interests the committee and is interested in the position. Hence, we insist repeatedly in this volume that the best searches pursue a process of active searching, not merely one of passive selection. Their efforts are directed not so much at screening out candidates, but rather at making sure that they have identified as many viable prospects as possible.

The Rice University search, whose story we present in Chapter X, was unusual in this regard. The search committee spent far more lead time than most committees in getting the search underway and in scouting around for prospective candidates. Under the enthusiastic leadership of chairman Ralph O'Connor, the search committee began not by reading resumés of applicants and nominees, but by consulting many leading university presidents in order to get a clearer sense of what sorts of people presidents are and what sorts of things they do. These "resources" were asked, for example, whether a place like Rice, which had always had a president drawn from the sciences, should once again have a scientist as president. The "resources" encouraged committee members to consider not only Rice's distinction, but also its unfulfilled potential. Many of the interviewees told committee members that it did not take a scientist or engineer to administer programs in these areas, and they should look for capable and energetic leadership, irrespective of academic discipline, current locale, or age. Young persons, not yet nationally visible, should be considered as well.

The Rice story also illuminates the ways in which members of a search committee can court a candidate. The Rice committee pursued their favorite choice for the presidency even after he had declared that he was not interested in becoming a candidate, and then won the support of the board and the campus for this unexpected appointment. Chapter XI develops this theme, examining the two-way process in which candidate and institution must each choose and be chosen. In the optimal case, the new incumbent, as a result of the successful conclusion to the search process, has made a start on understanding the new locale and on being understood by major players there. But even in the optimal case, there is never a guarantee of mutual success, for all judgments about candidates and by candidates about their own suitability and potential satisfaction are based on limited information and encumbered by myths and misperceptions. The final selection on both sides represents a leap of faith.

THE PLAN OF THE BOOK

The book is composed of five case studies, each followed by an analytical chapter.[13] Two of the cases are disguised: One, "Abbott College," is a small, highly selective liberal arts college, and the other, "Southern State University," is a flagship state institution. The remaining three institutions are named: the University of Florida, Winthrop College, and Rice University. These five chapter-length cases illustrate some of the substantial variety of approaches to the search process and illuminate the complex dynamics of search committees as they confront the controversies and quagmires of the search process. The chapters of analytic discourse, themselves peppered with examples drawn from the more than two hundred searches we have studied during our ten years of collaborative research, place problems of institutional succession in a wider context of political competitions, ethical dilemmas, and competing moralities.

For some readers of this book, the case studies may be too packed with details or too lengthy overall, and they will choose to skim these and pay closer attention to the more practical advice or theoretical analyses. Other readers will undoubtedly see the case studies as the heart of the book, as

---

[13] See Appendix for a discussion of our research methodology.

the stories that bring alive the complexities and the drama of the search process.

Earlier in this century, when sociologists began to do fieldwork (sometimes following the examples given by anthropologists) there was great excitement about the genre. Robert and Helen Lynd's two Middletown books aroused national interest. So did W. Lloyd Warner's Yankee City series; William F. Whyte's classic *Street Corner Society*; Herbert Gans's *The Urban Villagers* and *The Levittowners*; and the many studies of industrial settings, small towns, and urban ethnic enclaves.[14] Today that illuminating mode of work seems to be less frequently pursued. This is regrettable, for it has been our experience that, the more time we have spent, so to speak, in the field, the more complex we realize the search process to be and the less confident we become about generalizations. The more searches we have observed, the more we have become persuaded that there is no "typical" search process, even within a particular stratum or Carnegie classification of higher education. Searches reflect the enormous diversity of American academic subcultures and the idiosyncrasies of time, place, and commotion. Hence we do not attempt in this book to identify distinct types or classifications of searches or to trace frequencies of characteristics or procedures.

We should make it clear, as well, that this is not a manual about how to do a search.[15] In the pages that follow, we do not put forward prescriptions for the "one best search." Just as there is no one best leader for all institutions, so there is no *ideal* search process, no magic number of members of the search committee, no certain method of ensuring confidentiality, no sure-fire way of making the final arrangements for installation. To put the

[14] Robert and Helen Lynd, *Middletown* (New York: Harcourt, Brace, and Co., 1929); W. Lloyd Warner, *Yankee City* (New Haven: Yale University Press, 1963); William F. Whyte, *Street Corner Society* (Chicago: University of Chicago Press, 1955); Herbert J. Gans, *The Urban Villagers* (New York: Free Press of Glencoe, 1962) and *The Levittowners* (New York: Pantheon Books, 1967).

[15] Other authors, most notably John Nason, Theodore Marchese and Jane Fiori Lawrence, and Joseph Kauffman have provided colleges and universities with search guides which serve that purpose well. See John W. Nason, assisted by Nancy R. Axelrod, *Presidential Search: A Guide to the Process of Selecting and Appointing College and University Presidents* (Washington, D.C.: AGB, 1984); Theodore J. Marchese and Jane Fiori Lawrence, *The Search Committee Handbook: A Guide to Recruiting Administrators* (Washington, D.C.: AAHE, 1987); and Joseph Kauffman, *The Selection of College and University Presidents* (Washington D.C.: American Association of Colleges, 1974). Two other books that contain helpful advice about how to conduct a search are Thomas North Gilmore's *Making a Leadership Change* (San Francisco: Jossey-Bass, 1988), and Stephen A. Garrison's *Institutional Search* (New York: Praeger Publishers, 1989).

matter differently, a scrupulous search followed by magnanimous arrangements cannot guarantee a benign incumbency. Nor does a flawed search necessarily produce a "bad" outcome, although it invariably makes a rough start for the new incumbent. In the best cases, though, a transition in leadership offers a college or university—as it does a corporation or a country—an opportunity to stop, look, and listen: to stop and consider its past, present, and future circumstances; to look at its environment and its clientele; and to listen to internal constituents and to external suppliers, supporters, rivals, and enemies. In other words, the search is a time to take stock, to consider new alternatives, and having done so, to continue on course, to change directions only slightly, or to use the new leader as a signal that the institution will be making substantial changes.

Many boards of trustees and search committees fail to avail themselves of the remarkable opportunity for institutional learning that a presidential search can provide. When there is a rush to fill an anticipated or already existing presidential vacancy, trustees and members of search committees are often inclined to foreshorten the processes involved in the transition to a new leader.[16] Indeed, the word "search," although we use it throughout this book, is perhaps too elliptical, abridging—at both ends of the process of leadership transition—important work that makes it more likely that the process will be successful.

At the outset, many boards and search committees neglect to carry out to the extent that would make it useful the self-analysis that can both precede and be coterminous with the search. The search provides an institution with an opportunity to reexamine what Burton Clark has called the institutional saga.[17] Such a saga is never defined once and for all, and rarely, if ever, without differences of opinion. Colleges and universities have other chances for self-examination, particularly in the usually decennial review by the regional accrediting associations. But these can be taken in a perfunctory way by well-established institutions which may be chided by the accrediting team but hardly seriously damaged. It is through the process of leadership succession that colleges and universities seek to act

---

[16] For further discussion, see Gilmore, *Leadership Change*.

[17] See Burton R. Clark, *The Distinctive College: Antioch, Swarthmore, and Reed* (Chicago: Aldine, 1970).

upon their self-examination, to choose someone who, in their best judgment, will ensure institutional continuity or will promote change.

The process of leadership succession is also, many times, rushed at its end, almost as if it were an elopement or shot-gun marriage. As a result, the institution and the new president enter the relationship as virtual strangers. A new president is likely to have many naive ideas and misconceptions; most members of search committees are also serving in this capacity for the first time; and all parties can suffer from romantic notions about what lies ahead.

A presidential succession does not terminate when a final candidate is identified or appointed. Although the search is officially concluded, the process of leadership transition is ongoing.[18] First-time presidents are often astonished to find how different their position is from even the position of academic vice-president or dean of faculty; this can be true even within the same institution, and of course all the more true for someone who comes in from outside. And even an experienced president may rely unduly on that experience and misinterpret the differences between the former and the current locales.

We hope that our examination of many aspects of the search will help to make presidential successions more fruitful for institutions and for those who serve them. We hope as well that the stories we tell in this book can contribute to an understanding of contemporary moralities and expediencies in academic cultures and the wider political culture in the United States. Like perhaps no other event in the life of an institution, the search for the president reveals the politics, protocols, and promise of the American academic enterprise.

[18] For some excellent advice on how to ease this period of transition, see *On Assuming a College or University Presidency: Lessons and Advice from the Field* (Washington, D.C.: AAHE Publications, 1989); with essays by Estela Mara Bensimon, Marian L. Gade, and Joseph F. Kauffman.

CHAPTER I

Do Searches Matter?

W HEN WE HAVE TOLD colleagues about our research on searches for college and university presidents, we have encountered two very different reactions. Some people are immediately excited by the topic. Appreciating the fascination that this research holds for us, they have wanted to engage us in lengthy conversation about it. For the most part, these people have been candidates, trustees, or members of search committees, or they have an interest in the leadership of their alma maters or the institutions where they are working. Directly or vicariously, they have become acquainted with the chanciness and the vicissitudes of the search process, the anxiety and enthusiasm it can engender among participants, and the controversies generated by conflicts of personalities and purposes. They recognize that the search process has all the excitement of a wake, a wedding, and a birth rolled into one.

Other people, however, have been perplexed by our having spent so much time looking at something they think odd, wondering why we find this topic worthy of research, or even interesting. Many of them said to us that they believe that searches are unimportant because the presidency is unimportant, for it matters very little who holds the position of president of a college or university.

It is to this latter group of people that much of this first chapter is addressed. Their doubts about the importance of the presidency are neither trivial nor unusual.[1] Indeed, one of the interesting and important argu-

---

[1] Nor is the debate about whether leaders really matter limited to the arena of higher education. In his essay, "Where Has Greatness Gone?" (*Midwest Quarterly* 27, Winter 1986, pp. 129–148) the historian John C. Burnham contends that large parts of the American population have become convinced that it is great forces that are important and not great men and women. John W. Gardner, an eminent leader at the national and at the local level, and for decades a student and commentator on leadership, presents a cogent discussion of leadership in *On Leadership* (New York: The Free Press,

ments in the study of higher education in recent years has been over the question, "do presidents make a difference?"[2] In this chapter, we begin by addressing this question, and then turn to the related question: "Do searches for presidents matter?"

DO LEADERS MATTER?

In 1974, Michael D. Cohen and James G. March published *Leadership and Ambiguity: The American College President*, a work of exemplary provocativeness. Having examined forty-six presidents in a stratified sample of four-year institutions—public, private, large, and small—by interviewing these presidents and those around them and by perusing diaries, time budgets, newspapers, and archival records, Cohen and March conclude that leadership is principally mythological. "The presidency is an illusion. Important aspects of the role disappear on close examination. In particular, decision making in the university seems to result extensively from a process that decouples problems and choices and makes the president's role more commonly sporadic and symbolic than significant. Compared to the heroic expectations he and others might have, the president has modest control over the events of college life. The contributions he can make can easily be swamped by outside events or the diffuse qualities of university decision making."[3] Cohen and March compare the president of a college or university to the driver of a skidding car. There is little the president can do to change the course of events, and "whether he is convicted of manslaughter or receives a medal for heroism [is] largely outside his control."[4]

In all of their writing, Cohen and March, like Tolstoy writing about generals in *War and Peace*, emphasize the role of circumstance and chance, and the degree to which outcomes reflect continuing organizational pro-

1990). For a less historical, more contemporary outlook, see Warren Bennis, *On Becoming a Leader* (Reading, Massachusetts: Addison-Wesley, 1989).

[2] For an excellent discussion of the academic president, see Commission on Strengthening Presidential Leadership, Clark Kerr, Director, *Presidents Make a Difference* (Washington, D.C.: AGB, 1984) and Clark Kerr and Marian L. Gade, *The Many Lives of Academic Presidents* (Washington, D.C., AGB, 1986).

[3] Michael D. Cohen and James G. March, *Leadership and Ambiguity: The American College President*, Second Edition (Boston: Harvard Business School Press, 1986), p. 2.

[4] Ibid., p. 203.

cesses and not human intention. Calling higher education an "organized anarchy," these authors see decision making on the campus as occurring in a set of "garbage cans," into which individuals toss both problems and solutions. The problems and solutions may bear little relationship to one another; the latter are "an answer actively looking for a question."[5]

We should make it clear, however, that theirs is not a simple-minded Marxist view that material or economic circumstances are determinative. Nor is theirs merely an effort to debunk and demystify cults of leadership. *Leadership and Ambiguity* stands in marked contrast to widely prevalent notions of rational processes of leadership, for instance, the concepts of management by objectives or strategic planning. Whereas these management techniques assume a capacity for rational planning, Cohen and March recommended the use of intuition and brief ventures into foolishness as aids to creative planning. In fact, James March has sought throughout his scholarly career to bring a sense of freedom, even relaxation, to the commonly stressful lives of university presidents and other leaders. He wants them to recognize how easily they can become the victims of the expectations about leadership. Even as Americans distrust and seek to contain power, we have an abiding faith in the ability of leaders to help us. March sees leadership as more likely if leaders can laugh at themselves, be less terrified of their predicaments, and not be the prisoners of others' expectations of them.

Cohen and March's arguments are developed further by Robert Birnbaum, who has written extensively about the college presidency and the search process. Birnbaum declares that, while most presidents "will properly fulfill the requirements of their roles . . . they do not leave a distinctive mark on their institution."[6] In one research study, Birnbaum found that college presidents believed that they were doing better than their predecessors, who, in turn, believed that they were doing better than the president before them.[7] If the presidents were reporting reality accurately, higher education would be in a state of continuous improvement! Birnbaum, like Cohen and March, contends that the notion of heroic leader-

---

[5] Ibid., p. 82.

[6] Robert Birnbaum, "Presidential Succession and Institutional Functioning in Higher Education," *Journal of Higher Education*, Vol. 60, no. 2 (March–April 1989), p. 132.

[7] Robert Birnbaum, "Leadership and Learning: The College President as Intuitive Scientist," *Review of Higher Education*, Vol. 9 (1986), 381–395.

ship is a disabling myth, adding to the stress already weighing presidents down, rather than encouraging them to become more intuitive and experimental in the anarchic, nearly ungovernable settings in which they often find themselves. These researchers are in agreement in emphasizing the importance of symbolism in higher education; correspondingly, they see searches as serving important ceremonial functions. However, glancing at the academic landscape as a whole, they doubt whether the general caliber of presidents, assuming it can be assessed, makes a significant difference.[8]

We find Cohen and March's and Birnbaum's arguments fascinating and regard their elucidation of the symbolic aspects of the governance of higher education as both quixotic and compelling. We take exception, however, with their argument when carried to its extreme. That is, we do not think presidents are fungible people, like "light bulbs," necessary but "interchangeable," one "indistinguishable" from another.[9] While we agree that not every president makes major changes in the short-term or long-term viability of the institution he or she serves (and change in itself is, of course, not necessarily a good thing), we believe that there is a significant number of presidents who do change the course of the colleges or universities they head. The successes and failures of these presidents are most visible at the margins, at those institutions enjoying flush times and those whose very survival is precarious. And many more presidents affect, for better or for worse, the lives of the individuals with whom they have worked, including those they have dismissed as well as those they have recruited and promoted. Clark Kerr and Marian Gade refer to the trustees of institutions of higher education as *The Guardians*;[10] the presidents of

[8] It would take another book as long as this one even to begin disaggregating questions as to how a leader's impact can be assessed. Alexander Astin has for years been asking colleges and universities to assess the "value added" to their students through the educational process, and the assessment movement has become more active in the 1980s. Still, the impact of particular presidents long outlasts their tenures, and judgments of momentary success have to be weighed against often long-deferred consequences in plant and personnel. For a bibliography of memoirs, autobiographies by and biographies of college and university presidents, see James A. Robinson, "Lieutenants to Learning: A Bibliography of Participant-Observation by University Presidents," *Journal of Higher Education*, Vol. 59, no. 3 (May–June 1988), pp. 327–351. Moreover, one cannot judge the impact of the president merely by looking at the institution headed by the latter without taking account of the surrounding academic ecology. Consider, for example, the president who opposed political intervention in faculty appointments and dismissals, who was dismissed and whose institution suffered at the hands of the legislature, but who also gave an example toward which other institutions might rally.

[9] James G. March, "How We Talk and How We Act: Administrative Theory and Administrative Life," Seventh David D. Henry Lecture, University of Illinois, 1980.

[10] Kerr and Gade, *The Guardians: Boards of Trustees of American Colleges and Universities, What They Do and How Well They Do It* (Washington, D.C.: AGB, 1989).

4

colleges and universities are also guardians, and in failing in that capacity they can cripple an institution or they can help preserve it.

A retrospective glance is illustrative. In the relatively small and conservative state of Indiana, Indiana University, under the leadership of Herman B. Wells, became one of the least provincial of flagship campuses and a major institution academically in many fields, for example, anthropology, African studies, and folklore. Similarly in Michigan, in the face of the national renown of the constitutionally established University of Michigan, John Hannah made Michigan State University an international resource, not only in agriculture, but in area studies more generally—a university whose faculty entrepreneurs were encouraged to start subcolleges and programs across departmental lines. These and other academic mountains that rise above the hills and valleys of public higher education could not have become nearly so preeminent without presidents who had great visions and aspirations for their institutions, were persuasive with foundations, alumni, and federal and state officials, and could attract faculty members and students from beyond their immediate catchbasins.

Not infrequently today, one hears the lament, "where have all the great presidents gone?" Looking back wistfully to transformational leaders such as Herman Wells and John Hannah, or to Charles W. Eliot who presided for forty years over Harvard's change from a provincial college to a research university, David Starr Jordan who created Stanford, and Robert M. Hutchins who used the base of the University of Chicago to challenge the subspeciation of academic departments, some observers of American higher education wonder why there appear to be no comparable giants today.[11] In an essay in *Science*, Steven Muller, a political scientist and former president of the Johns Hopkins University, addresses the question of why presidents today lack the charisma of some of their notable predecessors. In the university as in society, Muller comments, things have become much more complicated. More players have a say and have won the right to say it; institutions are bigger, with more constituents carrying more messages and applying greater pressure. Altogether, there is less leeway for presidents to maneuver.[12]

In "The University Presidency: Comparative Reflections on Leader-

[11] Laurence Veysey's *The Emergence of the American University* (Berkeley: University of California Press, 1965) remains a fine account of the founding sagas of the research universities.
[12] Steven Muller, *Science*, August 14, 1987.

5

ship," a David D. Henry Lecture which followed that of James March, Martin Trow argues that it is in the interest of presidents to play down their authority, which is so easily seen as authoritarian.[13] Moreover, at any moment in time, the diverse segments of their institutions are responding to competing pressures, notably pressures for excellence and distinction and pressures for equity and access. The presidency is the point where these pressures meet and compete. Trow uses a telling metaphor to suggest that the anarchy observed by James March is only apparent:

> I suspect that observers have been looking at the university president's role as if it were a cross-section of a thick cable, made up of many differently colored strands or wires, each strand representing another program or activity, and all together in cross-section representing a heterogeneous collection of issues, solutions, and problems, showing little coherence or purpose. But in the research university, this model is misleading. For if this rope is cut along the dimension of time, we see that each strand extends backwards and forwards, moving along in its own coherent, purposeful, even rational way—each marked by its own set of purposes which are largely insulated from other strands, even as they intertwine. So what appears as a random or haphazard collection of events, problems, evasions, and solutions, when viewed in cross-section at a given moment, looks more like a set of purposeful programs—each being pursued in relative isolation within the boundaries of the same institution, when viewed along the dimension of time.[14]

It is the president, Trow argues, who tends these strands of university policy and artfully weaves them together.

Along the same lines, Kerr and Gade see the importance of the presidency as growing despite the decline in formal, hierarchical authority: "The presidency becomes more important to the institution as a whole as one check and balance on power incursions against the long-run welfare of the institution, whether these incursions come from outside forces or from students or faculty or staff or even individual trustees." The college or university president must attempt "to defend institutional autonomy, to manage conflict, to integrate separatist forces, to offset small group ef-

---

[13] Ninth David D. Henry Lecture, University of Illinois, 1984.
[14] Ibid., p. 30.

6

forts at inefficiencies and exploitations, and to advance programs over attempted special interest vetoes."[15]

In the public sector of American higher education, college and university presidents must defend their institutions daily against the attacks and incursions that will make them mediocre. At the same time, they must lobby for the public funding necessary to maintain and improve their capacities for research and teaching. In both endeavors, the president is a central figure whose actions can enhance public relations or threaten the curtailment of public support. When Kenneth Keller became president of the University of Minnesota in 1985, for example, he worked with the regents and with his fellow campus administrators on "Commitment to Focus," an effort to concentrate on what the University could do well and to discard those programs and services (including dentistry and veterinary medicine) which were exceedingly costly and which had few customers. Although there was an instant outcry at what was regarded by many as "elitism," it was not the dispute over academic priorities which doomed Commitment to Focus and caused Keller's resignation. Instead, Keller's presidency and the proposed academic policy failed because of the disclosure that Keller had spent over a million dollars on renovations (many of them badly needed) to the president's office and his official residence.[16]

Similarly, in the private sector of American higher education, many colleges and universities, especially those not heavily endowed or fortunate enough to have a large applicant pool, depend on their presidents for their institutional visibility and viability. In recent years, even the wealthiest institutions have been scrambling to build new facilities in response to market pressures of competitors and to repair existing facilities badly under-maintained in the inflationary period of the 1970s when fuel costs rose precipitously.[17] The wealthiest institutions are also in competition across the board for the recruitment of minority students, faculty members, and administrators; the established ones among them face competi-

[15] Kerr and Gade, *Many Lives*, p. 119.

[16] See Richard Broderick, "A University at Risk," *Twin Cities*, August, 1988, pp. 85–71, and Kenneth H. Keller, "For the Record," *Twin Cities*, July 1988, pp. 47–53.

[17] When A. Bartlett Giamatti, professor of Renaissance literature, was made president of Yale, he discovered that Yale, despite its huge endowment, could not afford to coast on its eminence. The university was running a deficit, buildings were in disrepair, and the low pay of the staff ("low" in comparison to Yale's competitor universities) facilitated unionization and a crippling and divisive strike.

tion from those newly enriched—for example, Emory, with its Coca-Cola money, or Trinity University in San Antonio, with oil and other wealth. And even these mighty institutions increasingly compete for students and faculty members with the so-called Public Ivys,[18] the national public universities which offer the atmosphere of a private liberal arts college or university at low tuition and primarily public expense: the Universities of Virginia, Michigan, and Vermont; the University of North Carolina at Chapel Hill; and in addition smaller places such as the College of William and Mary and St. Mary's College of Maryland.

In funding, too, private institutions now face competition from public universities which have broken away from the once implicit contract that the independent sector would be allowed exclusive fishing rights in philanthropic waters. There is now hardly a public university that does not have its University Foundation seeking support from corporate and private donors. This competition in the academic stratosphere affects the market share for the more local private colleges and universities, which find themselves competing in a more national and even international market for students and for faculty. It is the tuition-dependent private colleges which have suffered the most from the cuts in federal support for Pell Grants and other student aid programs.

The health of the public sector does not benefit as the private sector shrinks and perhaps becomes weaker as well: it is rather a win/win or lose/lose situation. The public sector can more readily defend its academic freedom and its relative freedom from micro-management against the state civil service and against local politicians—often a combination of the two—when the leaders of public higher education are able to mobilize support for their emulation of the leading private institutions. Clark Kerr has noted that Berkeley's achievement has depended in part on the distinction of Stanford and the Ivy League. The University of Illinois, which has suffered from political interference in the past,[19] is better off because of the presence of Northwestern and the University of Chicago.

[18] See Richard Moll, *The Public Ivys: A Guide to America's Best Public Undergraduate Colleges and Universities* (New York: Viking Press, 1985).

[19] On the dismissal of George D. Stoddard as president of Illinois for defending ''pink'' professors, and on his quarrels with particular state legislators and Regents, see Nicholas J. Demerath, Richard W. Stephens, and R. Robb Taylor, *Power, Presidents, and Professors* (New York: Basic Books, 1967), pp. 219–220.

The private residential liberal arts colleges, mostly with student bodies of fewer than 2,000, have been and are likely to remain principal sources of the faculty of the research universities. Reed and Swarthmore, for example, have long been famous for the scholarly distinction achieved by their graduates, all of whom at Reed and most of whom at Swarthmore work on a demanding senior project. But the same is true for less visible Midwestern colleges such as the College of Wooster or Hope College, whose students work with faculty members to present papers in the sciences and then continue in doctoral programs in the research universities.[20] In this regard, as in many others, the small scholarly liberal arts colleges are a model and resource for all of higher education.

In 1980 David Riesman, in association with Sharon Elliott Fuller, studied a small number of liberal arts colleges to see what was keeping them afloat or improving their situation in the face of demographic decline of the high-school graduates on whom they primarily depended for students. Everywhere they looked, the president had made a difference. Their findings matched those of other observers who have concluded that the prosperity of a number of private liberal arts colleges that have maintained themselves without assured ecological moorings has been due to the ingenuity and pertinacity of their leadership. J. Wade Gilley, Kenneth A. Fulmer, and Sally J. Reithlingshoefer examine twenty colleges and universities "on the move" and conclude that "the hand on the helm, or *the president*, is perhaps the key factor in the forward movement of each of these institutions. . . . the importance of leadership to a school's success is a factor well recognized on all twenty campuses."[21] Ellen Chaffee's *After Decline, What? Survival Strategies at Eight Private Colleges* examines the accomplishments of what she referred to as "turnaround" presidents at private liberal arts colleges. Among those she presents is the presidency

[20] Both the so-called Wesleyan Studies made more than thirty years ago and the report issued at Oberlin College in 1985, "Educating America's Scientists: The Role of the Research Colleges," found that many academic careers which end up in the great research universities begin in liberal arts colleges. See Robert H. Knapp and H. B. Goodrich, *Origins of American Scientists* (Chicago: University of Chicago Press, 1952); and Robert H. Knapp and Joseph J. Greenbaum, *The Younger American Scholar: His Collegiate Origins* (Chicago: University of Chicago Press, 1953), and David Davis-Van Atta, Sam S. Carrier, and Frank Frankfort, "Educating America's Scientists: The Role of the Research Colleges," Oberlin College, 1985. See also Carol H. Guller, "Ph.D. Recipients: Where Did They Go to College?" *Change*, Vol. 18, no. 6 (November–December 1986), pp. 42–51.

[21] J. Wade Gilley, Kenneth A. Fulmer, and Sally J. Reithlingshoefer, *Searching for Academic Excellence: Twenty Colleges and Universities on the Move and Their Leaders* (New York: Macmillan, 1986).

of Virginia Lester at Mary Baldwin College (1974–1985).[22] In the small town of Staunton, Virginia, Lester managed to sustain this women's college of seven hundred undergraduates in the face of the precipitous decline in the number of women choosing single-sex education and in the face of competition from better-known women's colleges in the area, including Sweet Briar, Hollins, and Randolph-Macon Woman's College. Lester inaugurated an adult degree program for older women and a school for exceptionally gifted precollegiate girls. Somewhat similar strategies were employed at Chatham College by president Alberta Arthurs and her successor, Rebecca Stafford, to keep Chatham alive.

Many cases could be written about presidents who have rescued private colleges that looked as if they might founder. One such story is that of Bradford College in Haverhill, Massachusetts, once a small women's junior college which had become four-year and coeducational. In 1982, the Bradford trustees chose as president Arthur Levine, a thirty-two-year-old researcher and writer on higher education, then a senior fellow at the Carnegie Foundation for the Advancement of Teaching. In "Bradford College: Curriculum Reform and Institutional Renewal," Paul Byers Ranslow and David Charles Haselkorn report the strategies Levine and his recruits used to work with faculty members toward a new curriculum, and then to market it to undergraduates and prospective students.[23]

One of the most dramatic examples of the importance of leadership for the survival of an institution can be found in the succession dramas at Antioch College.[24] We report a part of that story in some detail, because it suggests the difference that presidents can make, and beyond that it illustrates some of the tensions besetting contemporary searches. From its inception, Antioch has had a roller-coaster history of presidential catastrophe and rescue. Antioch College was founded by members of the Christian

[22] Boulder, Colorado: National Center for Higher Education Management Systems, 1984. Riesman and Fuller also examine Virginia Lester's presidency in "Leaders: Presidents Who Make a Difference," in Janice S. Greene and Arthur Levine, eds. *Opportunity in Adversity: How Colleges Can Succeed in Hard Times* (San Francisco: Jossey-Bass, 1985).

[23] In Greene and Levine, eds., *Opportunity in Adversity*, pp. 215–234.

[24] Our discussion of Antioch draws heavily from Clark, *The Distinctive College*, a work resting on archival research combined with fieldwork. Clark, one of America's leading students of higher education, shows how what he terms the "saga" of several colleges was the work of a single founder or transformational leader. To read Clark's book is to be reminded of how difficult the presidency could be for many in the nineteenth century, not only on financial grounds (hundreds of colleges expired altogether) but also due to the combat among Protestant sects.

Church in 1853, who managed to persuade famed Horace Mann to leave Massachusetts at age fifty-six and begin a new college in Yellow Springs, Ohio. Twelve years later, Horace Mann was dead, and Antioch College had its first experience with what was to become a series of exercises in resuscitation. Mann was succeeded by nine presidents and seven acting presidents. During one period the dean performed the duties of president, and at another time (1881–1882) Antioch College closed for a year. The Antioch we are familiar with today is the legacy of Arthur Morgan, a self-educated water resources engineer in nearby Dayton, who, having been a trustee, assumed the presidency in 1919. Morgan took advantage of the college's near bankruptcy to put into practice ideas drawn from his reading of the works of Edward Bellamy and other utopians, writers whose visions he had been pondering for many years. It was Morgan who developed Antioch's famous "co-op" program, which not only attracted students who could be housed in two shifts and saved Antioch from looming bankruptcy, but also became a model of experimentation, drawing adventurous students and faculty from all over the nation.

Even in the relatively quiescent 1950s, Antioch's distinctive character attracted radicals, who defined the College as at war not only with collegiate values of fun and games, but also with "strictly academic" traditions. The college developed a strong participatory ethos, with a "town meeting" format for deciding college matters. Many of Antioch's alumni went on to become national leaders in academe, law, the arts and sciences, and politics. But Antioch's future was not assured. During the 1960s and 1970s, Antioch's resources were stretched to near bankruptcy. James Dixon, M.D., an Antioch alumnus and public health physician, began a network of Antiochs, located in such diverse places as Keene, New Hampshire, inner-city Philadelphia, San Francisco, Santa Barbara, and Los Angeles, California, and the Antioch School of Law in Washington, D.C. These "add-ons" to Antioch College created "Antioch University," an institution that soon was over-extended and under-managed. Dixon was succeeded in the presidency by William Birenbaum, former president of the College of Staten Island in the City University of New York system and author of a left-liberal critique of higher education.[25] With the support of the board

[25] Birenbaum, *Something for Everybody Is Not Enough: An Educator's Search for His Education* (New York: Random House, 1971).

11

of trustees, Birenbaum moved the headquarters of Antioch University to expensive New York City, where he already lived, a city without an Antioch campus. The Yellow Springs campus believed that the network campuses and the new presidential arrangements drained its own limited resources, while the network Antiochs begrudged the large overhead they paid the college, claiming their assets were being used to pay off the college's deficits.

In the 1970s, Antioch College's radicalism was no longer so unique nor so inviting, and applications plummeted. Even while the Antioch center in Keene, New Hampshire, and some of the West Coast centers prospered, the home campus of Antioch festered in grievance and near insolvency. When Birenbaum resigned the presidency, some of Antioch's influential trustees realized in the mid-1980s the need for new leadership that, as in the days of Arthur Morgan, would resurrect an almost lifeless college. Robert Aller, an alumnus and newly elected chairman of the Antioch board of trustees, became co-chair and de facto head of the fifteen-person search committee charged with finding this new presidential leadership. Working with the committee was consultant Ruth Weintraub of the Academy for Educational Development.

After a long and difficult search, the Antioch search committee narrowed the list of prospects to two finalists. One of these, Alan Guskin, then chancellor of the University of Wisconsin at Parkside, was not at all sure he wanted the position of president of Antioch. Indeed, he thought much of the time that he was half-crazy even to consider it, but was certain he would not take it unless his selection could be legitimated by campus representatives beyond the search committee. Whoever became president of Antioch, he realized, would have to make some very tough, even cruel, decisions to regain solvency for the debt-ridden, mismanaged university, and would stretch legitimacy to the limit. The other finalist was also an experienced academic administrator. As second-in-command at a university, he was unwilling to have his candidacy exposed since there could be no assurance he would be chosen. Thus the question for the search committee was how to have a meeting with campus representatives such as Guskin requested, while maintaining the confidentiality that the other candidate required.

Ruth Weintraub, Robert Aller, and members of the search committee went to Yellow Springs and talked with students, faculty, and staff about the need for confidentiality. If the names of the two finalists were to become publicly known, they explained, Antioch might end up with no choice, or possibly no president at all. Reluctantly, the students on the search committee and the student newspaper reporter accepted the arrangements, and the campus visits took place with the two finalists meeting in confidential sessions with selected groups of campus leaders. The dates of these meetings were announced in the student newspaper, but the names of the two finalists were not given. After both candidates had visited the college, Alan Guskin was selected as the next president of the university.

Guskin's first decision was to concentrate his own efforts and the system's resources on the home campus at Yellow Springs. At the close of the search process, the Antioch board had made clear its desire that the new president establish the university's headquarters and his own home in Yellow Springs, and give top priority to the revival of the college. One consequence was the very hard and painful decision to drop the Antioch School of Law, located in Washington, D.C. The School of Law was begun in the early seventies in an effort to reform legal education and the system of justice in the nation's capital. The decision to stop subsidizing the School of Law aroused great controversy, not least because the Law School had concentrated on recruiting black students and on providing as part of its curriculum legal aid to Washington's inner-city residents, in both civil and criminal cases. Still, Guskin was able to turn attention toward revitalization at Yellow Springs, replacing faculty who had left or become demoralized, and adding new facilities and rebuilding the battered plant, the battered spirits of faculty, and the college's reputation, all in the pursuit of a contemporary restatement of the combined visions of Horace Mann and Arthur Morgan. Although it is too soon to know for sure whether Guskin will succeed in this endeavor, the prospects for Antioch look brighter than they have for many, many years.

Certainly Antioch is a college where presidents have made a difference! Not all institutions are so marginal in terms of their existence, of course; not all presidents will make the difference between the institution's life or death or even between its distinction or mediocrity. But even for institutions not precariously perched, the difference between an effective and ineffective president can matter a great deal. As the chief spokesperson for their institutions, all presidents have the opportunity to set a tone or style of operation; to help their institutions learn about their environment and their particular niche in this environment; to help develop and articulate agendas for their institutions; to affect quality; to mentor and educate, energize, frustrate, or enervate those who work with them. All presidents are the focal point of their institutions for students, faculty, administrators, staff members, alumni, parents, local citizens, government officials, and foundation heads; and they must find a workable balance among these often divergent and contentious constituents.

DO SEARCHES MATTER?

Just as there is argument as to whether *presidents* make a difference, so there is corresponding debate as to whether *searches* matter. Can a search be organized so that it will identify the person most appropriate for the institution? Does a "good" search produce a "good" president? Or is the outcome of a search basically random? Is the search merely a ceremonial activity, having little or no bearing on the quality of the person selected at its conclusion?

We believe that the search matters, both for its process and for its outcome. This is not to suggest that there is an inevitable connection between the success of the search process and the success of the person chosen by that process. As in all other human enterprises, consequences are not necessarily related to intentions. A search conducted with wild irrationality may nevertheless produce an effective incumbent, while another search conducted according to what is generally considered good practice may end up with a disappointing blowhard, a charismatic faker, or a secret alcoholic. What is optimal, however, is both a good search process and a successful selection.

First, a look at the search process itself. As Robert Birnbaum argues persuasively, the search process for a college and university president is an important institutional ritual, a significant ceremony in the life of an institution. The constitution of a search committee, the specification of the criteria sought, the selection of individuals to meet with the final candidates under consideration—all are indications of "ownership" by the in-

14

stitution's stakeholders and contestants. Participation in the search is often regarded as a statement of an individual's or constituency's status in the institution.

Not surprisingly, then, the search for a college president is viewed as an occasion for major constituents of the institution to seek to have their voices heard. The demands for participation in the search are frequently clamorous, yet when permission is granted, the actual amount of participation is minimal. In the 1983 University of Florida search, for instance, when the schedules for the campus visits of finalists for the presidency were circulated, members of several groups inquired why they had not been given special meetings with the candidates. Yet the actual turnout of faculty and students at open forums with candidates for the presidency was, in the words of a university administrator, "embarrassing." Rarely were more than fifteen people in attendance; at one meeting, the audience was made up of only six people who were not members of the search committee or the press. The demands for participation may, thus, be mostly ritualistic: constituents want to know that they are entitled to be part of the process, even if pressures of time and business make their participation unlikely, or even if their interest is cursory or negligible.

As soon as a search is announced, constituents quickly bring to it their own perspectives and special interests. Hence, the search functions as a crucible; or, to use Cohen and March's analogy of decision making, the search process becomes a garbage can, a repository into which constituents toss their hopes, desires, fears, frustrations, anger, and, most importantly, their various solutions, whether or not these are appropriate to the selection of a president. Similarly, some candidates seem to think, again to use Cohen and March's analogy, that *they* are solutions to any problem, and that every search that is advertised is a "trash can" into which they can get their name placed. They are candidates everywhere, believing themselves suited to every presidential vacancy that appears.

Nowhere is this trash-can phenomenon more evident than at the outset of the presidential search process when the search committee is attempting to come up with a statement of qualifications for the presidency. No group wants its issues submerged, and the result, as often as not, is that every mobilized individual's or group's special interest is added to the list, whose very size would be a deterrent to serious candidates if it were taken seri-

15

ously. No guidance is offered as to which qualifications are to be given weight and which are peripheral.

An example is the following job description from the *Chronicle of Higher Education*:

> The university seeks an individual who possesses the following traits: sensitive to the teaching and research components of the university; skills sufficient to articulate Eastern to its external constituents; collegial in governing style yet assertive in leadership; an understanding of the role played by a regional, comprehensive, state-assisted university; a commitment to the importance of understanding other cultures; a personal style marked by approachability, accessibility, and self-confidence; an ability to structure a university to maximize its human potential; a record of attracting capable, energetic, and enthusiastic faculty and staff, including an appropriate balance of women and minorities; experience and success in planning, fiscal management, and resource allocation; skills necessary to lead resource development; commitment to the intellectual and personal development of students; and an ability to articulate a vision for the university.[26]

The description of the person sought is reminiscent of the comments of a Yale University trustee in 1950, when Yale was searching for a president. Yale's new president, he suggested, should be a

> public relations man and fund raiser, a man of iron health and stamina, married to a paragon—a combination Queen Victoria, Florence Nightingale, and best-dressed woman of the year—a man of the world, but with great spiritual qualities, an experienced administrator who can delegate authority, a Yale man and a great scholar, and a social philosopher who has at his fingertips a solution to all of the world's problems. I don't doubt that you have concluded that there is only One who has most of these qualifications. But, we have to ask ourselves—is God a Yale man?[27]

[26] Advertisement for the presidency of Eastern Washington University, *Chronicle of Higher Education*, Vol. 36, no. 16 (January 3, 1990), p. B102.
[27] Quoted in Demerath *et al.*, *Power, Presidents, and Professors*, p. 56.

16

Many search committees spend long hours deciding on their statements of qualifications for the presidency, only to put them aside after they have been printed and circulated, never to look at them again. These statements seem to serve the same function as a party platform; activist constituents fight to have their virtuous desiderata included, but the platform, once determined, has only minimal bearing on the final outcome of the election.

Often, the search process serves as an indication of how people at an institution feel about their college or university, revealing their aspirations or their misgivings. In 1989, when Northeastern University was looking for a president to succeed Kenneth Ryder, many faculty members in arts and sciences hoped they could recruit an academic star whose presence at the university would serve as a statement that Northeastern was no longer only a commuter, "first generation" institution, but had become a research university competitive in some departments with the academic giants of the area. When the Northeastern search concluded with the selection of an internal candidate, executive vice-president John Curry, faculty members openly expressed their disappointment.[28]

Similarly, when Winthrop College conducted its presidential search in 1986, members of the Winthrop faculty hoped to have as president someone whose cachet would bring the college greater academic respectability, perhaps someone who had been the second in command at Duke, the University of Virginia, or the University of North Carolina at Chapel Hill. When the three finalists brought to campus hailed from less eminent institutions, many faculty members were sorely disappointed. In the 1983 University of Florida search, nominations for the presidency included former United States presidents and other notables, individuals not nominated because they were necessarily well suited for the university post but because of the supposed status their name recognition would bring the institution. Some colleges and universities start out with an inflated insti-

[28] Curry has sought to show that he is not a clone of his predecessor, nor a colorless "bureaucrat," as his opponents have charged, by setting out in his inaugural address proposals requiring the university to work with the Boston public schools. He has committed 100 Northeastern scholarships to first graders in Boston public schools, provided they graduate from high school. See Anthony Flint, "At Northeastern, new head offers 100 scholarships," *Boston Globe*, December 1, 1989, p. 29.

tutional ego: "Surely everyone will jump at the chance to be president of our college." In contrast, other colleges and universities begin with what could be called a "Groucho Marx" complex. Groucho Marx once said that any club that would have him as a member must surely not be worth joining. These colleges and universities have so profound a sense of inferiority that they are apt to conclude that no truly competent person could want to be their president.

At some institutions, the search is used as an opportunity to develop an institutional "logo," that is, a statement about the institution. The new president is seen as the representation of what the most influential participants in the search believe that the institution is, or hope that the institution will become. One such search, whose symbol mattered enormously not only for the institution but for the nation and even abroad, was Gallaudet College's 1988 search for a president. Gallaudet, in Washington, D.C., is the nation's only collegiate institution for the deaf. Three finalists for the presidency were interviewed on the Gallaudet campus: I. King Jordan, then the dean of the College of Arts and Sciences at Gallaudet, who is hearing impaired; the superintendent of a school for the deaf, also hearing impaired; and Elisabeth Ann Zinser, then vice-chancellor for academic affairs at the University of North Carolina at Greensboro, who declared that she was prepared to learn sign language if chosen. After a lengthy discussion by the search committee and trustees, Elisabeth Zinser was the selection for president. Zinser has impressive, and for Gallaudet, relevant credentials, including a doctorate in educational psychology and a record of administrative accomplishment.

Hardly was the appointment announced than the campus coalesced in opposition to the selection, insisting that the new president be a deaf person. Students occupied the Gallaudet administration building, demanded an end to classes, and marched to the Capitol to enlist Congressional support. Gallaudet depends heavily on federal subsidy for its operating budget. Jesse Jackson, in the midst of his campaign for the Democratic presidential nomination, immediately offered support, and hearing impaired people from all over the country rallied and came to Washington. In the course of less than a week, it became virtually impossible to bring a "hearing" person to Gallaudet's presidency. The faculty, the majority of whom

18

were soon brought to the students' cause, might recognize that Zinser would be an effective representative for Gallaudet, but such expedient considerations could not overcome the importance of the symbolism that the hearing impaired are capable of fulfilling significant and visible leadership roles.[29] The board of trustees then settled on I. King Jordan, who had been turned down in an earlier vote.[30]

The Gallaudet presidential search committee and the consultant, Nancy Archer-Martin, who assisted the search, had recognized the existence of a growing movement of deaf pride analogous to the civil rights movement or the demands for equity for the handicapped. However, they had failed to realize the intensity of support for the movement. As the Gallaudet case dramatically indicates, the search process is important not only as a symbol but also for the opportunities for learning it provides. In the best of searches, the members of the search committee and the institution's governing board develop an appreciation for the points of view of the various constituent bodies, the problems that they foresee, and the perspectives of outsiders.[31] Thus, as a consequence of discussions that have arisen at the outset of the search, as well as during its course, the search committee may end up with a conception of what sort of candidate would be best for the institution at that time somewhat different from what they assumed at the outset, or may identify new priorities they want the new president to address. Such was the case in the Rice University search which we describe in Chapter X. After members of the search committee had conducted intense exploratory conversations with distinguished educators across the country, they moved away from their initial assumption that

[29] Other student demands included the resignation of the chairman; a majority of the board to be hearing impaired; and no reprisals. The first and last of these demands were readily acceded to, and the change in the composition of the board to a majority of deaf persons and a deaf chairman will soon be accomplished. For an excellent analysis of the issues dealt with in the Gallaudet search, see Harold Orlans, "The Revolution at Gallaudet: Students Provoke Break with Past," *Change*, Vol. 21, no. 1 (January–February 1989), pp. 8–18. Also see Elisabeth Zinser, "Reflections on Revolution and Leadership by Surprise," *Educational Record*, Vol. 69, no. 2 (Spring 1988), pp. 22–25. On the Gallaudet story and the history of American Sign Language, see Oliver Sacks, *Seeing Voices: A Journey into the World of the Deaf* (Berkeley: University of California Press, 1989).

[30] Publicly, he and the other finalist withdrew when the protest first erupted, but Jordan returned as a candidate as the protest swelled.

[31] Sometimes in the life of an institution the decennial review of its programs by the regional accrediting association can help to provide such an up-to-date perspective. We discuss in Chapter IX the use of outside consultants to help a college or university look freshly at itself.

the president of Rice University had to be a mathematician or scientist, as all previous presidents had been, and were willing to consider someone like George Rupp with the most unlikely background of theology.

The best of search processes are invitational to the most attractive candidates. The intelligence and specificity of the questioning by members of the search committee can be impressive to thoughtful prospects who have not yet decided whether they want to become candidates. In contrast, messy searches generate bad press and discourage prospective candidates, particularly those who are not in desperate need of a job, that is, those the search committee most wants to interest in the presidency. This is of special concern because of the relative paucity of capable and experienced leaders who are willing to consider a presidency today. In *The Many Lives of Academic Presidents*, Kerr and Gade report that one-half of the academic vice-presidents interviewed in their study—those people generally assumed to be in line for the presidency—did not aspire to the total exposure of the presidency, what we might refer to as the fulcrum position. Instead, they preferred the less visible position closer to the academic side of things, while leaving to others the more public political and fiscal tasks of the presidency:

> The position of president has deteriorated; it mostly involves raising money and recruiting students. . . . There is year-round open-season on the president and little protection—many potential enemies and few friends, and too much 'humiliation.' . . . The position of provost is the 'highest post with academic respect.' 'It is a warm and cozy place, not cold and windy.'[32]

Kerr and Gade found, similarly, that the senior professors they interviewed, also once a source of presidents, declined interest in the top administrative position. Many of these professors had opportunities for influence, sociability, and also earnings outside of the academy, at a pace of

[32] Kerr and Gade, *Many Lives*, pp. 17–18. On December 1, 1989, we had the opportunity to meet with a group of chief academic officers—provosts, academic vice-presidents, deans of faculty—some of whom wanted to become presidents, while others did not. What was interesting to discover was that many of them had been drawn against their preferences, along with their presidents, into the public and political arenas, helping with fundraising, courting legislators or system heads, working with alumni—all on top of their internal duties. What some of them seemed to be saying was that the tasks of the presidency, because of their sheer magnitude, are beginning to be delegated even to those who still, in many cases, see themselves as faculty members on temporary service, still teaching at least one course and expecting to return to their tenured faculty positions.

20

their own choosing—"perks" far more desirable than the uncertainties of the presidency.[33]

The best searches serve to legitimate the final choice of the search committee and trustees so that a new president can have a smooth entrée to the presidency. Many searches, however, are fraught with missteps that leave constituents on the campus enraged about the search and hostile to its outcome. The search ends up an abysmal failure, not because the wrong person has been chosen, but because someone who might have been right for the institution is rendered ineffective by the traumas connected with his or her succession to the presidency. The outcome of a search that appears, from the outside, as an admirable choice may be soured by the suspicion of faculty, students, administrators, or the community toward the mode in which the choice was made. If a search is viewed with mistrust by formidable constituents, the president who emerges from it may be handicapped in establishing his or her legitimacy. One example is the search at Auburn University which resulted in the selection of Hanley Funderburk to the presidency being vacated by the scholarly historian Harry Philpot. Working with a board of regents commonly regarded as supine, governor George Wallace encouraged the appointment of Funderburk. Funderburk had been head of the Montgomery commuter campus of Auburn University and had support from faculty in engineering and agriculture, but was opposed by faculty in the liberal arts and sciences. When Funderburk's appointment was announced, there were immediate faculty protests. The Auburn faculty were furious at their exclusion from the process and the non-consultative imposition of a president by George Wallace. Throughout Funderburk's tenure he was never able to overcome the illegitimacy with which his presidency was viewed. Eventually, after

---

[33] This "insider's" view of the presidency is markedly different from that of many outsiders to higher education. In many local communities, the college or university president is one of the most important local personages, a symbol of power and prestige who seemingly occupies an enviable position. Visible are the prequisites: sometimes a sizable mansion—something which for many presidential families in a time of rising costs for housing has been more curse than blessing. There is the assigned car. The salary often looks attractive, although if one calculates the number of hours that presidents typically work, their salaries turn out to be meager indeed. On presidential compensation, see Mark H. Ingraham, *The Mirror of Brass: The Compensation and Working Conditions of College and University Administrators* (Madison: The University of Wisconsin Press, 1968). See also, for the current scene, the article by Carolyn J. Mooney and Scott Heller, "Benefits and Outside Income Boost College Presidents' Compensation, but in Some States, the Perks Sometimes Produce a Political Backlash," *Chronicle of Higher Education*, Vol. 33, no. 35 (May 13, 1987), pp. 1, 20–23.

a vote of no confidence in Funderburk, the latter's position became intolerable and he resigned.[34]

The 1984 University of New Mexico search was another example of the ravages that can result from an unsuccessful search process. In part to avoid virulent localism, such as efforts by the governor and other political powers in the state to assure the appointment of a chicano and a New Mexico resident, the New Mexico Board of Regents put the search in the hands of a search consultant. The executive recruiters they chose, PA Executive Search, had no previous experience with an academic presidential search, but did have a personal connection to the chairman of the board. When the presidential selection was announced, the faculty gave the news a stormy reception, believing that the regents' choice, John Elac, did not have the appropriate academic experience to be president and objecting to the secrecy with which his selection was made. The discovery by the local press that Elac was a personal friend of the search consultant who recommended him to the regents further fueled faculty opposition. Realizing that he could not have a successful incumbency under these circumstances, Elac withdrew. Thereupon, the second choice of the board, Thomas Farer, a law professor at the Rutgers branch campus at Camden, was offered the presidency. But Farer's stay in office was stormy and short; he, too, was forced to resign, with the remainder of his contract bought out by the regents.

As a result of this upheaval, the University of New Mexico's areas of real distinction, for example in anthropology and the arts, are overlooked; recruiting of distinguished faculty members becomes more difficult; and leading faculty already on campus are more ready to accept offers elsewhere. In situations of repeated leadership upheaval like this, the top administration becomes chaotic, and demoralization—always lurking in any going concern—sets in. It is possible that such a morass may attract a buoyant candidate who appreciates a challenge; however, since a public college presidency, especially in a state without strong traditions of academic autonomy, is a taxing situation at best, the problem of finding a new candidate who is at once ambitious and incautious is a formidable one.

[34] In many cases of this sort, the ousted president cannot recover, being viewed as "controversial" by search committees elsewhere. In Funderburk's case, this fate did not befall him: in 1985, he was named president of Eastern Kentucky University in Richmond, Kentucky.

Clearly, a president's life is difficult, even under the best of circumstances. Kerr and Gade report that the "average president works a 60–80 hour week. Much of this work time is spent in the evenings and on weekends." As a result of these heavy demands on their time, presidents cite common experiences such as "a sense of loneliness," "a sense of being driven," "a lack of time to read or think," "and a sense of being under constant observation."[35] In "The University and College President,"[36] William J. Bowen, vice-president of Heidrick & Struggles, Inc., Consultants in Executive Search, reports that forty percent of presidents have a tenure in office of about three years. He concludes that burnout is a principal factor in this high rate of turnover.

Rapid presidential turnover is costly to institutions and to society. Presidential searches are expensive and take time; new presidents, even those who have been president elsewhere, need time to learn about the institution and the position. Most learning takes place on the job. An "accident" of one sort or another—the suicide of a student, a rape on campus, racial incidents, sexual harassment of a student by a professor, an unexpected strike by buildings and grounds workers—can test the capacity for learning of the neophyte, and indicates the need to recruit people who have the endurance to stay in a taxing and exposed position while they learn and make the inevitable mistakes. And, of course, whatever they do or do not do, it will be considered a mistake by some constituencies.

In conducting our research for this book, we became persuaded time and time again of the importance of energetic, thoughtful, capable leadership for America's colleges and universities. Contrary to much recent criticism, we believe that American higher education is one of the most commendable aspects of American life, a magnet for students and faculty from all over the world. A great strength of our system is its enormous diversity.

We believe that capable leadership is necessary to sustain the collectivity, the collegium of colleges or universities. We believe, furthermore, that those presidents who can influence the academic, intellectual, and moral qualities of a campus are scarce human resources, and, hence, their identification and conservation is imperative. There is no magic formula for conducting the search for such presidents; changing conditions may

---

[35] Kerr and Gade, *Many Lives*, p. 28.
[36] Issued by Heidrick & Struggles, 1987.

mean that a well-conducted search will produce an incumbent who by the time of installation will prove quite unsuitable. Nevertheless, we believe that a search committee can become more than the sum of its individual parts, and not represent simply the lowest common denominator of its members, and thus be capable of finding, and in the best cases legitimating, a choice which no single individual on the committee could at the outset have envisaged.

CHAPTER II

"Abbott College"

MANY THEMES ARE illustrated in the "Abbott College" case study: the pressures for constituent participation in the search, the conflicts over confidentiality and disclosure, and the alternation of trust and suspicion vis-à-vis trustees, presidents, and other authorities in the culture generally and in academic culture particularly. Abbott College faculty members concerned themselves with their place in the search process, and sought to influence the type of candidates that could be considered as legitimate leaders for their college. Some of the faculty sought to wrench Abbott College away from its traditional, predominantly Protestant, male, and upper-class orientations. Restless with this rubric, which appeared to them unduly conventional and constraining, they used the slate of candidates to try to jolt the college, even though they were pretty sure it would not be jolted. On the whole, this struggle was carried on discreetly, without purposeful leaks to the student or the local press.

IMPORTANT DATES

Recent Abbott presidents	Curtis Rodgers, 1953–1969; Roger Thorndike, 1969–1984
Fall 1980	William Patterson comes to Abbott as vice-president for finance and planning
Spring 1982	Roger Thorndike on vacation, Patterson in charge
June 1983–January 1984	Thorndike on leave of absence; Patterson made acting president
October 1983	Thorndike announces intended resignation

25

January 1984	Thorndike returns to campus
January 1984	Faculty and students asked to select representatives to presidential search committee
February 12, 1984	First search committee meeting
March 1, 1984	Original deadline for applications and nominations for president
First week in March	Faculty representatives to search committee meet with faculty to discuss search process
March 13	Second search committee meeting
March 30	Extended deadline for applications and nominations
April 10	Search committee meeting scheduled for this date cancelled; re-scheduled for May 9
May 9	Third search committee meeting
May 10–June 4	Preliminary interviews of semifinalists
May 23	Fourth search committee meeting
June 4	Last preliminary interview
June 5	News story listing finalists' names appears in *Grand City Monitor*
June 6–11	Six finalists come to campus for day-long meetings
June 9–11	Faculty rally in support of Michael Knight
June 12	Final search committee meeting
June 13	Trustees name fourteenth president

CAST OF CHARACTERS

Roger Thorndike	Abbott's thirteenth president
William Patterson	Vice-president for finance and planning
Allen Pierce	Chairman of Abbott board
Martin Sloan	Chairman of Abbott search committee
Jim Willoughby	Secretary of faculty
Susan Levin	Affirmative action officer
Cynthia MacMillian	Semifinalist
Howard Fein	Finalist; director of educational studies, Northern State University

26

Charles Hammond   Finalist; dean of Pelham College

John Upshaw   Finalist; formerly a high-ranking government official

Michael Knight   Dean of the faculty, Prince College

Angela Rice   Finalist; vice-president for planning, North Central University

THE SEARCH

Abbott, a private liberal arts college located in Grand City, a large metropolitan area and the financial center of a midwestern state, conducted a search for a president in 1984. Founded in the Jacksonian era with the support of clergymen, Abbott College has long had high prestige. Places in its student body of 2,500 are eagerly sought after. The college has an immense library for an institution of its size, and a distinguished faculty respected for both scholarship and teaching. Alumni ties to the college are strong. Not only are most members of the Abbott board of trustees alumni, but so are many administrators and faculty members.

When the college's last presidential search took place in 1969, faculty and students shared the widespread assumption that the selection of a president was exclusively a board prerogative. Roger Thorndike was an Abbott alumnus and a member of the Abbott board of trustees when a small committee of trustees selected him to be Abbott's thirteenth president in 1969, a post he then held for sixteen years. Thorndike's predecessor, Curtis Rodgers, was reportedly approached about the Abbott presidency while he was dining at the New York Harvard Club. There had been no search process; the Abbott trustees simply had decided that Rodgers would make an excellent president for the college. In 1984, however, in part because of national developments and the way these were refracted at Abbott College, Abbott faculty members passionately believed that they should be active participants in the selection of Thorndike's successor.

Thorndike had been the first Abbott president with a Ph.D., and during the years of faculty-student unrest and often extreme politicization, he introduced coeducation and oversaw and supported the subsequent increase not only in women faculty members, but also the recruitment of minority (particularly black) students and faculty that accompanied selec-

27

tivity, visibility, and prestige. Helped by beneficent alumni and their corporate and foundation connections, Thorndike maintained the college's financial equilibrium, operating consistently in the black while neighboring institutions were experiencing unanticipated deficits and the accompanying upheavals.

Thorndike's tenure at Abbott was long—some faculty thought too long. In his last years at the college, his interest in his pressure-filled tasks seemed to wane. Many at Abbott wondered if the trustees or Thorndike might be thinking ahead to his retirement. In 1978, when Thorndike created a new administrative post, the vice-president for finance, many people speculated that Thorndike might be grooming a successor. The first person selected to fill this vice-presidency became seriously ill and resigned after only a few months at the college. A year later, Thorndike appointed William Patterson to the position.

Bill Patterson, the former chairman of the board of the state's largest bank, was highly regarded in state business and professional circles. His rise in banking had been rapid: he had become president of the bank at the age of thirty-eight and was named board chairman only five years later. Even so, Patterson's interests had never been limited to finance. As an undergraduate at Ivy League University and a master's student at Oxford, he had studied English literature and had seriously considered pursuing a doctorate in this subject. Later, in his early years in banking, Patterson had attended night school at the state university and earned a J.D. Not only Patterson's prominence, but his spirit of unassuming generosity and reputation for good judgment led to his involvement with many cultural and educational activities as well as service on the boards of many companies.

In the early 1970s, Patterson was nominated for the presidency of his alma mater, Ivy League University, and although he was intrigued by the offer, he did not wish to leave banking and decided not to pursue this candidacy. Several years later, however, at the age of fifty, Patterson was ready for a change. When his friend Roger Thorndike suggested that he become Abbot's vice-president for finance, Patterson accepted the offer.

Thorndike and Patterson worked well together, and Patterson quickly assumed many executive responsibilities. When Thorndike took a three-month vacation in 1982, he asked Patterson to direct the college in his absence. A year later, when Thorndike was having family problems and was granted a six-month leave of absence at his request, the Abbott trustees formally appointed Patterson acting president for this interim period.

Shortly after Thorndike began his leave, he announced that he was resigning from the Abbott presidency. He would return to the campus in January as planned, and would continue in office until the board had identified his successor, be it June 1984, January 1985, or June 1985. The announcement led to intensified discussion on campus. Some faculty were certain that Thorndike had been fired by the board; others were equally sure that Thorndike was simply ready to go elsewhere to begin a new life. But whatever the reaction to or speculation about Thorndike's leaving, there were no reservations concerning the importance of faculty participation in the choice of a successor.

The faculty's preoccupation increased because, although Thorndike's resignation had been announced in October, nothing was said about a search during the fall—an unusually long hiatus which led to suspicion even on the part of the most institutionally loyal faculty. Some faculty members surmised that board chairman Allen Pierce had become exhausted from settling matters related to Thorndike's departure and was dreading the prospect of launching a search. Others more inquisitively wondered what was going on and whether or not some back-room arrangement was being made among the trustees. They feared that Pierce as chairman, along with the rest of the board, would proceed with the selection as had been done in the past: making their selection, confirming the appointment quietly, and then announcing the *fait accompli*.

Had Allen Pierce hoped that the board might take such unilateral action, he promptly learned that so archaic a procedure was not acceptable in 1984. Jim Willoughby, secretary of the faculty and a former Abbott classmate of Pierce, sent a forceful letter to Pierce explaining that the faculty regarded themselves as entitled to have a voice in the selection of Thorndike's successor, and expected to have such a voice. This message, reiterated by Thorndike and Patterson, was hardly news to Pierce, who was aware from conversations with friends on other boards that the conduct of a search by trustees alone was no longer feasible. Such an imposed choice would create only turmoil, not a legitimate selection.

On a Friday afternoon in early January, Pierce telephoned Willoughby

29

and requested that he name three faculty members to serve on a presidential search committee. Willoughby responded that the faculty would conclude that three places were too few. Pierce agreed to raise the number to five and said he wanted the names of these faculty members by the following Tuesday. In effect that allowed only the intervening Monday for the decision. Both men recalled the ensuing conversation, with Willoughby saying, "That's impossible. That's not how faculties work," and Pierce responding that he had just chosen the seven trustees for the search committee! Pierce complained, "Faculties take forever to make a decision. As a surgeon, I have to make quick decisions every day." In contrast, Willoughby believed, as he later explained, that the faculty should have been told to "come up with a selection scheme that fits your habits of thought," and that sufficient lead time should have been allowed for this process to occur.

Willoughby called a faculty meeting to discuss how the faculty representatives should be selected, and after a lengthy discussion the faculty decided that the faculty senate should make these appointments. Later that week, the faculty senate met for two long afternoons, argued, negotiated, and compromised, until they had determined their slate of names. The five faculty chosen for the search committee were a varied group in terms of academic disciplines, personal styles, and tenure at Abbott. One faculty member was considered a conservative "solid citizen;" another was seen as a "provocateur." One faculty member had been at Abbott for more than twenty-five years, while another had come to the college only two years before. Two of the five professors were women. All were respected and liked by their colleagues.

Although the trustees had originally intended to include only faculty and trustees in the search process, they decided, on further thought, to have two student members on the search committee as well. Board chairman Allen Pierce asked the Abbott student government president to identify two juniors, one male and one female, to serve on the committee. The student government followed an elaborate selection scheme regularly used for deciding committee appointments. Interested students prepared written statements about their qualifications and then appeared before the student government for a thirty-minute interview. Ten days later, Pierce was given the names of two students. Both were active in student government, academically successful, and personally poised and articulate.

The first search committee meeting was scheduled for Thursday, February 12, at a downtown private club. The five faculty members, disturbed about what was expected of them and of the search itself, decided to caucus in advance of the session. Were they to be voting members of the committee or not? Several faculty feared that the search was a charade: there had been much speculation that the board had already picked Bill Patterson. This suspicion was fueled by the several months' delay before any public announcement of the search. Was the faculty being asked to participate solely to give the search the appearance of authenticity? The faculty members sounded one another out on how they felt about Patterson's candidacy. Most were not hostile to him and were open to considering him, but only in comparison to other candidates. The faculty discussed whether Patterson had the job in his pocket. The worst scenario discussed was that the search committee would simply be going through the motions of considering candidates, when, in fact, the trustees already had decided on Patterson; the best scenario was that the trustees were open to considering other candidates. Viewing themselves as the delegates of the entire faculty, the five faculty members were unanimous: they wanted to be voting members of the search committee, not to have merely an advisory role.

The first full search committee meeting was a dinner designed to acquaint members with one another and to allow the chairman, Martin Sloan, a trustee and businessman, to explain how the committee would go about its task. Sloan got down to business immediately. By his own account, he was tough. "I felt some things had to be decided fairly quickly." Prior to the meeting, Sloan had used John Nason's book, *Presidential Search*, to chart the course of the search. The charge of the trustees to the search committee was that they were to identify three to five strong candidates from whom the board could select Abbott's next president, and that this selection would take place at the board's May meeting. Sloan mentioned the importance of the search committee's consideration of women and minority candidates and explained that the trustees had decided not to employ a search firm but to have the search committee screen the candidates itself. He noted that the former assistant to the president, who had retired that year after thirty-nine years at Abbott, would serve as executive secretary to the search committee, acting as the paper-mover and scorekeeper.

Magic marker in hand, Sloan drew a series of arrows on a large note pad to depict the candidate screening process. The fourteen members of the search committee would be divided into three groups, with each group reviewing one-third of the candidate folders. The folders of the fifteen candidates receiving the highest scores in each group would be passed to another group for additional review. Five of these fifteen would then go to the third group for their consideration. When all three groups had reviewed all folders, only three to five top-ranked candidates would remain in the final cut.

When Sloan emphasized the importance of maintaining confidentiality, explaining that leaks of candidates' names could harm people in their present positions, the faculty representatives became alarmed. "Although we recognized the necessity of keeping names secret in the early stages of the search, we felt that at a certain stage they had to become known," one person stated later. The Abbott faculty wanted assurance that the finalists would visit the campus. Sloan would only say, "We'll have to wait and see." The faculty then wanted to know if they had a vote on the committee. Sloan assured them that they did and added that they had a veto. "We do not want to select any individual who is unacceptable to the faculty." But Sloan reminded the faculty that the final decision was the prerogative of the board of trustees.

Next, Sloan outlined procedures he had already initiated to obtain candidates. An advertisement for the Abbott presidency had been placed in the *New York Times* and the *Chronicle of Higher Education*, and Sloan had written college and university presidents in nearby states and at leading liberal arts colleges to request nominations. The deadline for applications and nominations had been set for March 1. The Abbott faculty would be invited to put forward candidates. And Bill Patterson had been asked whether he wished to declare himself a candidate. After consulting with his wife, Patterson had said that he did.

The faculty representatives had already come to the conclusion that several of the trustees on the search committee—notably board chairman Pierce—were strong Patterson supporters. No pro-Patterson leanings were expressed by the trustees at the meeting, and Sloan repeated several times that the contest was completely open, although he added that Abbott College was lucky to have such an excellent in-house candidate as Bill Patterson. Still, there was of course no decision as yet, and the task of the search committee was to identify the very best candidates possible. On this matter, the faculty members of the search committee were in complete agreement. They, too, wanted to evaluate Patterson's candidacy against others. "I believed that my responsibility to the faculty," one stated later, "was to see that we brought as good a pool of candidates as possible to Abbott College."

Although the letters and advertising undertaken by Sloan were standard, even routine, the uneasiness of faculty members concerning the whole process and its feared outcome was reflected in the fear that the position had not been advertised widely enough to attract appropriate candidates. Susan Levin, the campus's affirmative action officer, saw the search as an opportunity to promote an affirmative action agenda. She regarded herself as a spokesperson for women and blacks at the traditional college, and her expressions of concern about the search fueled the faculty anxieties. Believing that the search committee had failed to follow correct affirmative action procedures, she wrote to a trustee member of the committee, volunteering to assist the committee and referring to the college's affirmative action procedures she had helped draft a year earlier. These 'recruitment procedures' were to be used in the search for all new administrative staff members. The procedures called for the hiring plan, job description, pool of candidates, and final account of recruitment efforts to be cleared by the college's affirmative action officer, and stated that "once a candidate has been invited for an interview, the visit should be publicized accordingly." Levin wrote that the search for a president should provide a college-wide model of affirmative action. The trustee who received her letter sent it to Sloan, and Sloan responded by telephone, asking Levin to take the appropriate steps to ensure compliance with affirmative action requirements and inviting her to the next search committee meeting to report on her efforts at recruitment. When she offered to monitor the search, that is, to sit in with the committee, Sloan turned her down.

The faculty members of the search committee were pleased that Levin was placing additional advertisements of the Abbott position, but they still wanted to know whether the general manner in which the search was being conducted was "correct." Levin volunteered to explore what had been the role of faculty at other campuses, and whether it was the usual practice for finalists to be brought to campus to meet with the entire faculty and not merely with the search committee. While promising to find out how comparable institutions had organized their searches, Levin telephoned faculty at a nearby college for information about their recent search, and was able to report back that finalists had come to that campus for open interviews. Everyone had been pleased with the outcome of that process, because everyone had participated in it, the implication being clear that the Abbott search should follow the same open and participative process.

Knowing that their colleagues wanted information about the search, the Abbott faculty members of the search committee obtained permission from the search chairman to talk to the faculty about the procedures to be followed in the selection process. They asked the secretary of the faculty to call a special faculty meeting, and they invited the trustee members of the search committee to attend this session. When the faculty representatives to the search committee explained the format of the screening process, their colleagues immediately wanted to know what would happen after a few finalists had been identified. Would the full faculty get to meet these top contenders? Would the faculty representatives on the search committee take part in the final vote? Or would several unranked names be sent to the board of trustees for the trustees to determine the final selection? The faculty also expressed concern about what they saw as the "limited advertising" of the position. To some, this seemed "to confirm our suspicions that Bill Patterson was the predetermined choice of the trustees, and the search process was merely a show." Even if more extensive advertising were to be placed, the March 1 deadline would limit the possibility of any serious influx of candidates, the faculty members noted. Apparently the faculty's strong feelings about the application deadline impressed one of the three trustees who attended the faculty meeting sufficiently to lead him to telephone board chairman Allen Pierce and encourage him to extend the date by which applications could be made.

The freewheeling and, at times, heated discussion at this faculty meeting reflected widely divergent judgments concerning the respective roles of faculty members and trustees and the degree of trust the faculty put in the trustees. Older faculty members with strong institutional loyalty declared that the selection should be a matter for the trustees, with faculty only minimally involved; others, including younger, more vocal faculty who wanted to see substantial change at the college expressed the prevalent view that the search had been fixed, that is, that Patterson had been chosen, and that any faculty contribution would be merely a token. One observer of the meeting commented that he thought a good portion of the faculty attending the session was "paranoid" concerning the board's power.

Nominations and applications arrived throughout February and March. As candidates' curricula vitae were received, the secretary to the search committee directed them to search committee members, coordinating this paperwork from a small office, formerly part of the library stacks, located at the end of a corridor on the top floor of the administration building. Serving, as Sloan had stated, as the scorekeeper and paper-mover, this secretary played an important role in organizing the review process and ensuring the confidentiality of candidacies. Whenever she left her office, even for a few minutes, she locked the door behind her; when making telephone calls about candidates, she made certain that the door to the room was closed so that passersby would not catch a word of the conversation. Although a lot of people tried to "pump" her, she commented, she never felt any real pressure to divulge information. One administrator said that this was probably because of the secretary's personality. "She is too highly respected for anyone to have deigned to ask her an improper question. I thought she was an odd choice for that job. She'd been retired, and I wondered how good she would be at all that paperwork. But then I realized that, because of how proper she is, she was the perfect person."

With the second full search committee meeting scheduled for mid-March, the faculty representatives to the search committee again decided to caucus in advance. One faculty member asked about the wisdom of taking notes during search committee meetings, commenting that one of the trustees on the search committee was a lawyer, and records made during sessions might conceivably be subpoenaed later. Although this discussion was only half-serious, it suggested the initial mistrust that faculty felt toward the trustees.

The faculty members spent the remainder of the session drafting a letter to search chairman Martin Sloan outlining a "plan of operation which we feel will most appropriately and effectively assure full faculty participation in and contribution to the selection of the finalists." They recommended that the entire search committee meet to discuss the fifteen semifinalists; that the five finalists be determined by secret ballot, that these finalists be invited to the campus to meet with the search committee and the entire faculty, that any candidate not wishing to meet with the faculty at large be required to confer with faculty members of the committee in a separate session, and that, following the interview process, the entire search committee select the three names to forward to the board of trustees. The faculty concluded their letter by thanking Sloan for the one-month extension of the application and nomination deadline.

When the presidential search committee met on March 13, the first item of business was the report by affirmative action officer Susan Levin. Levin said that she had been in touch with the American Council on Education's Office for Women and a wide range of other organizations likely to know of qualified women and minorities, and she could reassure search committee members that these networks had now been used effectively to advertise the position. After her presentation, she was excused from the meeting. Next, the letter from the faculty was discussed, and Sloan agreed that the full committee should meet to discuss the fifteen semifinalists and that they would then vote by secret ballot. But Sloan refused to commit himself as to whether the finalists would be brought to campus. Until the committee knew who the finalists were and whether these people would be willing to appear in open interviews, Sloan would not give the faculty the assurance they wanted.

The third item for discussion was a letter one faculty member of the search committee had written to Sloan recommending that the only black member of the board of trustees be invited to serve as an ad hoc adviser to the search. All faculty, trustee, and student members of the search committee were white. The faculty member recommended that the position be ad hoc so as not to upset the even balance of trustees and nontrustees on the committee (seven trustees, five faculty, and two students). The proposal was discussed, and board chairman Allen Pierce strongly opposed it. Search chairman Martin Sloan disagreed as well, believing that making this change midway through the process would make it appear that they had not been giving minority candidates full consideration when indeed they had.

The next search meeting was scheduled for April 10 to allow time for reading material on candidates, which kept arriving up to the April 1 deadline. By that time, current academic deans furnished the largest crop of candidates, while the pool also included a number of current and former college presidents. Some individuals who had consented to become candidates after being nominated made clear that they did not want people at their home institutions to be used as references until such time as they became serious contenders, that is, finalists. One nominator expressed his own concern for confidentiality this way: "Let me ask that you use discretion in making inquiries concerning this nomination . . . the possibility of his leaving our college would cause consternation in some quarters if it were to become public."

When the executive committee of the board of trustees met on March 20, the trustees voted to ask the presidential search committee to present to the entire board no fewer than three and no more than five candidates for their final consideration. The executive committee did not state whether these candidates should be ranked or unranked. Search chairman Martin Sloan decided that they should be ranked, so that the board would be made aware of the search committee's assessments.

When several members of the search committee said that the scheduled meeting date of April 10 did not allow them sufficient time to read all the folders, the meeting was rescheduled for May 9, two weeks before commencement and the final board meeting of the academic year. During April, committee members reviewed folders and ranked them according to the rating scale Sloan had outlined. During this month, too, curiosity about the search heightened. One faculty member of the search committee recalled that a number of people tried to get her to say who the candidates were. "I thought this was a big nuisance. People would call me late at night to tell me things, mostly negative things about Patterson." On April 14, the student newspaper printed an editorial lambasting the trustees and the student representatives: "It is up to you, students and faculty, to take some aggressive action or else a day may come when the name of our new president will be sprung on the college without due and fair warning. Before school is over and summer brings the absence of your numbered voices, form panels, write letters, *demand* that you be informed and that your suggestions and questions are taken seriously."

Angered at this attack on the search committee in general and them in particular, the two students on the search committee wrote a letter to the student newspaper expressing their outrage at the "totally unfounded insinuations." They noted that "all of our procedures are public knowledge. The names of the candidates have been kept secret for the obvious reason of confidentiality." Later that month, the two students held an open meeting to discuss the organization of the search process. Approximately twenty-five students attended. Many students in the audience assumed that Patterson would be the next president, and most were favorably inclined toward his candidacy. Thanks to his periods of absence from the college, Thorndike had become a remote figure to students. Even when on campus, he had rarely attended student functions. In contrast, Patterson, as acting president, had inaugurated the practice of stopping in at parties and football games.

Generally, student interest in the search was minimal. One of the two students on the search committee said that the few students who bothered to ask about the search usually asked the following questions: " 'How's it going? Is Bill Patterson a shoo-in?' Next, they would inquire whether there were any black and women candidates. Finally, they'd want to know if anyone famous was a candidate. When told that there wasn't a celebrity among the candidates, they didn't ask anything else. Students don't know the names of faculty or administrators at other campuses, a student on the search committee commented, so the names of the candidates wouldn't mean anything to them."

Abbott's director of development said that many people from off-campus asked her about the search. "People would say to me, 'You must have some information,' and I'd say no. It became apparent that there weren't going to be any leaks and that saved a lot of trouble." A strong supporter of Patterson, the director of development said that she was approached regularly by alumni and parents who said, "What are you doing up there, for Pete's sake? You already have your man right on campus." When people would tell her of their support for Patterson, the director of development would suggest that they write board chairman Allen Pierce. One faculty member remembered seeing the "lobbying for Patterson" and felt it highly unfair. "No one was supposed to know who the candidates were. If we'd known, we could have lobbied for our candidates." Another faculty member said that everyone had "little stories about people in the community, stories that furthered our suspicion that Bill Patterson had it." He mentioned that a retired bank officer in his neighborhood had said that it was common knowledge that Patterson was Abbott's next president. Another faculty member reported that the minister at his church had introduced Patterson as "Abbott's next president." One faculty member on the search committee said that trustees were "blabbing at parties, saying that Patterson would be chosen president. I got very angry at that. They were predicting the outcome of the search and therefore putting pressure on the committee."

With the search process well under way, faculty members of the search committee were still disturbed that they had not been assured that the full faculty would interview the finalists. In addition, several Abbott administrators were irritated that no arrangements had been made for them to influence the search process. They would have preferred membership on the search committee; not having this, they wanted to make certain they would be able to meet finalists and to voice assessments of them.

The third meeting of the search committee took place on May 9, the first time all committee members were able to be present. Board chairman Pierce scolded one of the faculty members for her absence at the two previous committee sessions. Throughout the meeting, the two committee members exchanged barbs. Pierce, a surgeon in a metropolitan area one hundred miles from Abbott, had been Abbott's chairman of the board for eleven years. Deeply attached to the college, Pierce took the search very seriously. Pierce "shepherded the entire process. He was always there. He was really committed," one faculty member stated. Another person recalled the time when one meeting had gone quite late and Pierce stood up to leave at about 11:00 p.m. A faculty member chided Pierce about leaving before the session was concluded. Pierce replied that he still had a two-hour drive home, and he had to be in surgery the next morning at 7:00 a.m. No one questioned Pierce's loyalty to Abbott College or his conscientiousness, but some faculty wondered whether in his dedication to the college as he had known it, he was truly willing to consider blacks and women. One woman faculty member saw her role on the committee as that of "keeping sexist remarks to a minimum." She recalled that when Pierce referred to one woman candidate as "a real knockout," she quickly responded that she found this comment offensive. Feeling about Pierce's and other trustees' attitudes toward women candidates reached a peak when the candidacy of Cynthia MacMillian, a controversial figure in higher education, was reviewed. One trustee said "absolutely not," and several faculty demanded to know why. The trustee explained that he had spoken with several friends on other boards and they had said "not to touch her." The women members of the search committee said that they wanted to judge MacMillian for themselves. After considerable discussion, MacMillian's name was placed on the list of semifinalists.

The remaining semifinalists were chosen without much difficulty. One faculty member of the committee thought, however, that there had been insufficient discussion and that decisions had been reached too swiftly. Another commented that the session had been productive. Sloan had been very directive and had led the meeting "like a CEO."

Prior to the search committee meeting of May 9, one trustee committee member contacted an executive search firm he had used in his business and reported their advice concerning the screening of candidates, namely that the search committee divide into four teams with each team interviewing three of the twelve semifinalists. The full body would then convene as a whole to determine the slate of finalists. The committee agreed to proceed in accord with this recommendation and to ask the search firm to check eight to ten references on each of the finalists.

The time had come for a decision as to whether the finalists would be invited to the Abbott campus for open meetings. Several trustees agreed with the faculty that open meetings were important; others were concerned about the possibility of these meetings taking on a "circus atmosphere." One faculty representative commented later that trustees were wary of what might happen in open sessions because they had attended the spirited faculty meeting in March and had seen how outspoken faculty could be. One trustee thought that open meetings might mislead faculty to believe that their views on candidates would prevail. Another worried that making candidates known would be embarrassing to the losers. After considerable discussion, a decision was finally reached: all finalists would be invited to the campus for open interviews with faculty. No candidate would be dropped from consideration, however, if he or she did not wish to participate in the open forums.

Four teams were organized, each with a mix of faculty, students, and trustees. In late April, the three women on the search committee—two faculty members and one trustee—interviewed Cynthia MacMillian. Although they liked her initially, they thought MacMillian did not field questions well. Much as they wanted to warm up to her, they found they could not. At the May 23 search committee meeting, the women reported their impressions. The trustees were greatly relieved: there was not to be a fight on this issue. Committee members reported on other interviews as well, and decisions about the semifinalists were reached easily, with no major disagreements. The atmosphere changed, however, when Pierce announced that the board had voted to give the search committee a new deadline of June 13. The faculty immediately questioned the wisdom of this timetable: if the search committee was supposed to have a decision by June 13, they would have to complete their interviewing of semifinalists, decide whom to invite to campus for open meetings, schedule these day-and-a-half sessions, and evaluate all the finalists—all within the next three weeks. The trustees said that the deadline was firm. One faculty member's letter to Pierce expressed his sharp disappointment: "I am disturbed about the timetable of the entire operation. The selection of a president in June may very well be an outcome devoutly to be wished. But it is a fact that two months elapsed between the retirement of Roger Thorndike and the first overtures to the faculty regarding their participation in the search. . . . It was a month later before the entire committee met for the first time. Another month elapsed between the meeting scheduled for 10 April but never held, and the next meeting on 9 May. When this much time is lost at the front end and in the middle of the process, I think that more flexibility is called for at the other end."

The discussion of candidates at the May 29 search committee meeting proceeded much as it had at the May 9 session. Members of each team reported on the individuals they had met, and since other committee members had not seen these candidates, the consensus of the team was accepted virtually without argument. With Sloan directing the discussion, the committee decided on five finalists to bring to the campus for extensive interviewing by campus constituents. These five finalists were Bill Patterson, Michael Knight, John Upshaw, Charles Hammond, and Howard Fein. The committee agreed that a sixth candidate, Angela Rice, whose preliminary interview had not yet taken place, could be added to the list of finalists if the team so recommended.

Abbott College commencement exercises took place on May 24, and the campus emptied afterward. But even though faculty were off-campus, their interest in the selection of the president kept their communication network alive. The faculty were finally to have their long-awaited chance to participate in the search process.

On June 4, the search committee sent the faculty an interview schedule and a brief resumé of each of the five finalists. This announcement mentioned that a sixth person might be added to the list of finalists, depending on the outcome of a pending interview. Late that afternoon, a faculty member of the search committee received a telephone call from Abbott's director of public relations, Steven Schmidt. The city newspaper, the *Grand City Monitor*, had obtained a copy of the interview schedule and intended to print it, and the names of candidates, in the next day's newspaper. The faculty member thanked Schmidt for alerting him to this and then called Allen Pierce with the news. Pierce was furious. He was alarmed that this breach of confidentiality might seriously disrupt the process and might cause some candidates to withdraw. Faculty members on the search committee thought that a big fuss was being made over nothing. After all, they had told the candidates that these final sessions would be open. Getting this far in the process wasn't a stigma, one faculty member said. It was almost "a badge of honor."

Pierce telephoned the *Monitor* reporter to see if he could convince her not to print the story. "It's newsworthy; we're printing it," she replied. By the time Pierce called, the reporter had learned one additional piece of information: that the sixth finalist was a black woman. While Pierce argued with her about running the story, she tried to get him to tell her the name of this additional candidate. Neither Pierce nor the reporter achieved the end sought. Pierce then called search chairman Sloan to confer about what action they should take. Certain that the *Monitor* reporter would continue to try to track down Angela Rice's name, they decided to telephone all the search committee members to alert them to the likelihood of the reporter calling. Candidate Rice had explicitly mentioned her concern about publicity, noting that wide knowledge of her candidacy might jeopardize her present position.

One of the two students on the search committee was the first person the *Monitor* reporter called after she had the list of names. She probably thought she could weasel the missing name out of a student, the student commented, but she was wrong. The student guessed that the information about the candidates had "spilled over the top," leaked by trustees. Other members of the search committee were convinced that the *Monitor* reporter had obtained her information from a faculty or staff member at Abbott, since all had been sent the memorandum naming the finalists, and the memorandum had not stated that this information was confidential.

Sloan next telephoned the finalists to warn them of the forthcoming story. Many were unhappy with the leak. Howard Fein, by his own description an uncertain candidate, had scheduled his campus interview to coincide with his Abbott class reunion. When he arrived at the college, he discovered that, thanks to the newspaper story, his reunion classmates knew of his candidacy. When he returned home several days later, he was greeted with the news that his hometown paper had also printed a story about his Abbott candidacy. Some of his faculty colleagues were aghast, he said, but no real problems were created in the long run.

Michael Knight had not been completely comfortable with the open character of the Abbott search but had agreed to participate in the campus interviews. He had hoped, though, that knowledge of his candidacy would be kept "as confined as possible." When the *Monitor* story broke, Knight had not yet told the president of his college of his candidacy. The two talked, and although it wasn't a difficult conversation, it was not the way he would have wanted things to have happened. Even had the information about his candidacy reached his college by word of mouth, Knight would not have minded so much. The news story was somehow more indiscreet, he stated.

The story of the Abbott search ran on the top of page A17, under the six-column headline, "Abbott Narrows Presidential Search to Six Candidates." Names and brief biographical data on five candidates were given; mention was also made of one black female candidate whose identity was not known. As soon as the story appeared, several trustees complained about it to Pierce, pointing to this leak as an example of what they feared would happen if faculty were included in the search process.

Charles Hammond, dean of Pelham College, was the first finalist to visit the Abbott campus. When Hammond met with faculty members, he stated that he was not certain whether his own timetable would fit Abbott's. Hammond had just received an offer to spend a year at a research center. If Abbott were willing to wait a year, he would be very interested in the presidency. Some faculty thought a wait would be possible since Thorndike had said he could stay up to a year. But other faculty agreed with the trustees that the college needed new leadership right away.

Howard Fein came to Abbott a few days later. An Abbott graduate and trustee, Fein was director of educational studies at Northern State University. Fein talked with the search committee about their hopes for the college's future, and seemed, to many, to be leading a seminar. At the end of the session, Fein commented that he did not think he was interested in pursuing the presidency. One search committee member speculated later that Fein realized that his chance of being selected was not good. "His colleagues on the board probably let him know that Patterson had the inside track."

John Upshaw arrived at Abbott on June 8. Formerly a high-ranking government official, Upshaw was between jobs and seemed quite interested in the Abbott presidency. But the faculty members with virtual unanimity said that the likelihood of Abbott's appointing a black as president was very slim. The College was making a concerned effort to recruit black students, faculty, and staff (of 2,000 students, 90 were black; of 150 faculty, 7 were black). But the likelihood that the new college head would be a black man, not to speak of a black woman, was, if not outlandish, at least improbable. The students and faculty members on the search committee reported that they never believed that a black person would be chosen president; nevertheless, they liked the idea of bringing minority candidates to campus.

Michael Knight, dean of the faculty at Prince College, was the fourth candidate to visit the Abbott campus. Up to then, faculty had not seen anyone except Hammond who seemed presidential material, and Hammond had withdrawn from the competition. For the faculty who were not enamored of the idea of Patterson as their president, Michael Knight be-

44

came their man. "He charmed us all. I knew he had the faculty on his side when he began his talk with the comment, 'I haven't been this nervous since I defended my dissertation.' Every faculty member in the room immediately identified with him. 'He's one of us,' they thought." Like the other candidates, Knight spoke for ten to fifteen minutes and then answered questions from the audience. In his talk, he stressed the need for the president to know the academic enterprise of the institution well so that he could convincingly sell it to prospective donors. He described fund raising he had done at Prince College and criticized Abbott for its lack of aggressive fund raising. He spoke of the mission of a liberal arts college and the need for a humanistic education. The faculty were enchanted. One administrator said that they experienced "an almost evangelical conversion." Another said that Abbott was badly in need of resuscitation and revival and Knight seemed to offer this hope. "Faculty felt appreciated; morale soared." Not everyone was so totally taken with Knight, however. One of the student members of the search committee thought that Knight was providing all of the answers that he knew faculty wanted. A faculty member concurred: Knight was "pandering to us." Overall, however, there was an outpouring of positive feeling for Knight. Unfortunately, one faculty member commented, there had been no trustees from the search committee present at Knight's meeting with faculty to observe his performance in that setting.

Bill Patterson's interview followed Michael Knight's. Other than his having appeared before the three-person semifinalist interviewing team, Patterson had not previously been placed in the role of candidate, but had quietly gone about his regular business at the college. Many faculty members and administrators had commented positively on his handling of the situation, noting that he had kept a low profile and never seemed to be campaigning or lobbying. "He behaved like a perfect gentleman," one person said. The interview with faculty was his first time on the firing line. The room was full; the trustee members of the search committee were out in full force. Many of the faculty who were already favorably disposed to Patterson's candidacy had not bothered to come to the college on a summer day to hear him handle questions. The faculty who were not enthusiastic about Patterson as Abbott's next president had made a point of being there, and were armed with questions that were curves and fast

45

balls. Unlike Knight, Patterson had not prepared a polished speech. He talked generally for a few minutes and then answered questions. Patterson did not respond well, many people observed. Although he kept his composure, he seemed a little unsettled. When asked what he would do as president, he said that he thought the college was doing well at the present time and he would not anticipate making any major changes in the immediate future. "He is not given to exhortation, to utopian visions or any pretense of these," one person commented. Many of the questions focused on affirmative action. Patterson was pressed hard concerning his commitment to affirmative action. Some faculty had concluded that Patterson was insensitive vis-à-vis women and blacks, referring to a "confidential" draft of a memorandum Patterson had written a year earlier. Copies of this draft had recently begun to circulate among the faculty. Some faculty pointed to Patterson's language in the memo as proof of his disregard for affirmative action concerns; others said that the memo was only a rough draft and should not be taken as evidence of Patterson's beliefs.

The last candidate to visit Abbott was Angela Rice. She was interviewed the day before the final search committee meeting. Unable to get away from her home institution for a full day, Rice, the vice-president for planning at North Central University, arrived at Abbott in the evening, stayed overnight, and met with faculty in a brief session early the next morning. She was in and out of town quickly. No newspaper ever picked up her name. Few faculty members or administrators came to the session. For most, including members of the search committee, she was never a serious contender. She was a "statement." As a woman and a black, she was an unlikely contender, seemingly coming to Abbott more to gain experience in a presidential search than out of any expectation that she would be chosen as Abbott's new president.

With only a few days left before the search committee's final vote on the candidates, a small group of faculty announced a "pro-Knight rally." "We quickly decided to call our efforts pro-Knight, not anti-Patterson, for we didn't want to be seen as taking a negative position," one faculty member said. The faculty invited the members of the search committee to come to the rally. All of the faculty members of the search committee and one trustee member, Wayne Martins, himself an alumnus of Abbott and a faculty member at a liberal arts college, attended. About forty-five faculty

46

members and two administrators were at the meeting, an attendance several called remarkable since it was two weeks into the summer vacation. The first part of the meeting was given over to a discussion of Knight's interview, and the faculty were in strong agreement that he was a most attractive candidate. Later, trustee Wayne Martins called the meeting one of the most energizing sessions he had witnessed at Abbott. The faculty were demonstrating their concern and caring for the institution and were trying to take action to forward their own values.

Feelings about Patterson's candidacy were mixed. A small group of the faculty (some estimate five to ten percent; others guess as many as twenty percent) were strongly opposed to Patterson becoming the next president of the college. Others (probably ten to fifteen percent) were strong supporters of his candidacy. The remaining group of faculty had some positive feeling for Patterson, some questions about him, or no strong feelings one way or the other. Objections to Patterson fell into several categories. Some thought he was "a businessman for a scholar's job." They were concerned both that he would run Abbott like a business and that he would try to vocationalize the college. Others feared he would not be sensitive to women and blacks.

As the group of faculty discussed Michael Knight, the excitement built. The faculty seemed to come alive. After talking about how to convey their support to the full search committee, they decided to undertake three activities: to draft one letter for signature by as many faculty as possible; to have individual faculty write personal letters stating the basis of their support for Knight; and to divide up the trustees, particularly those not on the search committee, and have faculty members call them to alert them to the high level of support for his candidacy.

Other tactics were mentioned and discarded, including the possibility of picketing the trustee meeting, of holding a press conference, and of sending the "confidential" Patterson memo to the *Monitor* in an effort to make him look bad and therefore withdraw his candidacy. All of these actions were rejected: "We don't do those things here," one faculty member stated firmly. One administrator commented that she was surprised by the "politeness" of the Abbott faculty. Believing that the press would be their best strategic weapon, she was convinced that the only way they would prevail was if Patterson withdrew.

The faculty called their colleagues who were not at the meeting and asked them to come to the campus to sign a letter to the search committee supporting Knight. There were only two days left before the final search committee meeting. The level of activity was reaching a fever pitch.

Meanwhile, several members of the administration were considering what they should do to show their support for Knight. Twelve staff members signed a telegram to the search committee: only two of the top-level administrators (deans, directors) signed the telegram, while only one of the women staff and administrators did not sign the letter. Both in their sentiment about Patterson and their feeling about the letter, administrators were sharply divided. "No one in my zone signed that letter," one administrator stated. "It is tolerable, perhaps even desirable, to have a good piece of the faculty up in arms. But not the administration." Another administrator disagreed: "I work for the Corporation, not for the president. I feel obligated to express my disagreements when I feel something is opposed to the best interest of the college."

The full search committee met on Friday, June 12, to discuss the finalists. This was their last meeting. The board of trustees would vote on their recommendations the next morning. The faculty members of the search committee presented the letters and the telegram they had received supporting Knight. They had received twenty-nine individual letters and one letter signed by eleven other faculty. Next, the search firm's report on the finalists was presented. Because of the limited time that the firm had been given to work on the report, it was not complete: for one of the candidates, only four references were checked, with the fourth reference turning out to be a person who had nominated the candidate. The search committee discussed the finalists briefly and then easily determined the names of the three top contenders. Both Hammond and Fein had withdrawn from the competition; of the remaining four candidates, Rice was seen as the weakest of the group. To determine the ranking of the remaining three finalists, Upshaw, Knight, and Patterson, a secret ballot was taken. Much to the faculty members' surprise, when the votes were counted, Knight led with seven, Patterson was second with five, and Upshaw was third with two. Two trustees had joined the faculty to vote for Michael Knight. One of them was search chairman Martin Sloan. Sloan said later that he felt it important to convey to the trustees the full extent of the faculty's support for Knight. Sloan called Knight "an elegant, gentle man," and said that the search had produced two highly qualified individuals, one whose strengths lay in the academic area and one whose strengths lay in the area of finance.

Given the strong show of faculty support for Knight and the fact that only two trustees had met him, board chairman Allen Pierce decided that Knight should be invited to meet the board. That evening, Pierce called Knight at his home to ask him to come to the trustee meeting the next morning. Because he was out to dinner, Knight did not receive Pierce's call until almost midnight. The drive from his home to Grand City took two hours. To be at Abbott College for the 10:00 a.m. meeting, he had to leave home before 8:00 a.m. When Knight arrived at the college, he was told that he should talk for fifteen minutes and respond to trustee questions. Knight's meeting with the board lasted just over one-half hour. After he left the meeting, Knight and his wife, who had been waiting on the lawn outside, went out for lunch and then drove home. Their children greeted them with the news that someone from Abbott had called and left the message that the board had selected William Patterson as Abbott's next president.

The treatment of Knight, one trustee later commented, was "awkward and graceless," but it was better than either other alternative, not seeing him at all or delaying the board selection. The board had, in fact, been open to considering Knight for the presidency, he added. After Knight had left the meeting, the trustees had talked for a very long time about Knight and Patterson. Some trustees had been very impressed by Knight. Others found his style highly "academic" and could not imagine him handling the college fund raising successfully. Although a handful of trustees had been predisposed to Patterson from the outset of the search and were not prepared seriously to consider anyone else, most had open minds. Finally a vote was taken. On the first ballot, Bill Patterson was elected president by a solid majority of trustees. On the second ballot, the vote for Patterson was unanimous.

A week after the election of Patterson, the faculty members of the search committee met with interested faculty to review the search process. Twenty-six people attended the session. One faculty member reported that he had heard that the trustees had discussed Knight's candidacy at great length and that their first vote had not been unanimously for Patterson. Many faculty expressed disappointment that the trustees had interviewed Knight on such short notice, concluding that the board had not given him adequate scrutiny. Some of the faculty members of the search committee indicated that they wished they could have made the committee's report to the trustees, or at least have attended the meeting when the report was made, to ensure that the strong support of Knight was appropriately conveyed. Generally, though, while faculty were disappointed that their choice was not the final choice of the board, they concluded that their participation had not simply been pro forma. "We gave it our best shot," one faculty member said, "and we were pleased that we seemed to have affected the vote." Others commented that they were heartened by the fact that faculty assessments had been taken seriously: "We had our say and we said it."

In early July, two faculty members of the search committee wrote Allen Pierce that they believed it important that "we not forget what we may have learned from the experience, and that we glean from it what we can to instruct, inform, and guide us in the future." They expressed concern about the timing of the search process, criticizing both the overall timetable and the rushed nature of committee meetings. They indicated disappointment in the consideration given Knight's candidacy, mentioning that there had been no trustee present at his on-campus interview and stating that the trustees did not have time to give careful scrutiny to the letters of support for Knight from the faculty and administration.

In closing, they made two suggestions. First, they expressed a desire to see "a great mutual effort on the part of trustees and faculty to get to know each other as persons, principally in the context of what the college is mostly about, the education of students in a learning community." Second, they suggested that the trustees create an explicit system of accountability and periodic reviews of the president.

During the 1984–1985 academic year, faculty members reported little residual feeling about the outcome of the search or the procedural issues that had been debated during it. "We have our little scraps and then we all go to the same cocktail parties," one person explained. Another commented that if there were any lingering bad feelings, they were less among the faculty than among the administrators. But interest in the event per-

50

sisted. One administrator talked about writing a history of the search process. And midway through the year, the faculty senate drafted a letter to the board of trustees outlining their recommendations for future presidential searches. They stated that the composition of the search committee had been satisfactory and that bringing the candidates to the campus was a step they strongly endorsed. They mentioned that there had been concern about affirmative action and recommended that appropriate attention be paid to this area in the future. They noted that there had been substantial concern about whether sufficient time had been allotted for the process and suggested that scheduling of steps and determination of procedures should be the responsibility of the entire search committee. Finally, they recommended that the report of the search committee be delivered to the board by the full committee.

The secretary of the faculty added his own comment about the process. "The faculty started out with great suspicion and skepticism, with the concern that Allen Pierce might simply be trying to put his friend in. Somewhat kicking and squealing, the faculty went along. Finally, in the end, the committee members were friendly, trusting each other."

CHAPTER III

Getting Under Way

IDEALLY, THE TRUSTEES of a college or university will be constantly but non-obtrusively vigilant about the institutions they govern. They will know where the institution is going and what its various elements are. Thus, they will have a good idea about when a president should leave, perhaps even setting a date for the departure. Long before this departure, they will organize the search process for the president's successor, thinking about how they might widen the pores of the institution, so as to increase the flow of information during the presidential succession.

More often than not, however, boards of trustees find themselves faced with a presidential departure they did not anticipate or prepare for. Most presidential searches are organized on an ad hoc basis and managed by committees whose members are amateurs at this task. Rarely have trustees or other members of search committees had previous experience in conducting a presidential search. Rarely, too, are policies for the search for the new president ready when they are needed.

COMMITTEE STRUCTURE

As we just saw in the case of "Abbott College," the first issue to arise concerns the organization and membership of the search committee. Although it is widely understood that the college or university president is selected by, and serves "at the pleasure of the board," during the search for a new president the formal power of the board of trustees must invariably be supplemented by some form of participative consultation. The instances of small, exclusively-trustee selection committees are rare. (One example is the 1990 Harvard University search, chaired by Corporation member Charles Slichter.)

Most boards of trustees employ one of two committee structures for their presidential searches, the single search and selection committee, or the two-tiered advisory/selection process. The Abbott College search committee was an example of the former; the University of Florida search, described in Chapter VI, used the latter model. (There are a few notable exceptions. The New School for Social Research, in its 1982 search for a president, had a trustee search committee and two advisory bodies; one was made up of students and faculty members and the other was composed of deans. The 1989–1990 Carnegie Mellon Institute presidential search involved multiple committees: a trustee search committee composed of eighteen members; a faculty search committee made up of twenty-five members, including representation from the university's administration and staff; a student advisory committee of nine undergraduates and five graduate students; and a presidential search steering committee comprised of twenty-one members including trustees, faculty members and a student.)

In the two-tiered search process, the top tier generally consists of a selection committee chosen from the board of trustees, while the second tier is a campus-based advisory committee which includes faculty, administrators, nonprofessional staff, students, alumni, and members of the local community.[1] The campus-based advisory committee is typically responsible for soliciting nominations, and for culling the long list of candidates to a smaller group for further consideration. Often, the advisory committee interviews these finalists and then forwards their names (ranked or unranked) and the advisory committee's evaluations of them to the board selection committee. Typically, the board selection committee is responsible for making the ultimate decision as to who will be chosen president.

In some institutions, the two-tiered arrangement represents a reluctant transfer of certain aspects of the search to campus constituents, in response to campus pressures for participation. Such was the case, for example, in the search for a successor to William Friday as president of the University of North Carolina system. The UNC faculty wanted to be included in the search process; after considerable discussion, they were given an advisory, non-voting role. In such an instance, a campus-based

[1] The 1989 Texas Tech search was unusual in having its selection committee (its top-tier committee) include three faculty members in addition to four regents. This committee was advised by a larger campus-based search committee with twenty-one members.

committee, although advisory in name, may, in fact, determine the outcome, since the regent or trustee committee may not become active in the search early enough to see to it that candidates they might prefer are included in the group of finalists.

Today, many state colleges and universities are part of a state system, which sometimes means that presidential selection is handled by the board of the system and sometimes by a combination of the institution's own boards with some system involvement. In searches for presidents or chancellors of state systems of higher education, the search process is typically more dominated by the board than the search for a campus chief executive officer. Occasionally, in order to minimize the obvious political pressures playing on many public systems, the board of trustees or regents may seek to create a search committee that is independent of the board and of the competing institutions within the system. Such a procedure was followed by the trustees of the three-campus Montgomery College in Maryland when they selected Robert Parilla as president. The board put together an external committee, made up of the president of another multi-campus community college system, a campus head in a multi-campus system, someone from a state-wide office, and other people familiar with Montgomery College and community colleges more generally. This committee had no local college representation. All applications and nominations were sent to this external committee, whose members also sought out prospective candidates. This body reviewed the credentials of candidates and passed the names of twelve to fifteen persons to the board. Then a college committee, made up of faculty, administrators, and staff from the three campuses, was given the list, and they decided who should be interviewed and passed along their comments to the board. The board made its own judgments on the list. A small number of candidates had interviews with both the college committee and the board before the board made its final choice.

Sometimes, because of the culture of the state, the search will become political, no matter what committee structure is employed. In 1986, when the Massachusetts Board of Regents was seeking a successor to chancellor John Duff, Paul Ylvisaker, emeritus dean of the Harvard Graduate School of Education, was asked to chair a committee to find "the best person" in a national search. This selection committee's choices, all known through the state's open meeting law, included a nonacademic, James Collins,

55

among six semifinalists. A graduate of the University of Massachusetts at Amherst, Collins is a lawyer and was, at the time of the search, a Massachusetts state representative, with a special interest in precollegiate education. When the selection committee narrowed its pool to four finalists, Collins's candidacy was eliminated. The friends of Collins in the Massachusetts legislature, at the University of Massachusetts, and among the University of Massachusetts alumni set up an enormous outcry. The board of regents then decided to go outside the quartet of candidates presented by the search committee and to choose Collins as chancellor. Governor Michael Dukakis immediately intervened, replacing the chairman of the regents and, when he had the chance a few weeks later, naming three new regents. This new board reopened the search, reinstated the search committee's quartet of finalists, and chose one of them, Franklyn Jenifer, as chancellor. Jenifer, a biologist, was associate chancellor of the New Jersey state system.[2]

This Massachusetts story suggests a common danger with the dual-committee structure, namely, a struggle for influence between the selection committee and the advisory committee. Having become involved in the search in its early stages, the advisory committee may not wish to relinquish to the selection committee the most exciting and significant part of the process, the actual naming of the president or chancellor. Or the reverse may happen, with members of the board selection committee seen as interfering in the search before their turn comes, or accused of already having made up their minds, thus making the efforts of the advisory committee only pro forma. At its best, the two-tier pattern can serve to buffer the decision-makers against political pressures, while assuring the campus that it has had a say in the outcome.

The single search and selection committee is the most popular committee structure, especially at private institutions. Commonly, but not invariably, a member of the board of trustees chairs this committee, whose membership is drawn from the board and the campus. As we saw in the Abbott case, this single committee is charged with carrying out all aspects of the search, up to the identification of a single candidate or a small slate

[2] For an excellent account of this search, see Richard A. Hogarty, ''The Search for a Massachusetts Chancellor: Autonomy and Politics in Higher Education,'' *New England Journal of Public Policy*, Vol. 4, no. 2 (Summer–Fall 1988), pp. 7–38.

of candidates. Some search committees will be required to give the full board one nomination, whereas other committees will be told to give the board a ranked or unranked list of the three, four, or five finalists they have found most suited for the presidency.

COMPOSITION OF THE SEARCH COMMITTEE

Once the committee structure has been determined, an equally or more difficult issue is the composition of the search committee or committees. Many college and university searches have become politicized and faction-alized at their very outset by disputes over which constituencies should be represented and in what numbers. The faculty at Ramapo College lobbied successfully to increase their numbers on their presidential search com-mittee so as to include female and minority faculty because, when the faculty had voted for the three faculty seats the trustees had originally allotted them, their election had resulted in an all-male, all-white slate. At Springfield College, the trustees initially created only one committee, an all-trustee selection committee. When this body was announced, there was a great stir on the campus about constituency involvement. The un-rest was exacerbated by the fact that many people believed that an internal candidate had already been tacitly chosen (much as had been thought at Abbott College), because of his close ties to the retiring president. After the chair of the faculty senate met with the chair of the selection commit-tee, the board agreed to establish a sixteen-person advisory committee whose members would be chosen by their respective personnel groups (ad-ministration, faculty, staff associates, and physical plant), as well as in-cluding representatives of the student body and the alumni association.

As these two examples suggest, the membership of search committees is often decided for political reasons. The trustees place on the search com-mittee representatives of those constituencies they think would make the most noise if they were not included in the search. The composition of search committees, as Robert Birnbaum has noted, often represents ''a tacit negotiation that reflects the balance of influence on a campus.''[3]

Over the past several years, we have been asked many times what par-

[3] Birnbaum, "Presidential Searches and the Discovery of Organizational Goals," *Journal of Higher Education*, Vol. 59, no. 5 (September–October 1988), p. 494.

ticular committee membership we recommend. Our preference is to answer this question not by stipulating a certain size committee with representatives from certain constituencies, for we believe that the appropriate committee composition varies from institution to institution, and from one search to another within the same institution. Rather, we would suggest that the board of trustees begin by examining the multiple purposes of the search committee and then consider what qualities committee members must possess to ensure that these purposes are realized.

The most obvious reason for the existence of the search committee is to identify the individual best suited to serve as president of the college or university. Perhaps less apparent, however, are the attributes members need in order to be effective in achieving this end. To identify the "right" person for the presidency requires, first of all, a good understanding of the particular institution and the job of its president; the best match cannot be recognized, to use the analogy of a jigsaw puzzle, without knowing the shape of the place in the puzzle where the sought-after piece will go. The person who makes an outstanding president at one college or university might well be a disaster in the presidency of another.[4] Hence, one important quality that needs representation on the search committee is a good appreciation of the special nature of the institution and its presidency.

Closely related is another quality which members of the search committee must possess to be able to identify successfully the next president of the institution. They must be good judges of people. A trustee or faculty member who cares deeply about the institution and understands its peculiarities and idiosyncrasies intimately may, or may not, have the ability to "sniff out" a candidate in a short time. One must be able to see beyond the often highly polished presentation of self, or beyond a less polished or even awkward façade, to those personal qualities which can make all the difference in the long run. All too often the choice of the new president is based on very limited information. The amount of information gathered in interviews with candidates depends greatly on the capabilities of the interviewers and the perceptiveness of the listeners.

---

[4] For the alternating currents of hope and fear that drive search committees toward what they term "managerialism" or "hero-ism," see Thomas North Gilmore and James Krantz, "The Splitting of Leadership and Management as a Social Defense," *Journal of Human Relations*, Vol. 43, no. 2 (1990), pp. 183–204.

A second purpose of the search committee is to persuade those candidates the committee has found most appealing that the presidency is worthy of their consideration. We cannot emphasize enough that searches involve courtship quite as much as they involve selection. Although Alan Guskin, president of Antioch, had initially said that he would be crazy to consider that presidency, part of what captured his interest and persuaded him to consider Antioch seriously was the caliber of individuals on the search committee. The quality of the Antioch alumni he met during the search was a powerful statement about the best aspects of the college.

The search committee is often a candidate's first introduction to the institution. Yet we know of no search committee whose members were chosen because they made the college or university appear inviting to prospective candidates. We do know, however, of several instances when the behavior of a member or members of the search committee was sufficiently irritating that a candidate declined further interest in the search. One candidate told us that her ambivalence about remaining a candidate was greatly increased by the surly antagonism toward her of a member of the search committee of a selective liberal arts college. In another search, a student member of the search committee was deliberately rude, challenging each candidate about his or her willingness to spend time with students.[5] More commonly, however, candidates reported to us that they enjoyed meeting the student members of the committee. They said the presence of students on the search committee made the presidency of that institution more attractive. One person commented, "Their candor is refreshing. . . . A candidate can get a real feel for attitudes or morale on a campus through interaction with student leaders in the course of a search."[6]

Yet, the rationale for including students on presidential search committees is sometimes questioned. In the desire to keep the search committee reasonably small, every "seat" on the committee must be justified, and those filled by students are often seen as ones that could otherwise be filled by people with greater experience and longer exposure to the institution.

[5] Joseph A. Keane, dean of continuing education at Thomas Aquinas College, has written a humorous but damning article, "Why Deans Stay Put," with the subtitle, "Because of Search Committees," which itemizes one awful experience after another he had as a candidate. (*AAHE Bulletin*, September, 1988, pp. 8–9.)

[6] From private correspondence, June 22, 1989.

Occasionally, a student will be an unusually astute judge of character, picking up on nuances that other members of the committee have missed. More often, however, the chief contributions of the student members of the search committee are in the ways they can help further this second goal of a search committee, to persuade the candidate of choice that he or she would enjoy working at the institution.

The third task of the search committee is to legitimate the choice of the new president. For the outcome of the search to be considered legitimate, the search itself must be viewed as having been sufficiently participatory. The question thus arises as to who the stakeholders are; that is, who are the people whose support is necessary for the enterprise to go on? Or, to put the question differently, who are the people whose opposition will be a serious obstacle to the success of the new president?

For the search to be considered legitimate, important institutional stakeholders must be included in the search process. Nearly all search committees today include faculty members, who are arguably the best organized stakeholders of colleges and universities. Many faculty members believe that their stake in the institution is even greater than that of trustees, and, in fact, faculty members with tenure will outlast many, if not all, of the trustees, and two or three presidents as well. Hence, on almost all campuses, if the trustees brought in a president who would be found objectionable by the faculty as a whole, it would be a recipe for turbulence.

Eighty percent of the searches that we surveyed included students on their search committees. Often there were two students, one male and one female, or, as in the Rice University search described in Chapter X, one undergraduate and one graduate student. When Carleton College searched for a successor to Robert Edwards in 1986, there were four students on the fifteen-person search committee.[7] This meant, for one thing, that the search had to virtually suspend operations during the long stretch of summer vacation when the students were scattered.

Like faculty and students, administrators of colleges and universities are

[7] The Carleton search committee was made up of five trustees, the dean of the college, the vice-president/treasurer, four faculty members and four students. This committee was identical in structure to the committee that selected Robert Edwards as president, and three of the four faculty members on the 1986 committee had served on the earlier search committee. Since that earlier committee had not included a woman, a recently tenured female associate professor was named to the fourth faculty slot.

60

clearly stakeholders, and often they, too, believe themselves entitled to membership on the presidential search committee. As we shall see in the "Southern State University" and University of Florida searches, administrators are often included on large campus advisory committees, and occasionally there is a single administrative representative on smaller search committees as well. The 1988–1989 Babson College presidential search committee was unusual in having three administrators and only two faculty members on its twelve-member search committee, a ratio that would be deemed completely unacceptable at most institutions of higher education. At Babson, a college of business administration, the heavy representation of administrators reflected the institutional culture (as did the statement by search committee chair Elizabeth Powell that the committee would consider candidates from the business community as well as from academe), and serves as a reminder that what is considered a "legitimate" committee composition varies from institution to institution.[8]

While the practice of including faculty on search committees is now widely accepted, the wisdom of including administrators is debated. In part, the reluctance to include them is due to the fact that one of them may be a latent candidate (and we have come across such situations). In part, there is concern about there being a real or perceived conflict of interest in having administrators select their own boss. There is perhaps the realization that, because most administrators serve at the pleasure of the president, they might be tempted to make a deal with a candidate to vote for this person, in return for a guarantee of job security. Or if not doing this outright, they might well cast their votes for the candidate they deem most likely to keep them on. Moreover, those who set up search committees often seem aware that administrators can feel crowded or envious vis-à-vis their prospective superiors. But there seems to be almost no attention to the conflicts of interest among faculty members, that is, the wish of many not to be bossed, to have the president be weak, or at least be someone who will spend time raising money and not thinking about the quality of the faculty or the curriculum.

[8] Babson's choice as president, William F. Glavin, did, in fact, come from a corporate background. Glavin was vice-chairman of the Xerox Corporation, and had worked at Xerox since 1970. Prior to that, he had been at IBM for fifteen years. He had also served as a trustee at The College of the Holy Cross and a member of the Wharton School's board of overseers.

In some institutions, notably those that are unionized, there may be a distinction made between senior administrators, such as deans or directors, and professional staff. Frequently, this latter group is part of a union or professional association. In searches that are concerned about representation from all parts of the campus, one sometimes finds a representative of the senior administration and a representative of the professional staff.

Our own preference, in most situations, is not to have administrators on the search committee itself. However, in reflecting on institutional transition, members of the search committee can gain by drawing on the variety of administrators' perspectives and expertise early in the search process, as the committee—helped in some instances by consultants— confronts the question of what sort of leadership is now most needed, and also later in the search, as the committee evaluates the final candidate or candidates.

In addition to administrators, there are others on campus who could contribute greatly to a search committee's understanding of the qualities required in a successor. Librarians commonly have an excellent sense of the academic workings of the institution, including knowing which faculty members are the serious scholars and which are merely showmen.[9] The 1985 Williams College search committee, which included four trustees, four faculty members, and two students, came under attack from the campus's professional staff, led by the librarians, for failing to represent them. At some institutions, a dean of admissions or a dean of student affairs might be an excellent choice for a search committee because of their understanding of the institution and their skills in interviewing and listening, although they would probably not carry weight with the faculty, who often deprecate all administrators.

Some search committees include representatives of the administration, professional staff, non-professional staff (clerical, maintenance, food service, etc.), and local community, be that the city, town, or state in which the institution is situated, or the religious community with which it is affiliated. The New England College search committee, for instance, had fifteen members, including five trustees, three faculty members, a representative of their British campus, two staff members (a secretary and a

[9] See Wriston, *Academic Procession*.

62

member of the buildings and grounds crew), two students, and two alumni. The University of Connecticut search committee had twenty-four members, including the governor or his designate, and faculty, students, administrators, staff, and alumni.

By far the largest search committee we have heard of was the 1989 presidential search advisory committee at the University of Florida, a committee with forty-one members. In Chapter VI, we describe the 1983 search at the University of Florida which resulted in the selection of Marshall Criser as president. In that search, the university advisory committee was made up of twenty-five members, eight of whom were UF faculty. Six years later, however, when Marshall Criser left office, a new state law was in effect which severely restricts faculty membership on search committees.[10] According to this legislation, at least one-half of the membership of university advisory committees must come from business and industry, and the remaining members are to be apportioned equally from among the faculty, student body, administration, and other university employees. Hence, in order to have the five faculty representatives that the University of Florida faculty felt was the bare minimum they required, the committee had to have five students, five administrators, and five other UF employees, and twenty non-university members as well.

COMMITTEE SIZE

Whereas campus advisory committees in a two-tiered search tend to be large, single search committees vary greatly in size. In the Winthrop College search, the search committee had six members: one faculty member, one student, and four trustees. As we shall see in Chapter VIII, some members of that committee reflected afterward that the group was too small, and said they would recommend that future searches have one or two additional members, preferably drawn from the college faculty. More often, though, search committees err in being too large. As at "Abbott

[10] Many in Florida attribute the legislation to Florida state representative T. K. Wetherall, an unsuccessful candidate for the presidency of the University of West Florida whose candidacy was opposed by faculty members of that university. In an article in the *Chronicle of Higher Education* (Goldie Blumenstyk, "Florida's Universities Confront Huge Population Surge, Narrow Tax Base, Tough Politics, and Regional Funding," June 21, 1989, p. A13), this law is "privately referred to as 'T. K.'s Revenge.' "

College," the size of search committees is often swelled because faculty members complain of having too few representatives vis-à-vis the number of trustees, and lobby successfully for greater numbers. These added numbers do not necessarily serve the interests of the faculty, although they may satisfy the expectations and demands of influential individuals or departments, which, if united behind the outcome of a search, can help legitimate it with the rest of the faculty. However, since most search committees operate on the basis of consensus rather than by vote, what matters is not numbers but the power of persuasion or the power of veto of a forceful individual or individuals, or the power of information possessed by those search committee members who "do their homework" and attend all the meetings.

Looking back retrospectively at their searches, heads of search committees have frequently commented that the large size of their committees was a handicap during the search process.[11] It is obvious that the simple activity of scheduling meetings becomes more difficult for a larger group, with the result often being incomplete attendance at committee sessions or the delegation to subcommittees of various tasks, such as the review of candidate materials and even the initial interviews with candidates. In such cases, both understanding and responsibility tend to become diluted. Furthermore, when committee size grows, the mutual distrust with which members of a search committee often begin their work never disappears during the course of the search. In the best of searches, membership on the search committee enlarges the personal horizons of board members, faculty members, and students, by the ongoing contact they have with the others on the search committee. For this mutual learning to occur, the search committee generally needs to be small, within a range of between seven and a dozen members.

In search committees much larger than this, the trustee members of the search committee will typically sit with fellow trustees, the faculty members with other faculty members, and the different constituencies will interact largely with those people they already know and never become well acquainted with each other. Committee members may see the committee in terms of "them" and "us," a situation which is exacerbated when

[11] For the results of Glenn D. Williams's survey on this subject, see Williams, "The Search for Dr. Perfect," *AGB Reports*, Vol. 18, no. 4 (July–August 1976), pp. 39–43.

search committee members enter the process—as indeed many do—suspicious of each other's motives and intentions. In many searches, for instance, trustees underestimate the pragmatism of which faculty members and even students are capable, taking it for granted that faculty members will insist on selecting a candidate with a Ph.D. and a record of scholarship and teaching. Similarly, faculty members may be fearful of trustee collusion, wary that the selection may already be predetermined, or afraid that trustee priorities will be at odds with theirs. As we saw in Chapter II, such suspicions were pervasive throughout the "Abbott College" search. The feared differences between groups, especially between faculty members and trustees, are often accentuated by real, visible differences in language, dress, and socioeconomic backgrounds. Stereotypes and pre-judgments are especially difficult to overcome when the committee is large, and the opportunities for casual mixing and the chances for everyone (especially the shyer, quieter members) to speak, are infrequent. Committee members remain delegates from constituencies, a microcosm of the institution's own political and cultural schisms, unwilling and unable to negotiate differences.

A "dis-economy" of size can also dilute the sense of responsibility that individual members feel for the search endeavor and for each other. Our research indicates that leaks of confidential information are more common in searches with large search committees. This is undoubtedly partially due to the fact that more committee members means that there are more people who might leak information. But large size also means greater anonymity for members, so that it is more difficult to identify the person doing the leaking, and there is less sense of personal responsibility for the success of the search effort. If individuals on the search committee talk outside of the committee, they may not think that they are betraying particular others but rather some larger entity of which they are, or feel themselves to be, a peripheral or even antagonistic part.

One reason for the large size of many search committees is the belief that only women will push the cause of women, only blacks the cause of blacks—an understandable suspiciousness that is the legacy of prior powerlessness, but one which in many settings in the more liberal sectors of academic life is unwarranted. The result is an almost automatic increase in the size of search committees by a kind of Noah's Ark procedure. The

65

search committee for a new president at Evergreen State College—required when the former president, Dan Evans, was appointed to the U.S. Senate seat left vacant by the death of Henry Jackson—included an almost equal balance of men and women and became, in many respects, a "rainbow coalition." The result was a very large committee whose first effort to find a president failed. In the Williams College search for a successor to president John Chandler, the board decided that the faculty members chosen to represent the natural sciences, the humanities, and the social sciences should also be the representatives on the search committee. When they realized that all three of these representatives were men, they recruited a woman administrator to assure that women's concerns would be represented on the committee.

Similarly, at many large universities, the divisions are so great between colleges or schools, and even between departments within the same college or school, that faculty from one area, say agriculture, are not satisfied that someone from the faculty of humanities or the law school will "represent" them. The "two cultures" divide is a very rough and overgeneralized one, in that there are people in the humanities less humane than many people in the sciences, and many scientists with a broader perspective on people and events than most social scientists possess. Still, at some places it is politically important to have "both sides" represented. The Rice faculty chose its representatives to the presidential search committee in a two-stage process. First, they elected one faculty member to represent the humanities and social sciences and another faculty member to represent the physical sciences and engineering. In a second election, they chose an at-large representative from among the remaining candidates. All members of the Rice faculty could vote for all three positions. At universities with medical schools, there may be concern about representation from this area as well as from arts and sciences. When East Carolina University was beginning its presidential search in 1986, the ECU board of trustees asked the faculty to choose three representatives, noting that, ideally, one of these faculty members would come from arts and sciences and one would be from the medical school, and at least one representative would be a minority or woman.[12] At some institutions, relative seniority and relative

[12] Presidents of large universities joke among themselves about what is often their most difficult component, namely, their medical schools. Indeed, one well-worn joke presidents tell is of going to

youth rather than academic divisions are typical dividing lines. The Harvard faculty council, an outgrowth of the protest movements of the period from 1968 to 1972, is required by statute to include tenured and non-tenured faculty from each of the three divisions. Similar concerns about representation from "younger" and "older" faculty can be found on many campuses.

A search committee needs members who understand the institution in its present form and in terms of what is likely to ensue; who possess good judgment of others; who are good representatives of the institution to prospective candidates; and who are seen as "representative" by constituents and can thus make legitimate the work of the search committee. A search committee set up like a legislature to represent the various "districts" of the institution will not necessarily be more satisfactory than politicians and legislators generally are in legitimating outcomes. Similarly, knowledge of the institution can be ascertained in ways other than by enlarging the search committee. Later in this chapter we discuss the need for an institutional self-analysis prior to beginning the search for candidates. In the search for a new president of Skidmore College, whose retiring president, Joseph Palamountain, had served for twenty-two years, the search committee, guided by their consultant, took pains to meet with all department chairmen, with administrators, with buildings and grounds people, and many others in order to refresh and increase their store of knowledge concerning Skidmore.

THE COMMITTEE CHAIR

Although smaller committee size makes group cohesiveness more likely, another necessary ingredient is skilled leadership. One needs leadership to find leadership, leadership to recognize leadership in others. If the single most important act of a board of trustees is the appointment of a president, perhaps the next most crucial act is the appointment of the chair of the presidential search committee. Occasionally, a senior member of the

---

hell and being informed by the Devil that their punishment will be to have *two* medical schools! Soon after Charles W. Eliot was installed as president of Harvard University, he attended a meeting of the medical school faculty and was challenged as to his right to be there, for such an intrusion was apparently unprecedented. For many institutions, the medical school is much the most costly and, in terms of staff, also the largest semi-autonomous component.

faculty or an administrator will be asked to take on this responsibility, but more typically a trustee serves as the committee head. In some cases this is the chair of the board of trustees, and in many instances, the prospective chair of the board (the search chair earns his or her wings by this act of institutional service). Although many board chairs have made excellent heads of search committees, we believe it preferable for the board chair not to serve in this capacity. For one thing, any number of crises on campus may require the full attention of the board chair, who should in any case remain in the "backstop" position to deflect bad decisions or a poor selection.

In the Skidmore College search, the chairman of the board addressed the members of the search committee about the importance of their tasks and the salience of maintaining confidentiality against all pressures and temptations to divulge information, and then left matters in the hands of Judith Eissner as chair of the search committee. When, in the course of the search, she became chair of the board of trustees, another member of the search committee took her place as the committee head. It is commonly the chair of the search committee who sets the tone for the group, helping to develop the structure, timetable, and pace of the process. We have just seen the Abbott faculty's objections to the timing of their search, and it is not at all unusual to find searches slow in getting underway and rushed at the end. The chair of the search committee is responsible for seeing to it that the group remains cohesive while allowing for expressions of differences of opinion, and for exciting committee members about the prospects for the institution's future and alerting them to the potential hazards also riding on the outcome of their work. Throughout the course of the search, the chair must make certain that the energy and alertness of committee members are maintained, especially during such grueling times as when they are going over stacks and stacks of folders and need to take the most recent as seriously as the earlier ones, while keeping the earlier ones steadily in mind. What is required is both political astuteness and perseverance on a diurnal basis.

It is also commonly the search committee chair who acts as host when the committee meets with candidates. The chair is also host to search consultants when there is a contest to see which search consultant will be chosen. The best search committee chairs host discussions of the search committee in a manner that creates a spirit of mutual learning and an openness to new possibilities. In other words, the chair must be the "host" both for the committee and, in due course, for candidates being interviewed: always alert, neither dominating nor abdicating, preferably courteous. A chair can be too deferential, allowing bullying or obsessive members of the committee to take over, or too strong-willed, alienating committee members.[13]

Newton Minow, former chairman of the Federal Communications Commission and partner in a leading Chicago law firm, also an alumnus of Northwestern and its law school, chaired the search committee to find a successor to Robert H. Strotz, who had served as Northwestern's president for fifteen years. Like the many other practicing lawyers in large metropolitan firms who are able to shift some burdens to their partners and easily handle secretarial work in their offices, Minow threw himself into the search with the requisite energy. Unlike some on whom similar demands have been put, he found it useful, with search committee assent, to employ the executive recruiting firm of Heidrick & Struggles and its Chicago-based specialist on presidential recruiting, William Bowen. As we shall explore more fully in Chapter IX, a consultant can increase the reach of the committee and particularly serve the committee chair as confidant and adviser. When the Dartmouth board of trustees sought a successor to president David McLaughlin, Norman E. ("Sandy") McCulloch, devoted alumnus and retired Pawtucket, Rhode Island, businessman, could throw himself fully into the search, while continuing his chairmanship of the board. He also secured Bowen's help as consultant. For him, the search became an all-consuming effort, spurred by the hope that he could leave a transformed Dartmouth as a legacy to an alma mater which evokes passionate alumni loyalty.

Strong dedication, of course, is also possible among non-alumni. We describe in Chapter X the esteem that Ralph O'Connor, chairman of the Rice University presidential search, received from his fellow committee members for his energetic leadership in all phases of the process. Delaying

---

[13] For fuller discussion of the current inhibitions against taking charge on sociable occasions, see Riesman, Robert Potter, and Jeanne Watson, "The Vanishing Host," *Human Organization*, Vol. 19, no. 1 (Spring, 1960), pp. 17–27; see also "Sociability, Permissiveness, and Equality: A Preliminary Formulation," *Psychiatry*, Vol. 23, no. 4 (November, 1960), pp. 196–225.

what is often a rush to secure and consider possible candidates, he began the search with a weekend retreat and then helped the committee educate themselves about the tasks of a president, and about Rice's situation and potential. At a less well-endowed institution, Ramapo College, which had begun as a state college in 1969, board chairman John Dietze initiated a second search for a president after the first search effort had failed. Dietze established a new committee and convinced its members that Ramapo College could mount a national search and find a topflight person for the presidency. In the face of pressure to appoint someone from New Jersey, Dietze was able to persuade an energetic prospect, Robert A. Scott, at the time director of academic affairs of the Indiana Commission for Higher Education, to throw in his lot with Ramapo. Dietze personally made more than a hundred telephone calls to leading educators to obtain the names of prospects, and, when materials about candidates came in, he reviewed them with equal diligence.

THE CHOICE OF COMMITTEE MEMBERS

Just as there is no all-purpose answer to the question of who should serve on the search committee, so there is no one all-purpose method for selecting these committee members. Questions of choice are the most intricate because, as we noted earlier, the committee faces the overlapping tasks of pooling its best judgments and, if the outcome is not self-evidently compelling, defending that choice; and the committee is also a crucial window through which candidates will view the prospects of the presidency.

Often the members of the search committee are appointed because of positions they already hold, because they serve as chair of the faculty senate, or president of the student government, or head of the staff council. This means of selection to the search committee can present problems, however, if the person holding one of these positions is not personally or situationally best suited for the search committee. We are reminded of a search in a topflight liberal arts college where all four faculty members on the search committee were designated by virtue of the positions they held, rather than being chosen with the search in mind. All four had close personal and institutional ties to the dean of the college, and were united in supporting his candidacy, whereas many members of the board, including those on the search committee, would have preferred another inside candidate. The board was not prepared to make an issue of it, and hence announced that the dean was the unanimous choice of the board.

Sometimes, special elections are held to choose representatives for the search committee. Elections give constituents a sense of involvement early on in the search process and make it more likely that committee members will be respected by their peers. However, the result can be that those chosen regard themselves as representing a constituency rather than the entire institution. Search committee members may likewise feel beholden to the constituents that elected them "to office," a potential problem if this feeling of loyalty leads them to feel obligated to share confidential information about search activities. The election of committee members can be effective, however, when constituents understand the importance of the search and respect the need for confidentiality.

As mentioned earlier, the Rice University faculty elected three faculty representatives to the presidential search committee in two separate elections. These elections were preceded by a faculty meeting where all faculty were given a sheet of information explaining the importance of the search effort, the need to maintain its confidentiality, and the role expected of faculty representatives. The statement was forceful in emphasizing that the search would require a great deal of time, including considerable travel; that all committee members would be expected to hold all matters pertaining to the search in the strictest confidence; that committee members should approach their task with an open mind and without bias towards a preferred race, sex, academic discipline, vocation, or education; and that all committee members should make a successful future for Rice University as a whole their paramount objective and should not consider themselves as representing narrow interests.[14] A cynical or maladroit faculty might have discarded all this as an invitation to become co-opted, but given the culture of the campus, the statement conveyed to the entire campus, as well as to those who then became candidates, what the rules were by which the search would be governed.

The Rice search asked of its members, whether from the board of governors, the alumni, the faculty, or the student body, that they consider

---

[14] The full text of this statement is found in Chapter X.

themselves as voting, not for a faction, but for the public good, the common good, in the manner prescribed by Edmund Burke. Yet there is a sense in which the role of "representative" is Janus-like: the search committee member not only serves as the constituents' representative, but also as the guide for fellow members concerning his or her constituency's hopes and expectations.[15] If the search committee member remains too slavishly attached to constituent expectations, the search may be too constrained. But if the search committee members forget these expectations, the danger is that a presidential appointment will be made without recognizing the extent of constituent opposition that will develop. Ideally, search committee members keep in mind, alternately, if not simultaneously, the best interests of the whole institution and the implicit sanction of powerful constituency disapproval.

As studies in the larger political arena make clear, those who represent others possess and also develop somewhat broader horizons. Members of the United States Congress are constantly facing the charge that they have become Washingtonians, cosmopolitans, losing touch with the ordinary folk back home. At the height of the anti-Communist crusade, Samuel Stouffer commissioned interviews which allowed him to compare two cohorts, a sample of the general population and a subset of local leaders and elected officials. All were asked questions about the degree to which they were willing to tolerate dissent that might be termed sympathetic to Communism and the measures that should be taken to curb such political dissent. In his book, *Communism, Conformity, and Civil Liberties*, Stouffer reported that the leaders even of the more conservative organizations were more tolerant than members of the public-at-large, because their positions brought them into contact with others who thought differently. In Stouffer's interpretation, the orbit of a leader is wider than that of his or her followers, and people known face to face cannot so readily be demonized as when they are creatures known only vicariously.[16] We are not suggesting that knowing more types of people necessarily makes one more tolerant, but only that there is a tendency in this direction. Correspondingly,

---

[15] For a thoughtful discussion of the different meanings of "representative," see Chauncey A. Alexander, "What Does a Representative Represent?" *Social Work*, Vol. 21, no. 1 (January, 1976), pp. 5–9.

[16] New York: Doubleday, 1955.

72

our own observations in academia suggest that many trustees are more sympathetic to academic and liberal values than faculty and students believe them to be, and generally more sympathetic than the alumni or other groups from which these trustees are drawn.[17]

It does not take the subtle differences between the home guard and the cosmopolitan to create the potential for a rift between a search committee and the larger membership from which it has been drawn. A committee can easily develop its own cocoon. Search committees, which are ad hoc, that is, in place for this purpose only, are not as likely as more permanent bodies to become captives of their internal dynamics, but still it can happen. One of the most dramatic examples is the search at Gallaudet to which we referred earlier. It may well be that even the hearing impaired members of the search committee could not anticipate the explosiveness of the protests, which drew their strength in part from the growing nostalgia for the civil rights movements of the 1960s and the increasing campus confrontations over racist or alleged racist episodes. The Gallaudet search committee was hardly a runaway body, let alone a kangaroo court. In Elisabeth Zinser they had brought to campus a person who would previously have been unassailable and who at first was prepared to fight for the position in the face of opposition.

The search committee for a new president of Winthrop College included a single faculty member, already chosen by the faculty as their representative to the board of trustees. A senior professor of business administration, he was pursuing a second career after retirement from working in the Pentagon. When three candidates were brought to campus, the members of the arts and sciences faculty were decidedly upset by the choices presented them and petitioned the board to reopen the search. The Winthrop protests did not succeed, and the search committee's selection was grudgingly accepted by the faculty. Its importance for us lies in this similarity to the Gallaudet case, namely, the unpreparedness of the search

---

[17] Four decades ago, the football star "Red" Grange ran for the board of regents of the University of Illinois, in a sense on an anti-university platform, promising to get rid of the Communists on campus. Less overtly political has been the Michigan State University Board of Trustees, who have organized themselves separately to support the athletic interests against the wishes of the administration and the predominant part of the faculty. In contrast, some members of Harvard University's Board of Overseers have been elected on the issue of South African divestment, and regard themselves as "whistle-blowers" on the board, responsive to their electoral constituency, with its many faculty and student allies, rather than to the overall functioning of Harvard's governing boards.

committee, let alone the board, for the degree of faculty dissatisfaction with the choice.[18] The faculty member of the search committee proved to be neither a conduit for large faculty expectations nor a person with sufficient closeness to the faculty to assuage resentments or to legitimate the search.

Ideally, members of the search committee will develop a strong sense of cameraderie, based on their mutual respect and their extensive involvement in their common endeavor. There is a danger, however, that during the course of the search process these committee members will become closer to each other than to the constituents from which they were drawn. When search committee members form close attachments to the group and the group effort, there may be some attenuation of their sense of responsibility to their home bases. That attenuation is essential, at least to some degree, if the search committee is to come up with candidates who are not simply political trade-offs about whom no one is enthusiastic. But there is also the hazard that committee members will forget the degree of ignorance or mistrust among their constituents and lose touch with the political realities of their locale.

The trustee members of the search committee are ordinarily chosen by the person chairing the board, along with the person chairing the search committee. We know of no instance when trustee members of the search committee have been elected to this position by their peers. Trustees are generally named to the search committee because of the breadth of their contacts, their weight with their fellow trustees on the full board, and their geographic availability. With trustees as with other delegations, affirmative action considerations also may enter. Most trustees accept the appointment to the search committee because they realize that it provides one of their most important and interesting tasks, the one for which they will be well or badly remembered. Perhaps this is why dereliction of responsibility seems rare. It occasionally occurs, as when the wealthy donor who chaired a presidential search committee for a foundering liberal arts college took his annual vacation to Europe in the middle of the search, leaving difficult negotiations in abeyance. Overall, however, incompetence is a more common failing than neglect.

[18] At Winthrop, there was no organized protest by students, unlike at Gallaudet, where it was the student dissatisfaction even more than the faculty dissatisfaction which ignited the controversy.

In the preoccupation with what is deemed to be fair and equitable, the focus during the process of choosing members of the search committee is often on procedure, and not on the question of who has the best judgment, the widest orbit, the greatest capacity for quick learning, accompanied by thoroughness. The best committee members can state positions strongly without antagonizing fellow members; they are good interviewers; they have had experience in the assessment of people of whose behavior one can get only a limited "sample," either directly or through others, and can balance that judgment against the state of the institution in all its particularity.[19]

CRITERIA

In January 1989, Richard M. Cyert announced his intention to retire from the presidency of Carnegie Mellon in the summer of 1990, ending a seventeen-year tenure in that office. The university decided to use the long lead time for the presidential selection as a chance to "carefully consider the present state of the University, what they might want it to be, say, ten years from now, and how best to get there."[20] As its first major undertaking, the Faculty Presidential Search Committee produced a thoughtful document, "Carnegie Mellon University: The Search for the President." The report had nine "chapters," including sections providing "an overview of the University," "the principal constituencies and their responsibilities," "the organization of administration," "a brief financial report," and "a report on undergraduate recruitment." In a chapter entitled, "Is Carnegie Mellon different from other universities?" the document described the special character of Carnegie Mellon and the tensions confronting the

[19] Recent research on the success and failure of meetings is instructive. Lynn Oppenheim, of the Wharton Center for Applied Research, found that successful groups not only had the right people present; they also excluded people not directly involved. Too many people resulted in "dead weight" that kept meetings from being productive. Robert Sternberg of Yale University found that groups that were most effective had a balance among members "between intelligence, on the one hand, and social abilities, on the other. A group strong in either intelligence or affability alone . . . is handicapped." Successful groups also had "a high degree of diversity of both experiences and points of view." (Quoted in Daniel Coleman, "Recent Studies Help Explain Why Some Meetings Fail and Others Succeed," *New York Times*, June 7, 1988, pp. C1 and C9.)

[20] "Carnegie Mellon University: The Search for the President," a report prepared for the Faculty Presidential Search committee, John G. Fetkovich, Chair, by the Selection and Plans Committee, Dana S. Scott, Chair, March 17, 1989, p. 3.

institution and its new president. The closing chapter discussed the role of the president and the qualities of leadership sought. The exercise of preparing the document not only served as a forum for discussions at the university about its future, but the document itself alerted nominators and prospective candidates as to what made the presidency of Carnegie Mellon at once interesting and complicated. Similarly, in Clark University's 1984 presidential search, the Clark board prepared a sophisticated brochure which outlined the specific credentials and capacities being sought in a president and the future directions in which the board hoped the university would move.

In contrast to these institutions' workmanship, the lists of qualifications for the presidency drafted by many colleges and universities appear obvious and also arbitrary. Unless one is preoccupied with eliding state legislators and other political figures, it is arbitrary to demand an earned doctorate. Harvey Mudd College, for instance, which sends a larger proportion of its graduates to Ph.D. programs than any other American college, selected a president who has a background in engineering and an M.B.A. from Stanford, and was vice-president at Stanford, but has no earned doctorate. Sometimes the announcement asks for "demonstrated leadership abilities," as if these abilities exist in the abstract and not in relation to a particular setting and a particular institutional culture.[21]

There are instances where a college's presidential profile does say something definitive. Warren Wilson College is a small (five hundred students) Presbyterian college in rural North Carolina that has an intensive work program. In its 1985–1986 presidential search, the college called for a president who, among other things, "will represent, in daily activity and in the greater course of a life lived, an example of that devotion to service, spirit and mind judged characteristic of a college whose traditions inseparably conjoin intellectual effort, physical work, and integrity of the highest order." In the context of Warren Wilson College, where "college life" does not exist American-style, such a statement serves as both warning and invitation.

Some institutions are so well known that they do not believe that they need to say a great deal about themselves in their advertisements, al-

[21] This is a major theme of Michael Maccoby, *Why Work: Leading the New Generation* (New York: Simon & Schuster, 1988).

76

though they will commonly send prospective nominators a brief "biography" of the place. What is particularly striking is that in the lists of qualities sought, the ability to develop an administrative team is rarely included—another example of the way leadership is thought of in the abstract. When we have been asked about candidates by members of search committees, we are asked about their intelligence, their integrity, their skills in fund raising, and, occasionally, their readiness for participatory governance, but this latter quality is not put in the context of identifying, recruiting, and developing a team. The candidate is seen as an isolated individual—an outlook reinforced by the rarity of questions concerning the candidate's spouse.

It is common for searches to get under way without much discussion about the institution's situation or the qualities needed in a successor. Many search committee members believe, as a member of the "Southern State University" search committee said directly, that "we all know what we're looking for, and we'll know when we find it!" However, when a search consultant is employed, the consultant will almost always begin by working with the search committee to develop specifications for the position. The Academic Search Consultation Service (ASCS), headed by Ronald Stead, probably spends more time on this exercise than any other consulting firm, interviewing trustees, faculty, administrators, students, alumni and others about what they see as the major leadership priorities.[22] Typically, the ASCS consultants will talk with large numbers of people on campus over a period of several days, and then will prepare a summary report to the search committee which enumerates the implications of their findings for the search process.

This process of gathering diverse opinions can be revealing and healing. When Bowdoin College was uncertain whether to conduct a national search for a successor to Willard Enteman, or to offer the presidency to acting president Leroy Greason, interviews conducted by consultants Frederic Ness and Ronald Stead resulted in the decision to continue with the leadership Greason had already demonstrated. Ness and Stead had found that the faculty respected Leroy Greason and, on the whole, were

---

[22] As we discuss in Chapter IX, they then take on more of an advisory role to the search committee, becoming much less active than many other firms in identifying, interviewing, and researching the backgrounds of candidates.

content with the way that the college was proceeding. Perhaps these consultants also helped faculty members realize that there were not such wonderful prospective candidates "out there." By confronting the exalted expectations that many faculties have about who will become their president, the meetings with the consultants served as an exercise in cumulative realism for the faculty and trustees. Bowdoin again used a consultant—this time, William Olson of Russell Reynolds—in their 1990 presidential search which ended with the selection of Robert Edwards, a former president of Carleton College.

A search consultant, of course, is not necessary for—nor any substitute for—an institutional self-analysis. Many institutions that have not used consulting services have conducted successful institutional assessments which have served as the basis for their selection of a president. In the search which brought Dennis O'Brien from the presidency of Bucknell University to that of the University of Rochester, the trustees were initially surprised by many of the findings of their assessment. They recognized the degree to which Rochester, despite its large endowment and its distinction in such diverse fields as optics and history, had lost ground in relation to its competitors, and the trustees became persuaded of the importance of finding a venturesome president.

Commenting on the symbolic value of the discussions of the criteria for a new president, Robert Birnbaum notes that the process "provides a forum for interaction and influence in which members can begin to sense the different interests that each may have. It permits various constituencies to symbolize and confirm their status by ensuring that a criterion important to them appears in the written position description, and it allows all participants to test areas of consensus and begin the process of negotiating differences."[23] But such discussions are commonly short-circuited. Most of us find people more interesting than ideas, and search committee members quickly become impatient with abstract (and often pious) discussions of qualities; they want instead to examine the materials that are arriving from and about candidates, and want to meet the candidates themselves. The result of the short-circuiting is that the qualifications desired by every vocal person on the search committee get added to

[23] Birnbaum, "Presidential Searches," p. 495.

78

the list. Sometimes, even, these lists are alphabetical, giving no indication as to which characteristics listed are most desired.[24] Either the search committee does not want to show its hand to candidates, or perhaps committee members have not themselves reached an agreement about priorities. The large lists then turn into an impossible, self-contradictory ideal. As Alfred Kerr at Allegheny College has commented, the president they were looking for could be characterized as "Thomas Aquinas with a CPA and fund-raising experience."[25] When all candidates fall short of this ideal, as indeed they must, committee members are left to decide which qualities are the most important. Arguments about institutional direction—whether, for example, progress will be sought across the board or in specific areas—are thus made, not openly at the outset of the search, but buried in the evaluations of final candidates.

To illustrate from the previous chapter, Michael Knight was seen by the Abbott faculty as possessing the academic vision that "Abbott College" needed; William Patterson was seen by the Abbott trustees as possessing the requisite financial skills necessary to lead the college forward. Like many other institutions, Abbott College struggled over the question of which attributes were most desired while they were simultaneously considering the personalities and career histories of specific candidates. Not infrequently, the determination of the sort of person needed as the new president is made not after a thoughtful analysis of the institution, but in reaction to the predecessor president. If this president was beloved, his or her clone is desired. If the president was unpopular, his or her opposite is sought: a calm, conservative individual if the former president was regarded as pressing the faculty too hard or being too flamboyant or eccentric, or an "exciting" figure if the past president seemed dull or staid. This commonly results in a host of new problems, which then have to be compensated for the next time around.

Some candidates are indifferent about or tone-deaf to disagreements among search committee members and trustees concerning the future directions of the institution. But a superior candidate, already well-situated,

---

[24] In the Tusculum College list of "Leadership Characteristics," the presidential search committee noted that items were listed "alphabetically and, thus, randomly." Lycoming College similarly placed its "Presidential Leadership Needs" in alphabetical order.

[25] From letter of April 14, 1986.

may be put off by the recognition that trustees and search committee members have not resolved their differences, and that the new president will likely find the situation even more filled with traps and surprises than presidents commonly find when they begin their incumbencies. A careful assessment of the sort we are discussing here is also a protection for the committee and the campus against being captivated by a glamorous candidate, especially by a candidate whose style differs from or resembles that of the departing president.

Presumably, the main activity of a search committee is to search for potential candidates. To watch a number of search committees in action, however, one would not get this impression! We have heard many search committee members lament, at the conclusion of their search or as it nears completion, that they did not have any strong candidates because they functioned as a selection committee, not as a search committee. Following the dictates of affirmative action, the search committee advertised nationally, and perhaps wrote heads of the national educational associations to request nominations. Then they screened those names that came in from these various sources. Theirs was a passive stance, much as if the selection were that of an assistant professor in a field where the supply of people is abundant, rather than the identification of the chief executive officer of the college or university.

In some cases, this passive posture is the result of ignorance about how to identify prospects. The committee genuinely wants to seek highly qualified individuals, but does not give sufficient thought to how they should go about doing so, and instead relies on the familiar recruitment channels. Occasionally, this posture also reflects an attitude: we want someone who wants to be our president; we want someone who will actively pursue our job. Often this attitude is evident not only in the expectation that candidates for the presidency will be reading the want ads and applying themselves or arranging to be nominated, but also in the assumption that these people will be glad to write lengthy application statements, much as if they are applying for a fellowship or to graduate school. There is, of course, always a large number of people who think they would like to be a college or university president and have nothing better to do with their time than fill out whatever forms, no matter how lengthy, a search committee may require. At issue for the search committee, however, is whether these applicants are the sort of people they hope to find for their president. All search consultants have their stories about the crazy applications they have come across from people totally lacking in credentials or experience for a presidency. One of our favorites is the fellow who wrote, in response to an advertisement for the presidency of a small Catholic college, "Dear Sir: I am a devout Catholic. . . ." Several months later, the same search consultant who had worked with this Catholic college was employed by a Calvinist college to help search for their president. Among the stack of applications he perused was one from the same "devout Catholic." The letter began, "Dear Sir: I am a devout Calvinist."

CHAPTER IV

"Southern State University"

W E TURN NOW to the search for a president of a flagship state university which lives under the double directorate of its own advisory board and the System Board of Regents. Like other flagship campuses in state systems, especially in such poor states as "Dixie" (but as we shall see in Chapter VII, even in wealthier states such as Florida), the flagship campus must compete against other state universities, many of which have their own built-in constituencies in the legislature, on the board of regents, and in the state administration. When Paul Sharp was president of the University of Oklahoma, he said that he wished that his university did not have to play football against Oklahoma State, its land-grant rival. In the outcome of that somewhat fortuitous clash could lie the fate of millions of dollars, including legislative appropriations for new programs and buildings, and gifts from large donors.

When the search for a new president at "Southern State University" (SSU) began, the regents instructed the search committee to keep all information confidential, a proviso consonant with the state's open-meeting and open-records legislation. However, several leaks occurred by inadvertence, thanks to forceful investigative journalism by a SSU graduate. These leaks had devastating consequences for the career of one candidate, resulted in the withdrawal of another candidate, and raised the already high temperature of political conflict in the state system as a whole.

IMPORTANT DATES

March, 1981   William Ridgell announces resignation effective July 1, 1981

April 16   First meeting of Presidential Search and Screening Advisory Committee (PSSAC)

83

June 13	Second PSSAC meeting: review resumés
June 15	Deadline for applications and nominations
July 1	Third PSSAC meeting: 114 candidates culled to 14 to be given further consideration
August 8	Fourth PSSAC meeting: evaluate candidates; choose 9 semifinalists
August 14	News story: no women among semifinalists
August 28	News story: Dwight Stanton, Glen Lawton, James Smith, and Frederick Delaney are among semifinalists
August 29	Eastern State newspaper reveals name of Stephen Davis
August 30	Fifth PSSAC meeting: interview three candidates
September 9	Stephen Davis resigns presidency of Culpepper State University
September 12	Sixth PSSAC meeting: interview five candidates
September 13	Seventh PSSAC meeting: interview Stephen Davis; decide on four finalists to bring to campus
September 15	Official press release announcing names of four finalists
September and October	Finalists interviewed on campus
October 10	Eighth PSSAC meeting: final selection
October 17	Board of Regents makes selection

CAST OF CHARARCTERS

Earl Bryant	Chairman of search committee; corporate executive
Robert Bradbury	Finalist; director of governmental relations, National Education Committee
Douglas Comeau	Finalist; provost, University of the Southeast

Albert Hale	Finalist; dean, Northern State University College of Engineering
Dwight Stanton	Finalist; dean, SSU College of Law
Frederick Delaney	Semifinalist; president, University of the Northwest
Stephen Davis	Semifinalist; president, Culpepper State university
Glen Lawton	Semifinalist; vice-president for administration, SSU
James Smith	Semifinalist; president, Dixie State University
Grant Turner	Semifinalist; vice-chancellor for research, University of the Plains

THE SEARCH

Established just after the Civil War, "Southern State University" is the comprehensive land-grant university of the state of "Dixie." One of twenty institutions of higher education in the state, it is located in the small town of Collegeville, which is two hundred miles north of Warrenburg, the state capitol, and one hundred miles east of Carterton, a major city in an adjoining state. The university has an enrollment of twenty-five thousand. The population of the state is approximately three million.

Southern State University is deeply rooted in the state. Eighty-five percent of the lawyers in the state earned their law degrees at SSU's School of Law, and the state's agricultural and business development is closely linked with the university's departments of agriculture, forestry, and business administration. In public visibility, the president of Southern State University is probably second only to the governor of Dixie.

The university is a highly political institution whose governance system has undergone many changes, depending upon the desires of those in the statehouse. Currently, SSU is governed by the Dixie Board of Regents, the governing board for all state colleges and universities. The twelve-member board of regents meets monthly and is composed of nine gubernatorial appointees, one faculty member, one student, and the state superintendent of schools. The chancellor is the executive officer of the board of regents and serves at the pleasure of the board. In addition to the regents, each Dixie college and university has its own institutional advisory board which reviews, prior to submission to the regents, all institutional proposals having to do with such things as mission, academic programs, budget, and capital facilities. The SSU advisory board consists of eleven members, including seven lay citizens, one campus administrator, one faculty member, one student, and a member of the university's nonprofessional staff. The seven lay citizens serve for four-year terms, while all others have terms of one year.

In 1981, William Ridgell had been president of Southern State University for four years. When he announced that he was resigning to assume the presidency of Midwestern University, the news made headlines across the state. Ridgell's candidacy at Midwestern University had remained a secret up to his final interview with the Midwestern board. His departure did not come entirely as a surprise, however. A year earlier, word of his candidacy at another state university had made its way into the Dixie press and this had put the SSU board and the university on notice. An administrator who had worked closely with Ridgell commented later that "we knew he was leaving after he had been here six months. He was, and probably still is, under consideration for everything." Ridgell's short tenure and obvious ambition irritated many state residents. When he resigned, a major newspaper in Dixie ran a nasty editorial entitled, "Young Man in a Hurry." One person told us that Ridgell was perceived as having used his four years at SSU to further his career. In the future, he added, "ambitious carpetbaggers need not apply."

No sooner had Ridgell announced his resignation than a state senator asked the senate to pass a resolution urging the regents to select a Dixie native as SSU's next president. The resolution was referred to the Senate Education Committee where it was laid to rest. In early April, however, another bill was passed that had direct impact on the presidential search process. Introduced months before it was known that Ridgell was leaving, the bill stipulated the manner by which presidents should be selected. "The institution's advisory board, with the addition of six other persons— three appointed by the advisory board and three by the regents—shall serve as a search and screening committee, operating under guidelines established by the regents." Shortly after passage of this bill, the regents specified the guidelines to be followed at Southern State University. The three SSU advisory board appointments to the search committee were to be members of the SSU faculty; the mandate of the seventeen-member SSU Presidential Search and Screening Advisory Committee was to present to the regents at least three and no more than five candidates for the presidency.

Although the Presidential Search and Screening Advisory Committee (PSSAC) was large, it was smaller than the search committee that had nominated William Ridgell for the presidency in 1977. That search committee had twenty-five members. "I threw up my hands in horror when I heard about the size of the group," commented lawyer Lewis Findley, the chairman of that search. But the committee had conducted a successful search, bringing finalists to the campus to meet a few selected faculty and administrators, and maintaining confidentiality throughout. The 1977 search had been SSU's first experience with campus participation in executive selection. Ridgell's predecessor, Robert Cain, who had served as the president of SSU for ten years, had been chosen president in 1967 after a search conducted entirely by the regents. The faculty had been introduced to Cain only after he had been nominated for the presidency. Students had not been included at any stage of the process.

By 1981, constituency participation in university decision-making was firmly established. To select the three faculty representatives for the search committee, the advisory board asked board member Henry Otis, an engineering professor at SSU and chair of the faculty senate, to provide a list of six faculty members from which the advisory board could choose three. Otis met with the faculty senate's executive council. They discussed the need for a fair distribution of faculty from the various colleges within the university and they made certain that a female faculty member was included on their list. They did not think about appointing a black faculty member, however, an oversight that came back to haunt them later. From this list of six names, the advisory board chose three faculty members, two men and one woman, to serve on the PSSAC: a professor of agriculture, the chairman of the philosophy department, and an associate professor of biology on the faculty of the Medical School. In early May, the regents announced their appointments to the search committee. The group included five lawyers, four business executives, the president of a private university in the state, and president of the SSU student government, the president of the SSU staff association, and the SSU dean of arts and sciences.

The first meeting of the PSSAC was scheduled for May 16. Realizing that their faculty colleagues would soon be departing for the summer, the faculty representatives on the search committee decided to hold an open faculty meeting on May 14 to give faculty members an opportunity to talk about desirable qualifications for the new president. The meeting, held under the auspices of the faculty senate, was attended by thirty-four of the thirteen hundred SSU faculty. One faculty member commented that he wanted someone with an extensive background as a teacher and scholar; another said that the university needed someone who could work well with the legislature; others talked about wanting someone who would stay in the presidency for more than three or four years. The issue of affirmative action was raised, and the composition of the search committee came under attack. Of the seventeen members of the PSSAC, only two were women and none was black. When the discussion turned to questions about how the committee intended to operate, the faculty made it clear that they wanted to meet candidates before they were recommended to the regents. Here, the faculty representatives were somewhat at a loss. Because the search committee had not yet had its first meeting, they could not reassure the faculty about committee procedures. But they promised to carry the input of the faculty to the full search committee meeting later that week, and to keep faculty informed, within the limits of confidentiality, about the progress of the search.

The first meeting of the PSSAC was held in the student union building on May 16. After the committee members had introduced themselves, the chancellor passed out a document entitled "Policies and Procedures for the Search Process." The two-page statement stipulated that twelve members constituted a quorum; that all meetings of the PSSAC had to be called by the committee chairman with at least forty-eight hours' advance notice; that persons appointed to the committee would serve until the charge had been fulfilled and any resignations would not be filled. The document also described how applications and nominations would be handled. All candidate papers were to be sent to the chancellor's office where they would be coordinated by the director of personnel for the regents and then transmitted to the search committee. These papers were to be understood to be the property of the regents. Within ten days after the search committee had made its final report to the regents, all papers of the search committee were to be returned to the regents. No duplication of any materials was permitted.

The "Policies and Procedures" document explicitly noted the need for confidentiality: "Confidentiality of applicants' names and their background is the responsibility of each person who accepts the file of an applicant or candidate. Each member of the committee must understand that preservation of confidentiality of information can impose a personal liability on that member which is not covered by the insurance of the state." A member of the regents staff noted later that the question of legal liability was, in fact, unclear, but this language had been added to the statement to cover the regents should something happen and to underscore to committee members the importance of confidentiality.

In order to preserve confidentiality and to save the expense of large quantities of duplication, the search committee agreed that all seven campus members would use one copy of the files. Initially, these papers were kept in the office of Dean Driscoll, a member of the search committee; later, search documents were also placed under lock and key in the rare book room of the library. All off-campus members were sent copies of candidate papers. For purposes of voting on candidates, each candidate was assigned a number, and this number, rather than the person's name, was used on ballots and in the minutes of meetings.

Lewis Findley, a member of the advisory committee and chair of the previous SSU presidential search, commented on the previous search, noting the importance of selecting a president with the ability to manage, good judgment, familiarity with financial affairs, and good skills in public relations. After he had concluded his remarks, a faculty member on the committee asked if they could discuss qualifications for the president. In response, a businessman on the search committee who is a large donor to the university referred to Findley's statement and said that it described the desirable candidate sufficiently. "We all know what we're looking for," he said, "and we'll know when we find it." The discussion ended there. Later, one person said he had wanted to discuss criteria but had not felt he could raise the issue again. "So we were seventeen people looking for seventeen different things," he added.

Copies of all applications received as of May 15 were distributed, and times for future meetings were discussed. One committee member asked that meetings be held late in the day, and preferably mid-week. Others stated a preference for weekends. Search committee members hailed from all parts of the state, and several lived a four- to five-hours' drive from the university. The search committee members agreed to try to achieve some balance of meeting times, some weekends and some weekdays. The next meeting was set for June 13, beginning at 9:00 a.m. in the University Hospital.

On May 17, one day after the search committee meeting, a story about potential candidates appeared in the Collegeville newspaper, the *Collegeville Sun*. News reporter Whit Barlow had contacted two former SSU administrators, Sam Moorehead, president of the University of the Northwest, and Robert King, president of Windsor University, to ask them if they were aware of the SSU vacancy and if they were candidates for the position. Moorehead said that he was not interested in the position himself but had nominated someone for it; King responded that it was premature of him to say anything at all since he knew nothing about the search.

Barlow's aggressive news reporting had just begun. A 1978 SSU graduate who had been a reporter on the SSU student newspaper, Barlow's beat for the *Collegeville Sun* was Southern State University. In search of news, he regularly attended university faculty meetings and other open forums held on campus. Administrators were accustomed to Barlow's calls for information about campus events, and several commented that they found his reporting responsible and of high quality. "He always got the facts straight," one person said.

Four years earlier, when Ridgell was named president of SSU, Barlow was a general news reporter, and he had been scooped by the Warrenburg paper on the news of the Ridgell selection. "I was determined not to let that happen this time," he said. Already, he had been first to break the news of Ridgell's selection to the presidency of Midwestern University. When Barlow had heard from a Midwestern newspaper reporter that Ridgell was rumored to be a top finalist for the Midwestern presidency, he had telephoned the Midwestern regents office to find out when the final selection of the president would be made. Barlow had then called the local

90

airlines, not identifying himself, and had asked to confirm Ridgell's reservation to Midwestern. When the airlines clerk gave him the time of Ridgell's flight, Barlow drove to Carterton to greet Ridgell at the airport. Ridgell's mouth had dropped open, Barlow said. When Barlow had asked his destination, Ridgell had responded, "no comment." In that evening's newspaper, Barlow reported the facts: Ridgell's statement, his flight, and the timing of the Midwestern selection.

On May 20, the *Salisbury Herald* printed the news story, "28 Considered for SSU Post." The story said that the deadline for applications and nominations was June 15 and that the Dixie chancellor had said that the regents had already received twenty-eight nominations and applications. On Sunday, May 24, the *Collegeville Sun*'s editorial was entitled, "An Open Letter to the PSSAC." In what was obviously a reference to Ridgell, the editorial stated that the search committee should seek someone with "genuine affection" for the university, not someone who saw the SSU presidency as an attractive job to be cast aside when a new, more lucrative job offer appeared. Ideally, the editorial stated, the new president should be a native of the state.

One other news story related to the presidential search appeared that weekend. Butler attorney Joseph Walker, president of the state NAACP, issued a statement protesting the fact that there were no black members of the PSSAC. In the press release, Walker said that he was "shocked, dismayed, and disappointed by the lily white committee. The board obviously ignored the recent report by the Committee on Civil Rights; the prevailing attitude that blacks are acceptable in only one broad category at the university (athletics); the gross underrepresentation of blacks at the university; and the feeling expressed by so many blacks that they feel unwelcome at the university." Walker stated that he had appointed a special task force to address the committee composition. The same news story noted that the Dixie chancellor had said that neither he nor the regents had heard directly from Walker. The committee composition was determined by the Senate bill, the chancellor explained, which allowed only seven of the seventeen members of the search committee to be appointed. All other seats were filled with members of the SSU advisory board, and at the time there were no black advisory board members. Approximately six percent of the state population was black and nine percent of the SSU student body was black.

Walker's statement appeared in newspapers across the state. Nothing more was heard about the special task force. No changes were made in the committee membership. A member of the chancellor's staff said they had been sensitized to the issue, however, and would make certain in the future that the institutional advisory boards had black members.

The second meeting of the search committee was held on June 13. Prior to the session, committee members had been sent resumés of sixty-four candidates and had been told to rate them on a one-to-three scale. The committee members presented their votes, and some candidates were eliminated immediately while others were discussed further before a decision to drop them was reached. After a lengthy session, fourteen candidates were identified as prospects warranting additional consideration. A third search committee meeting was set for July 1.

The date of the next search committee meeting was also the date of the changing of the guard at SSU. President William Ridgell departed for Midwestern University on June 30. Dr. Charles Thompson, a retired SSU administrator, had been selected by the regents to serve as president until the person chosen by the search process could come on board. Thompson was no stranger to SSU or to the office of the president. He had been president of Fairhaven College, a small college in the state, for seventeen years, and when he stepped down from that post, he had served as assistant to SSU president Edward Fenner in the 1960s. On two separate occasions Thompson had served as acting president when SSU presidential searches were in progress. In recognition of his service to the university, the regents named Thompson president rather than acting president, making him officially the eighteenth president of Southern State University. The appointment achieved two important results. First, it placed the university in competent hands, allowing the search committee to do its job without feeling rushed to find someone to take charge of the institution. Second, because of his advanced age, Thompson was clearly not in the running for the presidency. There were, therefore, none of the liabilities of having the acting president perceived as an inside candidate.

Although Thompson was not an internal candidate, others at SSU were. No sooner had the request for nominations gone out to the faculty than speculation began about who would be the next SSU president. One of the first names to be mentioned was that of the vice-president for academic affairs, Preston Caldwell, who had come to SSU just two years earlier. Well-regarded by the faculty, Caldwell's administrative post made him highly visible within the university. However, Caldwell declined to have his name entered as a nominee. Unbeknownst to people at SSU, Caldwell was already a candidate elsewhere. Later that year, he resigned his SSU position to accept a university presidency in another state.

Another vice-president whose name was mentioned frequently as a likely candidate was Glen Lawton, vice-president for administration. Lawton had spent most of his professional life in Collegeville. Coming to the university in 1961 as an assistant professor of business economics, Lawton was soon appointed acting dean of the College of Business, then assistant to the president for planning, and, finally vice-president for administration. Locally, he had been a member of his church choir, president of the Collegeville Housing Authority, active on the Collegeville planning commission, and a one-term member of the City Council. "Everyone knows Glen Lawton," one faculty member said. "You can't find a nicer guy anywhere." Nominated by several people for the SSU presidency, Lawton said that he would be glad to be considered for the position.

Dwight Stanton, dean of the SSU College of Law, was also nominated for the presidency by several people and was also quite interested in the position. Unlike Lawton, Stanton was a relative newcomer to SSU, having come to the law school as dean only two years earlier. According to one member of the law school's search committee, Stanton, then only thirty-three years old, was "probably the top candidate for a law school deanship in the country. He had another offer elsewhere. We felt extremely lucky to get him here." Stanton held both a law degree and an Ed.D. in educational administration. A specialist in labor law, he had served as senior staff assistant to a justice of the United States Supreme Court, as a member of a law school faculty, and as an associate dean of a law school prior to coming to SSU. Probably from his days as a student-body president, Stanton's wife commented, Stanton had been interested in administration. A college or university presidency was a career goal he had identified a long time before. But neither she nor her husband had expected him to be a candidate for the position quite so soon. Stanton had always assumed that there would be another step first: that he would move from a dean-ship to a vice-presidency or provostship prior to becoming a candidate for a presidency. But there he was with the SSU presidency vacant and many people telling him he should be a candidate.

That Stanton's name should come to mind for the presidency, when he had been at the university for only two years, reflected the high profile he had energetically sought. When Stanton first came to the SSU deanship, he spent a good deal of time cultivating relationships with the major Dixie attorneys. "The big law firms were not hiring our people," one advisory committee member explained, "and Stanton started asking them what we could do to strengthen the curriculum. As he responded to their answers, he developed tremendous support for the law school." Another member of the search committee commented that the relationship between the law school and the state bar association had been very poor when Stanton arrived at SSU. "In two years, he turned it into a love affair." Among the popular programs that Stanton had initiated was a series of short refresher courses for lawyers, held at the law school on Friday afternoons and Saturday mornings. The courses concluded with participants sharing a buffet luncheon and then walking down the hill to the SSU football games. Stanton had also been active on the SSU campus, speaking forcefully about quality in education, working to set up a day-care facility for the law school, and developing a reputation for tightening standards. When Ridgell's resignation was announced, Stanton spoke with a number of people about his potential candidacy for the presidency. When he decided to become a candidate, he wrote a note to Dixie Governor Smallwood saying that he was informing him, as a matter of courtesy, of his interest.

The major business of the third meeting of the PSSAC, held on Wednesday, July 1, was culling the large number of applications and nominations to a small number of individuals to whom the committee would give serious consideration. The search committee had received 52 applications and 127 nominations. Of this latter group, 64 individuals had expressed willingness to have their names entered into the competition.

The entire list of candidates was given to search committee members. Chairman Earl Bryant read the candidates' names and, after each one, asked for discussion. It quickly became apparent that the care with which committee members had read candidate files varied greatly. Some had read

94

the resumés and accompanying materials in detail; others seemed only to have scanned the materials quickly. One faculty member later commented that he was irritated by the casual treatment a few non-campus members had given this information. Four hours after the meeting had begun, the number of candidates who would be reviewed further had been reduced to fourteen.

Looking back later on this screening of candidates, one member noted that some applications almost got lost in the grading of folders. "One thing that helped a candidate was when someone knew him or had met him or had heard about him second-hand." Another committee member recalled that there was "one guy from the midwest. No one knew him. I thought he was probably pretty good, but he was eliminated because he didn't have a sponsor. Everyone had to have a sponsor. If a candidate didn't, he didn't make it to the finals." Another search member added, "It only took the slightest comment, so long as the candidate wasn't someone's candidate, to be eliminated. Gone for good. Meanwhile, the search committee members' candidates were percolating through the process."

During this session, various members of the committee attempted to "find out who other people's candidates were." There was no question about whom the lawyers on the committee favored: Stanton was their choice. When Stanton's name was raised, one of the lawyers in the group called him "the new messiah." The praise for him was so extravagant that one campus member of the committee found himself backing away from Stanton's candidacy. "I wanted to say, 'there are undoubtedly other people out there equally as good.' "

After determining the list of fourteen semifinalists, the search committee members decided that the semifinalists should be contacted by telephone and asked to provide the names of three or more references. All agreed that this business should proceed expeditiously so as not to slow down the work of the committee. Chairman Bryant asked the campus members of the committee to consider possible arrangements for the campus visits of finalists.

Immediately after the meeting had ended, the faculty and staff representatives to the search committee met to draft a progress report on the search to distribute to the SSU campus. Their memorandum stated that the PSSAC had identified 14 semifinalists from a list of 114, and noted

95

that 12 of these 14 were persons who had been nominated, that is, their candidacies had been proposed by others. Six of the 14, the memo continued, have some direct connection to the state or the university.

As Bryant had requested, the campus committee members sketched a possible two and one-half day schedule for candidate visits to the university. The question of whether these campus visits were desirable or necessary was not considered. Open campus interviews had first occurred in the state during a presidential search at another institution a year earlier, and the pattern had been carried through for all subsequent searches.

Meanwhile, James Harcourt, director of personnel for the board of regents, was gathering reference information about the fourteen semifinalists. Harcourt had been asked by the chancellor to coordinate the activities of the search process and to serve as the chancellor's representative on the search committee. The position was a delicate one: relations between SSU and the board of regents had been troubled over the years, and there was some distrust of anyone who represented the chancellor and, hence, the regents. According to one campus member of the search committee, candidates whose names were submitted by the chancellor were eliminated very early in the process. While members of the search committee were glad to have Harcourt do the necessary paperwork in preparation for meetings, some of them—in particular, the faculty members of the search committee—were skeptical about his being the person to convey information about candidates, especially when he was reporting information he had received over the telephone. Harcourt was very aware of his position, and noted to us after the search had concluded that he had tried to be extremely careful about what he said in search committee meetings, knowing that his statements might be construed as the position of the board of regents. Although most members of the search committee liked Harcourt personally, they were wary of the regents "interfering" in their proceedings. James Harcourt was watched very closely, one person noted.

The fourth PSSAC meeting was held on August 8 with fifteen new folders set before committee members for their consideration. After some discussion, the group agreed to advance one name from the fifteen to the semifinalist list. Since the previous meeting, one of the fourteen semifinalists had withdrawn his candidacy, having accepted the presidency of

96

another university. With the addition of the one new name, the list of semifinalists again stood at fourteen.

A vote was taken on the fourteen semifinalists and the list was reduced to nine. The committee decided to interview these nine candidates during a two-day period and, based on these interviews, to decide whom to invite back for campus interviews. Since the advisory board was meeting on August 30 to review President Thompson's budget request, the search committee decided to arrange three candidate interviews for that afternoon and the remaining six interviews for September 12. In the interim, search committee members were given the green light to inquire discreetly about the nine finalists. The student government president and several faculty members of the committee made calls to colleagues at the home institutions of the semifinalists to learn more about them.

Six days after the August 8 search committee meeting, the *Warrenburg Times* ran a news story entitled, "SSU chief candidates narrowed to eight." The opening paragraph of the article stated: "The list of Southern State University presidential candidates has been informally narrowed to eight semifinalists, none of whom is a woman." The second paragraph quoted student government president Steve Lester as saying that there were still some in-state people but no women among the top eight finalists.

Lester felt awful about the news story. Like others on the search committee, he had received numerous telephone calls from the newspaper reporters asking him for information about candidates. A faculty member said that committee members were badgered constantly by reporters. "They would call sometimes once a day to ask for little pieces of information or to confirm something they had heard." When Lester had been pressured for information, he had responded that the proceedings of the meetings were confidential. But, early one morning, the telephone rang and woke him up. The caller, a local reporter, had a more sophisticated approach than many. " 'I know you can't give me names,' he said, 'but tell me what it feels like to be the only student member of the search committee.' " Lester said that the reporter got him talking, and somewhere deep into the conversation, the reporter asked, "Are there any women candidates? Any people from in-state?" Lester gave the answers, and as soon as he'd hung up the phone, realized he had said too much. "All I could think of was, well, at least I didn't give out any names."

That afternoon, the story hit the press, and immediately thereafter, Lester received a letter from Chairman Bryant saying that Lester had acted inappropriately in divulging this information. "I wrote him and the chancellor an apology," Lester said, "and I said it would never happen again."

On August 23, the column "What's New in Dixie," a regular gossip column of the *Warrenburg Times* began: "Two SSU officials are still said to be in the running for the Southern State University presidency. They are Law School dean Dwight Stanton and vice-president for administration Glen Lawton." The information was accurate: both men were among the final nine candidates. Whether the information had come from the search committee was uncertain, for both had been widely known to be candidates. But a story written by Whit Barlow, which appeared in the August 28 *Collegeville Sun*, contained information that was unquestionably confidential. Citing "a source close to the selection process," the news story stated that the search committee would be interviewing SSU dean Dwight Stanton, SSU vice-president Glen Lawton, Dixie State University president James Smith, and University of the Northwest president Frederick Delaney in the first round of interviews. The news story included brief synopses of the vitae of each of these four candidates. All four men had connections to the state: Stanton and Lawton worked at SSU; Smith, a Dixie native, had served as Dixie State University's president since 1974; Delaney, a Dixie native, was a graduate and trustee of Dixie College.

When the *Collegeville Sun* story appeared, Lester said that he knew that some people must have thought him responsible, "but I wasn't." The identity of the source close to the selection process was never known. Off-campus members of the search committee speculated that the information had come either from Lester, or from the staff member on the committee, or from the faculty committee members. The campus members of the committee said that they had heard that a secretary in the law office of one search committee member was talking openly with the press. Later, reporter Whit Barlow explained his method of getting information. His source was not on the committee, he stated, but was someone "close to the committee." It was not difficult to get rumors, and then Barlow would have his source confirm information by answering yes or no to the questions he put forward. Then Barlow would attempt to validate what he had gleaned by calling candidates directly. Obtaining the credentials of candidates was easy: without offering any explanation of why he wanted the information, he would simply call the person's secretary and ask for a copy of the person's resumé. No one asked why or refused to send the vita. Barlow was scrupulous about not printing a name until he was certain it was accurate.

Barlow's story about the four finalists was picked up by newspapers across the state. The big news locally was the candidacy of Dixie State University president James Smith. DSU, located in Butler, is the second largest university in Dixie. DSU and SSU have always competed for students and for funds, and this competition became especially heated when both universities had succeeded in obtaining medical schools several years earlier. The state could barely fund one medical program, and each university wanted the lion's share of appropriations. For the president of Dixie State to be a candidate at Southern State was seen by many DSU loyalists as a defection.

Prior to the appearance of the news story, Smith had told his advisory board of his nomination for the SSU presidency. The news story, which Smith called "a scream, not a leak," did not hurt his position seriously. Some Dixie State University supporters were upset, but people on his campus urged him to stay, and, overall, he experienced an outpouring of good feeling. Whether Smith was ever a serious contender for the SSU presidency was uncertain. While some members of the PSSAC commented that they had included Smith on their list of finalists as a courtesy to two members of their committee who were personal friends of Smith, other committee members said that Smith was a strong leader and might make a good president were it not for the SSU-DSU rivalry.

On the SSU campus and elsewhere in the state, rumors about the search were rife. One search committee member reported that her husband, also a faculty member at SSU, often came home with stories about the search that he had heard at his office. Sometimes they were totally without substance; but other times, they were entirely accurate. Another committee member missed several committee meetings because he was away on vacation. When he returned home, his first news about the progress of the search came, not from a committee member, but from his neighbor, a lawyer in Collegeville. In early August, the Dixie chancellor sent all search committee members a memorandum urging confidentiality and noting that leaks could have the undesirable effect of causing promising candidates to withdraw their applications. Shortly thereafter, chairman Bryant spoke to the committee about the need to maintain strict confidentiality. These words apparently made an impact: Whit Barlow found that he could no longer get information from his source. The leaks had been plugged.

Whereas the candidacy of Dixie State president Smith was big news around the state, the candidacies of Dwight Stanton and Glen Lawton caused a stir more locally, on the SSU campus. Law dean Dwight Stanton had made a favorable impression during his two years at the University, and was widely known on the campus. His position on day care had attracted the interest of the Women's Concern Committee; his willingness to be a speaker at campus symposia had won him the support of many liberal arts faculty. Although comments from the law school were somewhat mixed—Stanton's efforts to upgrade the curriculum had insulted some older faculty—most of the younger law professors expressed their high regard for him.

Such was not the case with Glen Lawton. After Lawton's candidacy became known, committee members were astonished at the enormous reaction, some assertively positive but most aggressively negative. There were no fence-sitters on Glen Lawton. The deluge of calls about him surprised committee members. Lawton, too, was surprised by the passionate reactions. Neither he nor anyone else had realized that he would be such a controversial figure. The lesson learned from the reaction to Lawton's candidacy, one search committee member later commented, was that you cannot become president of an institution in which you have been the chief financial officer. As the vice-president for administration, Lawton was seen by many as responsible for financial decisions that, in fact, had been made by the entire administrative team. Many faculty and administrators feared that if Lawton were president, there would be a continuation of the policies of the Ridgell administration, in particular the financial cutbacks.

"I don't know how well known it was across campus that I was a candidate until the news story appeared," Lawton said. He took a noncommittal position when queried by the press, referring reporters elsewhere for information. Dwight Stanton also tried to keep a low profile. Prior to

100

the news story announcing his candidacy, he had informed the law school faculty that he was being considered for the presidency. He wanted them to learn this from him rather than from the newspaper. A colleague at the law school said that he noticed that, once Stanton's candidacy became public, Stanton became more measured in his statements. Stanton said his reaction was to lay low. "From August until the search ended, I was as committed a law school dean as you ever could find." Suzanne Stanton said that when the news of her husband's candidacy broke, they found themselves in a fishbowl. "I couldn't go anywhere without being asked about it." She recalled the remark made by her newspaper boy when he came to the house to collect for the week. Obviously trying to make polite conversation as Suzanne Stanton wrote her check, he asked, "How is the campaign going?"

On August 29, the name of still another candidate became public: the *Culpepper Gazette* broke the story of the candidacy of Culpepper State University president Stephen Davis, stating that he was one of either four, or eight, or nine candidates who remained in the SSU competition. The news article noted that Davis, in his third year as Culpepper State's president, had been a finalist the year before for the presidency of the University of the Mid-Atlantic, but had withdrawn from that competition.

In preparing the news story, the *Culpepper Gazette* reporter had contacted the chancellor of the Culpepper system to ask him what he knew about Davis's candidacy at SSU. The chancellor was quoted as stating that he had never spoken with Davis about his interest in the position. The new chairman of the Culpepper State University board of trustees was also quoted as saying that Davis had not told him or other trustees about his candidacy, adding that he worried that CSU might be hurt by uncertainty about the president's position.

The headline in the *Culpepper Gazette* the next day read, "News of other school's interest in Davis irks CSU trustees." "Several of the trustees contacted Saturday made it clear that they were not happy with the fact that Davis had not told them he was a candidate for the presidency of Southern State University," the story said. The vice-chairman of the CSU board called Davis's commitment to CSU "questionable," and the chairman said: "If he can better himself, he ought to do it." The news story also quoted Stephen Davis. In a press release, Davis stated that the *Gazette* story "came as a surprise to me. I was asked by Southern State University some time ago if I might be interested in being a candidate. A little correspondence has taken place, but I have never been informed that I am being seriously considered, much less a finalist." Davis concluded that his "time, energies, and talents" were dedicated to serving Culpepper State University.

The campus members of the SSU search committee met on August 13 to plan the screening interviews with semifinalists. In their recommendations to the full committee, they noted that "entrance into and departure from the interviews should be handled so that the candidates do not meet each other." They also stipulated the importance of confidentiality. "Hosts must be constantly aware of confidentiality. The news media must be avoided now. When full campus interviews are conducted, then the names will be available, but not now." After the interviews, "one and only one person on the PSSAC should be authorized to telephone the persons who wrote letters of recommendation. The PSSAC needs to know for sure that there are no unmentioned skeletons hiding in closets."

The fifth meeting of the search committee was held on August 30, with the first portion of the session devoted to search committee business and the latter part of the meeting set aside for interviews with three semifinalists. In the business meeting, one committee member announced that he had just been appointed to the board of regents and was therefore resigning from the search committee to avoid any perception of a conflict of interest. After business was finished, the interviewing began. In the midst of one of the three interviews, one PSSAC member became aware of voices outside. When he went to investigate, he found that three members of the student newspaper staff were eavesdropping on the sessions. The journalists, two reporters and one photographer, were peering in the louvers of the door. The committee member explained that the meeting was an executive session and asked the students to leave. He told them that the search could be damaged by leaks and it would become open later, at a more appropriate stage of the process. When the students refused to move, claiming that they were on public property, the search committee member called the campus police and told them that the students were not allowed to stand close enough to the door to hear the interviews. Although he added that the students could try to interview candidates afterward if they wanted, he tricked them by letting the candidates out through a back door the students did not know was there. Three days later, a student newspaper editorial titled "Waiting in silence" lambasted the search process for keeping "thousands of people in the dark about a decision that will affect them for years to come." The editorial attacked the composition of the committee, drawing particular attention to the fact that there was only one student member and suggesting that the recently vacated seat be filled with a student. The editorial concluded: "It seems that too many people— particularly students—are being kept out of too much of this university's future, and that just isn't fair."

In early September, Windsor University president Robert King sent a letter to the SSU search committee and a press release to his local paper stating that while he was flattered to have been nominated for the SSU presidency, he wished to have his name withdrawn from consideration. Noting that he still had ties to Dixie and to SSU from the time when he had been dean of the School of Business, he declared, "I'm happy where I am." Moreover, the SSU vacancy occurred when he had been at Windsor for only a few years. Although he had immediately told his board chairman about his potential candidacy as soon as his name had emerged in the SSU search, King did not want to seem to be an eager claim-jumper. In addition, he told us, the extensive press coverage of the SSU search was a significant factor leading to his decision to withdraw. In fact, he was not one of the nine candidates chosen as semifinalists.

Elsewhere, the leak of the names of the candidates had more ominous consequences. Culpepper State University president Stephen Davis had not told his board chairman, with whom relations were already strained, of his having been nominated for the SSU presidency. A news story of September 7 reported that the chairman of the CSU board had declared that he had received a great many letters and telephone calls concerning Davis, presumably primarily antagonistic to Davis, and that he had talked on the telephone with the system chancellor about the problems created by Davis's candidacy. Two days later, Davis announced that he was resigning the CSU presidency effective June 30, 1982. In a letter to the system chancellor, Davis requested a leave of absence to begin immediately and to extend until June 30, to allow him to prepare for other professional activities. Davis stated that his resignation was not requested by the CSU

103

board, but resulted from his own decision that it was in the best interests of the university.

Several days later, the SSU search committee received a *Culpepper Gazette* news clipping about Davis's resignation that had been sent anonymously with the second and last paragraphs underlined in ink. The news story's second paragraph reported that Davis's resignation came on the heels of criticism by CSU trustees that he should have told them that he was a candidate for the SSU presidency. Next to this statement was scrawled, *"Only an Excuse."* The last paragraph of the story noted that Davis had created controversy and resentment during his tenure at CSU by reorganizing the university administration and abolishing the positions of two vice-presidents.

The anonymous missive arrived when the SSU search committee was holding its second set of screening interviews on Saturday, September 12. This time there were more extensive efforts to avoid exposure of the candidates. All prior announcements of the meeting, including letters to candidates and typed meeting agendas, noted that the interviews would be held in the Medical Center at the same place as previously. But privately, members were told that the sessions would take place in another, more secure location. This site, the architectural seminar room, was separated from the rest of the building by a long corridor and several doors, including one that could be locked. A security guard was posted outside. Candidates were brought to the building via a back door.

On September 12, five candidates were interviewed from noon to 6 p.m. The following day, Stephen Davis was interviewed at 10 a.m. Following the Davis interview, the search committee decided who to invite back for open campus visits. To reach the semifinalist stage it had been important for a candidate to have on the search committee someone favorably disposed towards him. To reach the stage of the final interviews it was essential to have a committed advocate. It was not necessary, however, for the full committee to agree that a particular person was a serious contender. Committee members were quite prepared to promote to the finalist stage a candidate who was strongly advocated by someone else, even if they thought him "a complete turkey," as long as their own candidates also became finalists. One committee member noted, in fact, that the more "turkeys" in the pool the better, for the low-grade competition made his candidate appear even more impressive.

At the outset of the search, the regents had charged the search committee to send them the names of three to five finalists, listed in alphabetical order and not ranked. Before voting on particular prospects, several members of the search committee declared that they favored inviting five candidates for public interviews, while others thought that four would be a better number. The judgment of the latter was confirmed because when votes were taken on the candidates, a substantial gap in tallies between the fourth and fifth led the group to agree to invite the top four: Douglas Comeau, provost at the University of the Southeast; Dwight Stanton, SSU law dean; Albert Hale, dean of engineering at Northern State University; and Robert Bradbury, director of governmental relations for the National Education Committee.

Following the meeting, a member of the chancellor's staff contacted all nine semifinalists to let them know their status. In his letter to the four persons chosen as finalists, he alerted them to the completely open nature of the remaining stages of the search. "It is important to understand that no pledge of confidentiality with respect to your identity can be offered from this point forward. In fact, we are announcing to the public the identity of each person who is still in active, open competition for the presidency." Any candidate who wished to be considered for the presidency was required to submit himself to the open campus interview. Of course, candidacies were already in the open, and no person withdrew at this point.

An official press statement naming the four finalists was released on September 15. When the *Collegeville Sun* reported that story the next day, the reporter, Whit Barlow, identified four of the five semifinalists the committee had interviewed but "rejected." Indeed, Lawton, Smith, Delaney, and Davis had all been named in earlier news stories. Despite his talents, Whit Barlow had not succeeded in learning the name of the ninth semifinalist.

On the day of the press release, James Smith wrote SSU search chairman Earl Bryant requesting that his name be removed from further consideration. In a newspaper interview the next day, Smith declared that he had never intended to leave Dixie State for SSU, and that he had been surprised to be chosen as one of nine semifinalists. When the reporter asked Smith who stood the best chance of being named the next SSU president, Smith gave Dwight Stanton's name. In response to Smith's letter, Bryant wrote him and apologized for the breakdown in the confidentiality of the search, noting that it "may have caused some awkward situations for you and for some of our other candidates."

The public exposure of his candidacy had indeed been awkward for internal candidate Glen Lawton. The leaks may have hurt his candidacy because of the outpouring of antagonism to him that had resulted, and, unquestionably, they had informed the campus that Lawton had not made it to the stage of finalist. As several people commented to us, it was an embarrassment for Lawton, who found it hard to believe that he was not even given a campus interview. Lawton said later, however, that even though he was not pleased by the public disclosure of his candidacy, he would still have been a candidate if he had been told in advance that the names of candidates would become public.

The publicity surrounding the search enveloped the Stantons as well. The intensity of the process built as the search became increasingly open and undeniably political. "About halfway through the search process, the search seemed to take over our destiny," Suzanne Stanton commented. In supporting Stanton, "people had used their trump cards, thrown in their chits. We were no longer operating on our own. Dwight couldn't bow out." During the final campus interviews, Suzanne Stanton declined an offer to tour the president's house because "by that time, it didn't matter what the house looked like." Several of the Stantons' close friends noted that the public nature of the search placed great strain on the Stantons. "It consumed their entire lives," one said. "They were constantly on display." During the course of the search, Suzanne Stanton developed a nervous stomach and heart palpitations; Dwight Stanton gained thirty pounds; and their young son began to have problems in school.

Open campus meetings with the candidates were scheduled for the end of September and beginning of October. In preparation for the campus visits, the four faculty members of the search committee sent a memorandum to their colleagues urging their participation in the open forums. It was explained that each of these forums would begin with a short statement by the candidate, followed by questions from members of the faculty senate executive committee, with the remainder of each session devoted to questions from the general audience. "Please remember that the candidates are observing and evaluating SSU at the same time as we are interviewing them," the memo cautioned.

Steve Lester talked with the student government leaders about the upcoming interviews and made certain that the sessions were advertised in the student newspaper. Brian McCarthy, the staff representative on the search committee, met with the staff council to formulate an agenda for the staff sessions with candidates. Responsive to what he saw as the interests of staff members and concerned that they not be voiceless at meetings with candidates, McCarthy handed out different lists of questions to various staff members. Recognizing that many people would be unable to attend the forums because they could not leave their jobs during working hours, he saw to it that the local newspaper and radio reporters would cover the sessions.

On September 24, Robert Bradbury was the first of the four finalists to appear on campus. His schedule, like that of the candidates to follow him, included separate "meet-the-candidate" hour-long sessions with faculty, students, and staff; a collective meeting with all of the academic deans; and individual interviews with the mayor of Collegeville, the executive assistant to the president, the director of alumni affairs, President Thompson, and each of the vice-presidents, including Glen Lawton. Candidates and their wives had dinner with search committee members and their spouses. Wives of candidates were given tours of the president's house and of the town, and were joined for lunch by the wives of the vice-presidents of the university. Suzanne Stanton and Beverly Lawton, the wife of Glen Lawton, found themselves sitting next to one another at lunch, and the situation was awkward for both of them.

Collegeville Sun reporter Whit Barlow attended all of the faculty, staff, and student forums and wrote lengthy stories about each candidate's visit. His stories were picked up by newspapers around the state. The SSU student newspaper sent its own reporters to the sessions, who, in addition to reporting what candidates had said, offered their own evaluations of the candidates' performances and the audiences' reactions.

"Reaction to candidate favorable," read the student newspaper headline to the news story about Bradbury's appearance on campus. "Bradbury was youthful and business-like in appearance; his manner was firm and soft gestures were used to emphasize points," the story said. "Bradbury's work in Washington for the past ten years has given him firm command of the national and international political scene. He is a self-proclaimed educational leader who seems to have a firm command of the functioning of a major university at all levels," the reporter concluded.

If student reaction to Bradbury was positive, faculty feeling was much less so. "Bob Bradbury would have to be described as someone coming to the presidency through a nontraditional route. This caused faculty to be turned off by him. Although I thought he did a fine job of answering questions, this criticism was pretty general," one faculty member of the PSSAC noted. Bradbury, thirty-nine, holds a doctorate in international politics and economics. Prior to becoming the National Education Committee director for government relations, Bradbury taught for six years (including his years as a graduate assistant) at Mountain University and served as assistant dean at the University of the North. Many faculty felt that Bradbury lacked sufficient experience with academic life, while others were irritated by his "heavy use of educational jargon." Staff members were also somewhat critical of Bradbury, thinking that he "spoke over their heads."

After Bradbury returned to Washington, he wrote PSSAC Chairman Bryant thanking him and the search committee for handling his visit with "dignity and organization." Bradbury also expressed his support for the open process in the final stages of the search. Whoever is named president, he explained, will have an important head start as a result, since he will know the campus and its problems, and, most of all, since he will be seen as the legitimate choice because of the full campus involvement.

"Familiar with issues" read the headline to the student newspaper story about Stanton's campus interviews. Stanton "can lay claim to experience and familiarity with the university that his three rivals for the position of president cannot," the story said. "His speaking style—candid, quick, friendly, usually specific and punctuated with gestures and an occasional off-the-cuff-joke—contrasts with the slow, deliberate speech of former president Bill Ridgell." Faculty members attending the open forum with Stanton were also favorably impressed. Stanton himself felt that the sessions had gone well. In preparation for the meetings, he had met with a small number of people at SSU, using them as his "kitchen cabinet." He knew that he had to be careful in approaching people for fear that he might be perceived as lobbying. But Stanton also felt that he had to be fully prepared for the campus meetings. "As an internal candidate, I had to do better than good. I had to perform at a ninety to one hundred percent level." The open interviews were crucial, he thought, because their ripple effect in terms of public sentiment made them a critical turning point in the search.

The interview with Albert Hale was scheduled for September 29 and 30. Hale, fifty-five, had been dean of the Northern State University College of Engineering for ten years. On September 21, news about Hale came over the wire service: on a fund-raising trip to the west coast, Hale had been stabbed four times in an apparent robbery attempt. Hale had lost twenty-five percent of his blood from the stabbing, but had managed to save his own life by fashioning a tourniquet from his tie to stop the flow of blood from his arm. The stabbing occurred on Sunday evening, September 20; on Tuesday, September 22, Hale was moved out of intensive care to a private hospital room; on Tuesday, September 29, he began his campus interviews at SSU. Although Hale acknowledged he was "not up to full speed," he kept his originally scheduled visit because it was the only free slot he had for the next month.

"Still recovering from wound" was the student newspaper headline. The newspaper story noted that Hale's interviews "drew mixed reactions. The engineer in Hale was apparent throughout his interviews; he constantly referred to computers, technological advances and photons, to the point that some members of the faculty expressed concern for his interest, or lack of it, in the humanities." Some faculty members referred to Hale's extensive experience in academic administration. Others paid more attention to what came across of his personal style and degree of energy. Thus, one professor saw Hale's manner as alienating, while several others said he seemed much older than his chronological age.

Douglas Comeau was the fourth and final candidate to visit the campus. When Comeau, forty-five, provost at the University of the Southeast, arrived at SSU, he found a dozen long-stemmed red roses in his hotel room. The card attached to the bouquet was signed by the president of the University of the Southeast and said simply, "Hurry back." Comeau was being courted by his own university.

"Gives candid answers" read the headline to the student newspaper article about Comeau. During the open forums with faculty, staff, and students, Comeau was forthright about his assessment of SSU's relationship to the Dixie Board of Regents. "The wraps must be taken off the president so that he can talk to agency heads," Comeau stated. Noting that he had not yet met with the chancellor or the regents, Comeau predicted that "we may find ourselves at serious odds." "He was completely and thoroughly turned off by the regents," one faculty member explained. "He felt that the way the regents relate to the university is not conducive to a thriving university. He really felt it was an impossible situation." The faculty were impressed with Comeau's directness and thought him highly knowledgeable about academic affairs. "He was so well liked," one faculty member said. "If he'd remained a candidate, I think he'd have been the one."

A day after Comeau returned to the University of the Southeast, he withdrew from the race for the SSU presidency. According to the *Collegeville Sun*, sources in Comeau's state reported that the governor had a long talk with Comeau when he returned home after his SSU interviews. In his letter to the SSU search committee, Comeau said that he was deeply honored at being considered so highly for the SSU presidency, "however, the unanticipated broad support that has been expressed to me to remain at the University of the Southeast leads me to believe that the wisest course of action is for me to withdraw my name from future consideration."

Comeau's withdrawal was a very great disappointment to the faculty and presented the search committee with a problem. The regents had charged the search committee with recommending three to five candidates. With Comeau no longer in the running, there were only three finalists remaining. Uncertain how to proceed, the campus members of the search committee met together to explore options. Several faculty members thought they should see if they could perhaps send only one name, Stanton's, to the board with the message that they had found only one of the three finalists an acceptable choice. Others wanted to see the search reopened, speculating that they had amassed a small number of qualified candidates because they had taken a passive posture, merely selecting from those candidates whose names had been submitted to them, rather than actively searching for people. Questions were raised about the wisdom of reopening the search. Would Stanton remain a candidate? Three faculty members volunteered to talk with Stanton about this possibility.

When the question was put to Stanton, his answer was unequivocal. He would not remain a candidate were the search to be reopened. The process had already been enormously stressful for him and his family, and he would not consider extending the ordeal.

On October 10 the search committee convened for its eighth meeting. Chairman Bryant asked the campus members of the committee to report on how their various constituencies had felt about the candidates. At each of the open forums, faculty, staff, and students had been given forms on which to evaluate the candidates. Stanton had been rated highest by most faculty, staff, and students. Comeau was their clear second choice. Hale and Bradbury had been cited by few people as their first choice and had been rated by a large number of people as unacceptable. Faculty attendance at the forums had ranged from a maximum of ninety to a minimum of thirty. Student attendance varied from a low of seventeen to a high of twenty-five. Staff attendance ranged from forty-five to fifty.

When Bryant asked the committee to vote on the candidates so that they could determine support for each of the three finalists, Stanton received fifteen votes to send his name to the board of regents, Hale received seven votes, and Bradbury received six votes. The faculty expressed concern about sending the names of all three persons to the board of regents. They said they did not trust the board to choose Stanton, and were afraid the regents would select the weakest candidate. The faculty members' fears were heightened by the rumor that when Ridgell was named president by the regents, he had been the third choice of the search committee. Chairman Bryant agreed to consult informally with the regents to see if the search committee could send them only one name, and a search committee meeting was scheduled for October 17 to discuss the results of this inquiry.

During the week before the next search committee meeting, search committee members received three letters from liberal arts faculty expressing concern over the "inadequacy" of the remaining finalists. "May I urge you to reopen the search," one letter stated. "We must all hope that

111

more able persons can be found to provide crucial leadership during these troubled times."

One search committee member, Townsend Taylor, a Warrenburg lawyer, was made nervous by the talk of reopening the search. Stanton was his candidate, and Taylor knew that Stanton would not continue as a contender for the presidency if the search process was extended. Furthermore, Taylor was concerned about rumors that former Governor Bill Wheaton was interested in being drafted for the SSU presidency, since the presidency would be an excellent launching pad for Wheaton to make another bid for the governorship or a race for the U.S. Senate. Taylor was a close personal friend of Governor Smallwood, and did not want to see Bill Wheaton set up so well. Taylor knew that the search committee had better act quickly. When the search committee had voted at the last meeting, only two members had failed to vote for Stanton. One was a businessman who was rumored to be irritated at Stanton because his nephew had not been admitted to the SSU law school. The other was an active supporter of Bill Wheaton.

Taylor also knew that the majority of the members of the board of regents had been appointed to that body by Governor Smallwood. Any concerns he might have had about the regents' vote were erased when Stanton told Taylor about his recent meeting with the governor. Stanton had needed to talk with Smallwood about some matters to do with the law school. When Stanton called Taylor afterward, he reported that during the meeting the governor never once mentioned Stanton's candidacy. But as Stanton was walking out the door, the governor winked at him. "When Stanton told me that," Taylor said, "I knew we were really rolling."

Three members of the search committee met with two regents to explore the possibility of sending the regents only one nomination. The regents quickly vetoed the idea, explaining that it would set a dangerous precedent: the board wanted the right to make the final selection. When the three search committee members reported what had been said, they added that they felt good about the regents' prospective selection. To make absolutely certain that the regents understood the extent of their preference for Stanton, several search committee members urged the committee to send the names of the three finalists in rank order. The regents had stated explicitly, however, that their list should be unranked. A member

112

of the chancellor's staff offered a compromise plan, recommending that they send two lists, one in alphabetical order as they had been told and the other, placed in a sealed envelope, with their preference stated. The regents could decide whether they wanted to open the sealed envelope. The committee felt certain that they would. The compromise was quickly accepted and Bryant wrote the letter to place in the sealed envelope.

On October 30, Stanton was invited to meet with the board of regents. Just as he had prepared himself for the meeting with the search committee by having close associates throw questions at him which he might be asked throughout the course of his campus visit as a finalist, so too he had learned a great deal about each regent, so that he would have some idea of what questions they might ask. When the first question was about Stanton's position on collective bargaining in higher education, he knew he had "a home-run-ball." Stanton's speciality was labor law, and his personal stand on unionization in higher education squared with those he knew were held by members of the board. With this as his first question, Stanton found himself completely at ease. "By the end of the session, I knew I had the job."

The board of regents voted to appoint Dwight Stanton as Southern State University's nineteenth president. He was the university's youngest president, and the first to be appointed from the university's own ranks since 1939. Within his first year in office, he made major changes in the administration, including asking Glen Lawton to step down as vice-president to return to a faculty post and filling the vice-presidential vacancy created by the departure of Preston Smith with the dean who had been on the search committee. By fall of the following year, there were additional changes at SSU and elsewhere. Lawton left SSU to become vice-president for administration at a larger, more prestigious university. Stephen Davis moved to Coastal State College as vice-president for academic affairs, having found that his resignation at Culpepper State had made him far too controversial a candidate for a college presidency. Robert Bradbury became the new president of the University of the Gulf of Mexico.

CHAPTER V

Confidentiality and Disclosure

FREDERICK G. BAILEY, the British anthropologist who has reported on preliterate peoples, has also observed the academic community and described the behaviors he found there. In *Morality and Expediency: The Folklore of Academic Politics*, he presents ten "masks" that people wear when they encounter one another in academic decision-making. Among these dramatis personae is Buck, who believes that "anyone will do anything, if the price is right;" Stroke, who wants to like and be liked, and deals entirely in human interactions; and Baron, who sees only two possibilities in every situation, "to screw or be screwed, and he aims to be the man who turns the screws." There is Rock, a revolutionary who opposes whatever exists; Patron, who believes in distributing resources to cronies; Sermon, who believes in eternal verities, whereas Formula believes in rules and regulations. Reason and Rational have difficulty dealing with people as they are, while Saint is sometimes successful at this, through his very innocence.[1]

Some of these "characters" (in the sense of "character" in a play) can cooperate, whereas for others, notably Rock and Baron, this is impossible. Bailey's metaphoric inventiveness and gift for interpretation fill his book with scenarios of encounters of these "characters" with one another, indicating the gains that can attach to being, for example, stubborn, either for virtue or for profit, but also the gains of other, more conciliatory modes. He sees veto groups entangled with one another everywhere in academic culture; they can do so interminably or surrender resignedly or even happily to the offerings provided by Baron or Buck. Some, like Stroke and Saint, live in a highly personal world; others, such as Sermon

[1] Chicago: Aldine, 1977, p. 129 and p. 134. Regrettably, this penetrating and witty volume is out of print.

and Reason, in a world of structures and codes.[2] Pondering the cogency of Bailey's account, the reader is astonished that anything ever gets accomplished in a committee.

And indeed, his "characters" can be discerned in the search for a president at every phase of the process: in the original discussions of how the search is to proceed, in the deliberations about what qualities are most desired in the new president, and in the last stages of deciding among the serious prospects. But nowhere is the drama sharper than when the committee has to confront the questions of confidentiality—concerning what they say to one another, what is said to them and whether information will be shared beyond the search committee.

It is impossible to grow up in America without receiving mixed messages about secrecy. On the one hand, secrets are a treasure, personal yet powerful, something to protect.[3] They are inextricably linked to the concept of privacy, to being able to keep to oneself one's own thoughts and feelings. The threat that "Big Brother" is watching engenders strong emotional reactions. Americans resist carrying identity cards, and in most states, the mainly male mobilizers of the National Rifle Association defend the right to carry lethal weapons as an extension of our prized individualism, which can be infringed upon only as one boards a plane. The Fifth Amendment "privilege" against self-incrimination allows individuals to withhold information about themselves in the face of what other democratic countries would regard as legitimate inquiries by the state.[4]

But even as Americans seem to revere privacy, we insist upon making many things public. The *National Enquirer* is both scorned and widely read. People become instant celebrities by telling all that they learned behind closed doors or in bed. Non-Americans are wary about dealing with American diplomats because the Americans have a world reputation as "blabbermouths," unable to keep a secret even when we have promised to do so. We ask questions which in other countries would be considered

---

[2] If he had been delineating subcultures among university trustees, no doubt there would be an overlapping, somewhat different cast of characters.

[3] For an excellent discussion, see Sissela Bok, *Lying: Moral Choice in Public and Private Life* (New York: Pantheon Books, 1978), and *Secrets: On the Ethics of Concealment and Revelation* (New York: Vintage Books, 1984).

[4] The Fourth Amendment, limiting "searches and seizures," also inhibits governmental authority in the investigation of crime. Both the Fourth and Fifth Amendments reflect the propaganda of the American Revolution against a tyrannical British monarchy, which by 1776 had in fact become more parliamentary than absolutist.

tastelessly intrusive. There is a specifically American generosity that places a premium on openness, on sharing thoughts and feelings, on being candid. Not only with spouses, but with friends and colleagues, concealment is almost akin to cheating. Judith Martin, "Miss Manners" of the syndicated column, frequently discourses on the problems of individuals asked intrusive questions concerning their personal lives, who want to know how to respond without giving offense. People regard it as friendly to inquire not only about one's health, but about matters that would once have been regarded as completely private, such as money and sex. People believe that their friends and even their acquaintances should level with them. To keep a secret is in a sense to maintain a privileged status in an egalitarian time.

The American ambivalence concerning secrecy is manifest in the tensions in our society over which matters should remain confidential and which should be disclosed. Although there are some Americans who believe that secrecy is *never* justified, most of us will give a privilege to negotiations to end or to inhibit a war or to engage in negotiations for control of nuclear weapons, as in the famous "walk in the woods" outside Geneva in the summer of 1982, during which the American negotiator Paul Nitze conferred with his Soviet counterpart, Yuli Kvitsinsky, out of the hearing of leak-prone colleagues, to forge an "original and provocative nuclear-weapons agreement." In domestic affairs, although all states have open-meeting and open-records laws on their books, there are major differences among them in scope. Most states, for instance, allow certain kinds of discussions to take place "behind closed doors," most notably labor negotiations seeking to end a labor dispute, personnel discussions, and decisions about the purchase of real estate, so that the state agency is not required to show its hand ahead of time. But even these few exceptions are not accepted as appropriate by all. In Florida, for instance, all of these matters must be conducted "in the sunshine," and the media and Common Cause in Florida are pressing to make the already far-reaching state disclosure provisions even more comprehensive.

SECRECY AND THE SEARCH

Not surprisingly, then, throughout the presidential search, boards of trustees and search committees find themselves contending with opposing

117

pressures over questions of confidentiality and disclosure. In some public universities, these tensions are evident in the seemingly contradictory state laws under which the search is conducted. In Minnesota, for example, the Data Practices Act outlines individual privacy rights, and under this law, the names of all candidates for a university presidency should remain confidential until the final stages of the search process. But Minnesota's open-meeting law requires the regents to meet in public whenever they conduct business, even if this business is the discussion of candidates for the presidency. The coexistence of such laws is testimony to our competing and oftentimes conflicting values over "the individual's right to privacy" and "the public's right to know."[5]

When a president departs, especially one who has been in office a considerable amount of time, trustees are sometimes surprised by the intensity of interest in the selection of a successor. Alumni who are loyal, and even some who have been alienated, rally around. Many faculty members bestir themselves. Administrators are understandably uneasy. In the public arena, as at "Southern State University," there may be strong repercussions at the state capital and in the local community where the college or university is situated. At every stage of the search process, journalists and broadcasters speak for their audiences in wanting to know who is "in," who is "out," and what is going on. Even before the board of trustees and the search committee begin their consideration of the institution's current situation and what they ought to be looking for in a successor, there are many who, out of interest or curiosity, want to eavesdrop on the impending conversations.

For many of the trustee members of the presidential search committee, the question of confidentiality is not novel. Trustees with corporate or legal backgrounds have experienced the need for confidentiality in their professional work. Privileged conversations take place between lawyer and client, doctor and patient, and (in practice if not always in law) journalist and anonymous source. Trustees may also have read John Nason's *Presidential Search*, in which Nason stresses the salience of confidentiality to

---

[5] For an excellent discussion of concerns for privacy, see Edward H. Levi, "Address before the Association of the Bar of the City of New York," April 28, 1975. Also see Judith Wagner DeCew, "The Realm of the Private in Law and Ethics," paper presented at the Bunting Institute, Cambridge, Massachusetts, September, 1988.

118

permit free discussion among members of the search committee and the board, and to make possible courting of candidates who believe that a public campaign would jeopardize their present positions. Nason writes, "The best qualified individuals are often the least inclined to submit themselves to being dressed and undressed in public."[6] His views are shared by most writers about searches. Joseph Kauffman, a former college president and former vice-president of the University of Wisconsin, states emphatically, "There is no question in my mind that the inability of search committee members to pledge confidentiality . . . prohibits a search from attracting persons who are relatively successful and satisfied with their present positions."[7] Ted Marchese and Jane Lawrence declare that, "in accepting committee membership, each member assumes a responsibility not to mention any candidate's name or status, or the content of committee conversation, to any non-committee person within or outside of the conversation. . . . By committee stipulation, the chair should be empowered to accept the resignation of any committee member who breaches these agreements."[8]

However, faculty members' understanding of and belief in the need for confidentiality, as one might expect, is not uniform. When Harvard University creates an ad hoc committee to decide on a candidate or candidates for tenure, both those chosen to serve on this committee from outside of Harvard and from within Harvard are pledged to confidentiality. Most requests for letters of recommendation in university life come with an assurance that the response will be held in confidence. At the University of Wisconsin-Madison, however, any candidate under review can have an open hearing on demand. Correspondingly, there is division on this issue within the American Association of University Professors.[9] On presidential search committees, faculty members, like students, will not necessarily regard themselves as agents for the institution rather than for a coterie. Hence, while most chairs of search committees, and often the chair of the

[6] Nason, *Presidential Search*, p. 25. John Nason had been president of two liberal arts colleges, Swarthmore and Carleton, both known for their aggressively participatory students and faculties.

[7] Joseph F. Kauffman, *At the Pleasure of the Board: The Service of the College and University President* (Washington, D.C.: American Council on Education, 1980), p. 23.

[8] Marchese and Lawrence, *Search Committee Handbook*, p. 14.

[9] See Ann H. Franke, "Disclosure of Tenure Evaluation Materials," in *Academe*, Vol. 74, no. 6 (November–December, 1988), pp. 36–37.

board as well, make it known at the first meeting of the search committee that it would be a betrayal of trust for search committee members to reveal their privileged discussions, promises of confidentiality are not always readily pledged, and, even when promised, confidentiality is far from being routinely accomplished.

In 1981, we surveyed the heads of search committees at sixty-five institutions about the extent of confidentiality that had originally been intended and had actually occurred in their recent presidential searches. We presented them with five scenarios—ranging from searches where complete confidentiality was maintained throughout the process to those where all search information, including candidates' names and the deliberations of search committee members, was publicly available—and then asked which of these scenarios most closely corresponded to their own search experience. Next, we inquired whether the disclosures that had occurred during their search had been planned or not, and how such disclosures had affected the outcome of their selection process.

We found that in the majority of searches there had been a compromise between the recognition of the importance of confidentiality at every stage and a fear that, without direct campus participation, there would be objections from the campus when decisions among finalists were made. Many search committees had concluded that their preferred procedure was to keep all information about candidates confidential until the point at which they identified a small group of finalists. Once this determination had been made, they warned these finalists that their confidentiality would be jeopardized when they were brought to campus, and that they needed to weigh this risk of disclosure and corresponding exposure on their home bases against their ambitions and hopes for success in that particular position. Some candidates were willing to take that risk for a variety of reasons, while others were unwilling and withdrew from the search. In the 1988 University of Minnesota search, for example, several "proposed finalists" withdrew from consideration because they were unwilling to be identified publicly as candidates. Similarly, in the 1988 University of Oregon search, two of three finalists refused to submit to the public campus visit and withdrew their candidacies. We also found that a few search committees made a sub-compromise, bringing to campus those candidates who agreed to come for open interviews, while holding in reserve a particular and desirable candidate who was unwilling to go public unless assured of selection.[10]

Campus Visits

Although most search committees believe confidentiality is important, the majority, as we noted earlier, believe that this confidentiality must give way in the final stages of the search in order to bring a small number of finalists to campus for open sessions with constituents. Search committees and boards of trustees fear that, even though campus constituents are represented on the search committee, these constituents will not consider the search legitimate unless they have had a chance to meet the finalists themselves. Faculty members, in particular, are accustomed to doing comparative shopping when they select their own colleagues, and, with the widespread democratization of governance, many expect that they will be able to do likewise vis-à-vis those final candidates for the presidency.

In Chapter VIII, we describe the debate of the Winthrop College search committee over whether or not to bring three finalists to the campus. Just as we saw earlier at "Abbott College," the faculty at Winthrop were insistent that such visits occur, while the trustees were less persuaded of their desirability. In the Winthrop search, it was the arguments for campus visits made by search consultant Ruth Weintraub that carried the day. But the campus visits did not assure the legitimacy of the final selection. When members of the faculty of arts and sciences circulated a petition after the campus visits, declaring in effect that none of the candidates was suitable and asking that the search be reopened, some trustees pointed to the faculty petition as proof that the campus visits were a mistake. It appears to us, however, that had there been no visits of candidates, the antagonism on the campus would have been much greater, and perhaps fatal to legitimacy.

One of the problems with campus visits, when used primarily to assure the legitimacy of the outcome, arises from incomplete inclusion of those who believe themselves entitled to a visit with the candidate. In a small college, a general show-and-tell meeting with anyone who wants to turn

[10] For more information about these survey results see Judith Block McLaughlin, "From Secrecy to Sunshine: An Overview of Presidential Search Practice," *Research in Higher Education*, Vol. 22, no. 2 (1985), pp. 195–208.

up can provide everyone with a chance to observe and often to be heard. However, on a large campus, with whom do the candidates meet? At a university with a medical school, does provision need to be made for adjunct medical faculty who may be influential practitioners in the area? With the faculty in agriculture in a land-grant institution which still has a sizable political base in this area? With buildings and grounds people, who might be planning a strike? With the mayor or other officials in a small town where the campus is located? In a society increasingly built on entitlements, unfulfilled entitlements can always be harvested.

In fact, as both the "Abbott College" and "Southern State University" accounts suggest, campus visits can become highly political occasions in which the candidate offers contending factions the opportunity to abuse each other in the guise of asking questions of the finalists. This is not an argument against the campus visit, but rather against believing that such a visit can insure legitimacy, not to speak of harmony.

In the Winthrop College case (Chapter VIII), the protesting faculty concluded that the successful candidate was the "least worst" of the trio, thus reluctantly ratifying a decision of the search committee and the board. In other cases, the search committee and the board genuinely want help from the campus in making what they have concluded is a difficult choice among several contenders. In such cases, campus visits become a means, not just for legitimizing the outcome, but for eliciting the reactions of campus constituents to the finalists for the presidency. Thus, groups on campus, after meeting the finalists in the various forums provided, may be asked to fill out forms, or their views may be solicited more informally. These opinions are then taken into account when the search committee or the board makes its final decision. In the search at Smith College, for example, after spending a full day with each of ten candidates, the search committee chose two finalists to bring to campus, either of whom they would have been happy to have had as president. The campus helped not only to legitimate but to make the choice. The majority of faculty members preferred Mary Maples Dunn, who had a down-to-earth, quiet confidence, to the other candidate, an alumna trustee and distinguished, forceful Ivy League professor.

In one search, campus administrators and members of the faculty advisory committee to the search were asked to put into writing their impres-

122

sions of each finalist, based on their meeting with these candidates during the campus visits. Told these assessments would remain confidential, the administrators and faculty members, almost without exception, expressed serious reservations about the abilities of one of the candidates for the presidency. Disappointed when this candidate was subsequently named president, they were horrified to discover that the new president was given the written critiques of him. Fortunately, the president behaved decently and made no attempt to get back at anyone. Even so, the situation was so distressing to the senior administrative staff that two took early retirement, and others began serious job hunting.

Campus visits are sometimes defended on the ground that they test the stamina of candidates and reveal their ability to handle themselves under pressure. (As we will see in Chapter VII, this argument is also advanced by advocates of sunshine searches.) When candidates have been senior executives elsewhere, their "grace under pressure" has presumably already been demonstrated, but a visit allows faculty members, students, and others to see and hear the candidates, to ask questions, and to observe demeanor. Those on campus who insist that candidates come onto their landscape may also believe that a candidate's willingness to do so shows good faith and indicates that he or she will accept the position if it is offered. After all, why else would someone want to go through such a strenuous and probing period? In fact we have met quite a few ambitious people who have gone through such rituals for practice, knowing that they would withdraw if the position were unexpectedly offered. They, in effect, use one campus to coach them for a hoped-for better one. Other people become candidates in order to manipulate their home-base, or another institution at which they are a candidate, by demonstrating their vendibility. In cases where the visiting finalist is simply using the campus as a dress rehearsal for a later performance, there is the risk for the campus that this person may appear more attractive than the finalist who accepts the presidency, thus weakening the latter's position by being viewed by the campus as a "second best" choice.

There is, to be sure, no foolproof way to determine whether or not a candidate will accept a position if offered. Candidates, and quite often salient family members, change their minds about a move without an element of disingenuousness toward the search. Still, the most careful

123

checks, and often the most pertinacious search consultants, can minimize the risks that a finalist will exploit the opportunity for a visit, not only for coaching, but also for leverage on his or her home base.

Many campus visits are structured in such a way so as not to be informative either for the candidates or for the campus. Repeatedly, finalists have told us of the shallowness of the questions they were asked. With their schedules calling for one-hour sessions with different groups of people, they never had the time to explore any subject in depth or to cover much new territory. The questions they were asked were generally the predictable ones: faculty members inquired about the candidate's commitment to affirmative action and position on the importance of the liberal arts, as well as on pay raises, tenure, faculty development monies, and parking places. Students—the few who showed up—might have asked about "diversity" on campus or about the candidate's feelings about fraternities; and in the more liberal milieux, they might ask about the candidate's attitude toward current political issues, such as divestment of securities in companies with ties to South Africa, CIA recruiting, ROTC, or women's issues.

Campus visits can serve an important purpose in helping presidential prospects learn more about the institution, a theme which we take up again in Chapter XI when we discuss the last stages of the search. If the chief reason for the campus visit, however, is to educate the leading contender for the presidency about the campus and to make certain that this person is accepted enthusiastically by the campus, then there may be no need to bring anyone but this top choice for a campus visit. Presenting several candidates to the campus as if they are all viewed by the search committee as equally well suited for the presidency, when in fact one of the finalists is overwhelmingly the committee's pick, is both deceptive and potentially dangerous. It deceives the campus in that it allows constituents to think that they are being asked to make a choice when one, in essence, has already been made. And, worse, it deceives the candidates who are not really serious contenders, asking them to expend time and emotional energy, and possibly risk negative consequences from exposure of their candidacy at their home institution. Women and minority candidates are especially wary of being used in this fashion, unfortunately often with good reason.

The practice of presenting more than one candidate to the campus when the search committee has a decided preference for one person can be dangerous, too, in that the campus constituents, based on very limited exposure to the candidates and far less information about them than the committee has in its possession, could conceivably prefer the finalist who is the least highly regarded. Although sequences differ among institutions, typically the search committee has interviewed a group of "semifinalists," has invited a smaller number of "finalists" back for longer discussions, and has gathered extensive information from and about these individuals. As a result of their work, members of the search committee can make a reasonable claim that they are "experts" in comparison to those not intensely involved in the search process. It seems to us that search committee members who then depend more upon the first impression of campus constituents in their brief encounters with the finalists than on their own considered judgments are denying their own expertise and being remiss in their responsibility. Hence, when there is a candidate who is the clear choice of the committee, instead of parading several finalists before the campus, just this one person can be invited to the campus. This individual is then presented as the candidate about whom the committee is enthusiastic, although no binding decision has as yet been made. In such a situation, the candidate is informed that if there were to be an unexpected outpouring of opposition from the campus, the offer of the presidency would be reconsidered. Conversely, even if there is no formidable opposition, the candidate would have the opportunity to conclude after the campus visit that the presidency was, by reason of opposition or for other reasons previously not fully realized, not attractive to him or her. The possibilities of awkward and embarrassing outcomes are evident, much like an imaginary wedding scenario where someone rises up and says that there is a reason why this man and woman should not be joined in holy matrimony.[11] But when the search committee and the candidate are reasonably confident about the prospective "marriage," it makes good sense to introduce the campus only to the one "intended."

Although all campus visits of candidates represent a move away from

---

[11] Obviously, in cases where the decision is made to bring only one finalist to the campus, all discussions about salary and other provisions about employment should already have taken place so that there are no later misunderstandings on these scores.

the confidentiality with which most search committees have attempted to conduct their previous activities, the amount of disclosure realized during the campus visit varies greatly from search to search. As we mentioned in Chapter I, when Antioch was conducting the presidential search which resulted in the selection of Alan Guskin, the search committee chairman, Robert Aller, was able to persuade the Yellow Springs campus and Antioch's satellite campuses that they could not find a suitable president if they insisted on knowing the names of finalists and on having candidates visit each of the centers as well as the home campus. In the end, two finalists came to Yellow Springs for confidential meetings with selected members of the Antioch faculty and administration. Aller gave the *Antioch Record* the news story that there would be campus visits, but not the names of either finalist. In a news story in the *Record*, Aller noted that, "As an Antiochian schooled in the tradition of open, consultative community, it hurts not to open it [the search] as much as I would like. But we want a good president and that overriding objective has had to take precedence over our desire to be more open." The student editors were apparently not persuaded: their editorial queried why, if confidentiality was the mode in searches, Antioch should conform. One of Antioch's central teachings, they argued, "is to question authority figures who tell us what we need." Nevertheless, the names of the finalists were never printed. Since the finalists did not visit any of the Antioch centers, two representatives from each center came to Yellow Springs for the confidential meetings.

Occasionally candidates for a college presidency will tell us that they were amazed to discover that, despite their participation in a campus visit, their candidacy never became known at their home institution. In some instances, the search committee has placed certain limits on the campus visit, such as that finalists will meet only with certain people at the institution (to whom they have stressed the importance of not disseminating broadly the names of finalists for fear that one or more of them will withdraw) and not in large forums open to the general public. In other searches, there is no apparent reason why word of their candidacy never made it back to the candidates' home base. Perhaps the usually vigilant media were inattentive. But as the trustees (and candidates) in the "Abbott" search learned the hard way, any time candidates are invited to come to a campus for open meetings with constituents, the institution and the candidates themselves must understand that the possibility of publicity is very real.

Complete Confidentiality

Nineteen percent of the searches in our sample had followed a policy of complete confidentiality, in which candidates never met campus constituents other than those on the search committee (and occasionally a few other highly placed administrators and faculty leaders), and no information about candidates was released other than the name of the person appointed president. It is our impression that, since our survey was completed, the number of institutions choosing to keep their search proceedings confidential from beginning to end has been increasing. Perhaps this is due to a dawning recognition that no search, even at an institution with high self-regard, has a guarantee of eliciting an array of marvelous applicants who are willing to have their candidacies known. These decisions not to have campus visits—or to have only the final choice of the search committee and the board come to the campus—may also be the result of an increase in the candidacies of people currently serving as presidents, due in part to the shorter term of presidents, in part to the young age of many first-time presidents, and, in part, to the paucity of desirable post-presidential positions. A survey conducted in 1988 under the auspices of the American Council on Education found that thirty-one percent of the presidents of major research universities had come to their present office from another presidency. The figure is seventeen percent for all types of colleges.[12] Some boards of trustees and search committees may also recognize that publicity, even about the finalists, would serve no purpose other than to create dissension and politicization on the campus, or further aggravate the turmoil already there.

When Pennsylvania State University sought a president, no one was brought to campus, and faculty, staff, and students learned of the choice of Joab Thomas only after his approval by the board of trustees. When Duke University conducted a search for a successor to Terry Sanford in

[12] See Madeleine F. Green, *The American College President: A Contemporary Profile* (Washington, D.C.: American Council on Education, 1988).

127

1984, Professor Arie Lewin, then the chairman of the faculty senate, was given the responsibility of delineating how a search might proceed. Lewin consulted individuals knowledgeable about searches, many of whom suggested that the committee should work with a search consultant. After comparing various possibilities, the Duke search committee chose to use the firm of Heidrick & Struggles. The eighteen-member search committee was chaired by trustee John A. Forlines, Jr., with professor of history Robert F. Durden as vice-chairman, and included other trustees and faculty members, a representative of the Duke employees, and a representative of the Durham area. Search committee members explained to their constituents on campus that open campus interviews with finalists would scare away promising prospects. After extensive inquiry and interviewing, the search committee recommended two individuals to the board of trustees, whose members then interviewed both. The person chosen, Dr. H. Keith H. Brodie, professor of psychiatry at Duke, former chairman of the department of psychiatry and a former acting provost, was a surprise to the faculty. At the outset, the expectation had been that Duke would recruit a candidate from outside, but as the search committee met with prospects, Dr. Brodie looked better—a scenario we have seen operate in other cases also, where the limitations of the inside prospects are well known, while those of extramural candidates come to light only on further scrutiny. Faculty members at Duke accepted the decision, receiving sufficient assurance from their colleagues on the search committee that they had interviewed some very able extramural contenders.

The University of Virginia also used executive recruiters for their presidential search, in this case the firm of Ward Howell. No finalists were brought to campus. Robert O'Neil, the person chosen president, was at the time of the search serving as president of the University of Wisconsin, and he insisted on complete confidentiality. In that case also, sufficient trust existed to permit the selection of someone, unlike previous incumbents, with no prior connection to the University of Virginia. Sweet Briar College conducted a presidential search with the aid of Millington ("Millie") McCoy of Gould & McCoy, an executive search firm, where only the finalist, Nenah Fry, was brought to the campus. Here again, campus constituents were prepared to accept the selection on the basis of her approval by the search committee and by the board of trustees.

The curators of the University of Missouri System asked Joseph Kauffman to advise them in their presidential search. Kauffman, a former president of Rhode Island College, was then executive vice-president of the University of Wisconsin System. He was able to court president Peter Magrath of the University of Minnesota, persuading him of the advantages of the Missouri position and, at least as important, assuring him that his candidacy would not be disclosed, risking his ability to lead in his then-current position or jeopardizing his reputation.

Similarly, when Michigan State University conducted its search for a successor to Cecil Mackey in 1986, it secured as a consultant Fred Ness, then working with the Association of Governing Boards' Presidential Search Consultation Service. Like all the consultants we know or have learned about, he emphasized the role of confidentiality in courting anyone already well situated. John DiBiaggio, then president of the University of Connecticut, had already publicly lost out in Florida's "sunshine" search (described in the next chapter). At first, DiBiaggio was unwilling to take the risk of the MSU candidacy. Ness made clear to him how seriously the search committee took his candidacy and assured him that all information would remain completely confidential and that, were there to be any unexpected leak, DiBiaggio would be informed instantly, so that he could prudently withdraw.[13] On this basis, DiBiaggio agreed at least to talk with members of the search committee.

A Michigan native, DiBiaggio knew the East Lansing campus, and did not need to take the risk of visiting it and perhaps being recognized and identified as a candidate. However, when his wife Carolyn wanted to see the university and surrounding community before the DiBiaggios made their decision about whether to move, she traveled to the campus using her maiden name and an assumed identity, pretending to be the parent of a prospective student. Carolyn DiBiaggio's "white lie" hardly raises ethical dilemmas. Deceptions of this sort are short-lived, and for those deceived are at most a matter of disappointment that they were not confided in. They belong with the routine concealment that makes social life possible and do not involve bribery or other forms of gross corruption.

The Drew University trustees were also able to win someone they

---

[13] Such an assurance allows someone to declare that he or she never was a candidate, but the credibility of this assertion can be open to doubt. In the next chapter we describe the embarrassment of Peter Magrath when, against his expressed wishes, the University of Florida named him in an open search as a contender on the basis of hope that he might consent, despite his repeated denials.

129

wanted for their presidency in 1989 because they could keep their search confidential. At the outset of the search, someone on the Drew faculty had suggested that the search committee consider Thomas H. Kean, the governor of New Jersey, whom the committee then dubbed a " 'wouldn't-it-be-nice-but-highly-unlikely' candidate."[14] Because the Drew trustees could talk in secret with Kean about this possibility and could wait for him for the eleven months remaining in his term of office as governor, they were able to make what had seemed "highly unlikely" actually happen.

Plugging the Leaks

Although many search committees plan to maintain complete confidentiality for much if not all of the search process, many discover that these hopes are not realized. Leaks of confidential information (names of candidates, discussions and votes of the committee concerning these candidates) can occur at every stage of the search process. As in the case of "Southern State University," the presidency may be the most important position in the local community and the college or university the most important source of local news. In that case, a young newspaper reporter rather easily penetrated the committee's efforts to maintain confidentiality. An enterprising journalist can place calls to likely candidates, check airplane schedules and hotel guest logs, and pursue the trail of reimbursements, photograph people entering buildings where interviews with candidates are being held, or check the license numbers of cars outside of the locale where trustees are visiting. Someone's secret is someone else's scoop.

Correspondingly, many leaks occur inadvertently, either because search committee members are unaware of what should or should not be discussed outside of search committee meetings, or because they are tricked by an ingenious reporter into divulging more than they intended. In the search at "Southern State University," a student member did not realize that items disclosed could be pieced together to build a larger story. Such seemingly simple mechanical matters as record-keeping or addressing mail can mean the difference between the maintenance or loss of confiden-

[14] Nancy S. Shaenen, chair of Drew's board of trustees, quoted in Pat Meisol, *Minnesota Alumni Association*, May–June, 1989, p. 20.

tiality. Correspondence that is addressed to a potential candidate's office rather than his or her home can cause problems if it is opened by a secretary who is not discreet or who becomes upset by assuming that the nomination suggests that a boss is considering leaving.

Various measures have been taken by search committees to avoid unwanted disclosure. Mindful of possible leaks if the business of the search committee was handled on campus, the lawyer-trustee who chaired the presidential search committee for Earlham College in 1983 reimbursed candidates for their expenses with checks drawn on his personal account, so that receipts did not pass through the hands of college secretaries and bookkeepers until after the search had long concluded. When the University of Rochester was searching for a president in 1983, search committee members never used the word "candidate," but referred to those prospects with whom they discussed the presidency as "consultants." Hence if word were to leak of their conversations, all concerned could say they had been exploring ideas in a consulting capacity. The Rice University presidential search committee flew finalist George Rupp to Houston in a private jet in order to avoid the chance that news reporters might learn of his flight plans prior to the announcement of his appointment. A private jet was also used by the University of Hartford search committee in 1988 when the members of the committee flew to the State University of New York at Potsdam to interview president Humphrey Tonkin and to talk with others at Potsdam about him as a potential president for Hartford. Here, though, the use of a private jet backfired; the jet was so much larger than any other airplane using this small-town airport that it aroused considerable attention.[15]

The circle of secrecy commonly extends beyond the search committee itself. Individuals who are questioned by search committee members concerning the capacities of a particular candidate are assured that their comments, both written and oral, will be kept in confidence, and these informants are almost invariably instructed not to divulge the fact that so-and-so is a candidate. In recent years, however, these assurances have lost some credibility, in large part because of cases in which courts have

---

[15] For a fuller listing of measures utilized by search committees to preserve confidentiality, see Judith Block McLaughlin, "Plugging Search Committee Leaks," *AGB Reports*, May–June, 1985, pp. 24–30.

131

insisted on opening records in response to litigation over claims of discrimination or violation of affirmative action requirements. A unanimous Supreme Court in *University of Pennsylvania vs. E.E.O.C.*, no. 88-493 (1990), in an opinion written by Justice Harry Blackmun, has declared that universities have no special privilege to maintain the confidentiality of tenure records against an inquiry from the Equal Employment Opportunity Commission pursuing a person's claim of discrimination based on sex, race, or national origin. There does not have to be a showing of likely discrimination. The goal of fairness to women and minorities takes precedence, especially, as Justice Blackmun handsomely declared, because faculty members should be able to express their judgments on tenure candidates with equal candor in public and in private settings. Whether women and minorities are in fact given an advantage seems open to doubt, since, when files are open, the network of the telephone may be closed and be perhaps more biased; moreover, institutions may hesitate to offer initial appointments to those whose gender or race makes them likely candidates for litigation if denied a permanent position.

It is in line with this stream of litigation that, when campuses of the University of California system ask outside referees to comment on scholarly qualifications of individuals, they warn the letter-writer that they will maintain confidentiality insofar as possible. The qualification arises because of continuing federal scrutiny for compliance with affirmative action mandates. The University of Minnesota has been under similar scrutiny for many years.

Yet, in the instance of presidential searches, we do not know of any case where challenge to the outcome has led to the opening of records and the revelation of letters of recommendation, perhaps in part because a presidency is such an idiosyncratic position that it is difficult to contend that the preference for one candidate over another is a violation of equal employment opportunity.

The process of investigating the backgrounds of candidates is fraught with the same tensions between confidentiality and disclosure experienced elsewhere in the search. The search committee wants to learn all that it can about the individuals under consideration for the presidency, yet it does not want to compromise candidates in so doing. When faculty members on a search committee telephone their disciplinary colleagues on a

132

campus where a candidate is currently serving, the colleagues, though urged to keep the conversation confidential, often mention their conversation to others, and the news gets out, in many cases leading to the candidate's embarrassment and sometimes also to the person's withdrawal. So too, student members of search committees may call student government representatives on a candidate's home campus with the same danger of a leak. How wide should the search committee cast its net to find sources of information about candidates, knowing that the wider the inquiry, the more material is gathered but the greater the risk of leaking? In the early stages of a search, some search committees limit their inquiries to the referees furnished by the candidates themselves. At some point when the committee has pared down its list of candidates to a smaller group of serious prospects, it explains to these prospects that further inquiries are needed, and while the search committee members will urge everyone they call to keep the conversation confidential, they cannot guarantee that their request will be honored. Confidentiality is almost certain to be lost in the small proportion of cases where a subset of the search committee comes to the campus on which the candidate is currently working, for this is likely to become known on that campus, even if the visit is handled with discretion. When the candidate has been assured that she or he is at the head of the list of finalists, the visit, while anxiety-provoking, may seem worth enduring.

In searches, as in other enterprises, governmental and corporate, leaks may, of course, be quite intentional.[16] Sometimes the motivation for leaking confidential information is simply the desire to be in the limelight, as

[16] Anthony Lewis, in his column in the *New York Times*, "Abroad at Home," has defended government by leak in terms of owing the country the truth, with the leak as the only way to maintain accountability. Trained in law and journalism, Lewis has written about ". . . the whole American tradition of leaks that keeps the system honest. . . . In fact, leaks play an essential and accepted role in getting information around Washington." Lewis was addressing himself to *U.S.* v. *Morison*, a prosecution of Loring Morison, a civilian employee of the Navy, who sent U.S. satellite photographs of a Soviet aircraft carrier under construction to *Jane's Defense Weekly*, and whose conviction the Fourth Circuit Court of Appeals confirmed under the Espionage Act of 1917. (The Navy knew and had agreed to Morison's doing freelance writing for *Jane's*, but regarded this particular publication as a breach of national security.) Lewis referred approvingly to the Pentagon Papers case, Daniel Ellsberg's leak of documents being put together for a history of the Vietnam war. In that case, the majority of the Supreme Court concluded that the Espionage Act did not apply.

These large dramas of our national life remind us, by comparison with the British Official Secrets Act, what is exceptional about America: the freedom Americans allow the media, even while a large proportion of the population distrusts "the media," just as it distrusts other powerful institutions.

133

in one large search committee where a representative of the nonprofessional staff members at the university found himself, for the first time ever, being pursued by news reporters, and he enjoyed his totally new status. People "in the know" often find that their possession of secrets gives them a special kind of power. Leaks may also be part of a calculated strategy to obtain a particular end. In one search, a faculty member of the search committee gave the press the names of the five finalists because he suspected that the board would not choose someone from this list but would, instead, appoint an internal candidate who had been rejected by the search committee. This breach of confidentiality caused an uproar and slowed the board selection process. Although no candidate withdrew because of the leak, several withdrew because of the delay. The leak gave ammunition to the board and to others who supported the internal candidate. Ironically, the breach of confidentiality, intended to strengthen the search committee's hand, thus resulted in the very outcome the faculty member had wanted to avoid: the internal candidate was named president.

When Brown University was seeking a successor to Donald Hornig, a scientist who had come from the faculty, some faculty members and students were eager to have a woman chosen as his successor. The *Brown Daily Herald* carried the scoop that there were two finalists: one, a Woods Hole biologist, and the other, Virginia Smith, economist and lawyer and then director of the Fund for the Improvement of Post-Secondary Education in the Department of Education. As a result of this leak, the Brown Corporation aborted the search, created a new search committee, and appointed William Bowen of the Chicago-based executive search firm, Heidrick & Struggles, to assist the re-search. This time, Howard Swearer, the president of Carleton College who had earlier declined to become a candidate, was persuaded in complete confidence to accept the Brown presidency.

At that time, members of the Brown Corporation had some interest in Vartan Gregorian, then provost at the University of Pennsylvania, but the matter was not pursued on either side. However, when Howard Swearer announced his resignation, the corporation, again using William Bowen of Heidrick & Struggles, actively courted Gregorian, then the stellar and successful president of the New York Public Library, which he had raised from near-bankruptcy to a national cultural icon. Gregorian had been "mentioned" by the press when Yale had conducted a search for a successor to A. Bartlett Giamatti, and was being courted by the University of Michigan at the same time that Brown was on the lookout. To all comers, Gregorian made clear that he was not a candidate. He and many members of the faculty and student body at the University of Pennsylvania had assumed that he would become the president there when Martin Meyerson left office, but Sheldon Hackney was chosen instead. The last thing Gregorian wanted was again to seem to come in second to someone else. The Brown Corporation could not afford to focus on only a single candidate, no matter how stellar. Toward the end of the process, word did leak out that, in addition to Gregorian, the corporation was considering Walter Massey, an eminent black scientist who had been dean at Brown and had then become the director of the Argonne National Laboratories and vice-president of the University of Chicago. Still, when terms could be worked out with Gregorian, the choice fell to him.

Lapses in confidentiality can occur, unthinkingly, long after a search is over. We recall a search in which the academic vice-president of one liberal arts college had been a candidate for the presidency of another. She had been promised confidentiality, and throughout the search it was maintained. In the end, she was not the choice of the search committee or board. Some months after the search had concluded, she was horrified to learn that the chairman of her college's board had learned of her candidacy, and also why it did not succeed, in a casual conversation with a trustee of the college where she had been under consideration. The gossiping trustee, the search long past, had not realized that the need for confidentiality had *not* passed. [17]

One might conclude from what has been said that the pressure to leak is greater than the restraints favoring the maintenance of confidentiality. This would be a false impression. Our interviews are full of instances where faculty members and students have resisted the pressures of their

[17] The enormous amounts of paper accumulated in the course of a search (often including records of telephone conversations) are frequently put in sealed archives. Many institutions, Harvard among them, are facing the question as to when these archives might be opened for scholarly work; in Harvard's case, the pressure comes not only from scholars, but also from the *Crimson* and student activists, much as, in federal government cases, activists make use of Freedom of Information legislation. In 1988, a Harvard committee chaired by former dean Franklin Ford concluded that Harvard's archives should be sealed for fifty years, with some flexibility allowed for in the case of projects of significant scholarly importance.

135

intimates and accusations of being compromised by their refusal to reveal the names of candidates. An episode in the "Abbott College" search is illustrative of the degree of restraint that can prevail. A faculty member at Abbott proposed leaking to the press a confidential draft of a memorandum that William Patterson had written, hoping that some of his language in the draft would be interpreted as sexist and that this would result in his embarrassment and subsequent withdrawal as a candidate. The person who suggested leaking the confidential draft shared the widespread faculty assumption that the trustees intended, despite some faculty opposition, to choose Patterson. But another faculty member, also opposed to Patterson's selection, prevailed. "We don't do that sort of thing here," he declared. The appeal was made to a common ethos at Abbott, rather than to a bonding specific to the search committee.

Some Consequences of Leaks

In 1983, when the University of California was searching for a president, the Berkeley student newspaper, the *Daily Californian*, objected to the secrecy that had been attempted in that search process. The newspaper quoted Ann Roark, the able education editor of the *Los Angeles Times*, as saying that, if it came to a choice between educational values and the values esteemed by journalism, her adherence lay with the latter. Other educational editors in the state took similar positions, with one reporter commenting, "It isn't as if it were a matter of life or death."[18]

We believe that leaks can be justified when it *is* a matter of life or death. Physicians are required to breach the nearly sacrosanct patient-physician privilege against disclosure if the doctor is convinced that the patient intends to do harm to someone else (today, for example, by infecting others with the AIDS virus) or even to the patient, for instance, through an attempt to commit suicide. A leak would surely be justified if one knew of a plan to launch a supposedly surgical attack with nuclear weapons. However, such justification cannot be claimed for efforts to achieve a journalistic coup that could lead to derailing a search. Perhaps even more significant for the ethical considerations at stake here than the possible damage

[18] Drew Digby, "UC wants presidential search to be press-free," *Daily Californian*, January 3, 1983, p. 1.

to institutions brought about by leaks that result in failed searches is the savage damage that a leak can cause to individuals. When the Culpepper State press broke the story of Stephen Davis's candidacy in the "Southern State University" search, resentment against him at his own institution erupted. A president who had focused on academic matters, he had offended some alumni whose chief interest was the football standing of the university, and he had angered some powerful politicians whose chief interest was patronage. Already regarded as an outsider in contrast to his locally rooted, home-guard predecessor, now he was also charged with disloyalty. His children were verbally abused in school. Garbage was left on the doorstep of the presidential home. A combination of local pride and vulnerability had mobilized people who thought that the president had decided that they were not good enough for him. Stephen Davis was forced to submit his resignation. Shortly thereafter, Stephen Davis learned that he was no longer being considered in the Southern State University search. When he began to look for other positions, he found that his recent experience had made him controversial. Even several years later, the controversy haunted him: repeatedly, he was dropped from serious consideration by search committees and search consultants reluctant to take a chance with someone who had previously had such bad press.

In 1981, president George Rainsford of Kalamazoo College (now president of Lynchburg College) was courted by another institution which assured him that his candidacy would be kept completely confidential. He told no one except the chairman of his board. When the news leaked and people at the college and in the locality were hurt and angry, the board chairman turned on the president and joined others in expressing his disapproval of the president's "disloyalty." In response, the president resigned. He had served with dedication for more than ten years.

When word gets around that someone has been an unsuccessful candidate in several searches, the reasons—each of which may be idiosyncratic—become irrelevant, and such individuals can easily be seen as "rejects." In other situations, candidates can benefit from disclosure. It did not hurt James Holderman, then president of the University of South Carolina, when he withdrew as a finalist for the presidency of Ohio State University on grounds of his dedication to the poorer state and the smaller flagship. The one leak that occurred in the Rice University search we describe in Chapter VIII is believed to have come from a candidate, not himself a president, who thought news of Rice's interest in him would help him at his home base. Candidates can exploit, as well as be exploited.

When candidates benefit or do not suffer, it still may not be correct to say in a cavalier way, "It isn't as if it were a matter of life or death." There may be consequences that are not immediately visible. We recall the case of a search for a new president for Oberlin College. One of the finalists became a candidate only when assured of complete confidentiality. When students broke into the search committee's files and leaked his name to the *Oberlin Record*, the news came out in his local paper even before he returned from visiting Oberlin. He withdrew from the search. He also withdrew from the prospects of a presidency, not wanting again to submit himself and his family to the hazards of a search. Perhaps that is an overreaction, but it is not unique to him; others who have felt betrayed in the course of a search have similarly pulled back. Not all of these individuals would be incapable of facing the publicity and other stresses of a presidency.

There is a further consideration that can be illustrated by the search in 1982 for a new chancellor of the Oregon State System of Higher Education. A reporter for the *Portland Oregonian* sat in on a meeting of the Oregon State Board of Higher Education when members of the board were discussing the finalists. The reporter had been permitted to attend the session on the understanding that the meeting was off the record; however once he returned to the newspaper office, his editors persuaded him, despite some misgivings on his part, to publish the ranking of the three finalists. The Oregon board had placed George Weathersby at the top of its list. Weathersby was then director of the Indiana Commission on Higher Education. William E. Davis, then president of the University of New Mexico, was ranked a close second.[19] Although Davis was asked to continue as a candidate while the Oregon Board negotiated with Weathersby, Davis declined and promptly withdrew his candidacy. Upon arriving home in Albuquerque, he was greeted by the newspaper headlines, "Job Hunting Prexy Turned Down by Oregon." The news of his candidacy in Oregon caused considerable consternation in some quarters. People in New Mexico felt put down, hurt, and angry that their university president was

[19] Davis is now serving as chancellor of Louisiana State University at Baton Rouge.

138

looking at positions elsewhere. Meanwhile, the talks with George Weathersby continued, with the publicity about his having been ranked first giving him leverage he might not otherwise have had to make demands, not only for greatly increased salary, but also that the state system's headquarters be moved from Eugene to Portland. After much public wrangling, including accusations against Weathersby for overreaching, the board was unable to come to terms with him and rejected his candidacy.[20] The Oregon board then called William Davis and asked him if he would reconsider his withdrawal and accept the chancellorship. Reacting to the negative publicity he had received in New Mexico, and believing that the Oregon job was still attractive for the same reasons he had become a candidate in the first place—that the position represented a professional advancement with a higher level of responsibility—Davis accepted the offer. In the course of five energetic years, whatever tarnish to his legitimacy Davis might have suffered for being regarded as "second choice" had vanished. Davis's political difficulties with the campuses and with the legislature accumulated as a result of his success in raising more money rather than out of any weakness in the initial installation—success and resulting opposition he graphically described in a "Point of View" column in the *Chronicle of Higher Education* after the new Democratic governor, Neal Goldschmidt, who appoints the trustees, asked for his resignation.[21]

In conversations with us and with search committees, Ruth Weintraub, former vice-president for executive search of the Academy for Educational Development, has advised search committees not to "fall in love" with any one candidate, lest that candidacy evaporate and all other prospects then appear wholly lacking in luster. In highly political situations, search committees will want to rank candidates, even when instructed not to, as in the "Southern State University" search, in order to make clear their strong preference for one person or to prevent the insertion of a political crony in place of the person or persons on whom the search committee has been in full agreement. However, there is a danger that the publication by design or through leak of a list of finalists may overstate the importance of the rankings. Often, there are not significant differences among those

[20] See *Chronicle of Higher Education*, Vol. 24, no. 8 (April 21, 1982).

[21] William E. Davis, "The Growing Politicization of State Higher Education Makes Jobs of Top College Officials Shakier than Ever," Point of View, *Chronicle of Higher Education*, March 9, 1988, p. A-52.

ranked first, second, or third. (In the Oregon case just described, the difference between Weathersby, ranked first, and Davis, ranked second, was one vote.) Nevertheless, if the list becomes public and the board decides to offer the post to number two or three, then the new president may be seen as compromised by suspected political considerations, and in any case as "second best," no matter how stellar. Moreover, when the rank ordering of candidates becomes known, those not ranked first may quickly withdraw, and if the number-one prospect then decides against accepting the position, there is no viable candidate left, and the search process has to be inaugurated all over again.

THE DILEMMAS OF CONFIDENTIALITY

For many of us in America, it is hard to tell a direct lie. It is in part our egalitarianism, along with our belief in openness as a virtue, that makes it awkward for Americans to be even mildly evasive or duplicitous. Yet sometimes evasiveness is necessary. Consider, for example, the situation of Stephen J. Trachtenberg, former president of the University of Hartford, who in the winter of 1987–1988 was the leading finalist for the presidency of George Washington University. Rumors to that effect began to circulate in Washington and in Hartford. When a reporter for the *Informer*, the University of Hartford student paper, asked Trachtenberg if it was true that he was about to be named the new president of George Washington University, Trachtenberg responded that the rumor was ridiculous. This was technically true; the job had not yet been offered him, although the search committee had in fact indicated that they wanted him. Ultimately, though, only a vote of the board could make him president. Later, when his selection was formally announced by the George Washington University board, Trachtenberg explained to the *Informer* the dilemma he had faced. Although he felt obliged to answer questions from the media candidly, in this instance he had made a pledge to the George Washington University board that he would not reveal the fact that they were in the midst of discussions about the presidency.

The ethical dilemma faced by Cynthia Tyson in keeping secret her selections as president of Mary Baldwin College in 1984 was much more intense. The search committee to find a successor to Virginia Lester had promised complete confidentiality to candidates. The search committee

140

had met with the six finalists in Washington, D.C. Five of them were presidents elsewhere; none of them wanted the candidacy known at home base. Cynthia Tyson, the academic vice-president of Queens College in Charlotte, had reported her candidacy to the president of Queens, Billy Wireman, but no one else at Queens knew that she was considering a move.

When Tyson was chosen by the Mary Baldwin College search committee as its first choice, she was asked by Richard Ernst, a longtime trustee of Mary Baldwin and president of Northern Virginia Community College, not to inform her board of this until the Mary Baldwin College board could ratify the search committee's decision. The plan had been that the Mary Baldwin board would meet in an emergency session. However, the illness of the board chairman prevented that, and a month elapsed before the regular board meeting. During this month, because no vote had yet been taken at Mary Baldwin, Cynthia Tyson and Billy Wireman could not work with others to plan for Tyson's departure and make arrangements for a search for her successor. During those long weeks, Tyson had to deal daily with close associates from whom she was keeping her decision to leave. Matters were made marginally more awkward for her because on the very date of her flight to Staunton, Virginia, to the board meeting at which her appointment was to be announced, the *Charlotte Observer* broke the story. The newspaper had received a tip from the *Richmond Times Dispatch* and printed the news a day early, while Tyson was en route, unable herself to give the news to her colleagues. As an English-born and English-educated person, Cynthia Tyson might have found it somewhat easier than a comparable American not to confide in her immediate circle. Even so, whether in England or America, secrecy puts a strain on one's relations with close subordinates and intimate friends, who may be jealous, even bitter, concluding that they should not have been kept in the dark.

As we noted earlier, the dilemmas of confidentiality and candor have been ever present in American government and society. The two-hundredth anniversary of the Constitutional Convention celebrated in 1987 reminded us of the fragility with which the essential compromises were achieved that summer of 1787. What is often referred to as the "Great Compromise" of the Convention, the decision to have both a Senate and a House of Representatives, came about after bitter debates among the

141

assembled delegates. Benjamin Franklin characterized the issue simply: "The diversity of opinion turns on two points. If a proportional representation takes place, the small states contend their liberties will be in danger. If an equality of votes is to be put in its place, the large states say their money will be in danger." Then, in appealing for a compromise, he continued: "When a broad table is to be made and the edges of planks do not fit, the artist takes a little from both and makes a good joint. In a like manner here both sides must part with some of their demands in order that they may join in some accommodating position." Franklin followed these comments with the compromise motion of two Houses that was adopted by the Convention.[22] Compromises such as these could only have been accomplished under the bond and promise of confidentiality. So intent were the delegates on secrecy that they kept the windows closed and the curtain drawn in the room in which they were meeting, even in the hot Philadelphia summer. One day, the delegates arrived at the convention hall to find notes of a prior meeting that had been carelessly left behind. No one moved to pick them up, which would have marked him as the individual who had been careless in so essential a trust. George Washington rebuked the delegates strongly: "Gentlemen! I am sorry to find that some one member of this body has been so neglectful of the secrets of the Convention as to drop in the State House a copy of their proceedings, which by accident was picked up and delivered to me this morning. I must entreat you gentlemen to be more careful, lest our transactions get into the newspapers and disturb the public repose by premature speculations."[23] Characteristically, Thomas Jefferson, writing from Paris, strongly objected to the confidentiality of the proceedings as undemocratic. Prior to his own presidency, secrecy held no charms for that great propagandist of the American Revolution. Similarly, as we shall see in Chapter VII, public disclosure is often seen as desirable when viewed in the abstract, whereas those who are required to participate in public sessions soon recognize its liabilities.

[22] Quoted in Seymour Stanton Block, *Benjamin Franklin, His Wit, Wisdom and Women* (New York: Hastings House: 1975), p. 357.

[23] Recounted in Catherine Drinker Bowen, *Miracle at Philadelphia: The Story of the Constitutional Convention, May to September, 1787* (Boston: Little, Brown, 1966).

CHAPTER VI

University of Florida

O PEN RECORDS AND open meeting laws, also known as "government-in-the-sunshine laws," have proliferated during the past fifteen years. Although the exact stipulations of these statutes vary widely, all fifty states now have legislation on their books espousing the principle that the business of public agencies should be conducted in public.[1] Increasingly—largely the result of lawsuits brought by the media—these "sunshine laws" have been applied to higher education at the level of the board of regents and also to intramural decisions on the campuses of colleges and universities.

The benefits and costs of governing higher education in the sunshine are debated in the courts, the press, state legislatures, educational associations, and college campuses. Typically, the discourse in this area, whether in the pages of law reviews or in the press, has had an abstract, rhetorical quality. Hence, we made a case study of the 1983 search for a president of the University of Florida. Florida's sunshine laws are the most comprehensive in the nation, especially as applied to higher education. All aspects of the search—applications and nominations, letters of reference, the vitae of candidates, what is said about them in committee or in interviews with them, committee deliberations and committee votes—must be open to the press and the public.

The University of Florida, located in Gainesville, is both the "flagship" and the land-grant campus of the nine-campus State University System in Florida. Correspondingly, its president is a more visible personage than the presidents of the other university campuses and better known nation-

[1] For detailed discussion of the provisions of sunshine laws, see *Chronicle of Higher Education*, September 1, 1988, p. 4. Also see Harlan Cleveland, *The Costs and Benefits of Openness: Sunshine Laws and Higher Education* (Washington, D.C.: AGB, 1985).

143

ally than the system's chancellor at the state capital in Tallahassee. Within the Florida system of higher education, the University of Florida evokes the most intense alumni loyalties, and takes intercollegiate athletics, particularly football, with utmost solemnity. The university's 35,000 students distribute themselves across the state's largest array of academic programs, including some that have national distinction.

ROBERT MARSTON RESIGNS

In December, 1982, Robert Marston, president of the University of Florida, announced that he would resign as president effective September 1, 1984. Marston, an award-winning biomedical researcher, had assumed the Florida presidency on August 1, 1974, after having served as dean of the medical school and vice-chancellor of the University of Mississippi, and director of the National Institutes of Health. Although Florida's sunshine law had been on the books when Marston was selected in 1974, the search committee that recruited him had interviewed him in Atlanta, outside the reach of the state's sunshine law—and the state's journalists—in fact, if not in legal theory. Eight years later, however, no similar circumvention of the law was considered possible. Two recent administrative searches at the University of Florida had received extensive press coverage, and one of these searches, for the dean of the law school, had to contend with a lawsuit which was pending in the courts. Even without this cloud of litigation, there could be no doubt that the search for Marston's successor would be in the sunshine. The governor insisted on it, and the chancellor and the board of regents were in no political position to oppose the combined weight of the governor, the state legislators, and the media.

During Marston's presidency, private giving had grown from $3 million in 1974 to $24.9 million in 1981 and the university had become far more selective for undergraduates and for graduate and professional students. In 1981, the University of Florida ranked among the top twenty colleges and universities in the United States in the number of National Merit and Achievement Scholars. Many faculty members saw Marston's resignation as an opportunity to capitalize on Florida's sunbelt growth and the university's areas of distinction. The advertisement for the UF presidency stated, "The search committee wishes to consider the outstanding candidates in the nation."

144

THE SEARCH BEGINS

Like searches at many institutions, the University of Florida search was structured in two tiers, with a university advisory search committee responsible for identifying a pool of candidates and then winnowing this pool to a small number of finalists, and a board of regents selection committee appointed to oversee the search and to nominate a president to the board of regents. The board committee, chaired by Raleigh Greene, chairman of the Florida Federal Savings and Loan Association, had four voting members. The chancellor of the Florida system, Barbara Newell, was an ex officio member. The university advisory committee, chaired by Ellis Verink, a University of Florida professor and chairman of the Department of Materials Science and Engineering, had twenty-five members. Of these twenty-five, twelve were community leaders from outside the university; almost all were alumni, and many were lawyers. The other thirteen members of the advisory committee included eight faculty members, three administrators (a dean, associate dean, and registrar), one staff member, and one student.

The search was officially launched just before Christmas, 1982, when the board selection committee and the advisory committee met in joint session. After chairman Raleigh Greene explained that the search was to be conducted entirely in accord with the letter and spirit of the sunshine law, members of the regents' staff outlined the requisite procedures, including affirmative action, open-meeting, and open-record stipulations. Chairman Greene then charged the university advisory committee to develop a profile of the institution and the characteristics desired in the new president. Opening the discussion himself, Greene proposed that the new president should exhibit "broad management and scholarly achievements." Regent committee member Robin Gibson commented that the committee should seek someone already nationally established. Since the University of Florida is approaching national status, we "can't take a chance on the individual to develop national stature . . . we need someone who already has it."[2]

Thereafter, the university advisory committee, meeting on its own, marginally modified an announcement of the vacancy to be used in advertising the position. The changes reflected the special interests of individual

[2] From minutes of December 17, 1982, meeting of the University Advisory Committee.

145

members. An alumnus who had played football at the University of Florida suggested the addition of a statement about the university's athletic program. The chairman of the university's foundation wanted mention of the fact that the foundation, with the president as its effective voice, had succeeded in raising nearly $25 million.

As their last item of business, the joint committees dealt with the role of the press and of visitors in future meetings. The Florida sunshine law specified that the meetings were open to the press and public; the question before the advisory committee was whether these observers could also participate in the meetings. After some discussion, committee members decided that persons not on the committee would be allowed to address the chair only at the end of each session, and their remarks would be limited in length.

The University of Florida presidential vacancy was advertised in the *Chronicle of Higher Education*, the *New York Times*, and in Florida and national newspapers, with March 1, 1983, given as the deadline for applications and nominations. All advertisements included a statement about Florida's sunshine law, noting that all aspects of the search would be open to the public. To expedite committee business, the university advisory committee formed an executive committee of its Gainesville members to handle incoming mail and to refine a checklist for evaluating the resumés and other materials of candidates.

The Rain of Nominations

As candidate papers arrived, they were sorted into two groups, "applicants" and "nominees." Applicants included both those individuals who had themselves submitted letters of application and those persons nominated who, on being contacted by the advisory committee, agreed to apply for the university presidency. Nominees were those persons whose names had been put forward by others.

As is the case in most presidential searches, the University of Florida advertisement produced a flurry of paper. Applications came from the ever-present pool of people who regularly apply for positions: lawyers and business executives in situations where their candidacy, recognized perhaps as unlikely, will not bring them discredit with their peers, and pro-

146

fessors or administrators whose candidacy, while a longshot gamble, also poses no threat to them in their present job and may even bring some benefit. Florida's pool went beyond these standard opportunists and included bankers and management consultants, a superintendent of schools, a graduate student, and a cleaning lady.

When March 1 arrived, the board of regents found the candidate list disappointingly shy of eminent names. Hoping to garner additional nominations and applications, the deadline was extended, to April 1, 1983. Chancellor Barbara Newell placed some forty to fifty names in nomination and encouraged search committee members to do likewise. They, in turn, encouraged their colleagues to submit names. As a consequence, many of the major university presidents in the country were nominated, including John Silber of Boston University, Hanna Gray of the University of Chicago, Peter Magrath, then at the University of Minnesota, and Steven Muller of The Johns Hopkins University. In addition, a number of national political figures were nominated: Jimmy Carter, Gerald Ford, Henry Kissinger, Howard Baker, Griffin Bell, Cyrus Vance, Alexander Haig, Patricia Harris, Elliott Richardson, and others. The majority of the nominations came from the chancellor's office or members of the advisory committee.

Some committee members later questioned the wisdom of nominating "these big names." One stated, "It was done to draw national attention to the search, but I thought it damaged the credibility of the search from the very beginning." Another committee member called much of the list "window-dressing." A third person disagreed: "The list indicated the caliber of candidate we sought. We wanted a national leader."

A Drought of Candidates

Meeting twice in April, the executive committee reduced the size of the pool to be submitted for consideration by the full advisory committee from 350 total nominees and applicants to 87. Since the search guidelines set forward by the board of regents stipulated that only applicants would be interviewed, advisory committee chairman Ellis Verink telephoned more than 100 nominees to ask whether they were willing to become applicants. Some agreed to do so; more often, however, the nominees de-

147

clined interest in being considered, leaving Verink to interpret from their responses whether their expressed lack of interest was genuine or represented their unwillingness to risk having their candidacy publicly known. Since Verink's conversations involved only one member of the search committee, and hence did not constitute a meeting of the committee, they could be confidential. Verink's subsequent reports were required by statute to be public.

When Verink explained to the committee that the president of another state university had indicated that he was interested in being considered, but did not want his local clientele to be alerted, debate erupted among committee members. One committee member said that he felt "marginal on those who haven't even sent us papers," adding that "whoever becomes president will have to become a public person." Another committee member concurred: "Should we waste time if the candidate obviously doesn't want the job?" Other committee members argued on behalf of keeping nominees on the active list, even though the nominees denied interest in the University of Florida post. "Given that many candidates cannot afford to express their interest, can we eliminate them?" Several people suggested that they judge candidates' interest according to "just how a candidate says 'no.' For example, if good candidates don't express interest in the job, yet send extensive vitae and resumé materials, they might stay on the list; but if prospects neglect to return phone calls or to send a resumé, they might be cut."[3]

The Absence of Discussion

The full university advisory committee met for two days in early May to trim the list of selections provided by the executive committee. They placed fifteen candidates in a top category of "those receiving primary support," and twenty others in a lower group, "also receiving support." Two weeks later, the full committee met again and decided on a list of thirteen candidates, four applicants and nine nominees, to send to the board of regents search committee.

Interviewed after the search had concluded, committee members dis-

[3] See Lawrence Williams, "Search committee argues fate of those not wanting UF presidency," *Alligator*, April 18, 1983, p. 2.

cussed their reluctance to evaluate candidates in any detail in the public setting. "Everything said in meetings had to be couched in vague language," one committee member recalled. Several people described the instance when a member of the committee was aware that a certain candidate had alienated a number of people. Rather than risk being quoted in the press as having said this directly, the committee member said simply, "You might want to look into this man's background. I understand that several people left after he was appointed to his present position." This observation sufficed to alert committee members to the possibility that something might be amiss, and without more scrutiny, the candidate was dropped from the active list. More commonly, nothing at all was said, and candidates lost their place on the list due to silence. "If someone didn't receive positive support, his or her candidacy wasn't even discussed, let alone debated." Not having full information, committee members relied upon each other's judgment. When a university member of the committee said that an academic candidate was unsuitable, nonacademic members deferred to their intramural colleagues. Similarly, assessments of nonacademic candidates were conceded to the nonuniversity members of the committee.

One committee member thought that all this worked rather well, "because you could tell a lot from what wasn't said." But another disagreed: "I thought that this way of proceeding was wrong. Our decision-making should have been more important than protecting candidates."

The advice from the chancellor's office to speak positively was only once disregarded, when a nonuniversity member of the committee offered his judgment of a nonacademic candidate: "I don't think he is qualified for dog catcher, much less for the presidency!" Many people laughed. "It was refreshing to hear an honest statement," one member later remarked. The chairman quickly responded, "Perhaps this candidate has some redeeming quality we should consider," but no further discussion ensued, and the active list was cut by one.

On June 7, advisory committee chairman Ellis Verink submitted to the chancellor and the board of regents search committee the list of the thirteen persons the advisory committee recommended. Fearful that some of these candidates would be lost if they held to their search guidelines, the regents committee decided that nominees need not apply, but must only

149

agree to be interviewed. The regents committee also delayed their final selections from July until November to give the advisory committee more time for investigations into the candidates' backgrounds and interviews with them. The university advisory committee was told to get in touch with the thirteen candidates on its list to see if they would agree to be interviewed, to interview at least ten candidates, and then to recommend its top choices to the regents committee.

One of the thirteen candidates on the list was Peter Magrath, a nominee and then president of the University of Minnesota. The regents committee's last item of business was to drop Magrath's name from the list because of his expressed lack of interest. In the next day's newspapers, this bit of committee business was reported. One headline read: "Magrath takes self out of running for Florida job."

Magrath was only one of a number of nominees embarrassed by having his name appear in the news. As he told us, he had explicitly stated in repeated telephone conversations that he was not interested in the Florida position, and had even suggested to the search committee the names of other possible candidates. He added: "I suppose it was possible for somebody in Florida to conclude I was playing hard to get. . . . Nothing, however, baffled me more than having my name submitted to the Regents." He was then put in the position of having to withdraw from a competition he had never wanted to enter. One committee member explained, understandably but sadly: "We hoped that we could persuade him differently, and that his denial of interest in the University of Florida presidency was because of the public nature of the search. We kept him on our list until it became apparent that he would not come for an interview. To this day, I wonder whether, if the search had been confidential, he would have allowed us to pursue his candidacy. I was very disappointed that we couldn't get him."

Interviewing Candidates

The chairmen of the two committees, the chancellor, and members of her staff traveled extensively to meet the twelve leading candidates, to try to persuade them to agree to interviews in the sunshine, and to talk with others about their qualifications. When the July 1 deadline arrived for

150

candidates to accept the invitation to come for interviews with the advisory committee, only six of the dozen semifinalists had accepted. Three candidates had formally withdrawn; three others had refused to undergo the interview process in public.

The half-dozen interviews were held July 22–24, at a hotel at the Tampa airport. The six candidates included three Floridians: Robert Bryan, vice-president for academic affairs at the University of Florida; Robert Lanzillotti, dean of the University of Florida's College of Business Administration; and Marshall Criser, a Palm Beach attorney; and three candidates from out of state: John DiBiaggio, president of the University of Connecticut; Hans Mark, deputy administrator of NASA; and Jay Oliva, provost at New York University.

Just as the public setting had stifled committee discussions, the presence of the press at the interviews led to stilted exchanges with candidates. Committee members were uncomfortable asking direct personal questions that they might have asked in confidential settings. The outside candidates, DiBiaggio, Oliva, and Mark, were reported to have felt similarly unable to discuss freely their concerns about their candidacy or the university.

THE UNPLANNED VOTE

Late Sunday afternoon, after the interviews were over, one advisory committee member suggested that they discuss which candidates should be invited for interviews on the University of Florida campus. He proposed that, to reach a consensus, committee members list the names of all candidates they thought qualified to be president. Committee members proceeded accordingly and cast written ballots. When these were tallied, John DiBiaggio led with seventeen votes; Marshall Criser was second with fifteen votes; Robert Lanzillotti received eight votes; Robert Bryan had seven votes; Jay Oliva had four votes; and Hans Mark received three votes. Chairman Verink announced these results and adjourned the meeting.

As several committee members rushed to catch planes, others stayed on to ponder the implications of the balloting. The committee member who had suggested the vote declared that it was his intent to invite to campus only those candidates receiving a majority of votes; nine other committee members said that had been their understanding also. One person expressed anxiety lest this eliminate viable candidates, since only two, DiBiaggio and Criser, had received a majority of votes. In response, committee members noted that the regents had the power to interview any additional candidates from the pool if they desired, or even others not included in the half-dozen brought to Tampa. As the group deliberated about how to proceed, vice-chancellor Steve MacArthur reminded them that further discussion was inappropriate since the meeting was officially adjourned.[4]

Monday's newspaper carried the totals for each candidate. Several days later, an enterprising reporter appeared at the university office that was coordinating the paper-work for the search and asked to see the ballots. As required by the sunshine law, each ballot had been signed. Florida's sunshine law stipulates that all votes must be publicly recorded, and no abstentions are allowed, save for conflict of interest. A day later, a newspaper story listed the votes of every committee member. The most dramatic news items in terms of intra-university impact were the discoveries that Business School dean Robert Lanzillotti had not received a single vote from the campus members of the committee and that academic vice-president Robert Bryan had received no votes from nonuniversity committee members. All of the advisory committee members from the university had voted for Bryan with the exception of two, a tenured faculty member and a dean who reports directly to Bryan.

Somehow, this degree of visibility had not been anticipated, even though the sessions at the airport had been well-attended by the press, along with sporadic other observers, including a right-wing state senator who came to each interview, asked questions, and expressed his views. Some committee members had found the audience of reporters a distraction, since reporters scribbled notes throughout the interviews, and flash bulbs went off frequently. One committee member recalled that a reporter had leaned over her shoulder during an interview to see what she was writing even though, according to the sunshine law, personal notes that are not entered into committee records can remain private. But that ex-

---

[4] Minutes of July 22–24 meetings of the Advisory Committee.

perience had not prepared the committee for the revelation, as one member put it, of "individual members' feelings." Suddenly "people became very, very nervous." University members of the advisory committee hoped that their failure to vote for Lanzillotti would not affect their friendship with him. Faculty members and administrators on the committee and at the university wondered how the dean's vote would affect his relationship with his superior. Bryan commented that he and the dean met to discuss the issue and that, although the conversation was originally awkward, Bryan understood why the dean had voted as he did. Still, people watched the two men closely to see what effect the vote might have.

Ten days after the airport vote, chairman Ellis Verink received a letter from vice-chancellor Steve MacArthur declaring that the committee "had deviated from established procedure by ranking the candidates." That vote should be disregarded, and assessments of all of the six candidates should be sent to the board of regents committee.[5] A bit apologetically, one member of the university advisory committee commented, "we didn't intend to rank candidates, but of course that's what we did." Rather than simply accepting the airport vote as the search committee's getting a sense of the meeting, to see to what extent it made sense to pursue people for whom there was negligible support when the choice obviously lay between Criser and DiBiaggio, the chancellor's office decided that all six names should be kept alive as long as possible.

THE FRONTRUNNERS

In consultation with his committee, Ellis Verink prepared written "consensus statements" on each candidate. Each report was two or three pages long and enumerated the candidate's qualifications for the presidency. As the board of regents had specified, only positive characteristics were set forth, and no comparisons of candidates were provided.

In their attempt to be positive about everybody, the consensus reports read like public relations statements. Under the heading, "Affirmative Action and EEO," for example, Hans Mark was described as having "responsibility for compliance with the objectives of Affirmative Action for NASA. Therefore, he is thoroughly sensitized to the objectives of such a

[5] Carl Crawford, "List for UF Presidency back up to six," *Gainesville Sun*, August 11, 1983, p. 1.

program." Under the heading, "appropriate scholarship," the consensus report on Marshall Criser stated, "From a brief biographical sketch available, it is difficult to assess Criser's personal scholarship. It would be hard to imagine him making the success he has in the legal profession, however, unless he were a deep scholar of the law. Throughout his career he has also been a student of the educational process, having served both as a lawyer for a school district and as a member of numerous commissions on education and finally as a member and chairman of the Board of Regents."[6]

The consensus statements were presented to the board of regents committee in a joint meeting of the two committees on August 22. After the presentations, chairman Raleigh Greene asked each advisory committee member to name the one or more candidates he or she deemed qualified for the presidency. Criser was named by thirteen committee members, DiBiaggio by ten, Lanzillotti by six, Bryan by two, and Mark by one. Oliva was not mentioned.

In the ensuing discussion, advisory committee members spent most of the time talking about DiBiaggio and Criser. The two candidates could not have been more different. To the extent that there is a customary career line to a university presidency, DiBiaggio had pursued it. From a faculty position at the University of Kentucky, DiBiaggio had moved to a deanship at Virginia Commonwealth University, next to become vice-president for health sciences at the University of Connecticut, and, nine years later, to the presidency of the University of Connecticut.

Nominated for the University of Florida presidency by Barbara Newell and Jack Peltason, then president of the American Council on Education, DiBiaggio chose to retain his nominee status throughout the search, although he declared that he was happy at the University of Connecticut and was not actively seeking another position. DiBiaggio stated that he was intrigued by the presidency of the University of Florida because Florida offered greater opportunities than Connecticut, where demographic prospects were unpromising.

DiBiaggio had strong supporters among the university faculty members on the advisory committee who believed he possessed the requisite quali-

[6] From minutes of August 22, 1983, meeting of the University Advisory Committee.

ties for president: an appreciation of scholarship, an understanding of academic issues, a knowledge of administration. Since the Florida system is unionized, his supporters noted that DiBiaggio had worked effectively with a unionized faculty and had been successful in obtaining state, federal, and private funding.

Marshall Criser's resumé stood in sharp contrast to DiBiaggio's. An alumnus of the University of Florida College of Arts and Sciences and College of Law, Criser had been a member and chairman of the Florida Board of Regents. Although well-acquainted with the university from his days as a student and a regent, Criser had neither academic nor administrative experience in higher education. In corporate and civic life, his credentials were impressive: he had been president of Florida Blue Key (a prestigious university student leadership association), president of the Florida Bar Association, president of the Council of 100 (an organization of the state's leading businesses), and director of a bank, a corporation, and a hospital.

When nominated for the University of Florida presidency by Tampa attorney and advisory committee member Warren Cason, Criser was himself a member of the advisory committee. He withdrew from the search committee and formally applied for the presidency. Criser had ample experience in searches, having chaired four presidential and two chancellor searches during his years as a regent, including the searches that had produced both Robert Marston and Barbara Newell.

Initially, many of the university representatives on the committee had not considered Criser a serious contender; however, in the course of the search, a number of faculty members and administrators at the university became convinced that Criser's familiarity with Florida higher education, his knowledge of the state budgetary process, and his personal relationships with state political and business leaders would be significant assets for a president. In recent years, the boosters of the University of Florida had seen their premier position within state higher education increasingly at risk. Prior to *Baker v. Carr* (the one-man, one-vote decision of the United States Supreme Court), the northern part of Florida, which is primarily rural and culturally Southern, could more than hold its own in the state legislature. For the University of Florida, reapportionment meant that Alachua County, where the university is located, found itself with

155

fewer legislative votes than any other Florida county with a state university. Within the state university system, the emergence of newer, metropolitan universities in the population centers of the state also threatened the premier position of the University of Florida. The rapidly growing University of South Florida has its main campus in Tampa and outlying campuses (including prestigious New College) in Sarasota and St. Petersburg. Begun in the 1960s as upper-division colleges, Florida International University in Miami and Florida Atlantic University in Boca Raton, along with the University of West Florida in Pensacola, have now been granted full baccalaureate status. Like these other newer universities, the University of Central Florida, located in Orlando, has the advantage of a growing population base and a major international airport. Whereas the Florida legislature had once been dominated by alumni of the University of Florida who voted funding for their alma mater, with reapportionment and the growth of the new universities, the number of UF graduates in Tallahassee has seen a sharp decline.[7] It was not surprising, therefore, that faculty in Gainesville could reasonably conclude that Criser might serve them well in the competition for state funding.

The striking differences between the two frontrunners would seem to be the stuff of great discussion and debate. In fact, there was relatively little. Both men were praised by their supporters; neither was openly criticized. Although our later interviews with committee members revealed marked disagreements on several issues, most notably whether previous experience as an academic administrator was important, no conversations about this took place in committee session. When one nonuniversity member of the committee commented that skills were transferable from one sector to another, a tenured professor gestured toward the academic dean in their midst. The dean, he said, is a highly respected administrator, generally recognized as having talent for leadership. Then turning to a business executive on the committee, he asked him whether he would select the dean to be the CEO of his limestone company. A pause ensued; no one answered the query, or spoke to the larger issue of whether skills

---

[7] In 1968, there were sixty-seven alumni of the University of Florida in the Florida legislature. In 1978, this number had dropped to forty-two, and ten years later, in 1988, there were only thirty-five UF alumni in the state legislature. (For more information about intra-state competition in higher education, see Jack Wheat's excellent series, "Who's Calling the Shots," *Gainesville Sun*, October 28–November 3, 1988.)

are in fact transferable from the business sector to leadership of a university.

Similarly, when the board of regents asked advisory committee members to name the qualifications they most sought in the new president, the public nature of the search inhibited their discussion of priorities. All agreed that they wanted a president who would lead them to greatness, who could increase public and private funding, and communicate with faculty, students, alumni, and especially with legislators.[8] But arguments never took place about which qualities were the most important, especially since no one candidate possessed them all to the same extent. Such discussions translated too quickly into a discussion of DiBiaggio versus Criser for committee members to be willing to talk frankly.

MORE WITHDRAWALS, MORE INTERVIEWS

Shortly after the search committee meeting, two candidates, Jay Oliva and Robert Bryan, withdrew their names from further consideration. Jay Oliva wrote the search committee that he had given his candidacy serious consideration and had decided not to pursue the Florida presidency. University of Florida vice-president Robert Bryan stated that he had never actively sought the presidency but had allowed his name to go forward after several members of the search committee had urged him to this course.

On September 10 and 11, the board of regents selection committee scheduled interviews with the four remaining candidates. Prior to these sessions, all candidates met with chancellor Barbara Newell and vice-chancellor Steve McArthur to talk about Florida's system of higher education and the relationship of the university presidency to Florida politics. Since these meetings involved only a staff member and the candidate, they did not constitute an official meeting and could remain confidential.

When the interviews with the board of regents selection committee were over, chairman Greene proposed that the remainder of the search process not be strung out until the November date, but that a candidate be recommended to the board of regents at their September 21 meeting. Con-

[8] Warren Cason, quoted in Carl Crawford, "Criser, DiBiaggio favored again," *Gainesville Sun*, August 23, 1983, p. 1.

157

curring with Greene, regent Hyatt Brown proposed that they reduce the pool of four candidates to two, who would be invited to campus. Barbara Newell strongly disagreed, however, arguing that university faculty, students, and staff should have the opportunity to look at more than two candidates. After some discussion, the committee acceded to her request that all four candidates be invited for campus visits in October.

When we interviewed her later, Barbara Newell explained her insistence on campus visits by stressing the need for the campus to feel involved in the selection process. The choice of a president is a long-term marriage, she commented. Newell, as the chief representative of Florida's public higher education, wanted the choice of Gainesville's president to be a legitimate choice. Learning that DiBiaggio was seriously considering withdrawing his candidacy, Newell urged him to continue his participation in the search.

In retrospect, DiBiaggio attributed his decision to remain a candidate to stubbornness and a desire to see the process through to its end. DiBiaggio's decision to stay in the Florida search hurt him at home in Connecticut. It prolonged the outcome of the search well into the fall term and, as a number of people in Connecticut have reported to us, it made his relations with some of the Connecticut regents uneasy and complicated his ties to the governor and other state officials. In addition, his immediate subordinates suffered considerable anxiety, not knowing whether DiBiaggio would be staying or leaving.

Members of the advisory committee and a university staff member planned the two-day campus interviews with candidates. In the name of fairness and equality, all were invited for identical fourteen-and-a-half-hour schedules. Criser's visit was on the weekend of October 6 and 7; Lanzillotti's, October 13 and 14; and DiBiaggio on October 18 and 19. Shortly before Hans Mark's scheduled visit on October 20 and 21, he withdrew his candidacy.

When the schedule for candidate visits was released, members of several campus groups telephoned to inquire why they had not been granted special meetings with the candidates. They were told that the two-day schedule did not allow room for meetings with every constituent group, and that public forums were planned for this express purpose. Later, a university official commented that the turnout at these forums was embarrass-

158

ingly low. One forum was attended by only six people other than the public entourage of search committee members and the press.

THE PRESENCE OF THE PRESS

On Friday, October 21, several days after DiBiaggio's visit, a headline in the student paper, *The Alligator*, read: "UF insiders: Criser has job secured." The article stated that "it is a foregone conclusion that Palm Beach attorney Marshall Criser has the job locked up . . . at least 11 UF officials . . . said that they have heard that Criser is being touted as the next UF president . . . one UF administrator has said that several of the 'good ole boy UF alumni types' are behind the Criser for president speculation, several of whom serve on the four-member BOR [Board of Regents] selection committee." Later in the news story, several advisory committee members were quoted as denying these charges. "I don't think it's predetermined . . . if he [Criser] did not do well in the interviews, and if he hadn't had the broad support of . . . national education leaders, he would not be a candidate. The process was done in the sunshine. Everyone saw how the votes were cast. He developed the support of faculty on the committee and outside."

On Monday, October 22, chancellor Barbara Newell and board of regents chairman Murray Dubbin met with small groups of students and faculty members in Gainesville. The students expressed support for John DiBiaggio, stating their appreciation for his interest in meeting with students. Faculty members had reached no similar consensus. Some preferred DiBiaggio because of his academic and administrative experience. Others favored Criser, noting that his ties to influential people in Florida would enable the university to gain increased funding.

Meanwhile, letters vis-à-vis the candidates continued to pour in to the search committee. The visibility of the search encouraged the mobilization of opinion. Letter-writing campaigns were organized on behalf of both Lanzillotti and Criser. Criser, in particular, received massive written support from Floridians. The search committee received letters endorsing Criser from two former Florida chancellors, two former governors, and nearly every regent who had served in the past decade.

Opponents of the candidates used the media to make their feelings known. Criser was attacked because he was president of the board of a Palm Beach hospital that refused care to Medicaid and Medicare patients. The husband of a former University of Connecticut employee whom DiBiaggio had dismissed wrote Florida search committee members and newspapers vilifying DiBiaggio and alleging he had mishandled finances at the University of Connecticut. The Connecticut couple had connections in the Saratoga area, and created suspicions about DiBiaggio there. The chancellor's staff investigated these charges, found them groundless, and thus maintained the viability of DiBiaggio's candidacy, but not before several Florida newspapers had printed stories about the allegations.

Soon, local newspapers began to express opinions about the outcome of the search. On November 3, the *Alligator* endorsed DiBiaggio in an editorial: "All three [finalists] have their strengths . . . but only one—DiBiaggio—has the full complement of skills needed to successfully guide UF."[9] That same day, an editorial in the *Gainesville Sun* called upon the Florida regents to reopen the search, declaring that none of the finalists was "the candidate to assume the leadership of Florida's oldest, most prestigious university."[10] Noting that there were still ten months of Robert Marston's incumbency, the editorial urged the regents to continue looking for a president. Indeed, the long lead-time that Marston gave the University of Florida to choose a successor made such a reopened search possible, though unlikely.

On Sunday, November 4, the regents met to receive the regents selection committee recommendation that Marshall Criser be appointed president. There was little discussion. Although a number of the regents not on the selection committee had initially been skeptical about Criser's candidacy, the disagreements, negotiations, and deliberations had taken place prior to this session, in private conversations. The vote was unanimous. Marshall Criser was named eighth president of the University of Florida.

POSTSCRIPT

On December 9, 1988, Marshall Criser announced that he would resign from the University of Florida presidency effective March 31, 1989. Dur-

[9] "For a better university—DiBiaggio for president," *Alligator*, November 3, 1983, p. 6.
[10] "Hurrying the main event," *Gainesville Sun*, November 3, 1983, p. 4A.

ing his nearly five years as president, Criser had enjoyed seeing the University of Florida admitted to membership in the Association of American Universities, the select "club" of the nationally eminent research universities. He had experienced scandals in the football program and had weathered these as well as the outcry over his dismissal of a politically well-connected vice-president. He had fought for the university's autonomy against a legislature accustomed to interfere in almost every sphere of the university's administration. At the press conference where he announced his plans for departure, he remarked that "the cumulative demands of the totality of the position" had led to his decision to return to private life.

At the time of his announcement, the Florida Board of Regents was preoccupied by searches for the presidencies of the University of Central Florida and Florida Atlantic University, and it took a while for the regents' selection committee to get organized. There was delay also in naming the University Advisory Committee, understandable in the light of what we reported in Chapter III, namely, the 1988 Florida legislation stipulating the composition of presidential search committees. The law requires that at least half of the committee members must come from business and industry, with the remaining members divided equally among faculty members, administrators, students, and university staff members. Correspondingly, it was not until April 21 that the forty-one member UF Advisory Committee and the seven-member Regent Selection Committee held their first meeting. Prior to that, on April 1, Robert Bryan, who had served as provost under Marshall Criser, assumed the position of interim president. Bryan had planned to retire from the university in June 1989, but he postponed his departure to take on the interim post. He declared that he would not be a candidate for the permanent position.

Bryan's refusal would be tested in the ensuing months when a lobby of "locals" developed, hoping to draft Bryan for the permanent slot because the list of candidates for the UF presidency included few promising individuals. (Some of the names that did turn up were perennial applicants who had also been applicants at Florida Atlantic and in some cases before that, in the search several years earlier at Florida International University in Miami.) Chancellor Charles Reed then literally flew into action, traveling all around the United States, urging people who had been nominated to allow their names to go forward as candidates. Reed succeeded in recruiting several very capable candidates, including John Lombardi, provost and academic vice-president at The Johns Hopkins University, Marguerite Ross Barnett, then chancellor of the St. Louis campus of the University of Missouri, and Haskell Monroe, chancellor of the University of Missouri at Columbia. All of these candidates had reasons to consider looking around: Johns Hopkins was readying its own search for a president, and hence Lombardi's professional future at that university was not assured, and Barnett's and Monroe's candidacies reflected the bitter struggles among Missouri universities over their share of the limited state financial resources.

At one point in the search, just prior to the advisory committee's public deliberations about which candidates on their slate of five should be invited for another round of interviews, chancellor Charles Reed proposed that he telephone each advisory committee member individually to discuss the candidates privately. According to William Shade,[11] the Florida state university system's vice-chancellor for public affairs, Reed wanted to know which candidates were "tracking support from a variety of constituencies."[12] Immediately on hearing of Reed's intention, committee member Ralph Lowenstein, dean of the University's College of Journalism and Communications, and a passionate and indeed professional defender of sunshine laws, strongly opposed such a move as a violation of the law. Although a spokesman for Reed denied that these private one-on-one conversations were illegal, and said that they had occurred as a matter of course in other Florida searches, Reed decided against making the telephone calls because of the negative publicity they might bring the search.

The 1989 University of Florida search concluded with the selection of John Lombardi. Ralph Lowenstein declared in the *Brechner Report* that "Openness Works . . . the press was present for every comment and every procedure, and thus opened the process to a much larger, concerned audience."[13] But others seemed far less certain. Although pleased with the choice of Lombardi, several participants and observers of the search pro-

[11] One reader of this manuscript accused us of inventing his name, because it fits our discussion so well!

[12] Jack Wheat, "UF presidential talks going private," *Gainesville Sun*, September 30, 1989, p. 10A.

[13] Ralph Lowenstein, "Friend and Foe: 'Openness Works,' " *The Brechner Report*, Brechner Center for Freedom of Information, College of Journalism and Communications, University of Florida, December 1989–January 1990, p. 6.

162

cess questioned again the advisability of conducting it entirely in the open. A Florida legislator proposed legislation to exempt the early stages of the searches from the sunshine, and Charles Reed suggested that this deserved serious consideration. It had not been easy, he acknowledged, to persuade candidates to submit themselves to the full glare of the sunshine. "Really good people are very sensitive to the whole Sunshine thing."[14]

[14] Jack Wheat, "Bill aims to close search process," *Gainesville Sun*, November 23, 1989, p. 13a.

CHAPTER VII

The Significance of Sunshine Laws

T HE 1983 UNIVERSITY OF FLORIDA search began with high hopes for considering "the outstanding candidates in the nation." On the campus of the University of Florida and throughout the state, many people saw the opportunity to choose a successor to retiring president Robert Marston as a chance to bring greater national visibility to Florida's premier institution of higher education. Glancing northward to the University of North Carolina at Chapel Hill, with its eighteenth-century heritage and its current scholarly eminence, some Floridians thought, "Perhaps, if we could recruit someone like William Friday, younger, someone of national reputation, we could compete not only in a few areas but across the board."[1] The list of persons nominated for the University of Florida presidency included eminent leaders in education and politics, but the university's search committee quickly discovered that very few of these "outstanding candidates" were willing to be considered for the position. Six years later, in the 1989 University of Florida search, the search committee and the chancellor once again found it difficult to persuade individuals in whom they were most interested to become candidates for the University of Florida position. In both searches, the difficulty was not that the Florida presidency was unattractive. The difficulty in getting good candidates was that the route to the presidency lay in the sunshine.

Not surprisingly, then, much of the discussion about conducting searches in the sunshine focuses on how public disclosure affects the candidate pool. Advocates of sunshine procedures argue that public disclosure

---

[1] For current misgivings at Chapel Hill itself, in the shadow of William Friday's departure from the system, see Jack Claiborne, "Poised For Greatness? Some Friends Say UNC-CH 'Living On Its Reputation,' " *Charlotte Observer*, February 7, 1988, Section B, p. 48, discussing a consultant's report in which Chapel Hill is compared with better-funded and less constrained Michigan, Berkeley, and others.

benefits selection by winnowing out individuals unwilling to take risks for the job. The former dean of the University of Minnesota School of Journalism and Mass Communications, Arnold H. Ismach, declared in a column in the *Minneapolis Star and Tribune* that "A president of the stature the university seeks and deserves will be a strong, secure, and confident individual. He or she will be accustomed, as leaders are, to taking risks. . . ." Ismach declared that he wanted someone as a candidate for his university who was sufficiently ambitious to "willingly accept hurdles on the path to that ambition, including publicity."[2]

Many politicians and journalists, and, indeed, much of the public see a university presidency as not markedly different from a governorship or other high political office. University ceremonies, whether football games or commencements, add to the perceived attractiveness of the presidential office. Correspondingly, advocates of sunshine believe that candidates for a university presidency should be "hungry," willing to go through endless meetings and "photo opportunities" as part of the campaign for office. After all, the argument goes, public exposure is an essential characteristic of the presidency, and anyone who cannot stand the heat of press coverage should not be considered as a candidate for that job.

Some news reporters who cover higher education have recognized, however, that there is a difference between the compulsory exposure of the process of selection and the exposure requisite for the work and the life of a president of a university. No observant person would deny that the president of a major state university needs to be sanguine and emotionally sturdy. But defenders of sunshine laws make a common mistake in confusing the quality of fortitude that may be requisite *in* a presidency with qualities such as reckless ambition and lack of institutional loyalty, that would lead a well-situated president of one institution to enter a sunshine search at another.

As the Florida experience illustrates, most candidates who are willing to enter a sunshine search are not the individuals a search committee hopes to attract. Basically, they are people with little to lose. Persons who are well situated do not want to send a resumé which will become part of the public record, and thus risk harming their institutions or their careers. Occasionally, an exceedingly capable person will be in a position in which

[2] *Minneapolis Star and Tribune*, December, 1984.

public exposure of his or her candidacy will not be damaging, but most of the applicants are attracted to the search in hope of gaining prestige from having their names on the list of candidates, or because they are badly in need of a new job. As we saw in Chapter VI, one by one the most attractive nominees on the Florida list asked to have their names removed. John DiBiaggio was the only sitting president who consented to participate, and Jay Oliva was the only nationally known provost to indicate potential availability.

Nor, in a sunshine search, is it always clear who the real candidates are. In the 1983 University of Florida search, the sunshine law made it impossible for members of the advisory committee to gauge the extent of a nominee's interest. In the hope of retaining some reluctant candidates, the advisory committee maintained the distinction between applicant and nominee "to make clear to the press the state of a person's thinking"—a nominee being someone committee members hoped might be persuaded to come for an interview when assured that he or she was one of only a few finalists. This committee wishfulness proved a serious disservice to several persons, who saw their names repeatedly mentioned as candidates, despite their determined and unequivocal assertions that they were not. They had informed their trustees and other constituencies that they were not interested in the Florida position, and when their names repeatedly resurfaced in the news, their credibility became strained.

One of the persons treated this way was Peter Magrath, then president of the University of Minnesota, whom members of the Florida advisory committee frequently mentioned to indicate the caliber of person they were unable to recruit in the sunshine. Shortly after the 1983 Florida search had concluded, a completely confidential search, handled by a consultant, recruited Magrath as the new president of the University of Missouri system. Under similar circumstances, namely, confidentiality and the use of a consultant, Robert O'Neil, another president some people in Florida mentioned as someone they would have liked to have as a candidate, left the presidency of the University of Wisconsin for that of the University of Virginia. He stated emphatically he would not have participated in Virginia's search had his candidacy been disclosed. Perhaps if the University of Florida search had been confidential, Marshall Criser would still have been the choice of the advisory committee and the regents. Because the public process limited the pool of prospects, neither Floridians nor Marshall Criser will ever know who his competition might have been.

AN ABSENCE OF DISCUSSION

Not only does public disclosure lose prospects, it also sacrifices candor. As we saw in Chapter VI, Florida's sunshine law had a "chilling effect" on committee discussions.[3] In the public arena, there was virtually no discourse about which professional experiences and personal attributes were deemed essential for a new president. There also was no serious evaluation of the perceived strengths and weaknesses of the candidates themselves.

When J. Wayne Reitz, president emeritus of the University of Florida, surveyed members of the Florida advisory committee after the 1983 search was over, members agreed, almost to a person, that the sunshine law had inhibited clarifying discussion of the most salient issues. Search committee members had never debated, for instance, what the growing competition among Florida universities meant for the kind of leadership desired for the University of Florida presidency.[4] Could a national educational leader with political sagacity navigate effectively in the state's polit-

[3] Vanessa Williams, "Board confirms new UF head," St. Petersburg Times, November 5, 1983, p. 4B.

[4] Florida is not alone in experiencing this growing competition among public institutions of higher education for limited state funds. Analogous conflicts exist or loom in many other states between the flagship university—often located in a less populated place, like Tuscaloosa, Alabama, or Athens, Georgia, or Fayetteville, Arkansas—and the more metropolitan campuses of the same system, as in Birmingham, Atlanta, or Little Rock. The University of Illinois at Urbana-Champaign dealt with the same pressures by itself creating a system in which it is paired with and has some control over the Chicago campus. In Massachusetts, there is contention about whether the University of Massachusetts at Boston, twenty-five years old, would be better off independent from the flagship at Amherst or as the Boston satellite of Amherst. Presently, both campuses of the University of Massachusetts, along with the medical school at Worcester, are under the University of Massachusetts system.

Not until several years after the 1983 search did the Florida board of regents under Charles Reed's direction seek the help of outside consultants to have a look at the endemic conflicts between the excellence of the traditional flagship and the equity of the competitors. William Friday, the retired founding president of the University of North Carolina System, and Frank Newman, president of the Education Commission of the States, were invited to contribute their views toward a resolution of the competing claims. In an article in the Gainesville Sun reporting on this effort, Jack Wheat quotes John Folger, formerly at Florida State University and now director of the Education Policy Center at Vanderbilt: "You've got this aspiration that has exceeded the resources." He explained that there is "no income tax and a large number of retired people who want property taxes kept low." He notes Florida's wish to compare itself with the University of California's nine campuses, where Berkeley and UCLA and now San Diego are world-class, whereas in Florida, "you don't [have] any campus that comes close to any of the three," including the University of Florida, which "is clearly the strongest and most comprehensive university in Florida." (See Wheat, "UF, FSU must fight together for excellence," Gainesville Sun, pp. 1, 14A.)

168

ical waters? Or was the best recourse to choose a politically connected alumnus who knew "everybody" in state government and business and legal circles in Florida? Did the new president need to have contacts already established, or could he or she make them upon assuming office? The question of insider versus outsider, personified in the candidacies of Criser and DiBiaggio, was never directly addressed by the search committee.

One of the many ironies latent in the Florida story is the fact that Barbara Newell, chancellor of the board of regents at the time of the Criser selection, may have won and lost her job as a result of this insider/outsider issue. Newell was the first chancellor to have been chosen in a national public search, rather than coming from the University of Florida campus. Formerly president of Wellesley College and Ambassador to UNESCO, she was a cosmopolitan Yankee without Florida experience. In her diplomatic position with UNESCO in Paris, her sunshine candidacy for the chancellorship did not hurt her (nor would it have done so had she not been chosen, because her supporters could have written this off as due to sex discrimination). In contrast, sunshine helped bring to her candidacy the support of some female and male feminists who were eager for the choice of a well-known woman, rather than another "good ole boy."

At the time of the 1983 University of Florida search, however, the absence of a "good ole boy" at the seat of power in Tallahassee was probably inducement for some regents and members of the search committee to seek a native like Criser, who would have more influence in Tallahassee than Newell could muster. Not long after Criser's selection as University of Florida president, Barbara Newell resigned from the chancellorship. Some political observers say her resignation was connected to her apparent support of John DiBiaggio's candidacy over that of Criser; others suggest she had grown weary of contending with Florida politics and politicians. Whatever may have been the reasons for her departure, it was a well-connected "insider" who quickly filled her position: Charles Reed, then Governor Robert Graham's Secretary for Education.

In sequence, then, it seems plausible that the regents under Reed's leadership could choose John Lombardi, an "outsider," as Criser's successor. Some political observers have suggested, in fact, that an outsider may have seemed particularly desirable to some state leaders, so as to avoid having two "locals" competing on the same turf—the state government in Tal-

169

lahassee. But even in the 1989 search, with Reed available to offer on-the-job training in Florida politics, some local supporters of the University of Florida pushed to have then acting president Robert Bryan become the permanent president. Their argument was that Bryan knew the Florida political scene and therefore was best suited to win state support for the University of Florida. Again, the decision seemed to lie between an insider and an outsider; again, the debate took place in the press, not in the search committee.

Some proponents of "government in the sunshine" argue that public disclosure promotes good government by educating the general public concerning the issues facing state officials, thus leading not only to more legitimate outcomes but also, thanks to the airing of views, to sounder ones. As we have seen in the Florida searches, however, there was no discussion of the dilemmas and trade-offs inherent in the choice between an insider and an outsider. In the presence of the press and the public, the search committees and the regents did not debate the hard choices facing them. Indeed, they did not debate much of anything at all.

In public settings, representatives of competing groups typically make speeches designed to win them the allegiance of their constituents. "Behind closed doors," it is more possible for them to negotiate their differences by recognizing, at least in some measure, the legitimacy of their opponents' claims. It is in private that Senate-House conference committees agree on legislative compromises, in private that labor disputes are reconciled, in private that international conflicts are mediated. As we discussed in Chapter III, representatives of groups are generally more cosmopolitan than those for whom they speak; thus they have the capacity to become what their enemies would call "two-faced," that is, sufficiently demagogic vis-à-vis their constituents to remain in a position of influence, and sufficiently cosmopolitan to be able to be conciliatory to resolve what might otherwise be deadly differences.[5]

In the best cases, a presidential transition provides an opportunity for institutional learning. The search committee and the governing board examine the problems and priorities the institution faces, consider what sort of leadership is desired in light of these, and evaluate the credentials and

[5] See Stouffer, *Communism, Conformity, and Civil Liberties*. Also Riesman, "Orbits of Tolerance, Interviewers, and Elites," *Public Opinion Quarterly*, Vol. 20 (1956), pp. 49–73.

experiences of candidates accordingly. In the sunshine, however, discussions about missions and markets are truncated, if they exist at all. Likewise, discussions about candidates generally drop to the level of innocuous platitude. In the 1983 University of Florida search, background information that was gathered about candidates was reported to the full search committee in such vague language that committee members learned that something was dubious without ever finding out exactly what. Since committee members were instructed only to say positive things about candidates, they had to guess about what a candidate's weaknesses might be from what wasn't said.[6] However, negative comments concerning candidates did turn up in the press and in letters, and committee members found no way to interpret these, because they never acquired enough information to suggest, for example, that what one person might denounce as impolitic behavior might be interpreted by others as indicating a candidate's willingness to take a controversial stand when necessary, even at the risk of alienating others. Outside of meetings, committee members talked frankly, over the telephone or on walks to and from search committee meetings, despite the fact that such private talks may have been transgressions of the sunshine law. Court interpretations of the Florida statute indicate that conversation among any two or more people who are part of the decision-making process may be considered a meeting and thus must be open to the public.[7] Inside the meetings, however, committee members were reluctant to express their views, not wishing to offend either candidates they did not know or candidates who were friends, supervisors, or colleagues. As one person explained, "If I had said what I really thought, I might have lost a friend." Other committee members did not want to risk litigation, should a critical comment be interpreted as defamatory.[8]

[6] This happened also in the 1987 University of West Florida search where, when the advisory committee was discussing the six finalists for the presidency, the procedure was to bring up a topic, such as affirmative action, and have each committee member mention a candidate who was particularly impressive in this area. Not to be mentioned was seen as a sign of weakness. Why a candidate was not thought strong in this area was never directly stated and, hence, was never debated.

[7] There are no exceptions for this, not for labor negotiations, nor to settle a nasty dispute between two government officials. The rules are strict. When two state officials (including regents) meet, they constitute a meeting which cannot be held without due notice and must take place in public. See *Florida Freedom of Information Clearinghouse Newsletter*, Vol. 11, no. 10 (December, 1987), p. 1.

[8] When Riesman began studying defamation in comparative perspective fifty years ago, it would not have occurred to him or to other scholars that the fear of a libel suit would provide a serious

Of course, in and out of academic life there are pridefully and asser-tively independent people who enjoy polemics and combat, and who would be minimally inhibited from speaking their minds in public: they would enjoy offending powerful groups, and take their chances with suits for defamation. Some people relish fights, especially disputes that enjoy a large audience. Our research indicates, however, that members of search committees and boards commonly are more guarded in their public state-ments, not wanting to say things that might be harmful to candidates, hurtful to their institutions, or injurious to their own careers. Many of the members of the advisory committee in the 1983 University of Florida search whom we interviewed told us that they felt inhibited in the public sessions in expressing differences of opinion concerning candidates. Some people mentioned that they feared being misquoted or misinterpreted by the press. In our interview sessions in which we assured them of confiden-tiality, others spoke bluntly of their unwillingness to enter into a heated debate in the public setting because, as one person put it, fighting in public might mean losing in public. And not only could this prove embarrassing, it might be damaging professionally if the candidate the committee mem-ber was opposing turned out to be the next president of the university.

Concern about possible retribution extended to the actual voting as well. Several advisory committee members told us that committee mem-bers' votes had been affected by the sunshine, especially after the first signed ballots were reported in the state press. One committee member declared: "Everyone could see which way the wind was blowing. One per-son told me that he would be a fool to vote against the next president. I don't think there is any question that people would have voted differently if the votes had been secret."

The same reluctance to speak candidly in open meetings was present in the 1988 University of Minnesota search. On November 30, 1988, when the Minnesota regents met in public session to choose the new president

inhibition in such a setting. See, e.g., "Democracy and Defamation: Fair Game and Fair Comment I," *Columbia Law Review*, Vol. 42 (1942), pp. 1085–1112, and "Democracy and Defamation: Fair Game and Fair Comment II," *Columbia Law Review*, Vol. 42 (1942), pp. 1282–1318. Today the situation is radically different. The libel malpractice bar exists, primarily aimed at the media, small as well as large, but a presence in the land and available in a litigation-minded society, where juries have been "trained" to regard a million-dollar verdict as virtual peanuts and a socially useful spreading of re-sources! Cf., e.g., Rodney A. Smolla, "Why Does Libel Law Need Reform?" *Transaction/Society*, Vol. 26, no. 5 (July–August, 1989), pp. 67–70.

172

of the university from among three finalists, there was a minimum of discussion. This was not because there was a minimum of disagreement, for the final verdict was far from unanimous. Seven regents voted for Nils Hasselmo, then the provost and vice-president for academic affairs at the University of Arizona; and five regents preferred Robert Stein, the dean of the University of Minnesota law school. No regents voted for the third finalist, William Kirwan, then interim president at the University of Maryland at College Park, and soon to become the permanent president of that university. In the *Star and Tribune* the day after the vote, regent Elton Kuderer explained the reason for the paucity of discussion. "The problem is that anyone with serious reservations about a candidate, something detrimental, isn't going to air them in public. . . . In public, you're concerned about demeaning someone's character, concerned about libel."[9] Kuderer's remarks echo that of the United States Supreme Court in *U.S. v. Nixon*: "Human experience teaches that those who expect public dissemination of their remarks may well temper candor with a concern for appearances and for their own interests to the detriment of the decision-making process."[10]

Throughout the course of our study of the impact of open meetings upon the search process, we have been interested in the fact that the advocates and interpreters of sunshine laws—legislators, judges, and journalists—are among those people most resistant to having their own proceedings made public. Although Florida legislators have passed the most far-reaching sunshine laws in the country, they have been unwilling so far to have these laws apply to their own proceedings. Legislators can still gather for private discussions; their committee deliberations can remain entirely confidential. Judges, likewise, insist upon confidentiality for their own deliberations and for those of juries. And, in private conversations with us, newspaper reporters and editors have acknowledged that they would not like their own discussions of editorial policy or their meetings with superiors to be in the sunshine. It is as if sunshine laws are viewed as essential for the public interest when they are applied to others, but

[9] Quoted in Howard Sinker, "Hasselmo is new 'U' president," *Star and Tribune*, December 1, 1988, p. 18A.
[10] United States Supreme Court, *U.S. v. Nixon*, 1974.

recognized as a serious impediment to decision-making and a violation of privacy when applied to oneself.

In addition to the loss of candidates and candor caused by sunshine laws, public disclosure influences presidential searches in still another respect: the presence of the media alters the tone—and possibly the outcome—of the selection process. In the 1983 Florida search, the press treated candidates like politicians running for office. Interviews were turned into media events, responses to questions into campaign promises. The ongoing publicity about the search encouraged lobbying efforts and smear tactics, all of which were duly reported in the press. Partly because many journalists covering the search were young, inexperienced, recent graduates of the university, and partly because personalities make more popular reading than issues, news stories tended to focus on celebrities and trivia.

Whether, or to what extent, the media affected the outcome of the University of Florida search cannot be known. We have already mentioned that voting may have been influenced by the fact that the votes were made public. In the sunshine search, as in U.S. electoral politics, the potential of the press to influence opinion about candidates is very real. In the essay, "Thinking About the Press and Government," Gary Orren notes that "the challenging question is not whether the press influences policymaking, or even in general terms how much it influences policymaking. Nearly everyone, including journalists (at least privately), acknowledges that the influence of the press is substantial." He continues, "Within the span of a single generation, the American press has been transformed from a nearly invisible spectator to a principal actor in the American political arena, one frequently described as the fourth branch of the American government."[11] During a search process, editorial comments, selective reporting, and speculations about which candidate holds the lead are bound to leave an impression on search committee members and regents. Unlike juries, they are reading newspapers even as they reach their judgments.

SUNBURNED CANDIDATES

Journalists may also alter the outcome of the search when they act as investigative reporters. Some people argue, in fact, that sunshine helps the

[11] Quoted in Martin Linsky, *How the Press Affects Federal Policymaking: Six Case Studies* (New York: W. W. Norton, 1986), pp. 14, 17.

search in this regard; as a result of their investigative work, journalists may bring out information about candidates that members of the search committee may fail to gather on their own. Along these lines, attorney Marshall Tanick, representing the *Minnesota Daily* in its suit to open the meetings of the 1988 University of Minnesota presidential advisory search committee, declared: "Any skeletons in the closet of a candidate are more likely to be perceived if the closet door is open than if it is locked."[12]

This is not necessarily the case, however. In February, 1990, the *Chronicle of Higher Education* carried an account of the discovery that Joseph Olander, president of Evergreen State College in Olympia, Washington, and previously vice-president at the University of Texas at El Paso, had in both places used resumés saying that he was a member of Phi Beta Kappa when he was not, and that he had a master's degree in English, when in fact his degree is a Master of Arts in Teaching, a degree of somewhat less academic status.[13] Olander had been a highly visible candidate for the presidency at the University of Rhode Island several years earlier, attracting a great deal of publicity, as he had done again as a candidate at Evergreen State. But it was not until two faculty members at the latter institution investigated his credentials that the polishing of his curriculum vitae, what Olander later termed "technical omissions," was uncovered. Yet it is no crime to be a dramaturgical person, and the "grooming" of his curriculum vitae does not necessarily indicate that he was a mistaken choice. What the episode does suggest is that neither sunshine nor any other procedure can guarantee that all "skeletons" will be found out. The cynicism about what goes on "behind closed doors" can in fact lead toward a paranoia which disguises gullibility and innocence at the hands of those who can manipulate that very cynicism.

During the 1983 University of Florida search, one newspaper reporter traveled to the home campuses of several finalists to see if he could "dig up some dirt," as he put it to a faculty member he interviewed. His efforts were for naught; he found neither scandal nor innuendo around which to build a news story. In other searches, however, as in political campaigns, news stories are written about allegations and rumors, which, when finally

---

[12] Quoted in Dan Eggen, "Search for new U president goes to court on openness question," *Minnesota Daily*, September 22, 1988, p. 2, section 1.

[13] "Head of Evergreen State Leads Montana Search," *Chronicle of Higher Education*, Vol. 36, no. 21 (February 7, 1990), pp. 2–3.

found to be unsubstantiated, have already damaged the candidate by the mere fact of the accusation. The accusation creates suspicion, distrust, and, above all, controversy, and few boards want to select a new president who is surrounded by controversy. Moreover, these "candidates" in the academic search, unlike those in a political contest, may be undeclared, or altogether unwilling, contestants for the position.

Two of the six finalists in the 1983 University of Florida search were internal candidates—administrators at the university. In every search, internal candidates are in an awkward position in that they must attempt to conduct business as usual at the same time that they are being evaluated by their peers for the presidency of their institution. In the sunshine search, this position was made even more uncomfortable by the fact that many on campus knew that the two University of Florida administrators were candidates, knew what was being said about them, and knew who was, and who was not, voting for them. In an effort to spare the candidates embarrassment, only positive statements were made about individuals. Ironically, this reluctance of committee members to speak frankly about the weaknesses of candidates may have been a disservice to one of the two internal candidates whose candidacy was kept alive far longer than it would have been if discussions and votes had been confidential. Several search committee members told us after the search was over that one administrator would certainly have been dropped earlier in the process had it not been for the sunshine. Thus, this internal candidate invested time in interviews and in preparation for interviews and had his hopes raised about his eventual success, despite the fact that a negative decision had, in effect, already been reached.

For John DiBiaggio and Jay Oliva, the consequences of participating in a sunshine search were not limited to the eleven months of the search process. DiBiaggio was not trying to launch a major fund-raising campaign or initiate a comprehensive administrative or curricular reorganization at the time that his candidacy in Florida became widely known. Nevertheless, a president's institutional loyalty is an essential asset, and DiBiaggio's willingness to jettison Connecticut for a chance at Florida led to sharp questions about his loyalty from members of his board, state officials, and some people on campus. His position at Connecticut became tenuous, and yet when he wanted to consider other presidencies, he realized that his visible candidacy in Florida had limited his future prospects.

He could not afford to enter another search where his candidacy would become known on his home campus. That ruled out both those searches which brought candidates to campus for open interviews and those searches where, although the stated policy was complete confidentiality, leaks were likely to occur. DiBiaggio's participation in the Florida search had been tolerated at Connecticut, but a second "flirtation" would make him appear promiscuous. Moreover, having "failed" to win the Florida position, to be a public "also-ran" once again would make him appear to be a loser, or at least someone about whom two institutions had made a negative decision. Correspondingly, he chose not to enter several searches for which he had been nominated, even though the positions were very attractive. DiBiaggio was fortunate in that the regents of Michigan State University, delighted to find in him a Michigan native whose particular abilities matched their specific needs, were able to conduct their search entirely in confidence. Jay Oliva did not suffer at NYU as a result of his candidacy in Florida, and, indeed, shortly thereafter was promoted to the position of chancellor and executive vice-president. However, his experience in the Florida sunshine convinced him, like DiBiaggio, that this way of going about a search is "appalling," and made him determined never to participate in such a search process again.

Although Marshall Criser, as the successful contender in the Florida search, did not suffer the consequences of a public loss, he, too, was "sunburnt" by the sunshine process. The lack of respect accorded Florida's search process in national educational circles translated, probably unfairly, into a lack of respect for Criser. Criser was seen as a parochial choice, a political candidate in a political search. If Marshall Criser had been chosen in a confidential search, with the full support of the faculty members of the search committee, perhaps academics and others could have concluded that he was chosen for his potential effectiveness in gaining political support for the university in the north-south balance of influence in the state. Moreover, those who knew him well, rather than effusively supporting him in public, might have stressed in private that he was a quick learner and, despite his novice status, could become a capable administrator, drawing on his own and others' institutional loyalty to enhance the university's inner coherence as well as its support at Tallahassee.

In contrast, when Criser was named president, many observers of the search shrugged their shoulders and said, "but of course." They assumed

177

that the selection was predetermined; as one person commented cynically, "As soon as Marshall Criser's name emerged on the list of candidates, I knew that 'the fix was in.' " The fact that the search was conducted in the sunshine did nothing to dispel this notion, and it may in fact have contributed to the outcome by discouraging more competitive candidates and inhibiting discussions by the search committee and among the regents. One sitting president nominated for the Florida presidency told us that he had done some quiet checking around and then quickly withdrawn his name from consideration. The sunshine was enough to make him conclude that it was idiotic to become an open candidate while discovering whether or not the gossip was correct and whether or not someone of his stature and administrative attainments might have been able to become a serious contender.

Our field study of the Florida search process leads us to believe that the selection of Criser was not foreordained. Certainly there were members of the Florida search committee and the board of regents who had their minds made up for Criser from very early in the search. But there were others who were not enthusiastic about his candidacy and still others who were possible swing votes. Because of the public nature of the search process, those people who did not support Criser did not voice their objections to him. Those who were academicians would have been criticizing someone who stood an excellent chance of becoming their chief executive officer. Those who were businessmen and lawyers would have been expressing doubts about an influential state leader, or in many instances, their friend or a friend of their friends. Many of these friends and some would-be friends eagerly expressed their support of him, knowing that this would become public and therefore be to their credit with the presumptive winner. The very volume of this support not only made it easier for Criser's supporters to dispel almost unavoidably tacit opposition to him but, also, in the end, reinforced the widespread opinion that he had won the post because of cronyism.

PROTECTION FROM THE SUN?

Our conclusions about the hazards of conducting searches in the sunshine are shared by many individuals who have taken part in them, including

Marshall Criser. In 1988, in an interview in the *Gainesville Sun*, Criser noted, "If we look at presidential selections for the past 15 years, we'll see that there's no incumbent president who has been selected unless he or she has already made up their mind . . . to leave. . . . The problem is that once they let it be known they are willing to be considered on a short list, their alumni conclude they're disloyal, their staff starts looking for another job, the faculty become suspicious and they become ineffective."[14] The day after he left office, Criser, along with his three living predecessors in the University of Florida presidency—Robert Marston, Stephen O'Connell, and J. Wayne Reitz—wrote state officials and the chairman of the 1989 regents search committee, calling for the passage of legislation to exempt university presidential searches from the sunshine, and to repeal legislation stipulating the composition of the university advisory committee. As we noted in Chapter III, Florida law specified that at least half of the members of the university advisory committee were to come from business and industry, and faculty membership was limited to 12.5 percent of the committee.

Over the past few years, there have been repeated attempts to enact such an exemption from sunshine coverage for presidential searches. Many of these efforts have been led by University of Florida president emeritus J. Wayne Reitz and state representative Fran Carlton from Orlando. For both individuals, their strong belief in the importance of confidentiality in the presidential search process stems from their personal experiences of having served on a search committee. In Reitz's case, this was in his capacity as a trustee of Eckerd College, a small Presbyterian college in St. Petersburg, Florida. In that search, the search committee narrowed its pool of candidates to five finalists, four of whom were sitting presidents. The search committee chair then suggested having these finalists meet with the press. Since Eckerd College is private, it is not subject to Florida's sunshine laws and this disclosure would have been entirely voluntary. In response to Reitz's concerns about making the identities of the finalists public, the chair telephoned the four sitting presidents to learn their reactions to this proposed step in the process. All four presidents

14 Jack Wheat, "Criser: Close Search for College Presidents," *Gainesville Sun*, February 10, 1988, p. 1a.

declared that they would withdraw their candidacies immediately if their names were given to the press.

Fran Carlton, an alumna of the University of Florida, had supported the concept of sunshine searches until she experienced one firsthand as a member of the advisory committee in the 1983 University of Florida search. That experience persuaded her that sunshine searches are not desirable: "This is one situation where it [the sunshine law] really does not work to the advantage of the people of Florida, which of course is the purpose of the sunshine law."[15]

As with attempts in Texas and Iowa to modify open-meeting or sunshine laws on behalf of presidential searches, so too Reitz's and Carlton's attempts in Florida have repeatedly met with failure. Each time, when Carlton has introduced a bill to this effect, colleagues of hers in the Florida legislature have approached her, voiced their support for her efforts, and then told her that they regretted that they could not vote with her. As she explained to us, the legislators know that a vote to "close doors" would result in their being pilloried by the media. In a letter Carlton wrote to members of the Florida House of Representatives, Carlton commented, "Believe me . . . I am a realist. I know that many of you will not be willing to take the necessary heat from the media to make the needed changes. But we should!"[16]

As Carlton and her colleagues in political office know well, in Florida and across the nation the press has played a major role as vigilant defenders and enforcers of open-meeting and open-record laws. The Brechner Center for Freedom of Information, jointly sponsored by the University of Florida College of Journalism and Communications, the Florida Press Association, the Florida Society of Newspaper Editors, and the Joseph L. Brechner Endowment, publishes a monthly report "of mass media law in Florida." The report provides an update on legislation relating to freedom of information, gives a summary of court decisions in this area, and identifies all alleged violations of the state open-meeting and open-records laws. Whenever legislation has been introduced in Florida that would provide for an exemption from the sunshine, the Brechner Report has urged its readers to lobby actively in opposition. In many other states, as well, a

[15] Brent Kallestad, "Secrecy Bill Draws Protest," *Gainesville Sun*, February 6, 1988, p. 10A.
[16] Letter from Fran Carlton to House Members, December, 1988.

watchful media has questioned alleged violations of state open-meeting statutes and has brought higher education increasingly under the jurisdiction of these laws. In 1989, when Eastern New Mexico University refused to release the names and resumés of all applicants and nominees for its presidency, it was sued by the *Clovis News-Journal* for violation of New Mexico's Inspection of Public Records Act. In Georgia, a battle over whether the names of all candidates in the 1989 Georgia State University presidential search should be made public found the *Atlanta Journal-Constitution* and the Georgia attorney general on one side, demanding the release of names, and the chancellor and university on the other, insisting that confidentiality was crucial for the success of the search.[17]

SOME VAGARIES OF REFORM

Although Americans, like people elsewhere, notoriously distrust politics and politicians, the impulse to pass a law is strongest when some abuse of delegated powers is revealed. Freedom of information laws were strengthened after the Watergate scandal; anger at Congressional pay raises, honoraria and other perquisites have led to the strengthening of conflict-of-interest laws, which limit the recruitment of experienced persons to government service, facilitating the success of the young and the very rich. On the state level, we have seen in recent years the vastly increased use of the initiative, referendum, and recall as devices by which the public can express preferences directly via the ballot, rather than through elected representatives.

In *Direct Democracy: The Politics of Initiative, Referendum, and Recall*, Thomas E. Cronin describes the origins and current use of these various devices of "direct democracy."[18] The argument over whether democracy

[17] When the Georgia Supreme Court ruled in favor of the newspaper and the chancellor's request for a rehearing was denied, the university released information on the more than two hundred candidates for the presidency. By this time, a new president, John M. Palms, a physicist from Emory University, had been named, but the *Atlanta Journal-Constitution* nevertheless published stories based on the full list of candidates, questioning, for instance, why only one black man and no women were included among the twelve finalists.

[18] Cambridge: Harvard University Press, 1989. See also Patrick B. McGuigan, *The Politics of Direct Democracy in the 1980s: Case Studies in Popular Decision-Making* (Washington, D.C.: Institute for Government and Politics of the Free Congress Research and Education Foundation, 1985). While the first legislation permitting "legislative" decision making by ballot occurred in South Dakota in 1898, the leading state in this regard in recent years has been California. In 1986 California's public

181

is best served by representative or plebiscitary government dates from the founding of this country. Laws such as the initiative, referendum, and recall stem from the belief that representative institutions will inevitably be controlled by the bosses, the "interests," or the power elite, and will not be responsive to the interests of "We, the people."

So, too, with sunshine laws, where the belief is that government will become more "honest" with the public as audience to decision-making. But corruption is not so easily elided. When records and meetings are open, less is put down in writing and less said in public.[19] Rather than preventing skullduggery, sunshine laws lead to evasions and game-playing. As one respondent to Kerr and Gade's questionnaire commented, sunshine laws lead to "moonshine operations."[20] In searches conducted in the sunshine, search committee members avoid controversy altogether, or they talk off-the-record, outside of committee sessions, despite the fact that such conversations are "illegal." Such conversations take place in walks between meetings or during unrecorded telephone conversations. As a result, the public is no better informed about the real issues and no more confident about the fairness of decisions than had the entire process been conducted in secret. Indeed, the sense of concealment and illicit goings-on often heightens public cynicism. Sunshine laws thus seem self-defeating: They do not increase trust but provide temptations to indulge in duplicity.

Sunshine laws are often defended as a means of educating and informing the public. However, a sunshine search process can hardly be consid-

---

institutions of higher education were put in jeopardy by the "Fair Pay" referendum, which would have limited the salaries of all public officials to eighty percent of the governor's salary. This measure, had it passed, would have decapitated the administrative and academic leadership of the nine campuses of the University of California system.

[19] The Buckley Amendment, the federal statute named after its sponsor, former Senator John Buckley of New York, would seem to be an example of government by horror story. Buckley's law requires that schools, colleges, and universities keep confidential all records and recommendations concerning students; students, however, can see what has been said about them in teacher or counselor recommendations. Apparently Buckley believed that left-wing New York City schoolteachers were writing negative recommendations concerning college aspirants they judged to be too conservative, and students' access would curb this abuse. The outcome of this statute, however, is far different from the intentions which motivated it. Smart students waive their Buckley Amendment rights in order to give greater credibility to the recommendations written on their behalf. Moreover, the Amendment helped create a milieu of "letter inflation," akin to grade inflation, in which letters of recommendation become virtually weightless, thus privileging those students in schools and colleges whose sponsors know whom to telephone in a situation not monitored by the Amendment, not the sorts of students John Buckley had sought to assist.

[20] *The Guardians*, p. 77.

ered educational when important issues related to the search are not discussed frankly (or perhaps not discussed at all), and the presence of the media benefits the simplifiers and puts at a disadvantage those whose judgments are complicated and take longer to state and to comprehend.[21] Ironically, the more open a search is, in terms of public disclosure, the less openness, in terms of candor and argument, is practiced by all parties. Despite their promise of openness, sunshine searches reduce open access to talent and impede open deliberations about candidates. Unfortunately, then, the effect of the sunshine laws has been the promotion of the value of access to information to the neglect of the avowed purposes for which these laws were enacted—good government and good decisions.

In yet another respect, sunshine laws illustrate the near-universal "law" of unintended consequences. Although the supporters of open-meeting and open-records statutes argue that sunshine laws are a means of making the process of decision making public, thereby allowing more people access to governance, in many instances the outcome has been exactly the reverse. Recent experience suggests that, in many instances, when the search process must be conducted in accord with sunshine laws, less power is given to the large, representative search committee and more power accrues to the chancellor of the state system.

In 1987, when the University of Minnesota board of regents conducted a search for Kenneth Keller's successor, they discovered that they could no longer hold confidential meetings to discuss candidates for the presidency as they had done three years earlier, at the time of Keller's selection. Two court cases in those intervening years had widened the coverage of the state's open-meeting law, so that any meeting of the regents at which a quorum was present had to take place in public. Believing strongly that confidentiality was necessary in order to attract the most capable candidates, the regents asked the university's general counsel to devise a process that would satisfy the law while allowing the names of candidates to remain confidential. The procedure recommended and followed called for

---

[21] A monograph by Kiku Adatto compares the length of time given to presidential candidates' statements in the 1968 Nixon-Humphrey contest with the allowances provided in the Bush-Dukakis 1988 campaign, quantifying the change from minutes to seconds or "sound bites" by 1988, leading in turn to much attention by the media to the "handlers" (ignored in 1968) who framed and staged the "photo opportunities" and corresponding sound bites. See Adatto, "Sound Bite Democracy: Network Evening News Presidential Campaign Coverage, 1968 and 1988," Research Paper R-2, Harvard University, 1990.

the chair and vice-chair of the regents to meet privately with individual regents to discuss the full list of candidates; and a twenty person advisory committee to meet in private to screen candidates. Because this committee was not given decision-making authority, it was not deemed to fall under the state statute. When a small number of finalists was identified, these candidates were asked whether they were willing to participate in public interviews, and only those who agreed to do so moved to the final stage of consideration.

No sooner had the advisory committee held its first confidential meeting than litigation ensued. The student newspaper, supported financially by the Minnesota Newspaper Association, brought suit against the University of Minnesota on the grounds that the advisory committee was in effect a decision-making body since it would interview candidates and screen the total field down to five or fewer finalists for the regents to interview. An intermediate court dismissed the suit, and the state Supreme Court refused to hear an appeal. Judges in Minnesota must run for re-election, but it is ordinarily a perfunctory matter, and they are re-elected regularly. In any event, they were prepared to turn a stern face to criticisms from the media.

In 1988, when the University of Alabama system inaugurated the search for a new president of the flagship campus at Tuscaloosa, the *Birmingham News* went to court under the state's open-records law to secure access to the names of all finalists for the presidency and to interviews with these finalists. The lawyers for the chancellor and the regents protested this bid for disclosure on the grounds that "potential candidates currently holding prestigious positions simply will not allow themselves to be considered without an assurance of complete anonymity."[22] In the course of the court proceedings, the chancellor and board of regents revised their search procedure in a way that was even more systematic than what has just been described for the University of Minnesota. All conversations between the chancellor and members of the search committee would be premised on the role of these committee members as advisory to the chan-

---

[22] "In the Circuit Court for the Tenth Judicial Circuit of Alabama Equity Division, The Birmingham News Company, Plaintiff, vs. Thomas A. Bartlett, et. al., Defendants, Civil Action No. CV 88 504 403 MC," p. 2. To help argue their case, the University of Alabama system recruited Virginia Lester of the Richmond, Virginia, law firm of Hunton & Williams, as an expert witness. President of Mary Baldwin College from 1977 to 1985, Lester had subsequently graduated from Stanford Law School.

cellor, or, in effect, pro tem members of his staff. The search committee would have the function of reviewing all nominations and applications for the presidency and interviewing candidates. The deliberations of this search committee could remain confidential, under the condition that it would have no authority to reduce the number of candidates or otherwise screen the candidates. All information about the candidates and all comments made about candidates by committee members would be passed on to the chancellor. The chancellor would then have sole responsibility for selecting from the entire list of candidates the individuals or individual that he considered best suited for the University of Alabama presidency.

After the chancellor made his recommendation to the board, the board as a whole would interview and vote on the finalists or finalist. In compliance with state law, the board's meeting would be open to the public. Under this procedure there would not need to be more than a single finalist, whose approval by the board of regents would have been assured by the one-on-one conversations held with each regent. In such a case, where only a single finalist would be brought to campus with the board giving approval in an open meeting and an ensuing press conference, the press and other media would be almost completely elided.

Change along similar lines was proposed in Oregon in 1988, where legislation was introduced that would allow university search committees to proffer their recommendations only to the system chancellor, who would be authorized then to employ presidents. Search committees have reported to the Oregon Board of Higher Education, which is required by state statute to meet in public. However, communications with the chancellor are not subject to that state's open meeting laws. Again, the attempt was to find a way to keep the search process confidential in order to be able to recruit capable prospects who otherwise would not allow their names to be considered.

For cynics who believe that any law or procedure adopted by reformers can be evaded in one form or another, what we might call the "Alabama road" offers some evidence. The outcome may well be an improvement from the perspective of the hazards of sunshine, but it does not come without evident costs. A president chosen in the Alabama fashion may be regarded as someone preferred by the chancellor or by a powerful bloc within the board of regents, but the breadth and intensity of this person's support, in comparison with other potential contenders, will not be known, since there has been no airing, even in a small forum, of pro and con judgments. Thus a person chosen under these circumstances may have a more limited legitimacy than is the case in states where it is clear that the relevant committees, which include board members and faculty members, have agreed on the person chosen. In search of some privacy in the process, these university systems have been willing to give more and more power to fewer and fewer people. It is almost as if the "excesses" of plebiscitary democracy, illustrated by the effort to open everything up to everybody, has lead to the "dictatorship" of the chancellor.

Such a position is not necessarily enviable for the chancellor. Unable to share with a representative group the responsibility for recommendation, the chancellor becomes vulnerable to attack by those who do not like his or her decision. Additionally, there is always the possibility that the "Alabama road" may not give more power to the chancellor but to particular regents or legislators, who could lobby successfully for a candidate they want, quite outside what the chancellor proposes.

The political scientist Martha Wagner Weinberg, when she was teaching in the Sloan School of Management at MIT, developed a "case" involving the Massachusetts open-meeting law which she used as a teaching device. The case begins with a Massachusetts director of Common Cause seeing the open-meeting law as something which will provide a visible local victory for Massachusetts Common Cause whose membership has been dropping precipitously.[23] When the bill goes to the legislature, the only organized opposition comes from the Massachusetts teachers union and the Massachusetts Association of School Superintendents who fear that this law will distort the process of evaluation of personnel. The bill readily becomes law. Most students reading the case thus far conclude that good has triumphed over evil and that the nonpartisan organization Common Cause has lived up to its name.[24]

The next chapter in the story is a fracas at Concord High School be-

[23] Open meetings were one of four reforms (along with public funding of federal elections and regulation of contributions to campaigns for electoral office, disclosure of the activities of lobbyists, and disclosure of the outside income of public officials) that made up the "OUTS" program of the national Common Cause. "OUTS" stood for "open up the system." See Andrew S. McFarland, *Common Cause, Lobbying in the Public Interest* (Chatham, New Jersey: Chatham House, 1984).

[24] In correspondence with Riesman, John Gardner, the founder and first president of Common Cause, has expressed his opposition to the use of sunshine and open meeting laws in an undiscriminating way in searches for college and university presidents. (Letter of October 25, 1984).

186

tween local white students and inner-city black students bused to Concord as part of Boston's METCO program. A black resident of Concord, Charles Willie, a professor of sociology at the Harvard Graduate School of Education, trustee of the Episcopal Divinity School, and vice-rector of Christ Church in Cambridge, is asked to chair a nonpartisan commission to examine the causes of the violence and the general status of the METCO program. The Willie Commission holds fourteen meetings, three public hearings and eleven closed sessions. During the closed sessions, committee members interview witnesses to the incident in an attempt to determine what actually took place. They also talk with students, parents, and others familiar with the METCO program about racial relations at the high school. These meetings are closed so that individuals can speak with minimal fear of reprisal or public obloquy for saying unpalatable things, even, or especially, if they are true. Shortly after the Willie Commission has issued its recommendations, which are unanimously endorsed by the Concord School Committee, an assistant district attorney charges that the Commission acted in violation of the Massachusetts open-meeting law, and asks to have all minutes of the closed meetings made public. At this point, the sympathies of students reading the case begin to shift. Here, in the students' eyes and in our eyes, the virtue is in confidentiality, not disclosure, and the situation bears some resemblance to efforts to shield child victims of sexual abuse from the full glare of publicity if they testify concerning the alleged abuser. Martha Weinberg found that the concrete context forced students who had almost automatically thought the open meeting laws to be a straightforward and valuable reform, to reconsider, in the face of the particular episode, whether it might have unintended and undesirable consequences.[25]

CHECKS AND BALANCES

In *The Torment of Secrecy*, Edward A. Shils notes that "American culture is a populist culture. As such, it seeks publicity as a good in itself. Extremely suspicious of anything which smacks of 'holding back,' it appreciates publicity, not merely as a curb on the arrogance of rulers but as a

[25] On this theme, see also Richard Elmore, "Backward Mapping: Implementation Research and Policy Decisions," *Political Science Quarterly*, Vol. 94, no. 4 (Winter, 1979–1980): 601–616.

condition in which members of society are brought into a maximum of contact with each other."[26] Our egalitarianism, participative populism, hostility to cliques, and suspicion of conspiracy lead to the typically American belief that openness is not only to be expected but is the only moral and only democratic course.

Yet there are contrasting strains in American culture and politics. Unlike totalitarian governments where there is no respect for private boundaries, be these families, social groups, or religious organizations, our democracy ensures freedom from intrusion into many spheres of life. Charles Warren and Louis Brandeis wrote an influential article in *Harvard Law Review* in 1890 contending that there exists a right of privacy;[27] however, constitutional protection of that right has taken a long time to emerge and is still ferociously debated (at the time of our writing in terms of a "right" to an abortion). Concern for what Edward Bloustein has referred to as "the Right to Huddle"[28] is debated on the periphery of these larger struggles. In the case of governmental institutions, the "right" of privacy is seen to be at war with instant public accountability.[29]

Given the ever-greater visibility of state-supported higher education and the undiminished interest in "personalities" and "character," it is not surprising that the presidential search has become a battleground for the competing values of confidentiality and disclosure. Unfortunately, as we have seen, this often occurs to the detriment of individuals, the search process, and the institution. We believe that the concerns about accountability and arbitrary abuses of power can be better addressed in ways other than applying sunshine laws to the search process. Certain checks and balances are built into the search process, most notably in the membership of the bodies doing the searching, screening, and selecting. Almost all search committees today include faculty members, generally chosen by their peers, student representatives, usually student leaders, and often representatives of the administration and staff, alumni, and local community.

---

[26] Edward A. Shils, *The Torment of Secrecy: The Background and Consequences of American Security Policies* (Glencoe, Illinois, The Free Press, 1956), p. 41.

[27] "The Right To Privacy," *Harvard Law Review*, Vol. 4, no. 5 (December 15, 1890), pp. 193–220.

[28] See Edward Bloustein, "Group Privacy: The Right to Huddle," in *Rutgers-Camden Law Journal*, Vol. 8, no. 2 (Winter, 1977), p. 278.

[29] Bloustein writes: "Permeating much of the law of group privacy is an awareness that confidentiality assures associational success or efficacy by enabling individuals to be candid with each other."

188

The intricate efforts that go into building a search committee aim to elicit responsible representatives, make available a diversity of perspectives, and provide a protection against trustee collusion. The acceptability of a new president depends in large measure on the inclusion of these significant stakeholders in the search process.[30]

In addition, search committees are ad hoc, temporary bodies, entrusted for a short time only with representing the whole institution and some of its component parts. Search committee members serve on the committee for this trip only, then return fully to their previous statuses, which during the search committee's proceedings they have continued to serve. Hence, a runaway search committee which turns into a conspiracy is unlikely, and the committee members' limited term of service minimizes threats to democratic procedures. Likewise, while boards of regents are permanent governing entities, they have replaceable membership. Similarly, a president is not appointed for life, although to some who suffer under him or her it may seem so! Initial appointments are rarely for more than five years, if that long, and whatever the set term of years, the president serves "at the pleasure of the board." There is also in college and university life an analogue to the impeachment of public officials or to recall in states such as California, in that faculty votes of "no confidence" amount to a bill of impeachment or to a referendum leading to recall. Few presidents can remain in office when faced with such a vote. This was the case in 1984 at Auburn University, Alabama's land-grant institution, whose president, Hanley Funderburk, had the support of the late Governor George Wallace and of others in Montgomery, but could not hold out against the no-confidence vote and the public resignation of the highly respected academic vice-president Taylor Littleton. Presidential evaluations constitute another "check-and-balance" in the mixture of representative and participatory academic governance. As an instrument it, like a vote of no confidence, can be lethal, but it need not be, and everything depends on the circumstances and manner of its use.[31]

---

[30] For a general discussion of faculty members as principal stakeholders, and other stakeholders as well, particularly in the research universities, see Henry Rosovsky, *The University: An Owner's Manual* (New York and London: W. W. Norton, 1990), especially the discussion of privacy and secrecy versus sunshine on page 282.

[31] In *Exit, Voice, and Loyalty: Responses to Decline in Firms, Organizations and States* (Cambridge: Harvard University Press, 1970), Albert O. Hirschman presents a trio of alternatives which individuals

A search committee is not a permanent insider group. Its membership is known, is generally chosen by constituent groups, and is accountable to these groups as well as to the institution as a whole. Its process is known; only the contents of discussions and the names of candidates are kept confidential. When its task is accomplished, the search committee dissolves and its decision is available for all to see. In many respects, the search committee is like a jury. Its membership is chosen to be representative, yet its members are instructed to make a decision according to their own best judgment as "experts" on the case, and secrecy is understood as necessary to allow this process of deliberation to occur. As Sissela Bok comments in *Secrets*: "secrecy for their [the jury's] deliberations protects the members from attempts to influence them, increasing the likelihood of a fair decision; it allows the resolution of difficult conflicts even where the evidence is ambiguous, generating a degree of confidence in the final result that would otherwise be unattainable. Full publicity into every aspect of the deliberations might cast doubt on the most careful of decisions. The secrecy, moreover, is terminated as soon as a decision has been reached, and the verdict itself is open to public scrutiny and to appeal."

---

have when coping with corporate bodies from the family to the state. See further, "Exit and Voice: An Expanding Sphere of Influence," in *Rival Views of Market Society and Other Recent Essays* (New York: Viking, 1986), pp. 77–101. In the Auburn University episode, it was Taylor Littleton's well-known loyalty which made his exit speak with such a resonant voice. Had he exited quietly, with no evident conflict between loyalty and voice, his departure would have had limited impact. Similarly, Paul Ylvisaker's vocal resignation as chairman of the search committee to find a new chancellor for the Massachusetts Board of Regents because he objected to the board's choice of someone not included on the search committee's list of finalists brought an outcry from the press and drew Governor Michael Dukakis into the argument. See Hogarty, "Search for a Massachusetts Chancellor." To be sure, any departure, whether of a customer, an employee, or a family member, does say something, and may even echo, but what it says is often unclear.

CHAPTER VIII

Winthrop College

I N THIS AND THE NEXT CHAPTER, we turn to an examination of the use of consultants in searches for college and university presidents. Over the past several years, their use has become increasingly common as boards of trustees have come to recognize the difficulties of a search process and to appreciate that, as in corporate affairs in which many trustees are engaged, consultants can be useful. In corporate life, executives employ consultants regularly, often in the hope that they will be advised to do what they already want to do, thereby gaining legitimation. In academic life, consultants are still not routine, and are often viewed with great skepticism by many faculty members, students, and others. This chapter describes the search for a president of Winthrop College, a process conducted with the assistance of search consultant Ruth Weintraub, then senior vice-president of the Academy for Educational Development and director of the Academy's executive search division. At the conclusion of the search process, all members of the Winthrop search committee agreed that a consultant had provided essential help. As will be seen, however, it was not a search without controversy, including the not uncommon conflict between faculty members and the search committee seen as representative of the board of trustees. In Chapter IX we discuss differences among search consultants, identifying both the considerable support that a consultant can provide and warning also of the potential hazards connected with their use.

CONSIDERING A CONSULTANT

The presidential search at Winthrop College was already under way in September 1985, when Terry Peterson, the chairman of the search committee, decided to ask Ruth Weintraub to meet with the members of the Winthrop search committee in Columbia, South Carolina, to discuss the services she could provide. Ruth Weintraub was sometimes considered the doyenne of presidential search consulting, having been called in on more than a hundred searches for presidents and senior administrators in colleges and universities over a period of twelve years. A graduate of Hunter College, with a Ph.D. in political science from Columbia University and a J.D. from New York University, Ruth Weintraub was professor of political science and then dean of social sciences and dean of graduate studies at Hunter, prior to joining the Academy for Educational Development.

Winthrop College was founded in Columbia, South Carolina, in 1886. Its initial funding came from the Peabody Educational Fund, and the college was named for the Fund's president, Robert Winthrop. Five years later, the college moved to Rock Hill, became state-supported, and was renamed the South Carolina Industrial and Winthrop Normal School. In 1924, when the name was changed to Winthrop College, the South Carolina College for Women, it was the third-largest all-female college in the United States. Indeed, the fact that it was known as "Winthrop College" then, as now, has given it a certain cachet—the tone and quality of a private rather than a public institution.[1] In 1974, facing a serious drop in enrollment, Winthrop, like many public and private single-sex colleges, became coeducational. Currently, Winthrop College has a student body of over five thousand students, of whom approximately thirty percent are male. This is the largest enrollment ever for Winthrop, and has been achieved simultaneously with the college having raised its admission standards. At the undergraduate level, the College of Arts and Sciences has the largest student enrollment, followed by the School of Education, the School of Business, and the School of Music. At the graduate level, reflecting its history, the School of Education has the largest student enrollment.

Despite its location in the northern corner of the state, Winthrop Col-

[1] One of the three finalists for the Winthrop presidency commented to us that Winthrop's name had "marketing potential." It has "a private air about it," he stated. "It doesn't sound like Upper South Carolina State College, which of course it is."

For an analogous advantage of the avoidance of the term "state" in the designation of a small, primarily undergraduate institution, see the discussion of Ramapo College in Gerald Grant and David Riesman, *The Perpetual Dream: Reform and Experiment in the American College* (Chicago: University of Chicago Press, 1978), or compare the connotations of St. Mary's College of Maryland with Towson State College—both publicly-supported in Maryland, but the former with the "independent" cachet.

lege's student body is not regional, as are those of most of the other thirty-five state colleges, but draws heavily from around the state. In part, this is because of its high visibility in state educational circles: The college is currently the largest producer of teachers in the state (the University of South Carolina is in second place), and is the site of four statewide educational programs being implemented under the comprehensive South Carolina Educational Improvement Act of 1985. Winthrop College is also the only state college with an accredited business school at both the bachelor's and master's degree level, and has the only accredited art school in the state.

In June 1985, Philip Lader, president of Winthrop College since 1983, announced that he would resign from the presidency at the end of the calendar year in order to campaign for the governorship of South Carolina. Winthrop board chair Mary Sue McElveen appointed members of a presidential search committee and asked Terry Peterson, assistant to the governor for education, to chair this group. By state law, the governor of South Carolina serves on the Winthrop College board, but he had made Peterson his delegate. Peterson brought to the task his statewide visibility and corresponding knowledge of its politics, and also a doctorate in research and statistics and a corresponding knowledge of academic cultures.

The Winthrop search committee had begun its work in July. An advertisement for the presidency had been placed in the *Chronicle of Higher Education, Education Week,* and South Carolina and North Carolina newspapers; Winthrop faculty, administrators, and alumni had been encouraged to make nominations; and applications and nominations were beginning to arrive. The search committee had also held a "hearing" at the college, an all-day session arranged so that faculty, administrators, staff, and students could meet with the search committee and express their opinions as to what qualifications were most needed in Winthrop's next president. This meeting was well attended by senior administrators, but not by faculty or students.

Shortly after the first meeting of the search committee, Terry Peterson began to consider the possibility of a search consultant. A year earlier, he had served as staff to a search for an assistant commissioner of education and hence was well aware that chairing a search could require extravagant amounts of time for which his own busy schedule gave little leeway.

193

Moreover, he wanted to make certain that the search for Winthrop College would be fully national, and, appreciating the importance of networks in identifying prospects, he recognized that a search consultant at home in the national higher education scene would be helpful. Terry Peterson could also see the advantages of a search consultant in depoliticizing a search.

Terry Peterson was well aware, however, that the state prohibited the use of public funds for such a purpose. In this quandary of wanting a consultant without having funds to pay for one, Terry Peterson discussed plans for the search with a high-ranking executive of a firm that valued its role as a "good neighbor" of Winthrop College. This executive in turn talked with the chief executive officer of the firm. Peterson's wish that the search committee could employ a search consultant matched the chief executive officer's same hope, and he offered to provide the money to make this possible.[2]

SETTLING ON RUTH WEINTRAUB

With money for a consultant in hand, Terry Peterson called individuals in national education organizations and prominent leaders in higher education who were knowledgeable about presidential searches to ask which consultants they would recommend. Among those named were several firms with a sideline in academia but primarily working in the corporate field, and there was no consensus about which of these was best. Two not-for-profit agencies, however, were on everyone's list: the Academy for Educational Development and the Presidential Search Consultation Service. When Peterson reported his findings to the Winthrop search committee, the members were enthusiastic about the idea of a search consultant and agreed to interview representatives from the two firms cited the most often.

Thus it was that, in September, Terry Peterson called Ruth Weintraub to ask if she would meet with the Winthrop search committee to describe

---

[2] Terry Peterson commented later that, were other institutions to follow a similar course, he would recommend that one firm preferably not be the sole provider of funds, lest it be accused of some sort of conflict of interest. In Winthrop's case, this was not a problem because of the reputation of the firm making the donation.

the services she could provide. She agreed, and asked to be sent a Winthrop catalogue so that she could familiarize herself with the college.

The Winthrop search committee first met over lunch with a representative of the Presidential Search Consultation Service, a not-for-profit organization sponsored by the Association of Governing Boards of Universities and Colleges. They were favorably impressed with his understanding of the search process. Then they met Ruth Weintraub. Initially, several members of the search committee were taken aback by her New York brusqueness. "My initial reaction was that she came over real rough. She seemed obnoxious, although her brilliance shone through. In the end, I was sold on her. You just had to cut through her brashness and get down to the real person. She's a doer. She tells it like it is." Ruth Weintraub herself remembered criticizing one aspect of the search process the committee had delineated: their expectation that candidates would submit a 500–700 word paper on their philosophy of education. "If you are trying to discourage people, you're going about it the right way," she commented. Her remarks offended one member of the Winthrop committee. "I took exception to her criticism. I thought, 'I'm going to let her have it.' Then she challenged me, and I got the impression that she knew what she was doing. The fact that she was willing to come out and say what she thought impressed me." Still another member of the search committee declared, "She doesn't mince words, yet she's not abrasive. She doesn't offend anyone, yet she says things like she sees them. She was very positive; she seemed to know exactly how to go about a search and what we would need. And she got it across to us that we would be doing the choosing. She would only be guiding."

Ruth Weintraub's clear recommendation that the major decisions of the search would remain in the hands of the search committee dissipated the fear several members of the committee had that a consultant might "come in and take over." Ruth Weintraub made it clear that she would be an adviser and partner to the search committee members, not a substitute for them. After she left the meeting, the members of the search committee discussed the two consultants. Undoubtedly, both would be extremely helpful, they concluded. Perhaps somewhat to their own surprise, when each member of the search committee stated a preference, the majority indicated they liked Ruth Weintraub's outspokenness and directness and wanted to work with her. Terry Peterson telephoned the chairmen of three search committees that had employed Ruth Weintraub to check her references, and the decision was made.

On September 17, 1985, Ruth Weintraub signed a letter of agreement to serve as consultant to the Winthrop search. When she had first met with the search committee, she had suggested modifying the original advertisement. Explaining that the small-town location of Rock Hill might discourage prospects, she proposed the addition of a sentence: "Charlotte, North Carolina, with its international airport and cultural activities, is only 25 miles away." The convenient access to a city of half a million with Charlotte's cultural ambience might be an asset. Since the original advertisement had given a cut-off date for applications and nominations of September 15, a date that would not allow Ruth Weintraub time to prospect for candidates, the committee accepted her recommendation that the re-advertised date should be November 8.

Ruth Weintraub also talked with the search committee about what they were looking for in a president and made suggestions concerning the sort of person she believed would best serve the College. The committee should resist the temptation to choose someone from a large institution of high prestige who would be coming to Winthrop to retire. Instead, they should seek someone who had been in a rough situation and had solved a problem. "Get someone on the way up, not the way down," she said. Ruth Weintraub then asked the search committee, as she always did when involved with a search, if there were any "constraints" on whom they would consider. She was assured by the committee that they were open to women and to people from outside the state, although ideally the president would have a Southern connection. She became convinced that the search was not "fixed," and that the presidency of Winthrop College was not being treated as an item of political patronage.

THE SEARCH COMMITTEE

The more Ruth Weintraub saw of the Winthrop search committee, the more impressed she became with the individuals who comprised it. The committee had been appointed by board chairman Mary Sue McElveen, an alumna of the college who lived in Lake City, South Carolina. Mary

Sue McElveen was in her second term as a trustee, and was the only trustee ever to be elected as trustee both by the alumni association and the state legislature. The Winthrop College board of trustees has fifteen members (thirteen voting and two nonvoting). Seven of these trustees are elected by the state legislature for six-year terms; two trustees are elected by the alumni association for four-year terms; four trustees are ex officio voting members (the governor, the state superintendent of education, a member of the state senate education committee, and a member of the state house of representatives education committee). In addition, the board has two nonvoting members, a faculty representative and a student representative, who attend all meetings of the board, including executive sessions, with the right to discuss but not to vote on board matters. The faculty representative is the chair of the faculty conference; the student representative is the president of the student body.

Mary Sue McElveen's selection as chairman of the Winthrop board made history for the college, for although Winthrop had been a woman's college for most of its one hundred years, Mary Sue McElveen was the first woman ever to chair the college's board of trustees. Philip Lader's announcement of his planned departure from the Winthrop presidency came only three months after Mary Sue McElveen had taken over the board chairmanship. Although she wanted to be active in the search for Lader's successor, she did not wish to chair the search committee herself. Terry Peterson, the governor's assistant for education, who represented the governor on the Winthrop board of trustees, was her first choice. "Terry Peterson is the person who knows more about education in this state than anyone," she explained. Several other trustees praised Peterson's selection. "Terry is of such stature that everyone respects his judgment and industry. He is extremely knowledgeable." "He is highly respected by the board." Faculty members also respected Peterson, several people commented, because he had a doctoral degree.

In making her other appointments to the presidential search committee, Mary Sue McElveen strove both for balance and for small size. "I wanted to keep the committee small so that everyone could come to all meetings." Along with herself and Terry Peterson, she named four other members to the search committee: Elizabeth Singleton, a trustee and alumna from Myrtle Beach, South Carolina; Merritt Wilkerson, a trustee from Rock

197

Hill who served as secretary of the board of trustees; Gerald Perselay, a professor of business administration who was the faculty representative on the board of trustees; and Brett Smith, a junior at Winthrop majoring in business who was the student representative on the board.

WEINTRAUB AT WORK

In order to manage the search process more efficiently, Ruth Weintraub asked to have all the letters of application and nomination sent to the Academy for Educational Development offices in New York so that she could acknowledge them herself. Maeberta Bobb, assistant to the president of Winthrop, received the mail for the search at the college, made copies for each member of the search committee, and forwarded the files to Ruth Weintraub. Normally, clerical work of this sort would have been handled by a secretary; however, under the strict mandate of confidentiality, Dr. Bobb did the work herself. Upon receipt of nominations or applications, Ruth Weintraub immediately responded with a letter, noting that she would be in touch with the person later if further information was desired.

Many search committees, as in the dramatic instance of the search committee at Rice University, do not need search consultants to tell them that they should go beyond the prospects and applicants generated by advertisements. Search committee members may use their own connections in and out of academic life to generate nominations. Where some search consultants, however, can help is in the specificity of their inquiries. Hence when she had returned from her meeting with the Winthrop search committee, Weintraub sought to share with her staff her sense of what the Winthrop search committee was looking for.

Drawing on the experience of working with one another and also with a few small Southern colleges, Ruth Weintraub and her staff (Sarah White, assistant director, and Leah Greisman, senior consultant) began doing for Winthrop what among search consultants has become something of a routine in the hunt for leads. They explored whether, in previous searches they had assisted, there were any candidates not selected or who had withdrawn from candidacy who would be a good match for Winthrop. They also got in touch by telephone with presidents and other academic officers who had been selected in previous searches they had assisted, to see if these individuals might recommend anyone; and they made the rounds of other leaders in higher education, many of whom Ruth Weintraub in particular has come to know, to get their suggestions concerning prospects.

When the deadline for applications and nominations had arrived, Ruth Weintraub drew up the "master list" which included the names of all people who had applied, been nominated, or been suggested through AED's network calls.[3] Next to each name on the list was a letter (or letters) indicating the source of that name (applicant, nominee, or AED network). Approximately one-tenth of the nominations on the list came about as a result of the AED inquiries. People unfamiliar with searches might be surprised to learn how common it is for professors, many of them assistant professors with no administrative experience, to apply for a presidency they see advertised. Most of the applications to Winthrop were trial balloons of this sort, easy to dispose of, although a smattering of senior administrators had also sent in letters of application.[4]

As soon as nominations arrived, Ruth Weintraub, Sarah White, or Leah Greisman was on the telephone to the persons recommended, to tell them of the nomination and, where requisite, to tell them something about Winthrop College. Then they asked if the prospective candidates would provide the Academy for Educational Development with a curriculum vitae

[3] Although the deadline was included in the advertisement for the Winthrop presidency and was the official cut-off date for applications and nominations, Ruth Weintraub encouraged the search committee not to reject automatically any candidate whose name came in after this date (in the Winthrop search, none did) but to consider good candidates whenever their names were suggested.

This encouragement by Weintraub or by another consultant of similar outlook has been missing in a number of searches we have followed, where the search committee refuses to consider a latecomer candidate, even though not satisfied with the extant pool, on the ground that such consideration would be somehow unethical and violate an implicit contract with all parties. We do not refer here to one genus of latecomer candidate, namely, the acting president, who has firmly declared and had it declared on his or her behalf that he or she is not a candidate, only to take a liking to the position and directly or indirectly encourage a constituency of supporters. This can be a messy situation, and constituents as well as members of search committees are understandably uneasy when it occurs, even though the acting president may be an excellent fit for the permanent position.

[4] Most individuals who have made up their minds that they want to become a college or university president quickly learn that they will be helped by finding a sponsor, preferably someone widely known, who will at least nominate them, without necessarily doing more than that. We have talked with a few administrators who believe that there is something disingenuous about this circuitous route, and that if a person wants to be a president, he or she should not bow to the cliché that the office should seek (as would have been said in a pre-feminist era) the man. And there have been instances, even outside the sunshine, where applicants succeed; thus, at the community college level, and for many senior academic positions short of the presidency, applications are the routine and nominations the exception. Either way, chairmen of search committees like to report the total number when they announce the outcome of a search, as if the number was anything other than trivia.

and the names and telephone numbers of five people who could serve as references.[5] When some people were reluctant to comply, declaring that they were not interested in moving from their present positions, Ruth Weintraub attempted to persuade them to take a second look at the Winthrop post. If she thought someone was particularly well suited for the Winthrop presidency, she would persist until it was clear that the person was adamant in refusal. If naming five references was the stumbling block, she would waive that requirement in order to protect the confidentiality of the candidate. Here, her knowledge of higher education was helpful: occasionally she already had references for someone in her files; if she did not, she either knew enough about the person or knew people who knew the person well, so that she could assure the search committee that the candidate was worth keeping in the pool without conducting a reference check until much later in the process.

When the master list was complete, Ruth Weintraub sent a copy to Terry Peterson for his review. While its compilation was under way, she had been telephoning Terry Peterson or Mary Sue McElveen at least once a week and often more frequently. As Terry Peterson looked over the long list of potential candidates, Ruth Weintraub, Sarah White, and Leah Greisman examined every single one of the curricula vitae, cover letters, and letters of nomination that had arrived, and then met together to discuss the 308 candidates. Their aim was to reduce the full list to something on the order of twenty candidates whom the search committee could consider more closely. This order of magnitude they had found by experience to be a small enough number for a search committee to review in detail, yet a large enough group to provide diversity, a real choice, and the experience of vicarious review for committee members. The Academy consultants ended up with twenty-seven candidates who in their judgment deserved further attention.

[5] Quite commonly, those chairing search committees or the search committee secretary will write to people who have been nominated, sometimes with carbon copies to the nominator. Others may write the nominee, without letting the nominee know what in some cases may be multiple sources of nomination. Energetic search committee chairmen, like consultants, often begin not by letter but by telephone. We know a few senior administrators, presidents and others, who dislike this intrusiveness. (They refer primarily but not invariably only to those consultants who mainly work in corporate settings, who appear to know little about higher education.) However, there are many others more prepared to talk without previous notice to a search consultant rather than with someone chairing a search committee, since accepting discourse with the latter might seem to involve more readiness to make a commitment of interest.

The Winthrop search committee was not entirely comfortable leaving all of the screening and culling to the Academy for Educational Development consultants. Consequently, the three committee members who lived in Rock Hill—trustee Merritt Wilkerson, faculty member Gerald Perselay, and student Brett Smith—were delegated independently to look over the files and to pick out "stars." All three commented later that there was a sizable number of candidates one could eliminate without serious misgivings. Nevertheless, the screening was an exhausting task that it would have been irresponsible to take lightly. The files on candidates ranged from a one-sentence letter from an assistant professor—"Dear Search Committee, I hereby apply for the presidency of Winthrop College. Sincerely"—to a vast file sent in by a candidate who included with his letter of application a ream of press releases mentioning his name. It is common practice of search committees, in order to prevent contagion or prejudice by subsequent readers, to have each reader make selections without knowing the judgments of other readers, and this is how Merritt Wilkerson and Gerald Perselay proceeded. Likewise, Brett Smith read through the papers on his own, but then called Gerald Perselay to ask if he might talk with him about them. "I wanted to make sure my choices weren't way off the wall." As a student, Brett Smith had not had experience in reading through curricula vitae and recognized his own limitations in this area.

When the three members of the search committee received the list of twenty-seven names that the Academy consultants had identified, the Winthrop trio were surprised and pleased to see that, with only a few exceptions, they had settled on the same individuals who were on the Academy's master list. When all four lists were combined, there were only thirty-five names in total. Search committee members asked about the eight candidates they had identified who were not on Ruth Weintraub's list and were satisfied with her responses as to why she had not included them. None of them had been among anyone's top choices, in any case.

AN INTERIM PRESIDENT

Initially, the search committee had hoped the search would move so expeditiously that there would not be an interim period between the planned

201

departure of Philip Lader on December 31 and the appointment of a new president. In retrospect, they realized this judgment was unrealistic. Even a person chosen in the early fall probably would be unable to take over on the first of the year. As the search committee continued their work, they agreed to recommend to the board that an interim president be recruited, and they would take it on themselves to identify someone who would serve in this capacity.

When the question of an interim president was discussed at the search committee meeting, Ruth Weintraub recommended that the search committee agree that the person appointed interim president could not also be a candidate for the permanent position. Having experienced that situation first-hand in their last presidential search, when a college administrator who was named interim president was also a finalist for the presidency, the members of the Winthrop search committee were quick to accept this advice. Ruth Weintraub indicated that she would be available to help the search committee find an interim president. Indeed, the Academy for Educational Development has in other cases drawn individuals from a "stable" of retired presidents and other high academic officers who could be counted on to manage well in an interim presidency without eagerness for the position. However, search committee members did not need Ruth Weintraub's services, and proceeded rapidly on their own, considering a number of suggestions made by Winthrop trustees, faculty, and administrators. Speedily they identified Marcus Newberry as interim president. Newberry was vice-president for academic affairs at the Medical College of South Carolina in Columbia, where, several years earlier, he had served as interim president. This experience provided him with the perspective on how to behave during an interregnum, Terry Peterson commented. "There is a real science to being an 'acting.' Newberry kept things going but didn't go off in any wild directions. The College didn't lose momentum while it was searching." Mary Sue McElveen, chair of the board of trustees, signed a written agreement with the president of the Medical College of South Carolina to "borrow" Marcus Newberry for six months or less.

As the search proceeded, Winthrop faculty members knew that Ruth Weintraub had been engaged as search consultant, but they had not had a chance to meet her. When several of them expressed interest in talking

202

with her, the search committee decided that people on campus should have this opportunity, and asked Ruth Weintraub to visit the Winthrop campus. She came for the day on November 18, her schedule having been arranged in advance by the search committee and Maeberta Bobb.

NARROWING THE FIELD

As we will discuss in Chapter IX, some search consultants see their job virtually at an end when they have helped the search committee decide what to look for and have worked with the committee to broaden the pool of prospects. They may suggest questions for the search committee to ask candidates, but they leave the search committee in charge of pursuing prospects and checking their references.

This is not the way Ruth Weintraub and her cohorts work. In the Winthrop instance, AED staff members Sarah White and Leah Greisman checked references on the twenty-seven prospects they had identified—a task they considered the most important, most sensitive, and most interesting part of the search process. In the occasional cases where someone had not provided them with what they regarded as a balanced list of references—for example, when only administrators or only trustees had been named—they telephoned the candidate and asked for other people they could call. At this stage of the search, however, they stuck strictly to the references provided by the candidate so as not to disclose unintentionally someone's candidacy. Prior to the telephone interviews, Leah Greisman and Sarah White had settled on specific sorts of information they deemed most useful. When they called someone whose name had been given as a reference, they explained that the person they would be discussing was a "potential candidate" for the Winthrop presidency. They named the institution in order to allow the person on the other end of the line to answer questions concerning, for instance, ability to work well with the state legislature, or the need for strong academic leadership as well as managerial skills, in terms relevant to the prospective match or fit between Winthrop and the prospective candidate. The telephone inquiries to the five individuals named by each of the twenty-seven candidates were penetrating, asking for examples of academic leadership, for information about the candidate's ability as a speaker in large settings and small groups, and about previous relationships with a board of trustees, college administrators and staff, faculty, students, and alumni, as well as other aspects of the prospect's interpersonal relationships. They asked questions about the candidate's previous budgetary experience and the largest budget this person had administered, and for judgments on the candidate's standing in his or her academic field. Finally, they asked about a candidate's weaknesses, health and durability, and integrity. The two women sought to frame questions general enough to give the person on the other end of the line an opportunity to comment without constraint, yet specific enough to be sure that the information gathered for one candidate would be comparable to the information gathered for others. When a respondent was vague about something or seemed to avoid answering a question, Leah Greisman and Sarah White asked probing questions to see what they could uncover. The average telephone conversation took half an hour, with a range from fifteen minutes to a full hour.

The Academy consultants commented that they were repeatedly amazed by the candor they encountered. Not infrequently, Leah Greisman and Sarah White were given information over the telephone that was somewhat at variance with what had been stated in a letter of nomination or recommendation. In other words, the responses to their questions were rarely evasive and commonly judicious, with reservations and criticisms provided along with praise and endorsement. "Perhaps people know the Academy for Educational Development and so they know that their confidentiality will be maintained," the consultants explained. In addition, many individuals who were telephoned would not want to discredit themselves with the Academy for Educational Development, or perhaps even with the caller personally, by egregious misstatement, either on the side of malice or of euphoria about the candidate. Beyond all that, it is our impression that the telephone provides a kind of personalized impersonality that, when well managed by the inquirer, can in some cases be more evocative than a personal visit.

Leah Greisman and Sarah White took notes during their conversations with references, and then, as quickly as possible, turned these notes into sentences, trying to capture verbatim as much as they could, so they could present not only the information about the candidate but a sense of the sort of person who was providing it. While these inquiries were proceeding, a secretary was verifying the accuracy of the doctoral or other advanced degrees provided on the candidates' curriculum vitae. This is a precaution often omitted by people who assume that no one would be so foolhardy as to pose as a Ph.D. without possessing one, whereas there have been instances of brazen candidates misstating their institutions as well as their degrees, and assuming a presidency under false colors.

Both consultants reported that some of the references they called said that they assumed that the person under discussion could not be a serious candidate, because, of course, the Winthrop College search was "wired." Undoubtedly a "good ole boy" with the right political connections would be selected. When inquiries were made concerning a woman candidate, several respondents declared: "There is *no way* that the Winthrop board will appoint a woman." These statements were made so emphatically that Sarah White wondered if there could be some truth to them. Still, she trusted Ruth Weintraub's judgment, and Ruth Weintraub had assured her that the process was an open one.

THE PRESENTATION BOOK

Once all of the information on candidates was collected, typed, and summarized, the AED consultants met together to discuss each other's work and to prepare their "presentation book," the documentation on candidates that they provide search committees. The presentation book for the Winthrop search began with an introductory page explaining that the information it contained was "highly confidential" and warning that the contents of the book were not to be duplicated, and the book should not be left unguarded. Next, there was the master list of all candidates, and a list of the twenty-seven candidates identified as serious prospects. The remainder of the presentation book consisted of sections on each of these twenty-seven people. Each section began with a summary of the candidate's qualifications and an abbreviated curriculum vitae. This was followed by the AED consultant's summary of the candidate's education, experience, strengths, and weaknesses. Finally, there was an account of each telephone conversation the consultants had conducted concerning the candidate. A copy of the presentation book was sent to each member of the Winthrop search committee.

205

The members of the Winthrop search committee were impressed with the thoroughness of the materials they received. Several members noted that the presentation book provided them such vivid portraits of the candidates that they felt, after reading the materials in each candidate's section, that they "really knew" the person under discussion.

Two weeks later, in early December, Ruth Weintraub and Sarah White met with the search committee at the governor's mansion in Columbia to discuss the contents of the book. All members of the search committee had read the presentation book closely. "We slept with it for two weeks," Mary Sue McElveen commented. The purpose of the meeting was to select ten candidates for the committee to interview. Since Sarah White had done the bulk of the telephone inquiries, Ruth Weintraub asked her to come to the session so that she could respond to questions that committee members might have. Sarah White stated later that the members of the Winthrop search committee had scrutinized the materials carefully and were "shrewd in evaluating what they had read."

At the outset of the three-hour meeting, Ruth Weintraub suggested that, before any discussion of candidates, the committee should vote to see what consensus might already exist. She suggested that everyone should vote for all candidates they wanted to meet. After the secret ballot, they would then discuss not only the candidates about whom there was great convergence of opinion, but also any candidates who, although having minimal support from the full committee, had the strong backing of one or more committee members. By proceeding in this way, the prospect of premature foreclosure on a single candidate backed by the most influential or intimidating search committee members was minimized; on a secret ballot, people could support candidates they feared might be disapproved of by powerful committee members. As it turned out, the initial vote indicated that there was considerable consensus among the members of the committee. There was some argument about one candidate, but the small size of the committee and the encouraging tone of discourse created by Terry Peterson and Mary Sue McElveen gave everyone a chance to state an opinion and to argue with one another's views. When the search committee meeting ended, the committee had selected ten people to invite to interviews at a hotel near the Charlotte, North Carolina, airport.

INTERVIEWING THE SEMIFINALISTS

In her first mailing to prospective candidates, Ruth Weintraub had sent packets of information about Winthrop College. Now she wanted to give the ten candidates who would be interviewed further information, including Winthrop financial reports. "A candidate who would take a presidency without seeing financial information isn't someone you want," she stated bluntly. Back in New York, Ruth Weintraub made telephone calls to the ten candidates to invite them for interviews, and scheduled the ten sessions.

The interviews took place on January 2, 3, and 4, 1986, in Charlotte. Each interview lasted one and three-quarters hours; each debriefing session lasted fifteen minutes. Ruth Weintraub had insisted that the search committee have a debriefing session after each interview and a brief discussion at the close of each day. The search committee agreed afterward that these had been essential. Without them, candidates would have merged together in their minds. Ten candidates were the most they felt they could have evaluated successfully. One person commented that, in retrospect, eight might have been a more manageable number.

Prior to the interviews, Ruth Weintraub had provided the search committee with sample questions they might ask candidates and had asked the committee if they would mind her asking an occasional question if she felt an important area of discussion had not been covered. She explained that she preferred not to do much questioning and would only participate in the interviews if she felt something needed pursuing. During the debriefing sessions that followed each interview, Ruth Weintraub intentionally waited to offer her own judgments until all members of the search committee had given their reactions. They were pleased to find "no surprises." The members of the committee were "pretty much in sync" with each other and with Ruth Weintraub in their assessments of the candidates.

As the search committee proceeded in its work, and especially throughout the long weekend in Charlotte, a sense of community grew, with Ruth Weintraub very much a member of this newly-bonded group. Committee members not only developed considerable respect for each other, but also enjoyed their work immensely. By the end of the second day of interviewing there was a growing consensus about which candidates were the most suitable for Winthrop. At the end of the third day, after all the interviews were completed, Ruth Weintraub proposed that they vote by secret ballot in order to see what agreement existed. She suggested that the members of the search committee list all candidates in preferential order, with one indicating "first choice," two, "second choice," and so forth. Ruth Weintraub explained that, by proceeding in this way, she often found there was one candidate about whom there was near unanimity. Indeed, there was in the Winthrop search. Martha Kime Piper, the one woman candidate in the field of ten, headed the list. Serving at the time as chancellor of the University of Houston's Victoria campus, Martha Piper had previously been special assistant to the president for academic affairs in the University of Houston System and chair of the faculty senate at the University of Houston-University Park. Her Ph.D. was in science education from the University of Texas at Austin. Martha Piper's bachelor's degree was from Elmhurst College in Illinois.

"It was the biggest shock to me when I put her on my list of ten," one member of the search committee commented. "I didn't want a woman president. It took us a hundred years to get a woman as chairman of the board, and I didn't think we were ready for a woman president as well. But when I saw Martha Piper's credentials, I had to include her in the pool. If you'd not seen her name on her resumé and only seen her credentials, you'd rank her high. And when I met her, I had to vote for her." Another person commented that Martha Piper had come to the interview well prepared. "She dressed the right way; she called everyone by name; she had done her homework. She knew more about the college than many of us on the search committee and was able to ask cogent questions and discuss issues in a way that was impressive." "Martha Piper was a standout," a third member of the committee said simply. Martha Piper's mother and sister were Winthrop alumnae and her grandmother had worked at Winthrop as a dormitory mother, and Martha Piper brought her mother's yearbook to the interview. "That knocked the socks off the alumnae trustees," one person noted.

Two other names had enough support to be included as finalists. Both had ties to South Carolina. One was president of a small denominational college in the Midwest; the other, an academic vice-president of a state college in the Southeast. All members of the search committee had put

Martha Piper as one of their top choices, although they differed among themselves about the order of their ranking of the top three finalists.

VISITS TO THE CAMPUS

When the Winthrop College search committee had made its initial plans, no provision had been made for campus visits of finalists. Such visits had not occurred in previous presidential searches, and no one on the search committee had suggested them this time. When Ruth Weintraub came in, however, she immediately argued that campus visits were important. Unlike many search consultants who are skeptical of the idea of inviting candidates to the institution for open forums, Ruth Weintraub strongly believes in such sessions. She recommended that the Winthrop search committee invite the three finalists to the college to meet with the board of trustees, faculty, administrators, and students. To maintain confidentiality as long as possible, she proposed that the names of the three finalists not be released until the day of each one's visit. Most members of the search committee immediately took to the idea of campus visits. However, one member was apprehensive, afraid that people on campus might form superficial judgments concerning candidates, based on little information and limited exposure.

Up to this point in the search, confidentiality had been maintained. Although the state of South Carolina has open-meeting and open-record laws on its books, personnel matters, including presidential searches, can be handled in executive sessions. Numerous rumors had circulated on the Winthrop campus about various "candidacies," but almost all of these were erroneous, and none of the rumors made its way into the press. A reporter for the college newspaper, *The Johnsonian*, badgered the student member of the search committee, Brett Smith, to divulge the names of candidates. "Don't you want to be open with the students?" the reporter taunted. When Brett refused to give the names of candidates, he was castigated in the student newspaper for not "representing" students. Brett Smith responded that he certainly was representing them. He insisted, however, that his credibility to represent students lay in his ability to be effective as a search committee member, and that meant not betraying candidates by disclosing their identities.

Well before Ruth Weintraub called the three finalists to invite them to the interviews, she had been keeping in touch with them regularly about the progress of the search. (Ruth Weintraub explained to us that she has seen candidates become alienated and withdraw their names from consideration when they have been left in the dark as to the status of their candidacies.) In her conversations with them she tried to find out just how serious they were about the Winthrop position. If the position were offered them, were they likely to accept? She also obtained their permission to conduct additional, discreet background investigations beyond the five references they had already named.

Aware of her status as a woman, Martha Piper was interested in getting information from Ruth Weintraub. When Ruth Weintraub first called her to tell her that she had been nominated, Martha Piper agreed to allow her name to go forward on the condition that her candidacy remain confidential. As the chancellor of the Victoria campus of the University of Houston, Dr. Piper was concerned that her ability to lead her institution would be seriously compromised if she were seen as a potential "lame duck." Although she was interested in Winthrop in part because of her family connections to the college, she consented to be considered for the presidency only after reassurance from Ruth Weintraub concerning confidentiality. Martha Piper had never met Ruth Weintraub, but felt that she could speak candidly with her. When Ruth Weintraub called her about the campus interviews, Martha Piper asked her pointedly if the Winthrop search was "fixed." Was there a contender from inside the state who was the shoo-in for the presidency? Was there a real chance that they would hire a woman? Martha Piper told Ruth Weintraub that she had no interest in being an "affirmative action" candidate, someone who was included in the pool of finalists so that the search committee could say that they had considered a woman. Before taking the risk of possible disclosure of her candidacy on her home campus, she understandably sought assurance that the Winthrop search committee regarded her as a serious contender for the presidency.

The campus visits of the three finalists took place in late January and early February. The president of the small Midwestern denominational college was the first candidate to visit the Winthrop campus. Martha Piper visited next, followed by the candidate who was an academic vice-president. When the first finalist came to Winthrop, individuals on campus did not know his name or anything about him until they arrived at the room where the interview session was to take place, and were handed an abbreviated version of his resumé.[6] A number of faculty members and administrators criticized this procedure, complaining that, without any prior information about the person they were going to meet, they had no chance to think ahead of time about what questions to ask the candidate. Search committee members thought that this complaint was legitimate and decided to release the names and abbreviated resumés of the two remaining finalists, Piper, who had already arrived on campus, and the third candidate as well.

Maeberta Bobb, assistant to the president, planned schedules for each of the candidate's one and one-half day visits. The schedules for each of the three finalists were virtually the same.[7] All candidates and their spouses were given tours of Rock Hill and the president's house. Candidates met with the vice-presidents, deans, and executive staff, the president's faculty advisory council, department and division heads, the athletic director and alumni relations director, and with selected students. At the end of their first day on campus, the candidates and their spouses had dinner with, and then were interviewed by, the trustees, and these interview sessions were videotaped so that trustees who could not be present at all three sessions could see on video the candidate or candidates they had missed. On their second afternoon at Winthrop, the candidates met first with the entire search committee and then with Mary Sue McElveen and Terry Peterson to discuss their impressions of the college. At the end of their thirty-six hours at Winthrop, the finalists attended campus receptions open to all members of the Winthrop faculty and staff.

The schedules were deliberately full, Terry Peterson explained later, both in order to include everyone who wanted to meet the three finalists and to see how the three candidates performed in these various settings. The campus visits placed the finalists "in a very rigorous context, as bad as any of their bad days on the job. I was looking for them to fold, but

[6] The reason for this was never quite clear. This brief format had not been suggested by Ruth Weintraub, and may simply have been seen as an efficient way to proceed.

[7] The only difference was that the candidate and spouse with a school-age child were taken to see the local schools as part of their tour of the town of Rock Hill.

they all handled themselves very well," Peterson commented. But no one shone during this endurance test either, a fact that bothered many members of the faculty who had hoped to see impressive performances.

THE CAMPUS REACTIONS

At the conclusion of the campus visits, some Winthrop faculty members were seriously disappointed by the three choices for president. Philip Lader, the recently departed president, had been a charismatic figure. Although his selection to the Winthrop presidency had been controversial because Lader had no background in academe,[8] in his two years at the college he had won over many faculty members who now saw him as having given their college new visibility in the state. None of the three finalists was seen as having Lader's presence or his political connections. Additionally, none of the finalists had the distinguished academic pedigrees that many faculty had hoped their new president would possess.

Feeling that they had not been given sufficient information about the three finalists, several arts and sciences faculty members decided to conduct some inquiries of their own. They were able to locate people at Winthrop who knew people they could call at two of the finalists' home campuses, and, in Martha Piper's case, they discovered that someone on the Winthrop education faculty knew someone who had been in Martha Piper's doctoral program.

The search committee had anticipated that the names of the three finalists would spread across the campus, but they had hoped to avoid any publicity about their candidacies so that the candidates might escape having news stories get back to their own campuses. In a memorandum sent to all faculty and staff members, Mary Sue McElveen had explained, "We have been advised by Dr. Ruth Weintraub, the consultant, to maintain the strictest confidentiality possible during the interviews." As McElveen's memorandum explained matters, the visits would allow candidates to become more familiar with Winthrop College and would give faculty, staff, administrators, and students an opportunity to meet the candidates. Differentiating this search from its predecessors, she noted: "As you know,

---

[8] When Lader was appointed president, many faculty thought that he had gotten the job solely because of his friendship with powerful leaders in the state. Lader came to Winthrop from the chairmanship of Hilton Head Resort.

212

past presidential candidates have not been brought to the campus to meet faculty and staff; however, the trustees wanted you to have an opportunity to meet each one."

On January 30, the second day of the campus visits, a news story in the *Charlotte Observer* reported that three finalists would be visiting the Winthrop campus but did not give the names of these candidates. On February 3, a news story in the *Rock Hill Herald*, "Decision near on Winthrop chief," reported that two of the three finalists had visited the campus and the third finalist was scheduled to arrive that day. Again, no names were given; the news story stated that search chairman Terry Peterson "refused to name the three."

On Wednesday, February 5, however, the *Charlotte Observer* had the names. Potentially more damaging to these candidates than simply the mention of their candidacies, the news story also reported that there was strong criticism of these people at Winthrop. "Two faculty members who met all three candidates answered questions about the presidential search Tuesday on condition they not be identified. . . ." "One faculty member said he was not impressed by the three candidates . . . 'Many [faculty members] are not pleased with the selections. It seems there is some rather strong support for the woman [Piper], but I think [interim president] Marcus Newberry is far superior to all three,' he said. . . . Another faculty member said, 'The problem is that nobody seemed to create a lot of excitement. It's my belief that any of the three could perform the functions adequately, but we spent a lot of money on the consultant and I guess we expected more.' " The news story then proceeded to name all three finalists, briefly describe their backgrounds, and present quotations from their remarks to the faculty.

Although many members of the Winthrop faculty were unhappy about this airing of "family business," many agreed with the sentiments expressed in the news story. They were bothered by the fact that none of the finalists had produced what they considered serious scholarly work, and they were unimpressed with the institutions, all of them small and undistinguished, from which the finalists had come. "We had hoped to have someone with degrees from prestigious places, someone who had been the academic vice-president at Duke, Chapel Hill, or Virginia," one person remarked. In fact, one member of the search committee later commented that there had been attempts to interest such people in the Winthrop presidency but noted that these people already earned considerably more as second-in-command than the Winthrop presidency pays. (In retrospect, the search committee probably should have taken the opportunity to help faculty members appreciate the fact that someone who had been second-in-command in the academic stratosphere would be unlikely to come to Winthrop College, except as a last resort, and indeed, as a resort in the literal sense, whereas Winthrop's best chance lay in finding a person of promise who over time could improve Winthrop's quality other than through his or her reflected glory.)

The general sentiment of the Winthrop faculty who had met the finalists was that Martha Piper was the frontrunner. Some faculty members even thought that she stood so far ahead of the others that her selection must have been "wired." "She must have been included in there because someone wanted a woman," one professor commented. However, a number of arts and sciences faculty expressed serious reservations about her doctoral work having been in education, a field of study they did not consider fully "academic," and others wondered aloud whether, as a woman, Martha Piper would be able to work effectively with the largely and heartily male state legislature.

Complicating the picture, rumors began to circulate on campus that Winthrop's interim president, Marcus Newberry, might be persuaded to become a candidate for the permanent position. Although he had taken the presidency with the understanding that he would not be a candidate, his supporters on the faculty now said that Newberry and his wife had found Winthrop and Rock Hill very much to their liking and could probably be persuaded to stay on.

Several days after the *Charlotte Observer* news story about the Winthrop search, the weekly Winthrop student newspaper ran a front-page story on the three finalists. Since the *Charlotte Observer* had already revealed the candidates' names, the student reporters decided to pursue their own investigations into the backgrounds of these people. Winthrop student reporters telephoned the student editor of each finalist's campus newspaper and asked for student impressions of the candidate. These comments, mostly favorable, were reported in the *Johnsonian*.[9] The only men-

---

[9] The only negative remarks mentioned in the news story were that one candidate had been described by the student editor as "being weak on minority recruitment" and criticized for being "vague" about where the money from "a planned raise in student fees" was going.

tion in the *Johnsonian* of the Winthrop faculty's reaction to the three finalists was a statement that some faculty had told their colleague, search committee member Gerald Perselay, that they had reservations about Martha Piper's ability to lobby effectively for state funds. "However," the news story continued, "they didn't think it was something that couldn't be overcome."

The telephone calls to the student editors had alerted students at the finalists' home campuses to their candidacies at Winthrop. In Martha Piper's regularly scheduled meeting with student leaders of the University of Houston at Victoria, the student newspaper editor told her of the telephone call from Winthrop and asked her about her candidacy for that presidency. This call was the first that students had learned of Martha Piper's candidacy and they were upset to think that she might be leaving Victoria. Much to Martha Piper's surprise, without her asking, the students offered to keep the fact of her candidacy confidential, saying that they realized that this news could hurt their institution if released prematurely.[10]

The private college president who was a finalist for the Winthrop presidency was not so fortunate with his local press. His student newspaper, a daily, ran a special edition devoted to the candidacy of their president at Winthrop.[11] This intramural episode was not problematic, but coverage in the local newspaper was. The hometown paper had picked up the *Charlotte Observer* story from the AP wire service, naming the three finalists and citing the Winthrop faculty's dissatisfaction with them. Neither he nor other readers of the local paper had any way of knowing whether the faculty criticism was minimal or widespread, and the story was as embarrassing as it was unexpected.

MAKING THE FINAL DECISION

Although Ruth Weintraub had not come to campus for the interviews, she joined the members of the search committee for their deliberations in Columbia. The committee members talked briefly about the negative reac-

[10] This unusual personal and institutional considerateness on the part of students may reflect not only their respect and affection for Martha Piper but also the fact that the Victoria campus attracts large numbers of older undergraduates, including those in its student leadership.

[11] It is unusual to find a daily newspaper at a campus this size (six hundred students), and it must be hard for the student reporters to find subject matter to write about every day. This revelation of their president's candidacy must have seemed a real bonanza!

215

tions on campus to the three finalists, but the depth and extent of negative faculty reaction was not yet fully appreciated. Gerald Perselay, the sole faculty member on the search committee, was an atypical faculty member for Winthrop. He had become an academic late in life, after a career in the military; he was a New Yorker by birth; and he lived in Charlotte, North Carolina, rather than in Rock Hill. Indeed, it seems likely that the search committee, lacking a representative from the arts and sciences, may not have been sufficiently alert to the desire of many members of the faculty to distance themselves from Winthrop's traditional background in teacher education and applied arts, and thus may not fully have recognized the need to legitimate a candidate with a doctorate in education.

In their discussion of the finalists, members of the search committee wondered if they should try to find out more about these candidates by visiting their home campuses. Ruth Weintraub endorsed the idea in principle, but adamantly opposed their visiting the home campus of more than a single candidate. Such visits can put a candidate at serious risk, she explained. And while it is fair to ask the leading contender to assume this risk, since it is probable that this person will become the next president, it is thoughtless to expect others to put themselves in this vulnerable position. Should the campus interviews produce information that makes the leading contender less attractive, then it would be legitimate to seek to arrange a visit to the home campus of the contender next in line.[12]

After discussion of all three finalists, the search committee ranked Martha Kime Piper as the leading candidate for the Winthrop presidency. This choice was made despite concern on the part of a few members of the committee about having a woman as president. The college had only gone coeducational in 1974, and it still attracted twice as many women as men. Would a woman at its head—and the first woman to head a public institution in the Carolinas—perpetuate the very image they were trying to shake, that of Winthrop as a woman's college? In the end, the search committee concluded that the answer to this question was speculative, and that, in any case, even if a man were theoretically preferable, Piper was so

[12] Several candidates who have experienced these "home campus" visits have told us that, although they understand why a search committee would want to conduct these interviews, such sessions are unbelievably intrusive. Hence they should be done only when the search committee is reasonably confident that the candidate is their top choice and then should be carried out with as low a profile as can possibly be managed.

216

clearly the candidate best suited for Winthrop that the handicap of gender was not so formidable. The handicap of a doctorate in education was seen in the state as a whole as less serious (particularly in light of South Carolina's being in the midst of a popular educational reform effort), and it was outweighed in the minds of committee members by the fact that even those critical of the slate as a whole preferred Piper to the other candidates.

THE FINAL DAYS OF THE SEARCH

On February 16 and 17, two weeks after the end of the campus visits, three members of the Winthrop search committee—trustee chairman Mary Sue McElveen, search committee chairman Terry Peterson, and faculty member Gerald Perselay—traveled to Houston and its Victoria suburb to further their investigation of Martha Piper's background. On the Victoria campus, the members of the search committee interviewed members of the faculty, administrators, and students. They also arranged meetings with the president of the University of Houston system and selected others with whom they thought it useful to talk. These people included members of Piper's board of trustees, Piper's fellow chancellors in the University of Houston system, prominent business and community leaders, and the lieutenant governor of Texas. Altogether, the three members of the search committee talked with twenty-five people. They asked these individuals to evaluate Martha Piper in all of the areas that the search committee had established as important criteria for a new president, and they brought up questions dealing directly with the Winthrop faculty's expressed concerns about Martha Piper.

Almost everywhere they turned, the three search committee members heard high praise of Martha Piper. They were told that she did well in her dealings with the state legislature, and that the University of Houston system office delegated "much budget authority" to her. All the business and community leaders consulted said she was "outstanding" in her relationships with them. "They said she moved in all circles easily, be it a billionaire or millionaire or the average man or woman in the community." A former board member of the University of Houston stated that, "While you may find some candidates who are good, you will find none better than Martha Piper." The Winthrop search committee members re-

217

turned to South Carolina, as one of them put it, "totally persuaded by Martha Piper's qualifications," and convinced that they had hit upon the right person for the Winthrop presidency.

Meanwhile, Winthrop faculty members were sharing with one another their coolness at best, and dismay at worst, at the prospect of any of the three finalists becoming their next president. As they talked with each other and realized how many faculty members were uneasy about this, their sense of grievance grew. Fearful that their concerns about "the quality of the pool of finalists" would not be taken seriously and aware that a board of trustees meeting was scheduled for the afternoon of February 25, several faculty in the history department drafted a petition which they carried from office to office to ask for signatures. The petition stated,

> Over the past few weeks, we, the undersigned, have followed the search for a new president of Winthrop with interest and concern. Our feeling is that none of the three presidential aspirants who visited campus demonstrate[s] the vibrancy or has the qualifications we would like to see in the head of the institution. Indeed, there is a widespread feeling of concern with the possibility that one of these individuals might become president.

> Given these concerns and the excellent job that Dr. Newberry is doing as interim president, we are asking that you consider extending the search for a new leader for Winthrop. We all appreciate your allowing faculty to be a part of the search process, and certainly all of us share a common goal—the best possible president for Winthrop College.

The petition was circulated in a day and a half, on February 24 and 25, and then was given to Gerald Perselay to carry to the board of trustees meeting on the afternoon of February 25. Seventy members of the Winthrop faculty signed the statement; one professor wrote and signed his own somewhat amended version. All but four of the signers were members of the College of Arts and Sciences and School of Business faculties. Only two signers were in the School of Education. The organizers of the petition declared that, given the time limitation, the number of signatures—approximately one-fourth of the Winthrop faculty, with two-thirds of those signing full or associate professors—was an amazing level of response. "This was by far the strongest action ever taken by the faculty since I've been here, some sixteen years," one professor commented.

Looking over the petition in conducting research for this case, we were struck by the virtual absence of faculty from the School of Education. When we asked why this was the case, we received diverse answers. One member of the School of Education interpreted the petition as "sexist" and "anti-Education" in origin. Another person speculated that faculty members in the School of Education had not been approached to sign the petition because arts and sciences faculty sponsors assumed, for the most part correctly, that faculty in the School of Education were enthusiastic about the prospect of having one of their own as president. In fact, several members of the Education faculty said they had never heard about the petition until well after it was circulated. And one of the organizers of the petition drive explained that he and his colleagues in Arts and Sciences actually did not know many people in the School of Education. Even in a community of 36,000 in Rock Hill, and a college of 5,000 students, such chasms between the School of Education and the College of Arts and Sciences and School of Business are not surprising.

When search committee members met on the afternoon of February 25, Gerald Perselay presented to them the faculty petition he had been asked to deliver. The committee members also received the report from Terry Peterson, Mary Sue McElveen, and Perselay of their findings from their visit to Texas. First, the search committee considered the question of re-opening the search. They quickly dismissed the idea. Convinced that they had a good pool of candidates, they saw no reason to start the process all over again. They found additional encouragement in the fact that when faculty members and deans had been asked to rank the three finalists, they had come up with the same ranking as the search committee. (Gerald Perselay and Mary Sue McElveen had met with the deans after the candidates had visited the campus.) In other words, although faculty members wanted to see more candidates, all agreed that, of the three candidates, Martha Piper was the best choice. Had the campus ranked the finalists altogether differently, putting Martha Piper last of the three, a member of the search committee suggested to us afterward, perhaps the search committee might have become apprehensive about their judgments. The search committee members concluded, also, that the faculty signing the petition had insufficient information on which to base their judgments, because what had been found out as a result of the trip to Houston and Victoria was material not available to them. Altogether, everything the committee had learned about the qualifications and talents of Martha Piper convinced them that she "fit Winthrop. Other candidates might have fit Winthrop also, but she fit Winthrop the best." The good news from Houston overcame the bad news from the campus.

When the full board met that afternoon, trustees received the search committee's recommendation of Martha Piper and the rank order of three finalists, including the votes of each voting member of the search committee. The whole board considered the petition from the faculty and reviewed the finalists' qualifications. All trustees had either been present at the interviews of these finalists or had seen videotapes of these sessions. Then, as one search committee member reported, they "batted it back and forth. Everyone had something to say. It was a good meeting." At its conclusion, the board, perhaps with a certain pride in breaking precedent, named the first woman president of Winthrop, and the first woman president in the state of South Carolina and of a public institution in both of the Carolinas.

Knowing that this selection would be a serious disappointment to some faculty members, Gerald Perselay asked Terry Peterson and Mary Sue McElveen to come with him to a faculty meeting the next day (February 26) to announce the selection and respond to questions. The three search committee members decided that they would distribute at this meeting the report that Terry Peterson had prepared for the trustees of the "Visit to Dr. Piper's Last Two Work Sites and Follow-up Telephone Interviews." The report had two columns. The first column listed the "Desired Characteristics for New President;" the second column was entitled "Sample of Evidence That Demonstrates Candidate Has Characteristics." Although no names were given, the report included direct quotations and indicated their source (local businessman, state legislator, fellow chancellor in the system, etc.). For each characteristic listed, the seven-page report presented information that showed that Martha Piper excelled in that area. "This was probably more than we would normally have shared, but we decided to go public with that. Before, they had been operating on rumor and hearsay. This had created a whole dynamic by itself because there was no information countering it."

Faculty members listened politely as Gerald Perselay, Terry Peterson, and Mary Sue McElveen made their presentations. Afterward, one person asked angrily, "What happened to our petition?" Faculty members were upset by the selection, and convinced that it had been "a fait accompli." There was a strong sense that faculty views had not been taken seriously. And there was much irritation with Gerald Perselay, who they felt should "have represented us on the search committee," and had "let us down." There was anger above all at the search consultant, "because we spent good money on her and she turned up no one of quality."

Other faculty members, however, had much milder reactions. Some faculty, especially those in the School of Education, were delighted to have an "educator" at their helm. Others thought that they should "reserve judgment" on the actual selection and wait to see how Dr. Piper performed as their president.

A short while after the meeting, two members of the faculty individually approached Mary Sue McElveen and said that, if they had to do it over again, they would not sign the petition. "I did it without really thinking," one explained. A third person commented, in the course of our research, that he had felt "pressured" into signing the petition and later had regretted having done so. The organizers of the petition did not feel, however, that they had pressured anyone, noting that they approached senior faculty rather than junior faculty so that there would be no question even of subtle pressure.

REFLECTIONS ON THE SEARCH PROCESS

When asked for their criticisms of the search process several months after its conclusion, many members of the Winthrop faculty spoke of their displeasure at not having been given sufficient information about the three finalists prior to their visit to the college. One person suggested that faculty members might have been more impressed with the candidates had there been more information about the procedures by which the search committee had arrived at its selections, as well as more extensive curricula vitae of each of the finalists. Other faculty members with whom we spoke

221

observed that this search had been a significant improvement over previous presidential searches, both because the elected representative of the faculty had been a member of the search committee and because the campus visits had allowed all interested faculty to meet the finalists. Faculty members recalled how angry many of them had been when faculty had not been consulted in the selection of Philip Lader, and how opposed they had been to his selection. Yet two years later, these same faculty members praised Lader for his contributions to the college—the implication being that Martha Piper also might turn out better than anticipated.[13]

When reflecting on the search process, members of the search committee spoke enthusiastically about what they had accomplished, and expressed appreciation for the contributions of the individuals who had served with them on this committee. Despite the criticism by some faculty, all members of the search committee stated that they were very pleased with the pool of candidates from which they made their selections, and unequivocally delighted by the choice of Martha Piper. Regarding the decision to bring candidates to the college, however, there were differences of opinion on the wisdom of having had these campus visits. Most search committee members concluded that they would again recommend such visits. But at least one person is persuaded that the visits led to polarization of the campus, reflected in the faculty petition and the expressed bitterness at the time the choice was announced.

There were no disagreements, however, on the wisdom of using a search consultant. All members of the search committee thought that Ruth Weintraub had provided valuable assistance. "I have nothing but the highest praise for her," one commented. Another responded: "She was excellent throughout." When asked specifically how she had been helpful, members of the search committee said that she had known how to go about organizing the search and her suggestions had saved them time and,

[13] In a special insert to the alumni magazine dated July 8, 1985, trustees, faculty members, staff, and students expressed high praise for Lader. Board chairman Mary Sue McElveen stated: "Phil has done more for Winthrop in the time he has been here than any of us alumni or trustees could have believed possible." Despite the shortness of Lader's stay (and perhaps in some respects because of its shortness), there was no resentment at his departure to run for governor; on the contrary, some expressed hope that a governor who had been at Winthrop would be a boost for the college. If one compares this happy pride in a departing president with the bitter reactions to the departure of the president of "Southern State University," referred to in Chapter IV, we can see that it makes a difference that the president is a state resident and is not leaving the state for a presumably "better" one; in fact, Lader and his popular wife, Linda Lader, reside in Hilton Head.

222

quite possibly, mistakes. Her contacts in higher education had allowed them to reach much farther than they could have by themselves. Ruth Weintraub had convinced some people to apply who ordinarily would not have, turning "nominations" into "applications," including probably two of the three finalists. At the stage of investigating the backgrounds of the candidates, the consultant was able to check references more completely and more discreetly than the search committee could have and with a much faster turn-around, they declared. "She screened the files along with us and had a deep interest in us as an institution. She didn't want to match up two people who wouldn't be happy in wedlock."

POSTSCRIPT

On April 24, 1988, people at Winthrop College and many in the surrounding community were stunned to learn from local and state television and radio and then from an announcement circulated on campus that President Martha Kime Piper had died in a Charlotte, North Carolina, hospital of colon cancer complicated by the flu. She was only fifty-six years old. Although she had been sick off and on during that academic year, no member of the board, no one in the administration or staff, and no faculty member had been aware of the nature or severity of her illness. Martha Piper had apparently first learned of the cancer when she had exploratory surgery, followed by a colostomy, in June 1987, at the end of her first year at Winthrop.

Reactions on the campus ranged from shock and disbelief—President Piper had presided over a college administrative staff meeting only two weeks before her death and had seemed to several people there "to have vim, vigor, to be ready to go"—to sadness at the loss of someone so young and talented, to hurt, anger, and resentment at her having been so sick and so secretive about it. "She should have let people know of her struggle," one trustee stated. In her defense, a senior administrator noted that Martha Piper "was a very private person. She wanted to keep working, and nobody would have done anything if they had known she was dying. All college business would have come to a halt." In particular, he commented, Martha Piper had wanted to oversee the implementation of the Five Year Plan which she had initiated during her first year at the college.

The Winthrop Board of Trustees appointed vice-president Michael Smith as acting president and asked trustee Palmer Freeman, an attorney in Columbia, South Carolina, former state legislator, and newcomer to the Winthrop board, to chair a search committee to find a successor to Martha Piper. As had been the case two years earlier, the search committee was small and included one faculty member and one student. And again the search committee employed the services of the Academy for Educational Development, although in a more limited capacity than previously. Their consultant at AED was Richard Lancaster, who had come there in 1988 as vice-president and director of the executive search service when Ruth Weintraub had resigned her full-time post at the Academy and been named a Distinguished Fellow. Two finalists were brought to the campus for meetings with campus constituents and the board, and shortly thereafter, the trustees announced the appointment of Anthony DiGiorgio, academic vice-president at Trenton State College, as Winthrop's next president.

CHAPTER IX

The Use of Consultants

HAD THE WINTHROP COLLEGE search been conducted half a dozen years earlier, the idea of using a search consultant would hardly have occurred to anyone. The chair of the search committee might have consulted informally with retired presidents or other academic eminences within the college's geographic orbit. But it is highly unlikely that anyone on the search committee or board would have suggested turning to a national search firm or would have pursued the necessary funding to make this possible. Today, by contrast, the use of consultants in presidential searches is common. In recent years, institutions as different as Dartmouth, Juniata College, Louisiana State University, the New School for Social Research, George Washington University, the Pennsylvania College of Art, Hartford College for Women, St. Andrew's Presbyterian College, and Vassar have turned to consultants for assistance with their searches for presidents.

Higher education is a relative latecomer in the use of consultants in operations as well as in recruitment. The "Big Six" accounting firms often serve their clients as de facto consultants, as do many law firms, reassuring the executives who are their clients that they can do what they already want to do and legitimating the decision down the ranks. The leading business schools turn out few people today who intend to work their way up in a business, learning it from the shop floor up and the comptroller's office down; instead, they graduate specialists in finance or marketing or other fields, many of whom then enter consulting firms, becoming, in effect, generalists in the art of giving advice. In both the profit and nonprofit segments of American life, board members recognize the demands placed upon their institutions for accountability, and they and the administrators who report to them routinely resort to consultants in the hope of improving institutional performance and, in some measure, as a means of diluting their personal responsibility. In medicine, to give one example, doctors and patients alike are aware that no one doctor can know everything even in his or her specialty. Even without the swarm of malpractice lawyers in the offing, patient and doctor have many reasons to ask for a second opinion. Although it is omnipresent, and perhaps because it is, consulting is a chancy career in which one constantly stakes one's brains and reputation on the quick understanding of new settings.

Institutions of higher education, from small, precarious colleges to large universities, increasingly have resorted to consultants for specialized activities: for enrollment planning and admissions marketing; for data processing and information control; for planning a capital campaign and alumni giving programs; for improving the institution's logo and catalogue and other printed materials; for assessing the way the portfolio has been handled, and so on. Consultants are also frequently called in for such sensitive issues as the evaluation of a president. Indeed, James L. Fisher, author of the provocative *Power of the Presidency*, has contended that presidents, with the advice and consent of their boards of trustees, should have the right to choose their own consultants in an evaluation.[1]

Consultants are now being used in higher education for searches in all areas and levels of administration. Search consultants are believed to be helpful in providing a realistic sense of who is "out there" to be discovered, scrutinized, courted and persuaded. In the humbler institutions, private and public, many faculty members regard the presidency or even the academic deanship as an attractive prize, and assume that candidates for these posts are easy to find. In the more research-oriented universities, however, many professors soon realize that it is often more satisfying and even more lucrative to be a professor than to take on the responsibilities and headaches of administration. Major medical schools have been desperately looking for deans—individuals willing to spend their own energies finding room to maneuver among the barons of surgery or biogenetics, and the implacabilities of cost containment in the university-related hospitals. Law deans are easier to come by, but their turnover is fairly

---

[1] James L. Fisher, "Presidential Assessment: A Better Way," *AGB Reports*, Vol. 28, no. 5 (September–October 1986), pp. 16–21; and *Power of the Presidency* (New York: American Council on Education/Macmillan, 1984).

rapid. Engineering schools have great difficulty finding faculty at every level, and administrators in particular.

In the instance of Winthrop College, the chairman of the search committee, Terry Peterson, was well aware of how much time a well-run search requires and realized that a search consultant could help him cope with the simultaneous pressures of his job and the search. As assistant to the governor, he already had a full schedule when he agreed to chair the Winthrop search committee. An added advantage was that a consultant could also help to make it clear that the choice for Winthrop would not be a by-product of the political and patronage forces within South Carolina, but would in truth be a national hunt for "the best person." The use of a consultant would give the "Good Housekeeping Seal of Approval" to a process about which people are prone to cynicism.

ALL 'SHAPES AND SIZES' OF CONSULTANTS

Once having decided to use the services of a consultant, Terry Peterson had to determine who to employ. His options were many. A wide array of firms and individuals compete today for higher education clients. These include not-for-profit search firms, corporate firms with sidelines in not-for-profit work, smaller specialty firms, and individuals who regularly or occasionally take on search consulting in addition to their own administrative or faculty responsibilities.

In addition to the Academy for Educational Development, the best-known not-for-profit firms probably are the Presidential Search Consultation Service (PSCS), the Academic Search Consultation Service (ASCS), and the search service of the Association of Community College Trustees. PSCS operates under the auspices of the Association of Governing Boards of Colleges and Universities. ASCS, also based in Washington, D.C., was founded in 1988 by consultants formerly at PSCS. The Association of Community College Trustees maintains a search service for its member institutions.

In recent years, many of the leading corporate executive recruiting firms have developed a clientele among academic and other not-for-profit enterprises. Among those firms most active in higher education are Heidrick & Struggles; Korn/Ferry International, Inc.; Peat, Marwick &

Mitchell; Russell Reynolds; Spencer Stuart & Associates; and Ward Howell International, Inc. Other firms, such as Gould & McCoy, occasionally take on college and university presidential searches in addition to their corporate business. Additionally, a number of smaller firms which have spun off from these larger firms are competing for higher education searches. Among these are Auerbach Associates in Belmont, Massachusetts; the Educational Management Network in Nantucket; Ira Krinsky and Associates in Los Angeles; Leadership Development Associates in Washington, D.C.; Myer Enterprises, Inc., in Manchester, Massachusetts; and Perez-Arton Consultants in New York. Also available to consult on a search are many individuals—professors of higher education, present and former college administrators and presidents—who have experience managing one or more presidential searches.[2]

The preceding list of consultants is incomplete. As the demand for consultants grows, the supply increases. Although we have met representatives of most of the major firms now engaged in helping presidential search committees, there are many firms and individuals with whose work we are less familiar. As the cohort of search consultants increases, some consultants have become anxious concerning the new entries to the field, fearing an inexperienced competitor may behave in an unprofessional manner and give the entire industry a bad reputation. Such fears were especially acute as a result of the wide national publicity given the 1984 search at the University of New Mexico, where the consultant, PA Executive Search, produced a nominee, later elected president, whose previous ties to the consultant had not been disclosed. Indeed, when a suspicious press and skeptical faculty first suggested that there were such ties, they were denied; thus the New Mexico search was tainted not only by conflict of interest, but by the attempt at a cover-up. However, fears that this episode would lead to a general derogation of "headhunters" seem to have been unwarranted.

At first glance, the eagerness of major corporate search consultants to move into higher education appears puzzling. Typically, these firms base their consultation fees upon a percentage, usually one-third, of

---

[2] For further discussion of search firms, see Scott Heller's article, "A Headhunter Helps Dartmouth—And Many Others—To Find a New President," *Chronicle of Higher Education*, Vol. 33, no. 32 (April 22, 1987), pp. 1, 14–17.

the first-year cash compensation of the person recruited, plus the out-of-pocket expenses accrued in the course of the search. By corporate standards, the salary of the college or university president is low. Moreover, in comparison to most corporate searches, higher education searches require a great deal of time. Consultants in large firms which have a sideline in not-for-profit searches have told us about the complexity of higher education searches, where each search is different from the previous one. There are many players whose judgments must be taken into account, candidates for the presidency are increasingly harder to find, and salary is rarely a deciding factor in making a move. Since these large corporate firms with large overheads spend more time and earn less money on higher education accounts, we wondered why they bothered with higher education searches at all. Paradoxically, when we talked with some of the executive recruiters who have moved into the presidential search area, we discovered that it is their very intricacy that makes these searches inviting. Bill Bowen, Kennedy Langstaff, Stephen Garrison, and others have found that in higher education there is rarely a dull moment, although there are quite a few anxious ones. They have told us that they find academic searches stimulating because they enjoy visiting a campus, meeting with the members of the search committee, and coping with the many "publics" that higher education serves. Other consultants have become impatient with faculty members and campus "due process." However, while intrinsic interest might lead an ocasional consultant to do a presidential search, it is not sufficient to justify the increasing attention some of the major firms have given to this arena. For them, these searches have come to provide significant institutional advertising, prestige, and contacts. Many of the trustees serving on college or university boards also serve on corporate boards, and they may remember the consultants used in the higher education search when they are thinking about a consultant for a corporate search.

CHOOSING A CONSULTANT

The decision to employ a search consultant is ordinarily made by a board of trustees, the chairman of a search committee, or an entire search committee at the outset of the search process. (The Winthrop College search committee was unusual in having already begun search activities prior to considering the use of a consultant.) Corporate and other board members are likely to have had experience with consultants in their own professions or companies, where they have employed "headhunters" to identify new personnel. When board chairmen or search committee chairmen talk with colleagues on other campuses who have recently completed a search, they will frequently learn how helpful a particular consultant was. Or they might find out who was not helpful, or even occasionally encounter someone who has developed an allergy to all consultants, based on experience with one. The idea of a consultant can appeal to a trustee who has participated in an earlier search at the college or university and who recalls the unexpectedly protracted dilemmas and disappointments. The opposite can happen too, when the board of trustees concludes that the way they did it last time worked perfectly well, and they pull out the same advertisement used the last time to call for nominations and applications.

In deciding which consultant to employ, increasing numbers of colleges and universities use "shoot-outs" to compare competing firms and individuals. A shoot-out, in the lingo of recruiters, is an occasion at which a search committee or board of trustees invites several consultants to make competitive bids; these presentations resemble those made by advertising agencies competing for a corporate client. Often in one afternoon, representatives from the firms under consideration appear before the board or the search committee and discuss the services they would be willing to render. Typically, they also will provide written materials describing their firm and the names of the institutions they have previously assisted. In the case of the search at Duke, Arie Lewin, president of the faculty senate, working on behalf of the board of trustees, visited the New York offices of several firms which had expressed interest in working with Duke to talk with the person who would actually be engaged in the search. Those he recommended were then invited to come to Durham for a "shoot-out" before the full search committee, whose members then chose the consulting firm.

In February 1985, Joseph Palamountain, who had been president of Skidmore College for twenty-one years, announced his intention to resign effective June 30, 1987. George Colton, chairman of the board, asked trustee Judith Pick Eissner, Skidmore '64, to chair the search committee.

A former administrative social worker, Judith Eissner could pull free of other obligations to devote herself to the effort. Colton and Eissner recognized that, some time in the months ahead, Colton would retire as chairman of the board and Eissner would succeed him. Believing that it was best not to have the chair of the board also serve as chair of the search, they realized that this changing of the guard would imply also a change in the leadership of the search committee. Such a situation would seem to invite the use of a consultant to provide continuity. Indeed, in the fall of 1986, Judith Eissner became chairman of the board, and trustee James McCabe, who was a member of the search committee, was appointed as its head.

Rather than rush to appoint a president during the spring of 1985, as some had proposed, Mrs. Eissner concluded that it was better to use some of the long lead-time for careful preparation. First, she sought advice on how to conduct a search and "on ways of working with a consultant" from trustees who had headed search committees at other institutions, including Smith, Vassar, Oberlin, Colby, and Cornell.[3] As a result of these conversations, she became convinced that the services of a consultant would be helpful for her and for the other members of the search committee, not as a substitute for their own involvment in the search but as a means of intensifying that involvement. In these conversations, she obtained the names of numerous consultants, whom she then contacted to request their brochures and references. The consultants' materials included information about prior searches they had conducted in higher education, which allowed Eissner to make inquiries concerning their previous work. On screening these, the Skidmore search committee asked an unusually large number of firms, eight altogether, to make presentations at a "shoot-out," and, based on their impressions of these presentations, they selected three firms they wanted to see again. Finally, they decided to talk a third time with the one consultant whom they liked best. Altogether, they took almost as much time selecting their consultants as some searches spend selecting their president! But the time spent with consultants was not wasted. Their discussions at this early stage of the search process melded them into a working group, and in the course of choosing a consultant

[3] Judith Eissner, draft: "Reflections on the Skidmore Presidential Search," 1987.

committee members gained a sense of each other as persons, rather than as representatives of any one constituency. One could almost say that choosing a consultant, and arranging how the consultant would contribute to the process, was for them a rehearsal for meeting and evaluating presidential candidates.

Raymond Klemmer, a West Point graduate with an M.A. from Columbia, who had been an assistant professor of international relations at West Point, impressed the Skidmore committee with his energy and willingness to make the effort to understand the special nature of Skidmore College and help them create a truly probing search. When the leading consultants were invited back for a second round, he was the quite unanticipated choice. He had made it clear at the outset that he had never done a liberal arts presidential search. However, as a partner in Webb, Johnson & Klemmer, he had done fifty-six diverse presidential searches, ten of them working with search committees of nonprofit organizations. These include searches for the presidencies of Mount Sinai Medical Center (which includes a medical school) and of Memorial Sloan-Kettering Cancer Center (which has graduate academic programs).

The self-confidence the Skidmore College search committee found in choosing an unorthodox consultant seems to have spilled over into the way the Skidmore search proceeded. Once chosen, Klemmer went with search committee member Penny Kaniclides to talk with all Skidmore administrators. Then, Klemmer and Kaniclides were joined by the full search committee in interviewing faculty members heading departments and serving on several key faculty committees. In this way, they sought to find the qualities most desired in a new president. At the same time, they strove to impress on everyone the importance of maintaining confidentiality throughout the search. These interviews also allowed Klemmer to imbibe the college's commitment to its new liberal studies program and other aspects of its inner life, thus making him a more effective advocate for the college when he courted candidates. The sense of mutuality and sang-froid the committee developed helped it make the decision to bring only a single finalist to campus and to choose as Skidmore's next president David Porter, William H. Laird Professor of Liberal Arts at Carleton College. Porter, a classicist, had been chosen as Carleton's pro tem president while a search committee sought a successor to Robert Edwards. Porter had served only a few months when he became a finalist, and shortly *the* finalist, at Skidmore.[4]

Winthrop College chairman Terry Peterson went about selecting a consultant by asking people he knew for the names of the large executive recruiting firms and the smaller not-for-profit agencies. As we noted in the previous chapter, he found no consensus about the commercial firms, and thus invited only two consultants from not-for-profit firms to meet with the search committee. The committee then decided on Ruth Weintraub.

Another method of comparison shopping among consultants is to ask firms to prepare written responses to questions developed by the search committee. Nancy Archer-Martin, the consultant selected by the New School for Social Research presidential search committee, noted that the questions she was asked to address were particularly thought-provoking and required her to spell out in detail her mode of operation.[5] Based on the responses the New School committee received, they were able to narrow the list of possible consultants to a few individuals to interview.

Search committees have sometimes discovered to their dismay that the person who makes the presentation at the shoot-out will not actually do the work during the search. The firm will either give the assignment to another member of the firm or will delegate major aspects of the search to their research staff. Since the person chairing the search committee must work with the consultant on terms of candid mutuality, it is crucial to choose the individual who will act as consultant, as well as the firm. In the case of the Skidmore search, Ray Klemmer had brought with him to the interviews a young woman he expected to have work with him. Later, he

[4] Several months after the Skidmore search concluded, the search committee planned a dinner, both to get together with committee members who had become good friends over the course of the search, and to honor Raymond Klemmer who had assisted the search committee, in the words of Judith Eissner, "well beyond his specific remuneration." At the dinner, the committee members presented Klemmer with a framed map of the campus and a limited-edition china plate engraved with the Skidmore College seal.

[5] At the time of the search, the New School's once famed graduate faculty was in deep trouble, its accreditation threatened, its morale low, its earlier periods of eminence an implicit reproach. A search which involved many committees—students and various faculty groups as well as trustees—nevertheless proceeded with determination while maintaining confidentiality. Jonathan Fanton was lured away from his position as deputy to president Hanna Gray at the University of Chicago with the promise on the part of trustees that they themselves would contribute, and would also raise substantial amounts to make possible the revitalization of the graduate faculty. See Deirdre Carmody, "New School Graduate Unit Rebounds," *New York Times*, July 15, 1987, p. B3.

233

was told that if he were to do the search, he would have to do it entirely on his own, and he agreed.

DIFFERING POLICIES AND PROCEDURES

There is enormous variation among consultants in the timing and scope of their involvement, reflecting both the desires of the client and the operating procedures of the particular consultant. At one end of the spectrum, the consultant may serve as the confidential adviser to the chairman of the search committee without the knowledge of the rest of the committee. In one such instance, the consultant did not meet with the committee or handle directly any of the business of the search. Rather, he talked by telephone with the board chairman, who was also chairing the search committee, providing counsel as needed. This arrangement proved greatly reassuring to the chairman, who not only was the person most responsible for the search, but, as board chairman, would be destined to work closely with the person chosen.

Sometimes, as in the case of Rice University, a consultant or adviser is brought in at the beginning of a search to suggest how to structure the process, and then the search proceeds with no or only minimal further assistance. Joseph Kauffman, a former president and now an occasional consultant, was once asked to come to an all-day meeting with a board of trustees when the president was planning to announce his retirement, and the trustees wanted help in coping with the impending search. Kauffman outlined appropriate steps and identified questions concerning the institution and concerning the paths the trustees might pursue to increase their chances of a successful selection.

Occasionally, as in the "Abbott College" search, a search committee may employ a search consultant at the end of the search process to conduct background investigations on the finalists or finalist or to conduct a probing "psychological" interview with the leading candidate. Still other consultants regard themselves, in effect, as "staff" to the search committee, serving virtually in the capacity of an executive secretary or director of the search process.

The Academic Search Consultation Service sees its role primarily as guiding a process, while insisting that the search committee take respon-

234

sibility for every step along the way. At Evergreen State College, Ronald Stead came in as consultant to help inaugurate a new search after the failure of a search where confidentiality had been disdained. But Stead left the screening of the pool of candidates and the interviews with finalists entirely in institutional hands, and never met directly with Joseph Olander, who was chosen as president.[6]

Still other consultants manage the process tightly. They do a great amount of the searching themselves, depending primarily on their own resources rather than on the networks of people at the institution; they interview candidates privately prior to recommending anyone to the search committee; they take charge of most, if not all, of the checking of references.

Some consultants are quite willing to have members of the search committee review all materials sent in by and about candidates. In the "presentation book" which the Academy for Educational Development provided the Winthrop search committee, the consultants named all of the references whom they had called.[7] Other consultants, protective of the confidentiality of their sources, will not give out this information. They may distinguish between those candidates about whom the search committee has learned through their advertisements and requests for nominations, and those the consultants themselves have identified in their own networks and inquiries. To maintain the confidentiality of their sources, consultants sometimes present a composite statement containing what they have learned about a candidate from a number of sources, or they provide individual anonymous reports which do not give names and indicate only the connection of the respondent to the candidate.[8]

[6] Ronald Stead and his associates are perfectly willing to do more in the way of consultation and negotiation at the end of a search if asked. Thus, in one recent search at a private liberal arts college, the president-elect asked Stead's advice concerning appropriate levels of compensation, and Stead would have been willing to discuss this matter with the board chairman as well, if so requested.

[7] The presentation book came with the following statement about security: "These materials are highly confidential and have been prepared for the use of the Winthrop College Presidential Search Committee. They may not be duplicated and should not be left unguarded." The search committee was urged to shred the book after the interviews.

[8] An ingenious and relentless investigative reporter or other inquirer might be able to trace a report back to its sources by the clues in the anonymous report, much as can be done with letters of recommendation in which the connection of the recommender and candidate and other identifying information remains, even though the names are crossed out. But ordinarily, institutions do not pursue the issue to get behind the anonymous reports, but accept them on the basis on which consultants offer them.

235

We have yet to meet a consultant who does not believe in the central importance of confidentiality in the search. Indeed, one of the major reasons why some boards of trustees turn to a consultant is in the hope that this will help assure confidentiality. Heidrick & Struggles has handled sunshine searches for all three of Iowa's state universities, working out arrangements whereby material on candidates can be kept confidential in their Chicago office until the point where a small number of finalists (ordinarily five) must agree to surrender confidentiality in return for a serious chance to obtain the position.[9] In part, the reputations of consultants depend on their not harming or not exposing prospects or sources to whom they might want to turn again. Correspondingly, some consultants refuse to take part in a sunshine search in which all of their records must be publicly available.

Occasionally, thanks to precautions, widespread institutional loyalty, and good luck, campus visits can occur while still maintaining complete confidentiality. But since this cannot be counted on, search committees and consultants differ on the issue of campus visits. In the Winthrop College search, Ruth Weintraub persuaded the search committee of the importance of campus visits by the finalists. Indeed, some consultants believe that such visits are essential for the search to be seen as legitimate. Others, however, consider campus visits as something to be avoided, if at all possible. Still others seek to persuade the search committee to bring only a single finalist, the preferred person, to the campus, and then, if this person proves clearly unsuitable, to bring the next person in line. Ronald Stead and his colleagues at Academic Search Consultation Service recently have come to believe that this process minimizes damage to candidates not chosen, while providing groups on the campus a chance to voice opinions and to feel some ownership of the final selection.

What we have seen in recent years is, in effect, a partial collision between the continuing and perhaps increasing insistence on participatory as against representative democracy in the search and the increasing use of consultants, whose experience has led them to appreciate the impor-

[9] This arrangement has been attacked by the *Des Moines Register and Tribune* as an evasion of the state's sunshine law; however, the concession of bringing five finalists to the campus has nevertheless been maintained by the former chairman of the Iowa Board of Regents and his successor as a politically workable compromise—although from the side of the candidates it has meant that in recent years no sitting president has been among the finalists at Iowa, Iowa State, or the University of Northern Iowa.

236

tance of confidentiality. Hence one can imagine scenarios in which a consultant's advice in favor of confidentiality and against a parade of candidates on campus would engender suspicion that the consultant had something at stake that was not in the interests of the institution. In contrast, in the Skidmore search, Raymond Klemmer won the confidence of the members of the search committee, and the search committee was able, in turn, to persuade the leaders of the faculty to surrender their plan to bring several finalists to the campus. They were led to understand that their plan to "shop" among candidates would likely result in the loss of the search committee's first choice.

Help with Formulating Criteria

When Oberlin College suffered the death of its president and the need to find a successor, the chairman of the board, Dr. Lloyd Morrisett, became the chairman of the search committee. Morrisett has had extensive experience in academia, as a psychologist, as staff member of the Carnegie Corporation, and in recent years as president of the John and Mary R. Markle Foundation whose contemporary focus has been the support of research on the mass media. Plainly, Morrisett did not "need" a consultant to tell him and the search committee where to look for possible candidates. But he believed that a consultant, as a perceptive outsider, could offer a perspective on Oberlin and on what sort of person might be helpful to its future that no one closely involved with the college could credibly provide. In question, however, was whether the faculty of Oberlin College would permit any consultant to be used. As prideful guardians of the tradition of the "Oberlin Compact," which allowed them the de jure control which most good faculties possess de facto vis-à-vis selecting presidents, they had exercised this control in the past by managing to get rid of presidents they did not like.

Morrisett was able to persuade the faculty that the search committee could gain advice from a consultant without surrendering to the consultant the responsibility for the search process. For this sort of "minimalist" approach, Oberlin selected Frederic Ness and Ronald Stead, then the co-directors of the Presidential Search Consultation Service. Ness and Stead seemed appropriate choices because their approach is to begin by talking

237

with faculty members, administrators, and students on the campus in order to appreciate more fully the problems and opportunities confronting the institution in the present and the future. To the surprise of some, most people at Oberlin responded positively to the chance to talk candidly to Ness and Stead, experienced men who had themselves come out of academic life. It is unlikely that all of those interviewed would have responded as freely to one another, much less to a member of the board of trustees.

As with Oberlin, one important role which most search consultants perform is to help institutions define the criteria for a new president, both those set forth in advertisements and those which might have been rather impromptu or even semi-conscious notions on the part of the board and of constituents. Consultants can help introduce a measure of realism into these expectations. Our reading of the scores of announcements, both the shorter advertisements in the *Chronicle of Higher Education* and the longer descriptions sent out by search committees to nominators and prospective candidates, often reveals demands for qualities so fabulous as to be ludicrous. At times they are self-contradicting—in effect "wish lists" coming from both the concerned and the casual. Search consultants are not necessarily wiser than the ablest trustees and faculty members in framing such documents, but having seen a lot of these descriptions, they know what superlatives to avoid. They can also ask the committee to reevaluate criteria that have been taken for granted, such as specification of a certain number of years as a faculty member and/or as an administrator, or insistence on an earned doctorate, and, in many instances, a Ph.D. degree. If taken literally, this would eliminate prospects with degrees such as Ed.D., D.Sc., D.F.A., J.D., M.B.A., and D.B.A. Criteria such as these narrow the pool of viable prospects. Sometimes this is intentional, where there is fear of the candidacy of a state legislator or a retired businessman on the board and a wish to make clear that the search is open for politically unconnected outsiders. But at other times these criteria can be needlessly restrictive.

Help with Navigating the Search

If a search committee has not yet been formed, a consultant can help the chairman shape its size and composition. More typically, however, a con-

238

sultant is brought in after the committee has been created. In this instance, the consultant can help the committee establish procedures for the search process and outline reasonable timetables for their completion. As we saw in the "Abbott College" search, a search committee that does not plan well can find itself rushed at the end, hurrying the important final stages of the process in order to have a recommendation ready for the last trustee meeting of the academic year.

A consultant can also make committee members aware of the volume of paperwork with which they will be confronted. Often, two hundred or more applications and nominations arrive in response to advertisements in newspapers and letters requesting nominations. In many searches, out of mistrust of the priorities of others on the committee or out of curiosity about the search and eagerness to begin the process, all the members of the search committee read all the papers that arrive. However, it happens all too frequently that no one is in charge of responding to these materials; we have repeatedly run into nominees and nominators who have wondered whether their letters were lost, since two or three months had passed and there had been no response. It is generally the busier faculty members, trustees, and student leaders, the most visible and respected, who are chosen for search committees. When they apportion their time haphazardly, not only may there be neglect of the outsiders, but also weariness and boredom among committee members. Even so, there is much to be said for having all search committee members sample the initial harvest of applications and nominations, gaining a sense of each other's judgments as they develop their own, and learning that there are few luminous candidates, and that it may not be easy to find that perfect person for their institution.

While some corporate consultants are scornful of the importance many faculty members place on "process," members of search committees may be unwilling to delegate any review of nominations and applications to a consultant. Their fear is that the consultant will not sufficiently understand their institution to make the "right" selections. Such misgivings can be resolved by having committee members and the consultant take the same batch of folders and see to what extent they arrive at similar conclusions. Ray Klemmer used this procedure with the search committee at Skidmore College, and thereby won the committee's trust. When committee members trust the skills and experience of the search consultant,

239

the consultant can save the committee precious time early in the search process.

Sometimes a consultant will identify someone of promise that members of the search committee have overlooked. In one search, Millington McCoy of Gould and McCoy gave high marks to a prospective candidate (folders are sometimes rated A, B, C, or 1, 2, 3, etc.). Meanwhile, members of the search committee, reviewing the same materials, had determined that this person should not be given further consideration. When the members of the search committee compared their ratings with McCoy's, they decided, out of respect for her advice, to keep the candidate on their active list. When they brought him in for an interview, they were glad they had relied on the consultant's judgment. Several months later, this candidate was appointed president.

An energetic search committee chairman probably does not need to be told that even his or her alma mater will have to go after candidates, rather than assuming they will come forward on their own. The chairman may also know where to advertise the vacancy and whom to write to solicit nominations. However, as Stephen Garrison of Ward Howell told us, in recent years the "tried and true" methods of soliciting names of candidates have been breaking down. Athough advertisements can produce a great volume of applications, many of these are not worth pursuing. Similarly, letters soliciting names arrive like a tattoo on the desks of presidents of colleges and universities, the heads of the Washington, D.C. ("One Dupont Circle") higher education associations, and other individuals (Clark Kerr, Theodore Hesburgh, Harold "Doc" Howe, etc.) well known in educational circles. To the deluge of requests for names, these people will respond with different degrees of solicitousness and timeliness, and their rosters can easily become out of date.[10] Consultants make an effort to keep their own files up to date, and generally have a larger pool of potential nominators to contact than does the average search committee. Consultants can also bring to the search the persistence of a legendary salesman, a style with which committee members would be uncomfortable. One community college president told us he was approached about a

---

[10] Experienced academic administrators, hoping to become presidents or already in a presidency, recognize the value of letting their potential availability be known to individuals likely to be in the network of nominators and to leading search consultant firms.

240

presidency eight times by a search consultant. On the eighth call, he agreed to talk with a few members of the search committee. That conversation intrigued him more than he had expected, and he agreed to let his name go forward in the search. Eventually, he was offered—and he accepted—the new presidency. Few search committee chairmen and few members would have had the zeal (and many would not have had the time) to continue beyond the first, the second, or the third refusal. However, some consultants wear out their welcome by just such pertinacity, and we have met and talked with a number of college and university presidents who turn a deaf ear to all consultants because they feel they have been harassed by some.

Kennedy Langstaff of the New York office of Ward Howell International, serving as consultant to a thriving small denominational liberal arts college, was not satisfied when he had helped winnow the field to five candidates who were to be brought sequentially to campus. These closing events were occurring months after the search had begun. Realizing that during those months some of the people on whom he regularly calls for help in nominations might have acquired some new ideas, he made these rounds again, making sure that there was no new person out there who merited consideration, even at the last minute. Obviously, a late prospect would have to have special qualities. However, just as Ruth Weintraub extended the deadline for applications and nominations in the Winthrop case, so search consultants can suggest needed flexibility to search committees whose preoccupation with process may at times make them too legalistic.

One of the most improbable cases of a late prospect occurred in the Skidmore search. Just three days before the last round of finalist interviews, Judith Eissner was told that David Porter, a classics professor at Carleton College, was someone to consider. The presumptive deadline had passed. Even so, with the assistance of consultant Raymond Klemmer, it was possible to arrange for Professor Porter to spend fifty minutes with the search committee. The meeting took place late one evening after the committee had spent a full day interviewing finalists at the Albany airport. The immediate result was to place David Porter among the finalists, leading eventually to his agreement to have Judith Eissner, Raymond Klemmer, and a faculty member of the search committee come to Northfield, Minnesota. In the town's one hotel, they met with individuals from Carleton proposed by David Porter, not all of them admirers. Porter, a graduate of Swarthmore College with a Ph.D. from Princeton, was a celebrated harpsichordist who had spent virtually his entire academic career teaching classics. He had no administrative experience beyond chairing a department and serving for several months as the acting president of Carleton College, pending the outcome of a search in which it was understood that he was not a candidate. The other finalists in the Skidmore search were either seasoned presidents or chief academic officers. In such a situation, a search consultant could give support to a search committee prepared to take a gamble, or alternatively, fearing for the consultant's own reputation, warn against a gamble. In this case, the consultant on whom the Skidmore College search committee had gambled in turn helped that committee gamble on David Porter, and cooperated in helping arrange for his acceptance and installation.

Most consultants stay with the search process to the end. They are around when a small number of promising candidates has been identified and the search committee makes comparative judgments among the finalists. Sometimes, a particular committee member will have a strong negative reaction to a candidate, perhaps based on a single item of information, on geographical origin, or even appearance. Having seen many candidates, consultants are sometimes helpful in putting these reactions in perspective, with a disinterested sense of authority that takes away some of the burden borne by the chairman.

The importance of maintaining confidentiality has been discussed throughout the preceding chapters. Although a consultant is no prerequisite for, or assurance of, a confidential search, the consultant can help committee members appreciate the need for confidentiality, and can take various measures to avoid leaks during the search. One of the most common breaches of confidentiality occurs when faculty members on a search committee call their disciplinary counterparts or other people they know at the home base of a candidate, or students on a search committee call the leaders in student government at the candidate's institution. Almost invariably, these calls result in the word getting out at the candidate's institution that the person is considering leaving. Most consultants will take responsibility for checking references at least at the outset of a search,

242

before candidates have been sifted to a smaller number. Because they know whom to call and what to say, their calls are somewhat less likely to result in leaks. Similarly, trustees or senior faculty members of an institution known to be seeking a president may put a prospective candidate at risk when they are glimpsed on this candidate's campus. In one search for the president of a liberal arts college, the woman who chaired the search committee visited the campus of a candidate, a sitting president, under the disguise of a parent casing the joint on behalf of her college-bound offspring. To her dismay she was recognized in the airport on her arrival by a trustee of the institution she was visiting, and for days she was anxious lest there be suppositions leading to a leak. Fortunately, in this instance none occurred.

Considering Internal Candidates

Internal candidates raise some of the most delicate and vexing issues faced by a search committee. Should all or any of them at a particular institution be entitled to a hearing before the search committee? Should they be dealt with first and, if not seen as serious contenders, told that they are not in the running, so as to strengthen the assurances given to outside candidates that the field is open? How best can the lobbying on campus for and against an internal candidate be handled? No consultant can make the difficult process of considering internal candidates comfortable or easy, but a trusted outsider can contribute in various ways. In the process of talking with people on campus to learn more about the institution and the qualities desired in a new president, the consultant may learn something about how an internal candidate is regarded and get a sense of what the campus reaction would be to his or her selection as president. A consultant may help the search committee appreciate the strengths of an inside candidate who is so well known at home that he or she is overlooked in the search for someone new and exciting. In the corporate sector, where there is minimal participation from the ranks, it is common to choose someone from inside as the successor to a departing CEO, whereas in the more egalitarian setting of a campus, people not only tend to undervalue those they know, but have the power to act on their deprecations. To put it differently, the virtues of inside candidates are taken for granted and their limitations are

243

magnified. The consultant can help disabuse the trustees, the search committees, and campus constituents of the notion that somewhere out yonder is a person more exceptional than anyone they have come to know well.

Capable and ambitious academic administrators who are aware that their chances for a presidency at their home institution may be slim often look elsewhere for a better opportunity. When a board of trustees seeks to counter the premature departure of an outstanding internal prospect by assurances that he or she is under serious consideration for the presidency, both the board and the administrator recognize that, for the legitimacy of the selection process, this internal candidate must be tested against the competition. Only in unusual circumstances, such as immediate and evident institutional peril, would an inside candidate wish to assume the presidency in the face of the accusation that he or she has been "hand picked."[11] But how, then, can the potential competition be assured that they are not entering a rigged race? It is here that search consultants can be extremely useful. Assurances from them about the actual situation will carry more weight than any statements by search committee members. In one presidential search for a major university presidency, the leading candidate asked the search committee whether there was an inside candidate and was told there was none. Only after having been selected and having left his previous presidency did he learn that the academic vice-president at his new institution had been a candidate. He had been deceived. The credibility of search consultants rests on a reputation not tarnished by duplicity.

The Art of Asking Questions

As most consultants know and many members of search committees discover, it is not easy to conduct a competent interview, one which gives the search committee a good sense of the individual with whom they are conversing, and one that allows them to differentiate plausible candidates from one another. Search consultants, who have much more experience in interviewing than most members of search committees, can help the

---

[11] The derogatory term "hand picked" is one of those bumper-sticker epithets which, like "rubber stamped" or "closed doors" avoids the necessity for making specific judgments.

committee assess candidates' personal and professional capacities and past performance as a gauge of future performance. In such matters, the best consultants are skeptics rather than cynics. They have seen many people who look good, have dazzling resumés, and make wonderful first impressions, but who turn out to have little depth or staying power. Only after their selection does it become apparent that the past record of accomplishment of these candidates, if not inconsequential or even fraudulent,[12] was achieved at the expense of internal disarray or long-term damage. With these candidates, their greatest gift is self-promotion.

In the Skidmore search, consultant Ray Klemmer spent five hours with each of twenty individuals whom the search committee judged to be serious prospects. This is far more time than most search committees spend even with half-a-dozen finalists. The results of these lengthy interviews were summarized for the committee before they met with each candidate and served as a foundation for questions from committee members and candidates.

Consultants commonly seek to educate search committees in the art of asking questions.[13] They may proffer a sample set of questions and have members of the search committee review them and come up with others of their own. Some consultants assign questions to members of the search committee so as to produce variation, a technique which is best employed along with more casual conversation. If enforced mechanically, it would forbid exploration of interesting issues any one question may produce.

Some consultants believe it is useful to sit in on the search committee's interviews with candidates. Like Ruth Weintraub in the Winthrop search, they occasionally ask questions, or they may simply be present as silent

[12] In their *Search Committee Handbook*, Marchese and Lawrence note that consultants who check degrees, academic honors, and even employment history find a good deal of resumé inflation and elision—enough to justify having a capable search committee secretary check these matters at an early stage of a search if this can be done without jeopardizing confidentiality.

[13] January, 1987, saw publication of the first issue of *Questioning Exchange: A Multidisciplinary Review*. This journal seeks to bring together the various disciplines whose members are engaged in research based on questions or interviewing, or who are directly studying the art of asking questions. For example, some psychologists have sought to assess the imagination and intelligence of respondents by asking them to ask questions of the interviewer—much in the way in which search committees sometimes ask candidates to ask questions of the search committee, not only to allow the candidate to become better informed, but also to engage the candidate's level of knowledge and curiosity. *Questioning Exchange* also hopes to include work by philosophers of science, by counselors and therapists, and by anthropologists examining their own skill in asking questions and in assessing what is permitted or not permitted in different cultures.

witnesses so that they can talk with the committee later about their impressions. In the Skidmore College search, consultant Raymond Klemmer attempted to sit in on every session with a candidate, even in instances where the search committee itself split up into smaller, more intimate groups. He would shuttle from one subcommittee meeting to another and seek to have these meetings arranged in such a way that they were easy and natural for the candidates. Correspondingly, he was in a position to compare candidates across sessions, and to help the committee overcome the hazards of fatigue, when heads nod at the end of an over-long day.

Ronald Stead of the Academic Search Consultation Service helps the search committee frame questions, but ordinarily chooses not to be present at meetings with candidates, wanting to make certain that the search committee makes the final decision and does not turn to the consultant for validation of their action. Whether or not they attend the interviews, most consultants will help the committee structure the sessions and discuss how candidates will be assessed afterward.

Candidates have told us many times of search committees that are so new at the whole process of interviewing that it is the candidate who has to put *them* at ease. Consultants will sometimes have committees do a trial run of an interview, perhaps with one of their own number, or they will practice among themselves asking questions about a candidate they may never actually see. In the process, committee members may discover that differences among themselves do not run along expectable lines, such as trustees versus faculty, or scientists versus non-scientists, but reflect the idiosyncracies of the members. With simulation, committee members do not have to learn how to interview by practicing on the first one or two candidates.

Some search consultants keep in their own hands all reference checking on leading candidates. John Synodinos, now president of Lebanon Valley College but formerly a search consultant, said to us that he invariably "insisted" upon doing such checking himself for the sake of confidentiality and consistency, but in most cases such inquiries are made both by the search consultant and by the search committee chairman or search committee members. A number of consultants warn search committee members against the temptation to jump to a conclusion about a candidate in the first five minutes of an interview, urging them to keep questioning and

246

listening and testing their preconception. It goes without saying that consultants are subject to preconceptions too—and that these are not always wrong.

Because members of the search committee will have an ongoing relationship with whoever is chosen president, a search consultant can do some things that would be awkward or imprudent for committee members to attempt. Thus, one search committee hired a consultant to conduct probing personal interviews with a small group of finalists the committee was considering. Among other questions, the consultant asked candidates to tell her about situations where they thought they had done well and situations where they believed they had done badly. Naturally, one of her aims was to screen out candidates who believed they had done everything well, and to discover those who had a fairly robust understanding of themselves, of both their capacities and their limitations.

One small liberal arts college facing a precarious future asked several finalists to write essays about their vision for the institution and to spend a full day with a clinical psychologist. The successful candidate, who told us about this procedure, said that she had set two conditions in the psychological interview: one, that the psychologist's report be shared with her; and, two, that the report be shown only to the trustees. If selected, she did not want faculty members or others to be familiar with her psychological profile. Ordinarily, institutions should court candidates and not put them through a decathlon to prove their eagerness, but there are situations where one wants to weed out people who are not eager, someone who had to be coaxed to take the job, because only someone enthusiastic about the position and ready to take chances would possess the requisite tenacity. In this case, the winning candidate reported that she had learned from the clinical psychologist a good deal that was useful about herself. We can well imagine situations, however, where people with exemplary records as presidents in comparable settings would not be willing to undergo such scrutiny, believing that their records spoke for them.

Serving as an Intermediary

Most consultants are aware of the importance of keeping in touch with candidates concerning the progress of the search, even if no concrete decisions are as yet forthcoming. Many search committees behave abysmally in this regard, leaving candidates wondering if they have been dropped from consideration, placed on a "hold" list, or forgotten altogether. Some have commented to us later that, when they finally heard from the search committee, they were amazed to learn that they were still in the running, perhaps even considered a leading contender.

Although consultants vary in this regard, most seem to do a better job than most search committees do in communicating with candidates. Consultants recognize that it is in their best interest and that of the institution they represent when everybody with whom they speak, be they nominators or nominees, is satisfied with the treatment they have received. Consultants want to retain the good opinion of finalists who have not been selected in this particular search, for they may want to turn to them in a search they handle later. Moreover, the best consultants regard themselves as professionals, not simply as "guns for hire," and believe that they serve their clients best, and of course their own firms best, by behaving responsibly, ethically, and, insofar as possible, humanely.

Not all candidates realize this, and of course not all consultants live up to the norms set by those who are most judicious and discerning. However, where candidates' suspicions are not too great, a consultant can speak to them as an intermediary with a credibility that institutional representatives may lack. For example, nominators and prospective candidates often make assumptions about the sort of person who would be taken seriously as a candidate at a particular institution. Many women have had the experience of being courted, only to conclude that they were brought to campus, as in the "Abbott College" case, because of prevailing ideologies. The same thing is true, of course, of black or hispanic men or, as in one case in the Middle West, a man of Chinese origin who was at the time a banker. In both the 1986–1987 Dartmouth and Princeton searches, there was a widespread assumption that these institutions would insist that the president be an alumnus (and a "real" alumnus, that is, of the college and not of any graduate or professional school). In the Vassar College search, the assumption might have been made that Vassar would choose a man as a successor to Virginia Smith to emphasize Vassar's full coeducational status. To ask the search committee chairman whether one is a serious candidate or not is not easily done, for it would appear to be a suggestion that the search was lacking in good faith. In the Winthrop College search,

248

Martha Piper was reluctant to become a candidate because of her doubts about whether a woman would be seriously considered for the presidency. Ruth Weintraub's assurances were more persuasive than those by any member of the search committee could have been. Similarly, candidates may be reluctant to ask the search committee how things stand, but need to know, not only because of issues arising in their present locales, but also because they are candidates elsewhere and need to weigh competing opportunities. Yet they do not want to seem pushy or to expose an unseemly eagerness to the search committee itself. Candidates in this situation often turn more readily to the consultant, who may well be torn between a wish to keep this person in the available pool and hesitation about leading the candidate on. In several such instances, the consultant used the competing offer to a candidate as a means of prodding the search committee to come to a decision.

The Role of Go-Between

Consultants also have the task of doing their best to assure a search committee that the preferred candidate or candidates will accept the position if offered. But that can never be a certainty. Consultant Randy Myer estimates that in his general business probably one-third of the people who are offered a job decide not to accept it. Some finalists pull out because they are involved in more than one search, and another institution makes an earlier offer. The candidate's spouse may have second thoughts about the move, or their children may put up such a fuss that all considerations of relocating are discarded. And of course it may also happen that the campus and the leading contender cannot readily come to terms, with the campus concluding that the contender who is asking "too much" is not a good choice after all.

When a board of trustees has reached a decision about a top candidate, the consultant can serve as the go-between in negotiations between the trustees and the person offered the presidency. Ordinarily, these negotiations are conducted between the chairman of the board, who may or may not have chaired the search committee, and the winning finalist. This can be awkward, even destructive, on both sides. The candidate does not want to appear anxious or greedy concerning detailed arrangements for employment, and so may not mention items which later become major points

249

of contention or aggravation. The chairman of the board may know little about what arrangements should be discussed, or be so tired from the search that he or she does not want to haggle over details and prefers to leave everything with the assurance, "it will be worked out later."

To put questions such as compensation and benefits, presidential residence, academic appointment and/or tenure, plans for evaluation, arrangements regarding the spouse (role expectations, compensation for travel, staff, etc.), in the hands of a consultant can be advantageous to the board and the president. It means that the president-elect and the board chairman can focus on matters of institutional policy and practice, rather than on the personal concerns of the presidential family. The recently installed president of a small and struggling denominational college gave us a not untypical account of his own dismay in having to negotiate on his own behalf with the board chairman concerning his pay and his insistence on a post-presidential leave if he should be fired or if he himself should want to leave. This latter proviso, he assured the chairman, would make it easier for the trustees to fire him and make it easier for him to act as independently as a president should.[14] The board chairman had no idea at all that one should talk at the beginning of a relationship about its possible termination, but he was quite prepared to bargain with the president-elect about the latter's salary and other compensation. The new incumbent was also in a dilemma for, as he explained matters, he saw himself as representing the impecunious institution as well as his own interests, and unlike the real estate dealer who chaired the board, could not bring himself to haggle about pay. In such situations, a consultant as go-between can bring to bear in the negotiations his experience concerning what is appropriate. Where the expectations of the incumbent-to-be are excessive, or where they are overly modest, the consultant can help reach an accommodation.[15]

[14] See the discussion of the role of Francis J. Madden of Ward Howell International, arranging for a guarantee of three years' salary and bonus for an executive of a not-for-profit organization who was relocating from New York to California and who recognized that ". . . he had to please a board of governors rather than one boss, and that seemed too much risk to take without the guarantee." (Claudia H. Deutsch, "When a Handshake Isn't Enough," *New York Times*, February 4, 1990, Section 3, part 2, p. 29, discussing the use of consultants in arranging severance plans.)

[15] When an eminent liberal arts college in the East was searching for a president, one of the finalists, a former president of another college, was aware of the importance of the president's house. Although he considered the presidential residence to be much too pretentious, and knew that his wife would not be comfortable there, it was not something the finalist wanted to bring up with the chairman of the

250

By no means all consultants perform this role of go-between. Many consultants consider their work done when the selection has been made, and some consider their work virtually done when the search committee has come up with two, three, or four acceptable finalists. They do not themselves propose doing more, but prefer to go on to their other searches still awaiting completion, and neither the trustees nor the search committee ask them to do more. But in those searches where the consultant has served as intermediary in the final negotiations, both candidates and trustees have told us of their satisfaction with this arrangement. As one candidate reported, "The consultant saved us a lot of meetings. She served as broker. We didn't have to dance about." In addition to acting as brokers in the negotiations between the candidate and the institution, some consultants pay visits to the new president, to see if the incumbent is satisfied and the institution is satisfied. Such visits can serve as a check on the consultant's own judgment as well as an exercise in public relations. Consultant Ira Krinsky reports that in addition to helping with final negotiations, he offers to return soon after an appointment is made for the purpose of facilitating a planning session or retreat. The trustees and the new president set the agenda, and the consultant serves as facilitator, having learned a great deal about the institution and the new incumbent during the course of the search. Occasionally, the large executive search firms will also fulfill the function of out-placement, to help clients find alternative employment for personnel who need to leave for institutional or personal reasons.

HAZARDS IN THE USE OF CONSULTANTS

The preceding pages suggest the kinds of assistance a consultant can give a search committee and a board of trustees *in the best of circumstances*. Not all search consultants are equally good at what they do, however. Not all search consultants understand the world of higher education or know how to establish contacts within it. And no procedures are foolproof, even with the best of people guiding them.

---

board. The chairman had spent much more time and energy on the search than he had anticipated and was eager to get back full-time to his own company. Fortunately, the consultant turned out to be someone who understood the situation instantly and arranged alternative housing.

When Winthrop search committee chairman Terry Peterson asked for advice about consultants, he found great variation in how corporate consultants were regarded. Some individuals were highly praised, while others were thought not to have worked particularly effectively with the search committee. Our research corroborates his findings. The most experienced corporate consultants have cultivated an academic clientele, have become familiar with a great variety of "the many lives of college presidents," and can even muster patience and sympathy for the consultative processes in academe which are now the order, or more commonly the disorder, of the day. Yet with the great increase in the use of search consultants in higher education have come entrants unfamiliar with the culture or the language of academe. One search consultant told us that he despised working with search committees, preferring to do as much of the work of the search as he could all by himself. Were this attitude to be conveyed to the search committee, the consultant's usefulness would be destroyed. Another corporate consultant asked us what "ACE" (American Council on Education) was, because a candidate had been an ACE Fellow and he did not have the slightest idea what this meant.[16] He was having difficulty making sense of the calling cards of candidates, not knowing how to evaluate which items in the pages and pages of entries in the academic curricula vitae were relevant or even prestigious and which were mere fluff.

Faculty members often view corporate search firms as belonging to the trustees' world rather than to their own. A look at the glossy brochures of some of the leading executive search firms, with photographs of consultants in three piece suits striding briskly among the tall buildings of the major world metropolises, would not be reassuring to many in academia. Corporate consultants have the burden of making clear to the campus that they are not applying to the college or university a perspective appropriate to a manufacturing company, a bank, a hospital, or an art museum.[17] The

[16] American Council on Education Fellows serve for a year in the office of a president or other senior administrator at a campus—ordinarily other than their own—and participate during the fellowship year in meetings across the country with academic leaders. The aspirants for fellowships generally are faculty members who hope to enter academic administration. Being an ACE Fellow under a helpful presidential or senior administrative mentor helps the Fellow decide whether to pursue a career in academic leadership and gives the Fellow administrative experience and visibility.

[17] Of course there are enormous differences among corporations included in the Fortune 500 or any other listing, illustrated by the research now under way on "corporate culture." A corporation such

best consultants act almost like anthropologists, quickly sizing up a place, its values and mores, and then using this same perceptiveness and judgment in evaluating candidates. Their perspective can assist the search committee and its chairman so that the candidates they go looking for are neither so elevated as to be restless and unhappy if they do come, or so inconsequential that they will, at best, do no immediate harm. Corporate and non-corporate consultants alike can help with these judgments.

For this to occur, the consultant must acquire a fairly complete view of the institution. Consultants, however, can fall into the trap of seeing the institution primarily through the eyes of the board or search committee chairman and the members of the search committee. This is particularly a danger if the consultant does not personally visit the campus in an effort to discover divergent views within the institution, and to assess the weight of conflicting ideas of what sort of leadership is at the moment most desirable. Consultants generally accept their assignments from key players who themselves may not be alert to dissident factions or areas of quiet unhappiness and dissatisfaction on campus. Key players also may not fully disclose, nor fully appreciate, what they know. Since candidates depend in some measure on consultants for their understanding of the situation at the institution, an unwary consultant may mislead a candidate, encouraging a person to become president without telling him or her what may lie ahead in the way of opposition or demoralization.

By no means all prospective candidates welcome overtures from a search consultant. A recently installed president said to us that he had many inquiries from search consultants. As academic dean of a leading liberal arts college, he was an obvious prospect. To most of the inquiries he had responded negatively, for, as he put it, he wanted to hear from the principal, not the agent. Some consultants recognize that certain individuals might best be approached through someone they are known to respect. Likewise, some nationally prominent educators have said to us that they are tired of telephone calls from consultants who seem not to know their way around higher education and who ask for information about candidates that is readily available in *Who's Who* or other obvious sources.

The more experienced consultants know from previous searches the

---

as Hewlett-Packard may be more like some kinds of academic institutions than like General Motors or General Electric.

names of many of the people who apply or are nominated for a presidency. This familiarity with candidates is both a possible advantage and a potential hazard. On the one hand, a consultant can save the search committee the time and trouble of meeting with individuals who are entirely unsuited for a presidency or can recommend for the committee's consideration someone known from another search who may not, on paper, appear as impressive as in person. On the other hand, a consultant may himself or herself be biased against a person whom a search committee might find quite to their liking. We know, for instance, of a search consultant who met a candidate when the candidate was one of a small number of people considered for a university presidency. Later, the consultant and candidate met again, in a search at a very different sort of institution. Again, this candidate was deemed by the search committee to be one of a small number of finalists deserving a closer look, and was told by the search committee chairman that the consultant would be interviewing each of the finalists and reporting back to the search committee. However, when he heard from the consultant, rather than being asked for an appointment, the candidate was told that there would be no need for another conversation, since they had talked a couple of months earlier in regard to the other search. The consultant apparently felt that his earlier judgment was sufficient and did not take account of the fact that the presidencies at these two institutions were markedly different from one another and, therefore, another meeting with the candidate might be in order. It can also happen that a consultant, geared to establishing a successful record and wary of taking an unwarranted risk, eliminates a candidate about whom anything negative is known, including the candidate's having been turned down for unspecified reasons elsewhere. One candidate told us that a consultant had heard disparaging remarks about him from someone he had given as a reference. He got in touch with the consultant and urged the latter to check the validity of this strong denunciation. When the consultant made additional inquiries and discovered that his initial impression of the candidate was false, he returned the candidate to the roster of available prospects.[18]

[18] In one search where one of the national head-hunting firms was employed, a candidate for the presidency had recently been divorced. A trustee suggested to the consultant that the reasons for the divorce be investigated; the consultant responded that it was inappropriate to look into the private

A problematic situation arises when a consultant discovers that a candidate in a search he or she is assisting is also being recommended in a simultaneous search, assisted by someone else in the consultant's firm. A consultant from a large corporate firm explained to us the steps that are taken to avoid having his firm recommend the same individual to two different institutions. The firm's extensive computer network of names is programmed to alert the consultant whenever a person is being considered in another search. When a consultant tries to retrieve a file, he or she immediately learns from the computer if it is being used by another consultant. Once the consultant learns of this situation, he or she is required to talk with the associate who is using the file before considering the person as a candidate. In their conversation, the consultants discuss which institution they think this candidate would be best suited for, and then proceed to carry the candidate's name forward only in that search. In avoiding internal competition within the firm, the firm confronts a certain conflict of interest with both institutions and candidates. Had one or both searches not been using consultants (or had they been using consultants from different firms), they might well have kept the candidate on both search committee lists up to the end of the search process. Of course, if both institutions were to choose this candidate as the person they wanted for president, obviously one institution must be the loser. But the search committees and trustees have a chance to make their best competitive bids, and the candidate has the chance to make an independent judgment about which institution is more attractive, rather than having the decision made in the office of the consulting firm.

Another awkward situation can arise when a president or senior administrator whom a consultant firm helped place at one institution is a candidate in another search the consultant is assisting. Ordinarily, search firms have a "keep away" policy regarding anyone they have placed, which means that they do not recruit this person for another job until a number of years have passed after the original placement. In the case of college and university presidencies, search firms occasionally bend their own rules, however, noting that they only "enrich the pool" of candidates and

---

lives of candidates. The candidate in question was chosen, and not long after was accused in the local press of seeking homosexual connections among the young men on campus. Soon thereafter, he was asked to resign.

consult with the search committee and do not, themselves, recommend a final choice. Hence, when James McComas, who was president of the University of Toledo for only three years, was named president of Virginia Tech, John Richmond, who was the Heidrick & Struggles consultant to both searches, felt the need to explain what had happened. In the industry newsletter, *Executive Recruiter News*, he commented that McComas "did not come to the party through me" in either search, and when McComas became a finalist for the Virginia Tech post, John Richmond had asked him to explain that immediately to the University of Toledo trustees.[19] Apparently the Toledo trustees did not hold this against Richmond, for they hired him to help with the search for McComas's successor.[20]

Earlier, we discussed the value of consultants in assessing inside candidates, bringing detachment and helping compare them with outside nominees. There is, however, a danger that a search consulting firm will tilt toward an outside candidate, preferably a person they themselves discovered and brought to the attention of the search committee. If the committee settles on someone already on hand, the consultant may feel upstaged. In such instances, there may also be a feeling on the part of the search committee or the board of trustees that the consultant's fees and expenses were unnecessary because the consultant introduced no novelty into the search. However, the most capable search consultants recognize that they are performing a valuable service in persuading a search committee that an inside candidate is as qualified as anyone likely to be recruited from outside and possesses the enormous advantage of already knowing the scene.

Although search consultants seem generally to do a better job of staying in touch with candidates than do search committees operating alone, some former candidates have spoken to us about feeling "baited and trapped."

---

[19] *Executive Recruiter News*, September 1988, p. 7.

[20] The constraints on a big firm because of its being actually or potentially involved in more than a single search have been a mainstay of the advertising by John Lucht, who left Heidrick & Struggles to found his own firm, John Lucht Associates. Lucht advertises that he takes on only a single search in any competitive industry at any one time. (See Herbert E. Meyer, "The Headhunters Come Upon Golden Days," in *Fortune*, October 9, 1978.) He recently moved into the "industry" of higher education when he assisted the search for a provost at Worcester Polytechnic Institute. Executive search firms, like advertising agencies or other cohorts depending primarily on individual enterprise and talent, do not evoke enormous institutional loyalty from those who work for them. Hence, we may anticipate that, in addition to those already mentioned, other men and women will break away from one of the larger firms to go it more or less alone.

Search consultants pursued them until they became active candidates, and then left them hanging, uncertain of their status in the search. Suspicious that they were being urged to become candidates only so that the consultant could present an appealing slate to the search committee, they felt badly used. In other searches, a candidate has been left in the dark about his or her status in the search because the consultant has assumed that the search committee chairman is communicating with candidates and the chairman has assumed that the consultant is handling this aspect of the search. Occasionally, candidates have reported to us that they have heard from both consultant and chairman, and that it appears that each is unaware of what the other is doing or saying. Often this slippage comes about when both the search committee chairman and the search consultant are involved with many other activities in addition to the search, a situation that can sometimes be helped by having a capable executive secretary, free of ties that might threaten confidentiality, to work under the direction of the person chairing the search committee. Indeed, the chief reason for employing a search consultant in some cases is that the search chairman is such a busy person that he or she wants someone else to offer relief from the tasks of the search. However, some search consultants take on many searches at the same time, with the result that they, too, become overextended.

In his essay, "Executive Search Firms as an Alternative to Search Committees," Richard A. Mottram describes the modus operandi of some consultants who take over much of the work characteristically done by search committees. These consultants do a great amount of the searching themselves, identifying prospects through their own networks, pursuing prospects not actively in the market for a job, as well as reviewing the letters of nomination and application that come in to the committee. They then proceed to interview prospects by telephone and in person, check background references, and turn over to the search committee a "panel" or "portfolio" of finalists to be considered.[21] This approach saves enormous amounts of time for the search committee and especially the chairman. It also maximizes confidentiality up to the point of presenting finalists. But there can be danger in a too efficient, even too expeditious a search. The

[21] *Educational Record*, Vol. 64 (Winter 1983), pp. 38–42.

search committee may gain only a filtered sense of what their own institution is really like, what sorts of qualities might be requisite in a new president, and what sorts of people might be available for the office. They have no way of knowing, for instance, whether the finalists identified by the consultant are typical representatives of a larger cohort, or represent just about all the available possibilities.

However, most consultants are careful not to preempt the work of the search committee, and they understand that it is important for the search committee and the board to be involved and feel invested in the final choice. The best consultants are aware that a search can provide the search committee and the board with a chance for learning about the institution, about themselves and one another, albeit an opportunity commonly beset by anxiety.

TO USE OR NOT TO USE A CONSULTANT

It would be farfetched to say that every search can benefit from the use of even the most capable search consultant. There are a few situations in American higher education where the succession process requires neither the discovery nor the persuasion of candidates. The Jesuits and the Benedictines consciously prepare their members to assume top executive positions in colleges founded by and still under the influence of these Orders.[22] Even so, we can imagine one of the less prominent of the twenty-eight Jesuit institutions having to choose between drafting an unwilling member of the Order to take over its presidency and looking for a lay Catholic, much as at St. John Fisher College where a search in the academic year 1985–1986 led to the choice of a lay Catholic to succeed the traditional Basilian priest. There are also less organized networks of recruitment for some Protestant church-related colleges. For example, the Methodist Board of Higher Education in Nashville can make suggestions for the va-

[22] This practice has become more difficult in recent years since so many members of religious orders have left orders, although generally not the Catholic church itself. In fact, a number of former religious leaders have become top academic executives in secular as well as Catholic colleges. When the College of St. Catherine, still under the auspices of the Sisters of St. Joseph of Carondelet, was seeking a president in 1984–1985, they had a national search, and one of the finalists brought to campus was a member of a different order, an Ursuline nun who had wide administrative experience. "St. Cat's" was able to find an acceptable person from within, made legitimate by the national search.

258

cant presidencies of the country's many colleges founded by Methodists, for some of which the church tie is still significant.

Outside the areas where a church tie provides a kind of de facto consulting, it is still the case that capable chairmen of search committees have managed superbly without consultants. If the chairman of the board of trustees can find among fellow trustees someone with invincible energy, a capacity to commit time, an openness to learning, a willingness to endure frustration and to take infinite pains, a consultant is perhaps not so necessary. Still, one might prove helpful as someone with whom to share anxieties, check procedures, and serve as an additional precaution. We have met in person or in long telephone exchanges a number of search committee heads who come close to meeting these specifications. Several of them have had their sophistication concerning academia enhanced by service on committees of the Association of Governing Boards (AGB) or as AGB mentors to other board members. Where, as frequently happens, one of these individuals is also the board chair, it may be unwise not to choose a consultant because of the hazard of something coming up which will tax their capacities as board chairmen even while they are in the midst of the most stressful parts of a presidential search. In most of the instances to which we are now referring, this possibility had been thought of in advance: the chairman of the board was kept in reserve, also against vicissitudes of the search itself, and the person chairing the search committee had no other major board responsibility.

Moreover, in these matters much depends on the resources and visibility of the institution itself. Ralph O'Connor, when he chaired the Rice University search described in Chapter X, had behind him the name of a university instantly recognizable among leaders in American higher education, as well as the resources of the personal connections he and other members of the board and faculty members of the search committee could generate. Just as Harvard University, when it appoints a professor to tenure, can ask eminent persons in the prospective candidate's field to read a lot of publications and to come and spend half a day with the president and the relevant dean at Harvard to discuss what the department ought to do and whether this or that person is an appropriate choice, so Rice is a sufficiently illustrious name to permit Ralph O'Connor to impose his search committee colleagues on Derek Bok and on other eminent persons whom the search committee treated as "resources." Before beginning the search, Ralph O'Connor turned to Elizabeth Dycus, who had worked for president John Kemeny at Dartmouth and who had been executive secretary of the search for Kemeny's successor, asking her advice about the search process. She went along to the retreat in Kentucky where faculty members and trustees on the search committee began to look upon each other in a less adversarial way; thereafter, Ralph O'Connor, treating her as a wise person rather than as a formal consultant, would occasionally telephone her to share developments and concerns.

Some state systems have in-house expertise in the form of experienced individuals at the system level who can help a campus organize and conduct the search.[23] Such individuals, however, are not seen by candidates as detached and disinterested and therefore cannot perform the role of go-between in the same way as an outsider to the institution and system. When Gordon Gee (himself a former law school dean) became the leading finalist for the presidency of the University of Colorado System, he employed a Denver attorney to handle final negotiations on housing, provisions for the spouse, and related matters. Of course, such an opportunity is always available, but many finalists will not make use of what may be seen as too adversarial a mode.

In some searches, a consultant is not used for the wrong reasons. Considerations of cost, for example, have been a factor militating against use of a search consultant in a number of instances. Different consultants have different ways of calculating the price for their services, some charging a fixed price for each search, others having a sliding scale based on the ability of the institution to pay, and still others basing their fee on a percentage (typically one-third) of the compensation of the person who is to be installed. In public institutions, apart from legal constraints such as we saw in the Winthrop search, there is often fear that faculty members, politicians, or student and local journalists will make an issue of alleged waste

[23] Even as we write these lines, this is beginning to change. In the State University of New York system, each college or university has its own board of trustees, whose chief responsibility is helping in the selection of a new president, who must in the end be approved by the chancellor and the board of regents. The 1989–1990 search for a new president of the State University of New York at Binghamton used the consultation services of the Academic Search Consultation Service. Similarly, David Gardner, president of the University of California system, asked Ira Krinsky to assist with the search for a new Berkeley chancellor.

of "taxpayers' money" on a consultant. The rebuttal to such posturing—that consultants often save money by saving the time and sometimes the travel of search committee members—is often ineffective in preventing a public outcry.

In the private sector, too, we have found some search committee members who have resisted the use of a consultant as a luxury, not appropriate in light of the institution's prized frugality. If, however, one considers the potential benefits and potential costs in all aspects of an institution's functioning, including financial prosperity or anemia, the episodic financial cost of a consultant appears miniscule. Nothing is more expensive than a failed search, where the institution must pay the price of poor leadership and the board must again pay for a new round of advertisements, telephone calls, and visits to candidates.[24]

We have come across no instance where a search consultant has encouraged a search committee to be spendthrift. Search committees, however, often do cut corners both on cost and on time spent. They pack too many finalists into meetings at locations more convenient for them than for the finalists, leaving inadequate time not only for each interview, but for intervals of discussion before going on to the next interview. When candidates are brought to campus, there is quite commonly similar compression at a modest saving in the cost of lodging for the search committee members coming from a distance as well as for the candidates.[25]

We have made clear our judgment that it is wise for search committees and boards of trustees to consider employing a search consultant for assistance with their presidential search. As an outsider to the college or uni-

[24] Throughout our research, we have been struck by the difficulty trustees, coming out of the corporate world, have in firing a president who has proved to be a disappointing or even a catastrophic choice. They may give the president plenty of advice to fire So-and-So, and to do so instantly, and at least in their corporate capacity they present an image of themselves as tough and unsentimental. And some trustees are indeed ruthless, and capricious in the bargain. But most trustees, volunteers all, having formed ties to the president and to his or her family, will go to great lengths to avoid dismissal and, long before that, to avoid recognizing that they have either made a poor choice or that new circumstances call for another sort of president. We are referring here to cases where the president's failure makes it difficult for the person to move easily and quickly to a comparable position elsewhere, and where even a year's terminal leave pay would be cruel and unusual punishment. In academia the parachutes are hardly ever golden.

[25] In West Virginia, all sixteen state institutions come under the board of regents, and when any one of them has a search, a single state official, currently the attorney general, is deputized to attend all meetings with finalists on every campus. Because the attorney general has other work to do in addition to that for the regents, campus visits are often compressed and poorly timed to fit into the attorney general's schedule.

261

versity, a consultant can bring an added perspective on the institution and can serve as a liaison between candidates and campus. The consultant also brings long experience with searches—a familiarity with this enterprise few trustees, administrators, or faculty members can claim to possess. One candidate, a high-ranking official whose candidacy has been sought in many searches in recent years, told us that, given his experience with search committees and search consultants, he will not enter a search in which the search committee is working on its own.

A search, like a marriage, can have no guarantee of success, and the use of a marriage broker, though it may diminish romantic frenzy, provides no guarantee either. However, just as many marriages can be saved by wise counseling, many searches can be improved by wise counsel.

CHAPTER X

Rice University

N 1984–1985, RICE UNIVERSITY conducted a search for a successor to Norman Hackerman, who had been president for fifteen years. Hackerman had come to the presidency of Rice after he had been president of the University of Texas flagship campus at Austin. All the presidents of Rice prior to Hackerman, who kept his laboratory and worked periodically in it during his presidency, had been scientists or mathematicians. Rice astonished itself, Houston, and the observant educational world when Hackerman's successor was announced, for the search produced an altogether unexpected outcome in its choice of president. Moreover, the search which began, as we shall see, in a not uncommon atmosphere of suspicion between faculty members and the Board of Governors, concluded in a new sense of mutuality, inaugurating an era of good feeling.

This chapter is an account of how this choice came about. There is enterprise, imagination, even magnanimity in the story. It is an important episode, featuring a search committee unusual in the care taken in its selection and in the trust and cameraderie that developed among its members, and a dedicated and capable chairman. It illustrates, perhaps better than any of the other cases in this volume, the importance of looking in a wide orbit for potential candidates and then of actively courting serious prospects.

THE UNIVERSITY

William Marsh Rice, a fabulously wealthy oil man, created Rice Institute in 1891, drawing on three radically different models. One was New York City's Cooper Union (the Cooper Union for the Advancement of Science and Art), which, from its founding, has charged no tuition and, over time, has become more distinguished in art than in science. Another was Princeton, until recently the farthest north in the Ivy League that many Southerners tended to look. The third was Oxford, renowned for its many illustrious colleges. Rice quickly became the strongest school in science and engineering between California Institute of Technology (Cal Tech) and Massachusetts Institute of Technology (MIT). Presently, with 2,600 undergraduates, it is somewhat larger than Cal Tech but overall only a third the size of MIT, and it differs from both of these institutions in that two-fifths of its students are women—more than are found at most other science-oriented schools. In fact, as Rice greatly expanded its programs in the humanities and the social sciences, as well as in architecture and, more recently, in a school of music, it changed its name to Rice University. In recent years it has profited both from its ties to NASA and from the "culture boom" in Houston.

Despite increasing national recognition and growing attraction to students, particularly from New England, Rice remains to this day a regional institution. Just over half of its students are from Texas and two-thirds come from the South. Once a tuition-free institution, but forced to charge tuition in recent years by the ever-rising costs of higher education, the undiscounted price remains low and financial aid is available to all who can show need. Edward B. Fiske ends his comments on Rice in *Selective Guide to Colleges*, "Throw in the pint-sized tuition and ten-gallon endowment, and you have the best academic bargain in American higher education."[1]

LEGACIES OF THE PREVIOUS SEARCH

Rice University was presided over from 1907 to 1946 by Edgar Odell Lovett, from 1946 to 1960 by William Vermillion Houston, and from 1961 to 1968 by Kenneth S. Pitzer. In 1968, Pitzer left Rice to become president of Stanford University. When Pitzer announced his resignation, three of Rice's seven trustees had just come on the board.[2] After Pitzer's departure, the trustees asked three senior administrators to become interim admin-

[1] New York: Times Books, 1985, p. 421.
[2] Rice University has a bicameral structure, with a small board of trustees that has ultimate responsibility for the governance of the institution, and a larger board of governors that meets regularly with the trustees.

istrators of the university, and they asked the faculty to form a committee to assist with the search for a new president. No budget for their work and few instructions were provided for the prospective committee, which the faculty created by electing seven of its members. Two undergraduates and one graduate student were invited to participate as well, without a vote.

The group floundered, uncertain of its assignment. In January 1969 the chairman of the faculty advisory committee met with the trustees and asked for advice as to how his committee should proceed. The trustees responded that the advisory committee should collect the names of people qualified to be Rice's president and forward this list to the board. Nothing was said about numbers, or ranking, or the directions in which the board thought Rice should move. Nevertheless, the trustees indicated that no candidate who was unacceptable to the faculty would be chosen president.

Only two weeks later, just as the faculty advisory committee was starting seriously about its business, the trustees selected William Masterson as the next president of the university. Masterson was then president of the University of Chattanooga, a distinctly non-eminent urban commuter school, which that same year became the University of Tennessee at Chattanooga. Before going to the private and then faltering University of Chattanooga, Masterson had been professor of history and dean of humanities at Rice.

When the trustees, the trustee selection committee, and the board of governors met with Masterson to discuss his appointment, Ralph O'Connor, then a member of the board of governors, asked the chairman of the board of trustees what the faculty committee had to say about the appointment. The chairman responded, "We haven't talked to them yet. We are going to do that this afternoon." O'Connor and Masterson looked at each other with surprise. Masterson had apparently been quite eager to leave Chattanooga, where board members and the local community had been at odds concerning the school's orientation. But Masterson was not a fool. Addressing himself to the board chairman, he said that if the faculty did not enthusiastically endorse him, he could not become an effective president. He suggested that they stop the press release and meet with the faculty immediately. It was too late to recall the press release, however, and the story broke before Masterson could have this meeting. The Rice faculty was not in 1968, nor is it today, a contentious faculty. Indeed, the

265

atmosphere at Rice has been one of a certain degree of civility, perhaps just a bit Southern—a degree of equanimity rare among distinguished academics. Still, the faculty exploded on learning the news of Masterson's selection. There was seemingly no animus against him as a historian and not a scientist, as was expected of a new president, but he had not been a popular dean. Moreover, there was an expectation that Rice's next president would be a scholar like his recent predecessor. But Masterson had spent most of his professional life as an administrator and had published little.

Not only were the Rice faculty appalled by the choice of Masterson, they were angered by the manner in which he had been selected. Normally nonpolitical, they held strategy sessions to decide what to do, and called upon their colleagues to participate in an organized protest. When a formal vote was taken, ninety-five percent of the faculty voted to censure the board and to refuse to accept the appointment of Masterson. A student vote followed and produced similar results.

The trustees, who had expected their choice to be popular, were enraged by what they saw as an extravagant campus reaction. One faculty member recalled that it was like a place under siege. Masterson, viewing the battlefield from Tennessee, decided his presidency at Rice would not be tenable and resigned the position he had never held. The trustees then appointed Rice historian Frank E. Vandiver, an older man and one of the few faculty members who had defended the board, as acting president and began another search.

The troubles on campus had been widely publicized, making it difficult to attract good candidates. No prospects seemed in sight. Finally, several trustees and faculty members learned that Norman Hackerman, president of the University of Texas at Austin, was not getting along with a powerful member of his board and might be interested in leaving. It is reported that the first reaction to this news on the part of the Rice trustees was that no one would move from the wealthiest of all state universities with 40,000 students to well-to-do but tiny Rice.[3] Indeed, the trustees were

[3] We have often encountered this reaction when we have talked with members of search committees who have asked us for suggestions concerning a possible president. When we mention someone currently in an eminent position at an eminent institution, our interlocutor is likely to say, "So-and-so surely will not leave that place to come to lowly little us," or words to that effect. When we have the opportunity, we resist this common assumption about other people's situations and preferences, urge

able to persuade Hackerman to consider Rice, and the Rice faculty found him an acceptable choice. Finally, a new president was on board, but mistrust and hostility on the part of both faculty and board lingered for many years thereafter, down to the time of Hackerman's resignation.

PLANNING THE NEW SEARCH

Between 1968 and 1984, when Hackerman resigned, the entire board of trustees, most of the members of the board of governors and half of the faculty had turned over. Even so, the Rice faculty and governing boards were extraordinarily nervous about how to conduct a search that would avoid the blunders of the earlier time. When the governing boards chose Ralph O'Connor as chairman of the search committee, he was particularly alert to the delicate issues of process in presidential selection. Indeed, it was O'Connor who had raised the question of faculty consultation when William Masterson had been chosen. A Houston businessman, O'Connor was the son-in-law of the late George Brown, the largest donor in Rice's history. His professional life as an investor gave him sufficient flexibility so that he could devote the requisite time to a search. O'Connor began by reading everything he could find about how to conduct a search. Next, he telephoned individuals who, in recent years, had headed search committees at institutions similar to Rice. In Dartmouth's search for a president to succeed John Kemeny, O'Connor found a model which he thought would work for Rice, with some modification.

When Hackerman's resignation was announced on campus, Albert Van Helden, professor of history and speaker of the Rice faculty, approached the chairman of the board of trustees, Charles Duncan, concerning faculty participation in the search. Duncan invited Van Helden to have lunch with O'Connor and himself to discuss the composition of the search committee. The trustees had recognized that a single search committee made up of faculty members, students, alumni, and trustees would be requisite. However, wanting to maintain some control, O'Connor and Duncan proposed

---

search committees not to be afraid of rebuff, and encourage them to ask people whose current contentment may be for show, hiding a difficult situation of a professional or personal sort which could be improved by a move.

to Van Helden a committee that would include two faculty members chosen by the trustees from a list of six provided by the faculty council.

After the lunch, Van Helden discussed this proposition with about a dozen members of the faculty. Then he arranged another lunch with Duncan and O'Connor to share his findings. Van Helden brought two senior and highly respected members of the faculty, Neal Lane and Franz Brotzen, to the luncheon. Both men were former speakers of the faculty. The three faculty members explained to Duncan and O'Connor that the proposed mode of selection was demeaning: "It said, in so many words, that the trustees didn't trust the faculty." Moreover, to have two representatives would be too few. At this point there could easily have been a stalemate. As Franz Brotzen put it concerning himself, he went out on a limb. "I told the trustees that I would guarantee them they would get three people they could get along with, if they let the faculty do their own selecting. I promised them there would be no hotheads." The selection, moreover, would be by election, not appointment by the faculty council. As insurance to the trustees, the three professors agreed that, should a faculty member elected to the search committee prove uncooperative, then they themselves would work with O'Connor to find a replacement from the faculty. Furthermore, they would draft a statement for prospective committee members which would highlight the seriousness of the search committee's responsibility and the requirement of confidentiality. However uneasy the trustees may have been concerning the strength of these guarantees of cooperative rather than adversarial faculty choices, they certainly wished to avoid a confrontation, and thus accepted the recommendation for three elected representatives.

Van Helden as speaker of the faculty council called an open meeting of the council to discuss how the election should proceed. He circulated the *Guidelines for Membership of the Rice University Presidential Search Committee*—a remarkable document.[4] In addition to emphasizing the signifi-

[4] The text of this document was as follows:

1. Committee members must be prepared to devote a substantial portion of their time, from May 1984 through the Spring of 1985, to this search. It is essential that all members participate in all deliberations. Those with prior commitments to extensive summer travel, to major research or business projects, or to heavy administrative, teaching, or course loads may not be able to give the requisite time and attention, and should therefore not offer themselves as candidates.

2. The job of the Search Committee is to select a small number of finalists (3–6) from a pool of candidates, and recommend them to the Board. Each committee member will be involved in all

cant commitment of time, including travel, the guidelines declared that all committee members would be involved in all aspects of the search and that "such frank procedures within the Committee will only be possible if committee members hold all matters pertaining to the search in strictest confidence." The guidelines instructed committee members to begin their task uncommitted to any candidate and without any bias toward discipline, gender, race, or educational background. Prospective committee members were invited to think of themselves not as speaking for a particular constituency, "as representing narrow interests," but as responsible for considering "a successful future for Rice University as a whole their paramount objective." In many situations, such idealistic hopes would meet with a cynical response; as we shall see hereafter, in this case they did not.

After a lengthy discussion, the faculty decided on a two-stage procedure for choosing the three representatives. The first election would choose one person to represent the humanities and the social sciences and another person to represent engineering and the physical sciences. A second election would choose an at-large representative from among the remaining candidates. The university-wide nature of the enterprise was reflected in the fact that in the secret, preferential ballot where people would indicate first, second, and third choices, all faculty members could vote for all three representatives.

To stand for election, faculty members had to obtain a petition with twenty signatures indicating sufficient support. Eleven individuals did so. Each gave a short talk, outlining qualifications to serve on the committee and interest in serving in this capacity. Ten days after the open faculty meeting, the faculty voted by two successive written ballots. To speak for

---

aspects of this job, and he/she will, therefore, have access to all available information gathered by the Committee and be involved in all its deliberations. Such frank procedures within the Committee will only be possible if committee members hold all matters pertaining to the search in strictest confidence.

3. The Search Committee will consider candidates with many backgrounds, qualifications, and experiences. It is therefore imperative that committee members approach their task with an open mind and without any bias towards a preferred race, sex, academic discipline, vocation, or education. It is also imperative that committee members not enter into the search with a particular candidate already in mind.

4. Although the Search Committee will be made up of members of all components of the Rice community, these members are asked not to consider themselves as representing narrow interests. While differences of opinion are likely to occur, all committee members should make a successful future for Rice University as a whole their paramount objective. Under such circumstances the Committee will be able to do its job harmoniously and effectively.

"the two cultures" in a single university, the faculty elected William C. Martin, professor and department chairman of sociology (who had received his doctorate in a joint program in religion and sociology at Harvard) as the representative of humanities and social sciences, and G. King Walters, professor of physics and dean of natural sciences, to represent engineering and the physical sciences. C. Sidney Burrus, professor and department chairman of electrical and computer engineering, became the at-large representative. In the manageably small worlds of Rice's most respected faculty members, it turned out that all three men knew and liked one another. Indeed, Martin and Burrus had been the closest of friends, competing in weekly squash games, for seventeen years.[5]

By application process followed by interviews, the student government chose two student representatives, Garland A. Kelley, a senior with a double major in history and philosophy, as the undergraduate representative, and Alan Rister, a doctoral candidate in linguistics, as the graduate student representative.

The Rice alumni association named two Rice alumni, Catherine Hannah and Gus Hill, both former presidents of the alumni association and former members of the Rice board of governors, as alumni members of the search committee. The remaining members of the search committee were trustees: Josephine Abercrombie, C. M. Hudspeth, and Edward W. Kelley, Jr. Including O'Connor, four of Rice's seven trustees agreed to serve on the search committee, with trustee chairman Charles W. Duncan, Jr., joining the committee as an ex officio, non-voting member. All members of the search committee lived in the Houston metropolitan area.

GETTING UNDER WAY

On May 10, 1984, the day after the election of the faculty representatives, the newly constituted committee met at chairman O'Connor's home. Their charge was to present to the board of trustees a small group, no more

[5] The two men were featured in a *Houston Post* news story (December 20, 1985, p. H1) about male friendships. "They play squash together once a week and often meet for lunch to discuss everything from university politics to personal matters. As members of a search committee to select a new president for Rice, they recently spent many hours together. . . . The two men and their wives and families . . . attend the same church . . . , often meet for dinner on Saturday night and take out-of-town trips together. 'We share a real love for the academic life,' says Burrus . . . 'But that's superficial. The root of our friendship is centered around values and goals.' "

270

than five or six candidates, for interview and selection. Some committee members wanted to begin work right away, while others suggested waiting until September when the fall term would begin. Because Ralph O'Connor planned to be out of town in June, the committee agreed that June would be a vacation month.

Before starting their intensive work in July, members of the search committee accepted O'Connor's proposal that they hold a retreat in order to discuss what sorts of leadership were needed for Rice University and to get to know each other better. Josephine Abercrombie volunteered her Kentucky horse farm as the site for the retreat and, on May 19, the search committee members flew to Kentucky in private jets owned by some members of the committee—the first of many private and commercial jet flights they would take.

The two-day retreat turned out to be a critical event. One person put into words what many thought: "We went in as twelve individuals and came out a committee." Prior to the retreat, because they had been independently selected by faculty, students, alumni, and the board of trustees, there was no way of knowing whether the group might coalesce as a team, or work together at all.

On Saturday morning, committee members shared their hopes for the university. Their visions turned out to be similar. Faculty members had worried that the trustees might prefer a nonacademic person, perhaps even someone from business, for Rice's next president. There was relief in the trustees' promise, implicit in the early discussions and then stated outright, that they had no intention of selecting someone for the presidency of whom the faculty did not approve. All constituencies represented on the search committee would have to support the new president, "or it would be a total disaster." Correspondingly, the trustee members of the search committee were pleased to discover that the faculty members who were sharing the task were not pushing any particularistic interests, but were concerned for the university as a whole. Indeed, everyone at the retreat was ambitious for Rice, wanting a president who could make it more nationally known.

The retreat gave the student members of the search committee an opportunity to establish themselves as persons to be taken seriously. On the first day, chairman O'Connor turned to the undergraduate and asked

271

bluntly, "and what can you contribute to this committee, Garland?" A faculty member sitting next to Garland Kelley recalled thinking to himself, "poor kid!" Kelley paused, and then replied. "I've thought a good bit about that. Perhaps I've been asked to be on this committee as a token. But I don't intend to be a token. I think one of my biggest contributions will be that I don't have the disadvantage of hindsight that all of you do. I don't know what won't work, so I might just suggest you try it again."

One of the major aims of the retreat was to have committee members seriously confront their preconceptions and biases about the sort of person who might be chosen as the next president. "Did we *really* mean it when we said we wanted a scholar but the field didn't matter? Would we *really* choose a woman?" Gender and appropriate academic discipline were the issues most discussed and the most difficult for many members of the committee. Since its founding, Rice's national reputation, despite distinction in the humanities including music and anthropology, lay in its science, mathematics, and engineering programs. One of its four presidents had been a physicist; two were chemists; one was a mathematician. A few members of the search committee who had automatically assumed the next president would come from the hard sciences were surprised when the question of academic discipline was raised, whereas others said that they thought academic field was unimportant, and that perhaps it was time to have someone with a different background. The serious discourse led to an agreement to consider candidates regardless of academic field. Similarly, it had never occurred to some members of the search committee that the next president of the university could conceivably be a woman. They discussed this possibility at length and agreed to consider women on an equal footing with men.

The centrality of confidentiality in carrying out a search was a recurrent theme throughout the retreat. Of course this had been stressed in the guidelines as essential if all members of the search committee were to have equal access to information and to be candid with one another. The imperative need for confidentiality was also stressed by Elizabeth Dycus, whom Ralph O'Connor had invited to join the committee at the retreat. She had been the executive director of the search committee that had chosen David McLaughlin for the Dartmouth presidency. In delineating what Dartmouth had done, and to underscore the significance of confidentiality, she presented examples of what could go wrong as a consequence of rumors or of leaks from any committee member, and the ways in which even the most casual hint of names could damage or even destroy a search. "Elizabeth Dycus gave us lots of good advice," one Rice search committee member commented. Another added, "throughout the search process, we continually referred back to what she had said. She saved us a lot of trouble."

Recognizing both the enormous amount of paperwork and the concomitant need for keeping it confidential, members of the search committee at the retreat had agreed that the committee should speedily find an executive director to coordinate its activities. Ralph O'Connor asked whether anyone knew someone suitable for such a position, and one member of the committee suggested the wife of a faculty member. O'Connor called her to ask whether she might be interested in being considered, but she was unable to give the task the requisite amount of time. In the course of arrangements for the retreat, Elizabeth Dycus had met Karen Ostrum George, a Rice alumna (B.A. 1977, M.A. 1978) who worked for O'Connor's company, Highland Resources, Inc., and Dycus now suggested her for this task. Prior to the search, O'Connor had discussed with George how the search might proceed, and he wholeheartedly agreed with Dycus concerning George's competence. But he had demurred when it came to recommending George to the committee for fear of appearing to be giving preferential treatment to one of his own employees. He also had doubts concerning the appropriateness of having two individuals who worked for Highland Resources involved with the search. Indeed, prior to the retreat, he had asked George to help him think of persons who might be capable executive directors.

Several members of the search committee said that they did not think Karen George should be excluded from consideration merely because of her association with Highland Resources. Since O'Connor and George already had a good working relationship, such an arrangement could be advantageous. O'Connor consented to have the full committee interview Karen George with himself not present and, again without his participation, to make a decision whether or not to engage her.

The committee interviewed Karen George, offered her the position of executive director, and she began work immediately, arranging to be on leave from her full-time duties at Highland Resources, Inc. Moreover, largely based upon Elizabeth Dycus's advice, chairman Ralph O'Connor decided to base search activities in downtown Houston, three miles from campus, where adequate, secure space would be located and confidentiality better preserved. A search office was set up at Highland Resources, with Karen George's secretary handling typing and clerical work. Funds to cover expenses of the search were kept in a private account. Financial records were maintained in the search office and not turned over to the university until the search was completed. All committee papers were kept in the search office and were not allowed outside of the room. Committee members were expected to go to that office prior to committee meetings—which were held in a conference room adjoining the search office—to read curricula vitae, letters of reference concerning candidates, committee minutes, and anything else involving the search. All committee members were given keys to the search office and the office building so that they could come and go, day or night, at their convenience.

Ralph O'Connor and Karen George reviewed the extant literature concerning presidential searches, and all committee members were given copies of John Nason's handbook, *Presidential Search*, and other potentially useful material on searches. In mid-summer, announcements of the vacancy were placed in the *Chronicle of Higher Education* and the *New York Times*, with August 15 given as the deadline for nominations and applications. Letters requesting nominations were sent to all Rice faculty, students, administrators, and alumni, and in addition to the presidents of major universities nationwide and also to universities in Texas and the Southwest (athletic) Conference. On July 5, at the first search committee meeting held after the retreat, committee members discussed how to evaluate the candidacies that were beginning to pour in. Following a pattern common to many searches, committee members decided on three categories, with "A" indicating that the person merited further consideration, "B" that more information was needed, and "C" that the person was not a strong contender for the Rice presidency.

"RESOURCE" VISITS

Beginning in July and continuing through the fall, members of the search committee reviewed the materials pouring in concerning prospects, and made trips to visit those they termed "resource people." Individuals so defined were leaders in higher education, many of them presidents, and a few provosts or directors of research institutes, from whom the members of the search committee thought they could learn about the office of the presidency as well as solicit suggestions as to possible candidates. In some cases the "resource person" was also someone the search committee saw as a prospect for Rice.

Not every person identified as a "resource" had heard of Ralph O'Connor. But all were aware in a general way of the distinction of Rice University, and a certain comity among members of the elite group of research universities, the Association of American Universities, to which Rice had just been elected, provided entrée for O'Connor and his fellow committee members. All trips to resource persons, by either commercial airlines or the private jets of committee members, were made by four or five members of the search committee, including at least one faculty member and one trustee, and, when possible, a student and an alumnus.

These resource visits had several purposes. One, of course, was to solicit the names of prospective candidates and to gather more information about people who had already been suggested. A second purpose was to learn how these educational leaders viewed Rice, what they saw as Rice's strengths, weaknesses, opportunities, and challenges. Still another purpose was to learn more about how successful presidents saw themselves and their jobs. Rice search committee members asked questions such as, "How do you deal with faculty deadwood? What do you look for in subordinates? How do you get in touch with departments not in your field? Is a major fundraising campaign a good idea or not?"

"It was like having a grant to study American higher education," one search committee member commented. "It was thrilling." These discussions went beyond the somewhat abstract agreement at the retreat that people from various disciplines, and women as well as men, could be considered for the presidency. On the visits, several committee members who had remained uncertain about the idea of a woman president shifted their position when they met and were greatly impressed by the three women presidents they visited. At least one of them was regarded as a conceivable candidate, but she made clear that she had no intention of moving. More generally, the horizons of committee members were broadened so as to consider alternative styles and approaches to the presidency.

Although the search committee members began their collective effort wanting to find someone who could lead Rice to national greatness, that vision did not translate readily into the biographies of specific individuals. In talking with the resource people, they were repeatedly told not only to be imaginative in thinking about candidates, but to look for someone young and exciting, with lots of enthusiasm and energy. "Look for someone who is a real comer," was a frequent message. This translated into willingness to find someone who could not be guaranteed to stay forever at Rice—someone other institutions would seek to recruit—rather than someone they could be relatively certain of retaining. In other words, they should be willing to recruit someone not already famous, but who would become famous in the course of helping Rice become a national model for others.

Consonant with this advice was a related judgment that a prospect's scholarship was more important than experience in management, academic or corporate. Search committee members had asked each resource person whether, other things being equal, they should prefer a person with a scholarly record and some evident potential for leadership, or a person with proven leadership but only a meager scholarly record. The answer was always to go with the scholar. One resource person summed it up well with the comment: "There is a sociology to academia and one must have lived and succeeded in it to be accepted as a leader in it."

The question of academic discipline also came up on these visits, with most resource persons assuming that, because of its history and reputation, Rice would be looking for a scientist. But even those who made this assumption cautioned the search committee not to "lock in" to any one discipline. "Don't look for disciplines; look for an individual."

The resource people were also asked about individuals, including questions concerning individuals who had been nominated and who, on paper, looked interesting to the committee. Several resource people spoke at length about the need to court "prospects" and not to treat individuals as "candidates." "Don't ask if someone is interested in the presidency until you really have to have an answer. And even then, don't accept no, but assume that the person can perhaps be persuaded." Those resource persons in whom the committee was interested were given the opportunity to speculate about their own potential interest in Rice in a situation that

276

might be called tacit courtship. In several cases where Ralph O'Connor asked for the privilege of a return visit, some resource persons insisted that such a visit would not make sense if its aim was recruitment, thus pulling away from an ambiguous situation in which the resource persons felt that they might be leading the Rice committee on.

These resource visits served a significant additional function. Like the retreat, these excursions brought search committee members together and helped them get to know each other better and to talk through their different notions of leadership. On their way to the resource visits, the search committee members discussed how the search was going and thought aloud about what questions to ask. En route home, they discussed their visits and the important insights they had gained. Just as the resource visits themselves proved educational, the discussions on the trip back to Houston furthered the search committee members' understanding of Rice University. Trustees, faculty, students, and alumni who had simultaneously heard the advice concerning Rice and the nature of the presidency, naturally discovered that they had "heard" not quite identical things, and sought to understand and come to terms with their differing interpretations and reactions to what had been said.

Throughout the late summer and fall, members of the search committee met almost every week to report on their visits and to discuss applicants and nominees. When the members arrived at committee meetings, black notebooks, prepared by Karen George, were placed around the conference table, each with the name of a search committee member on its front cover. Serving as place cards, the notebooks (which included a one-page summary sheet of background information on each candidate gleaned from *Who's Who* and other reference works), were placed in a different location at each meeting so that no individuals or groups of individuals always sat together. Likewise, although search committee chairman Ralph O'Connor sat at the head of the table at the first committee meeting, he changed his seat at every session thereafter.

O'Connor was sensitive not only to seating arrangements but to the dynamics within the group as well. When he concluded that one trustee was pushing a candidate too hard and his assertiveness was preventing others from freely expressing themselves, he took the trustee aside and asked him to play a less dominant role. The importance of this nonpublic intervention also cannot be overestimated. We have witnessed intimidation of the shy and diffident by imposing trustees, and, of course, most of us have the experience of being intimidated at one time or another, especially if our views are not well formulated, let alone guaranteed to stand up in combat. O'Connor's leadership gave each individual a sense of playing a significant part in the collective enterprise. As one member declared: "He kept it fair in letting everyone have a voice." Said another: "He made certain that no interest was ever slighted." "He's my hero," said a third committee member. In addition to his alert and sensitive leadership of group meetings, O'Connor's enthusiasm about the task was infectious. From the outset, he told committee members that their participation in the search effort was the single most valuable contribution they could make to Rice. Throwing his own energies fully into the work, O'Connor persuaded his committee colleagues that they were making history: this was an opportunity for Rice to leap to the forefront of American higher education. O'Connor helped search committee members believe that they had "a sense of mission."

When the deadline for applications and nominations arrived on August 15, the search committee had received 370 names, all but 60 of them nominations. Up to this point, no oral inquiries had been made about anyone. When committee members shared their ratings of each person on the basis of the materials collected by Karen George, majority rule prevailed unless someone on the committee thought a prospect looked particularly promising, in which case Karen George was asked to gather additional background information. On the basis of this work alone, without any telephone calls, the list of 370 names could be reduced in a rather cursory way to 120. At this point, in cases where the biographical material Karen George had provided was deemed insufficient, committee members began to make telephone calls to individuals who might provide additional information. All committee members, including the two students, participated in the calling. During each call, the caller explained that the matter was extremely confidential and requested that no mention of it be made to anyone. Sometimes, calls consisted of asking about a whole string of rather well-known academics, none of whom was presented as someone in whom Rice was particularly interested, but rather as a sort of foray into who might be "out there." And indeed, the Rice search was still in its early stages, so that it was likely that the prospect about whom committee members were calling was still unaware that he or she had been nominated. Apparently it worked: the committee did not learn of any leaks from these calls; the persons who were called seemed to appreciate the need for secrecy.

Early in the search, there was an incident which was thought to be a breach of confidentiality and turned out not to be. Just before leaving on a trip to visit "resource people," Karen George left a big stack of papers on her desk for her secretary to xerox for search committee members. On top of the pile she wrote "Trish," her secretary's name. The next afternoon, when Karen George called Trish to see if she had received any telephone messages, she asked her whether she had completed the xeroxing. Trish responded that she had not found the papers; there was nothing on top of Karen George's desk. Neither woman could figure out what had happened and, after a thorough search of the office, they began to worry that someone had somehow gotten into the office and stolen the papers. Two miserably anxious days later, the mystery was solved. The Mexican employee who cleaned the offices at the end of the day had seen the note on the stack of papers and had thought it said "Trash." In the process of picking up the papers to throw them away, she had second thoughts and put them aside to ask Karen George about them the next time she saw her. The papers were retrieved; the crisis was over.

In October search committee members visited some additional resource people and began to meet also with a small number of prospective candidates. As before, visits were paid to individuals who could serve both as resources concerning academic leadership and as likely prospects for the Rice presidency. Although, in most of these cases, no effort was made to disguise the double purpose of the visits, the fact that the word "candidate" was never used not only made it unnecessary for those who were visited to commit themselves (unless they were absolutely certain they could not consider becoming candidates) but also protected them from harm in case of leaks. Based on the report of the three or four members who had visited particular prospects, six people were invited at different times in the late fall to come to an off-campus location in Houston to meet with the entire committee.

279

CRIES AND WHISPERS

The three faculty members of the search committee had to cope throughout the fall with rumors concerning those supposedly being considered for the presidency. Some names were accurate, good "educated guesses;" others, one search committee member commented, were "patently ridiculous." The faculty trio had decided in advance how to answer tricky questions so that they would give consistent responses and not be caught off-guard. When queried about candidates, the faculty members on the search committee replied, "I haven't heard that rumor," "I'd heard that one, too," or "that's a new one on me." One frequently asked question was whether any candidates from inside the university were in the running. Several Rice administrators and faculty members had been nominated, and had been considered alongside other nominees. When the question about internal candidates was posed, the faculty members responded that each candidate was being given the attention he or she deserved, a remark that occasionally drew smiles.

One much more serious and potentially debilitating rumor was that the search was "fixed." After much anxiety and thought, the faculty members on the search committee decided to respond. In a memorandum sent to all faculty and administrators, Martin and Burrus (Walters was out of town) stated that virtually all of the rumors were erroneous. The search was proceeding well, and the committee was keeping to its original schedule. The memorandum declared that rumors were hurting the process.[6] Most faculty members reacted sympathetically to the memorandum. One faculty member complained that the memo trod on academic freedom; a few others suddenly got interested, asking "who's gossiping, and what about?" But most people were reassured, and rumors subsided.

In addition to their memorandum, Martin, Walters, and Burrus gave periodic reports to the faculty at regularly scheduled faculty meetings. Faculty members were assured that the search committee and the trustees would be in a position to announce a new president so that there would be

[6] It may appear farfetched for the faculty members to have claimed that rumors were doing any harm, although of course people might be harmed on their home campuses if the rumors spread there of their candidacy at Rice. The rumors could also be a serious matter if the names being tossed around were of well-known, glamorous figures, since it might turn out that the reality of the person who would become the next president could not live up to the advance billing of celebrity.

no interregnum. At one meeting, after the three search committee members had deflected several questions about candidates, one professor stood up and said that, if he had known that the three faculty members on the search committee would be so discreet, he would never have voted for them. At the end of the meeting, he stood up again and jokingly pleaded, "Won't you give us just *one* name?"

In casual encounters throughout the search process, Martin, Walters, and Burrus were quizzed about the search by colleagues. However, they reported that they never experienced any disagreeable pressures to divulge information, as against more casual inquiry. Their colleagues respected their need to maintain confidentiality. "We knew they had to be different people. It was a chapter of their lives they couldn't talk about," one professor commented. Another explained that the faculty had enormous respect for these three men, and if they said that everything was going well, their word was trusted.

To make accidental leaks less likely, Ralph O'Connor decided to give aliases to the candidates being brought to meet with the search committee. These code names were used in the discussions of candidates, and hotel and airplane reservations were made in these names. O'Connor thought up the code names and then asked the members of the search committee to figure out the rationale for each. "It pepped up the process a little," he commented. It also proved helpful. At one point in the later stages of the search, two members of the search committee were talking about a candidate they had just interviewed when they realized that they might have been overheard. But because they were calling the person by his code name, "Baseball," no one could figure out whom, perhaps even what, they were discussing.

THE COURTSHIP OF GEORGE RUPP

"Kentucky" was the alias given George Erik Rupp, a reference to the former, much admired basketball coach at the University of Kentucky, Adolf Rupp. Rupp's name had come up in the conversations with "resource people" concerning the sorts of individuals who might be considered by Rice. When it was first mentioned early in the search process, Martin said he "perked up, but my feelings were those W. H. Auden attributed to Joseph

281

when told Mary was pregnant. 'Yes, it may be so. Is it likely? No.' "
Martin was certain that Rice University would never name a theologian
as its next president. Others reacted similarly to the nomination of Rupp.
One committee member said that, although George Rupp looked attractive on paper, he still assumed that they would select a scientist.

In October, when four members of the search committee were planning
a trip to the Boston area to talk with another prospect, they decided, almost as an afterthought, to try to arrange a visit with Rupp, who was dean
of the Harvard Divinity School. Gathering that they were looking him
over as a possible candidate, Rupp responded, when they telephoned him,
that he was not interested in being considered. The caller persisted, and
asked if committee members could simply meet with him informally to
talk about Rice, perhaps at Rupp's home so that the visit could remain
confidential. (The official home of the dean is just across Francis Avenue
from Rupp's office.) Rupp finally agreed, and four members of the search
committee spent an hour in conversation with George and Nancy Rupp.

Reflecting on this meeting after the search had concluded, Ralph
O'Connor said that Rupp had made it clear at this meeting that he was
talking with them only to be courteous. Rupp had explained carefully that
he could not possibly consider the presidency of Rice at that time, since he
was embarked on a capital campaign, and there were other things he
wanted to do for the Divinity School which would be jeopardized if there
should be any suggestion that he might be leaving.

Even if committee members had not been told that they should not take
"no" for an answer, they were aware that Rupp had taken an early administrative position as vice-chancellor of Johnston College, a no longer extant
experimental college of the University of Redlands, when he was only
thirty-two years old. In light of this trajectory, it was not irrational to
suppose that the notion of becoming a college president had not been entirely alien to the lives of George and Nancy Rupp, nor were they immune
to the call of educational adventure.

On the side of the search committee, "that visit did it," as one member
explained: "Rupp just bounded into the front ranks." King Walters, professor and chairman of physics, was the faculty member on the trip, and
the fact that he returned so favorably impressed led Sidney Burrus, professor and chairman of electrical and computer engineering, the person

282

elected at large, to conclude that Rupp was worth serious consideration. Catherine Hannah, alumna representative, reported that, following the advice resource persons gave, she had not paid attention to Rupp's field of academic specialization; rather, it was "the man himself that came through so strongly." When the search committee reduced the list of prospective candidates and then reduced it again, Rupp's name remained on the active list, despite his strong denial of interest.

In early January, the search committee re-evaluated the top group of candidates and came once again to George Rupp's name. "Rupp had said, 'No, this isn't a good time for me,' and we really hadn't known how to deal with that, so we'd said, 'Oh, okay.' " But, just maybe, they thought, he could be persuaded to become a candidate, telling themselves, "Perhaps we hadn't sold ourselves strongly enough."

Both Bill Martin and Ralph O'Connor placed telephone calls to Rupp to ask him if members of the search committee could come to Cambridge to talk with him again. Martin made his call on a Friday afternoon; told that Rupp was out of the office, he asked to have him return the call. On Sunday morning, the disappointed O'Connor telephoned Martin to report that he had just spoken with Rupp and that the latter's answer was still no. Then, a few minutes later, Martin received a call from Rupp, who said that he had received the message that Martin had called and was returning his call. Since this time it was perfectly clear that Rupp was not being called to permit another courtesy visit but was being actively sought as a prospect, Martin judged that Rupp had to be, if ever so slightly, interested or else he would not have returned the call. Recognizing this glimmer of hope, and appreciating that in any case he had nothing to lose, Martin did his best to persuade Rupp to reconsider and to look more closely at Rice. Like the other faculty members on the search committee, Martin spoke as a dedicated institutional loyalist. He said to Rupp that Rice was in a unique position: It was wealthy and small; it had not yet achieved its potential; it was therefore able to leap forward in a way that universities in the Northeast could not. Rice's next president could have a real impact on American higher education. It was the chance of a lifetime.

In his first conversations with the Rice search committee, Rupp may not himself have believed that, as a non-scientist, he stood much chance of becoming president of Rice, and thus would not want to be distracted from his ongoing work by playing with a fantasy. Martin's call changed that. And Rupp's own situation was somewhat changed, for he was far enough along in his fund-raising for the Divinity School to make it possible for him to think about something else. Ralph O'Connor and Martin made the trip to Cambridge on January 22 and were able to persuade the Rupps to come to Houston the following week to meet with the full committee. Two trustees, one of them board chairman Duncan, could not arrange their schedules to be there, but all the rest of the committee met with George and Nancy Rupp on January 29. There was general enthusiasm about the possibility of Rupp as Rice's next president.

After the Rupps' visit, one of the trustees observed, "If he weren't a minister, he'd be perfect." C. M. ("Hank") Hudspeth, a trustee on the search committee who is an attorney in Houston and has taught at Rice, went to the library and checked out Rupp's most recent book, *Beyond Existentialism and Zen: Religion in a Pluralistic World.*[7] Since Hudspeth is regarded by faculty members and trustees as a careful scholar, his statement that he was impressed by Rupp's book removed misgivings. He convinced the search committee, one person recalled, that, although a man of religious sensibility, Rupp made decisions based on rational principles, not on dogma.

Bill Martin, by now a strong supporter of Rupp's candidacy, went to the library with another purpose, namely, to see to what extent presidents of institutions distinguished in science and engineering were themselves scientists or engineers. With the benefit of a 1970 American Council on Education report and the 1983 *Gorman Report*, each of which ranked the top twenty schools in science and engineering, Martin then consulted other reference books to find out who had been their presidents in 1970 and in 1983. In each year, some three-quarters of these institutions—including MIT, Berkeley and Harvard, Johns Hopkins, Stanford, Michigan, Chicago, and others—had presidents from backgrounds outside of science and engineering. Martin also looked up the age at inauguration of these individuals and of other outstanding college and university presidents. Their average age was forty-six, and several had been as young, or younger than, George Rupp, who was forty-two.

[7] New York: Oxford University Press, 1979.

284

Martin duly reported these facts to the search committee, further fueling the growing enthusiasm about George Rupp. As one person put it, "they had struck oil!" But there were two trustees who had not seen Rupp, and the Rupp enthusiasts were aware that some sort of exchange between George Rupp and selected faculty members and administrators at Rice would be requisite on both sides. George Rupp had to be convinced. Moreover, because of the unexpected nature of the "oil" they had struck, they would be helped by some confirmation that their prospecting had not strayed too far from their mandate. Yet the search committee recognized that, as had been made clear from their first conversation with Rupp, they would lose him as a candidate if complete confidentiality was not maintained. There was little risk of leaks in the third visit to Cambridge, arranged for February 13, when the two trustees could talk with George and Nancy Rupp. So as "not to step on any toes," the chairman of the Rice board of trustees, Charles Duncan, telephoned Derek Bok, after securing Rupp's permission, to let Bok know that Rice was talking with Rupp.

There was, however, a hazard to confidentiality when O'Connor began to talk to individuals who had known and worked with George Rupp. When the search committee had narrowed down its list of prospects to eight, there had been some preliminary inquiries in which George Rupp's name was mentioned to knowledgeable persons along with other names, some serious and some not, along with a request that the telephone call be confidential. The graduate student member of the search committee, Alan Rister, looked up old Green Bay catalogues to identify the names of those who had worked with Rupp during the two years he was there, and O'Connor then telephoned both those who had reported to Rupp and those he had reported to. All that he learned reinforced his and the committee's judgment that Rupp was right for Rice. There was no breach of confidentiality vis-à-vis Rupp from any of these telephone calls.

But how could the Rupps be brought to Houston, and actually to the campus, without the news getting out? Just a short time earlier, they had experienced the first and, for all practical purposes, the only leak of the search. The name of a candidate who had met with the search committee and visited the Rice campus had appeared in Houston, Washington, and Boston newspapers. The source of the leak was never known. Some search committee members speculated that the candidate himself had released the information because it was advantageous for him to be viewed on his home campus as a serious contender at Rice. Shortly after the press coverage, the candidate had withdrawn from the Rice search and accepted the post of provost at his home university. Others noted that the candidate's visit had involved a large number of people on campus, and the likelihood of leaks was quite high. "The great amount of exposure, and the fact that the visit got into the press taught us something. It was too great; we had tried to be too inclusive."

When word of the earlier candidate's visit appeared in the press, a student newspaper reporter scented a possible story and began to do some investigative reporting of his own. Making a list of putative candidates, the reporter telephoned these people and asked them if they were on Rice's short list. The Rice search committee learned what was going on when several of these people called the search committee to ask about their standing in the search. "It was awkward, and in a couple of cases, embarrassing," one search committee member commented. Ralph O'Connor quickly made an appointment with the student newspaper editor and explained the damage that leaks can cause. O'Connor discovered that the student newspaper staff was angry because they thought the search committee had given the information about the candidate's visit to the *Houston Post* and not to them. O'Connor explained that this was not the case and promised them that he would give them the scoop on the appointment of the new president. The student reporters agreed, in turn, to stop their pursuit of leaks about the search. (The fact that they were prepared to do so suggests something about the quality of Rice, although in fact even at campuses with more assertively rebellious students, arrangements of this sort have sometimes been agreed to.)

Determined to forestall further leaks, the search committee determined that when Rupp came, he would meet with a restricted number of individuals, smaller than the number who had met with the previous candidate. Those included would not be "certain people who were perceived as security risks." In a way, the previous leak turned at this point into an advantage, for it legitimated this level of secrecy. As one faculty member explained, the campus had seen the consequences of too much exposure.

Meanwhile, in Cambridge, George Rupp was uncertain whether or not he wanted to leave Harvard Divinity School and to become president of

286

Rice. Born in New Jersey, he had earned his undergraduate degree at Princeton, his Bachelor of Divinity degree from Yale, and his Ph.D. from the Committee on the Study of Religion at Harvard—a committee that includes faculty from arts and sciences and from the Divinity School. Thereafter, Rupp had moved to the experimental Johnston College, at the University of Redlands, where he had been a faculty member and vice-chancellor. In 1974, Rupp had returned to Harvard as assistant professor of theology; two years later, he had been promoted to associate professor and chairman of the department of theology. In 1977, Rupp, again the adventurer, had moved to the University of Wisconsin at Green Bay as professor of humanistic studies and dean for academic affairs. This campus had begun in 1968 as "Environmental U," as a *Harper's* article termed it, a wholly interdisciplinary program, primarily for undergraduates, focusing on "Man and His Environment." Two years later, he was back at Harvard as John Lord O'Brian Professor of Divinity and dean of the Divinity School.

When first approached by the Rice search committee, Rupp had been dean for five years, and he was planning a capital campaign and handling sensitive administrative issues within the school. His position as professor and, for the years immediately ahead, as dean, was secure; his work continued to be challenging and enjoyable. Yet Rice was interesting enough so that the Rupps were prepared to consider a move.

As he had made clear, Rupp could not consider a visit to Rice and Houston without assurance of confidentiality. It was good fortune that he had already scheduled an out-of-town trip for fund-raising and meetings with alumni, which enabled him to add Houston to his itinerary without telling anyone at Harvard Divinity School, not even his secretary, of the reason for the Houston stop-over. Nancy Rupp, assistant librarian at Buckingham Brown & Nichols School in Cambridge, found her brief absence from work more difficult to explain. Confidentiality was as important to her as to her husband, since she was being considered for a promotion and did not want to jeopardize her chances should they stay in Cambridge.

At the end of his visit to the Southwest, George Rupp, along with his wife Nancy—alias Mr. and Mrs. Kentucky—arrived in Houston on January 29. They met with search committee members, with selected faculty members and administrators, and with the board of trustees and the board of governors, leaving for home the morning of January 31.

The visit to Houston had intensified the Rupps' interest; moreover, they were confident that their interviews in Houston had gone well. Although there were definite advantages to remaining in Cambridge—Nancy could accept the likely promotion; their two daughters could continue in their schools; George could bring to conclusion some of his current projects at Harvard—the prospects at Rice had become increasingly inviting.

They were expecting to hear any day from the search committee. Days passed—not so many days, but they seemed long—without any word from Houston. As happens regularly, more even than many sensitive search committees appreciate, finalists at this point begin to wonder. The Rupps asked themselves whether they had been mistaken about the reception they had been given. Was perhaps someone else being interviewed? More seriously, had another person been offered the position? After their interest had successfully been incited, the courtship had seemed to end. The Rupps were climbing down from their emotional high, concluding that Rice must no longer be interested.

At this point, George Rupp received a telephone call from Bill Martin. "You're probably thinking that nothing is going on down here. You're wrong; you're still very much a strong candidate." Martin explained that the committee was moving as fast as possible. They were not simply holding him in reserve.

Rupp told Martin that he was grateful for the call. Rupp concluded from what Martin had said that the search committee members were discussing his candidacy with a few crucial individuals in order to be certain of wholehearted support, not simply of lukewarm approval or mild skepticism. In fact, Rupp had made it clear that he would not come to Rice if there was a dissident faction. He would have to be the choice of the entire board.

Rupp's reaction was an enormous relief for Bill Martin. Since Martin cared so deeply about Rice and had come so badly to want Rupp to be its next president, the days since Rupp's visit had quite possibly been more agonizing for Martin than for Rupp. Martin had developed a chronic stomachache and would get up in the middle of the night to write memos to himself. After one sleepless night, Martin's wife had told him that she did not think he had worried this much when he was first in love with her! Martin feared that, "if Rupp was warm at all, he was going to cool off as the time dragged on without an offer." Finally, Martin had decided that, if he were in Rupp's position, he would want to know that he was still under the most serious consideration, even if nothing definite could be reported.

In fact, Rupp's guess as to the reason for the delay was correct. George Rupp would initially appear to many to be an odd choice for the presidency of Rice University, not only because his discipline is theology and he would be coming from a divinity school, but also because of earlier association with "far out" interdisciplinary ventures. Correspondingly, members of the search committee wanted influential faculty members and members of the board of governors fully to understand their enthusiasm for Rupp. While maintaining discretion concerning his candidacy, they wanted to make certain there would be strong support for him should he be chosen and in turn choose Rice.[8]

CLOSING IN

In late February, just a few days before the search committee was to give its final recommendation to the board, a small group of trustees and governors accompanied by one faculty member of the search committee flew to Cambridge for one last serious visit with the Rupps. This was their chance to deal openly with any remaining questions that board members might have. George Rupp's relaxed manner and personal charm put the group quickly at ease. After the meeting the committee was ready to go to the board.

Given the original instructions to the search committee that they present a small slate to the board of trustees and governors, a few people wondered about the wisdom of presenting only one candidate: "It was

[8] Viewed in retrospect, many initiatives appear less bold than at the time they were taken. Consider, to begin with, the fact that Rupp had Ivy League degrees and would come, not from numerically small and immensely distinguished Cal Tech nor from large and immensely distinguished MIT, but from Harvard, shortly to embark on its 350th anniversary celebration. As mentioned in the text, Rice had only just been elected to membership in the Association of American Universities. Academicians are not above name-dropping—and in George Rupp's case, his prestigious credentials were accompanied by his very real accomplishments, evidenced in his scholarship and in his reputation as an academic administrator.

almost as if the search committee had picked the new president, not the board." However, since five of the seven trustees had participated in all search activities, and all seven trustees had interviewed Rupp, it was generally felt that there was no need to recommend additional candidates. On this issue, with the strong endorsements of Rupp in hand, there was no serious disagreement.

A special meeting of the two boards was called in early March to receive the search committee's nomination and formally to elect the next president. Prior to the session, Ralph O'Connor asked each constituent group represented on the search committee to select one individual to serve as spokesman, to tell the boards their impressions of Rupp. The three faculty members chose King Walters; the two students settled on the undergraduate, Garland Kelley; and the two alumni selected Catherine Hannah. Each person described his excitement about Rupp's candidacy. Hannah commented on George Rupp's age. "I knew some people were thinking, 'forty-two years old . . . that's pretty young,' and I wanted to respond to that. I said 'we're bringing you all the potential you need to go into the twenty-first century.' " Hannah later commented that she is 63 years old, but "older people don't necessarily think old. I was willing to take a risk on someone young. It's better to do that than to do something second rate." After Walters, Kelley, and Hannah made their presentations, board members directed questions to all members of the search committee, and chairman Charles Duncan then asked if there was anything further anyone wanted to say. After a few more comments, the faculty, student, and alumni members of the search committee were excused from the meeting. Their discussion with the boards had lasted almost two hours.

Ralph O'Connor walked the search committee members out to their cars and promised that he would let them know the outcome of the meeting as soon as he could. That night, each received a call. By unanimous vote, Rupp had been elected president of Rice University.

Charles Duncan telephoned George Rupp and offered him the position. Rupp responded that he was excited by the prospect; however, he was not prepared to accept without first discussing the move with the elder of the Rupps' two daughters who was spending her junior year of high school studying in a Düsseldorf *Gymnasium*. George and Nancy Rupp had discussed the move with their younger daughter, who had become enthusi-

290

astic about moving to Houston, not least because, when Ralph O'Connor had visited the Rupp home and had learned of her interest in horses, he had promised that she could have her own horse if they came to Houston. However, for the Rupps' older daughter it would mean moving for her senior year, when she had expected to graduate with her class. Her parents had not wanted to arouse either her anxieties or any possible hopes until there were definite plans to discuss. Now that plans were pending, George Rupp did not want to spring the news on her without giving her a chance to discuss it with him. He arranged a weekend trip to Düsseldorf, talked with his daughter, and returned home impressed with her maturity and relieved by her willingness to enter a new school. He had explained to her that it could be Houston's magnet school which is large and teaches an array of foreign language courses (George and Nancy Rupp had been assured about schooling by search committee members and by their own visit to Houston.

If George Rupp, by this time eager to accept the Rice opportunity, was relieved by his daughter's flexibility, the Rice trustees and search committee members were relieved by his only briefly delayed acceptance. We asked search committee members: Suppose there had been a hitch, and he had not accepted, what then? The way the Rice search had proceeded, there was no one in reserve. It would have been back to the list of eight and the fuller list of twenty, and perhaps an inquiry beyond them; the aim would have been to find a new person to court wholeheartedly, as George Rupp had in the end been courted. Any delay in filling the post might have been thought a small price to pay for finding someone on whom all could agree.

THE ANNOUNCEMENT

The trustees made arrangements for Rupp to come to Houston. The announcement of Rupp as Rice's next president was planned with the same care that had distinguished the search. In order to avoid premature publicity either in Houston or in Cambridge, Rupp was flown to Houston in a private jet so that enterprising reporters could not check airplane reservations for names. Rupp was scheduled to meet with the full board and then to appear for a press conference. An executive faculty meeting, that is, a

291

meeting at which no students, press, or other visitors could be present, was planned to take place simultaneously with Rupp's meeting with the press.

Despite these attempts at confidentiality, the news leaked: some woman, who did not identify herself, called a *Houston Post* reporter and announced the forthcoming appointment. Apparently able to verify the information, the *Post* ran the news story the morning that the announcement was made on campus.

The leak "was probably a good thing after all," several people later commented, "for it prepared faculty for the shock." When Bill Martin, King Walters, and Sidney Burrus stood up at the executive faculty meeting, they were besieged with questions about whether the news story was accurate. The three search committee members said that it was, and then described their own reactions to Rupp. They explained that they had been greatly surprised to realize how impressed they had been with him when they had first met him. With each encounter, they respected him more and liked him better still. By the time they had finished talking about Rupp, they had created an atmosphere akin to a pep-rally.[9] When Rupp appeared in the doorway, a number of people stood up and applauded. Rupp answered questions from the faculty, and when the session was over, some faculty members in the humanities had tears in their eyes. "The fact that he was a humanist hit me between the eyes," a history professor stated. "I thought, 'the Board had really meant it when they said that academic subject wouldn't be a criterion.' " "He's good," another faculty member said. "He's spectacular," someone else replied. The three faculty on the search committee left the room euphoric. One of them declared, "We've done something bold and fantastic for Rice."

[9] For sharp contrast, compare the reactions of faculty members at Winthrop College to the three candidates who had been brought to campus without prior preparation, without cheerleaders, without even the unintended benefit of a tiny leak.

CHAPTER XI

Reaching Closure

S THE CASES in this volume attest, the search process grows more and more intense as it unfolds, as the pool of candidates narrows, and as the decision about a new president is imminent.[1] It is in these final weeks and days of a search that the stakes seem the highest; that critical actions are taken; that the success of the selection process is being determined. As search committee members agonize individually and collectively about which candidate best fits their institution, or lobby among themselves for votes for their favorite contender, they often forget that the candidates are themselves struggling with feelings about the search. Some candidates badly want the presidency and anxiously await news as to their standing; others are trying to weigh the relative advantages of their present job or present locale against the attractions of a new position; some are groping with an attempt to reconcile their own professional and personal interests and desires with those of their spouse and their family.

The search for a president of Rice University, delineated in the previous chapter, illustrates the two-way nature of a presidential search process. In the early stages of the process, the search committee looks inward to the institution, to see what nature of leadership is desired and to create a receptive climate for that new leadership; it also looks outward to identify prospects who either are presently well situated or have other opportunities and, while they might not "need" a presidency, perhaps can be persuaded to consider it. As the search process continues, the search committee must keep in mind not only what the representatives on the search

[1] In a draft of this chapter, we discovered a typo: in place of the word "president" we found the word "present," making the sentence read, "as . . . the decision about a new present is imminent." Although we corrected the typo, this earlier sentence also describes what happens in the search process.

293

committee may want, but also what prospective candidates may be interested in knowing.

The best search committees recognize that they are both buyers and sellers. From the very outset of the process, these search committees realize the need to court candidates. The members of the Rice search committee, for example, knew their institution was attractive. Rice University was thriving, and a good president could help make it better still, and certainly better known. Yet they did not assume that the best prospects for the presidency would seek them out, or that the presidency of Rice was so attractive that it would sell itself. While many search committees see themselves in the role of selectors or of judges among contestants for the "prize" of the presidency, the Rice search committee simultaneously pursued the dual tasks of choosing and of being chosen. The former objective required them to identify prospects and learn as much as they could about the match between these prospects and Rice, while the latter objective required a sagacious combination of considerateness and pertinacity. Overanxious pursuit might, to the pursued, sound a note of desperation, as if there were real undisclosed problems which had to be addressed immediately. Less enthusiastic courtship might lose them their candidate.

As the search process drew to a close, members of the Rice search committee recognized that they still had dual tasks. After interesting George Rupp in the university, the search committee had to persuade all the trustees and influential members of the faculty that they were making a good choice. Here, they served first as cheerleaders for George Rupp, and then as advocates of Rupp to the Rice community, being careful all the while not to overpersuade or overpromise, lest a backlash ensue. This combination of external negotiation with George Rupp and intramural negotiation within the institution (and governing boards) depended upon the maintenance of confidentiality, much as in the case of arms control negotiations between the superpowers, where leaks can undercut delicate and inchoate webs of connection being created by the negotiators in private.[2]

___

[2] The choice of Harvard's Divinity School dean as Rice's new president has some of the elements of a journalistic coup. After a certain time, however, the kudos from this coup will have evaporated, and it will undoubtedly be hard for George Rupp, even with the full support and transitional welcome he has received, to prove as spectacular in the presidency as the selection itself seemed at the time. A president chosen after a less benign and admired search may have a more difficult time at the outset, especially in the absence of an informal welcoming committee from the search committee itself, but

294

Boards of trustees and members of search committees must bear in mind throughout their search that they are seeking to create the conditions that will attract capable candidates, will legitimate their choice of the person named the new president, will make the new president effective once in office, and will allow them to retain the president when other search committees come calling.

THE TREATMENT OF CANDIDATES

In recent years colleges and universities, along with other not-for-profit enterprises, have become more publicity conscious as they seek a competitive advantage in ever widening orbits. Positions such as director of public relations and vice-president for external relations are cropping up at institutions public and private, large and small, and campus press offices have grown in size and importance. Surprisingly, though, many institutions seem to forget that the search for a president is one of their best opportunities to enhance public relations. Advertisements of position vacancies place the institution's name—and often a description of its locale, clientele, and attractive features—before a national audience. As the search gets under way, the treatment of candidates can win respect or engender ill will for the institution.

A search can be an opportunity to make friends for the institution, by treating nominators, prospects, and candidates with courtesy. Too often, as the search committee focuses on its own internal concerns, candidates are treated with insensitivity. Often those who have been nominated are asked whether they are interested in being considered for the presidency, and having responded positively, they may hear nothing at all for weeks on end. Worse still, a finalist may be brought to the campus for interviews, become intrigued about the possibility of being president of that college or university, begin to speculate with family members about the requirements of the move, only to learn by hearing the news on the radio or reading about it in the newspaper that someone else has been selected. In such cases, which are all too frequent, candidates are likely to regard the

---

may later win approval on her or his own merits and make the search committee look better in retrospect than perhaps it deserves.

institution with unconcealed animosity, and to communicate these feelings to their friends.

The opinions candidates form about an institution develop from the treatment they receive from the very beginning of the search process. The reader will recall that in the Winthrop College search, prior to bringing in Ruth Weintraub as search consultant, the search committee had planned to ask all appplicants and nominees to submit not only a curriculum vitae, but also a list of five references and a lengthy statement of educational philosophy. Weintraub advised the committee that if they wanted to turn people off, this was the way to go about it! Surely for many desirable prospects who are currently well situated, she is correct. Some search committees will justify asking candidates to provide them with extensive information by saying that they have so many names that this is a form of weeding people out. It is—but it weeds out all the wrong people! Prospective candidates not desperate to leave a current position will not place themselves in the position of supplicant. Younger, less well established people might toy with the idea of using a search to gain experience. However, if as commonly occurs, they are asked to provide five letters of reference, they may be hesitant to impose on busy people to have them write letters for a position they may be unlikely to get and that they are not at all sure that they want, and at an institution that has not indicated that it is serious about them. Established people are unlikely to commit the time it takes to write lengthy statements in pursuit of the hope that the institution will be seriously interested in them and that they in turn will be attracted to it.

In the first search for a president of Evergreen State College to succeed Daniel Evans, the search committee asked nominees and applicants to provide five letters of recommendation that specifically addressed their eight criteria for the Evergreen presidency, and to write separate statements of their educational and administrative philosophies. They further stated that the search committee would "not consider incomplete application files." The Evergreen State College search committee chairman justified the procedure by reporting to us that a number of impressive applications had been received. Of course, there will always be a large number of people who have nothing to lose by going through the sort of motions that the Evergreen search committee required. Search committees—and the press—seem invariably at the end of a search to report the number of candidates who were considered, as if this said something about the desirability of the institution, the thoroughness of the search, or the high quality of the person chosen. If it says anything, it may be testimony to the inefficiency of the search and the unrealistic expectations generated all around. The problem is never, even for the most woebegone institution, to find candidates, but rather to find ones who are well suited to the needs of the institution. In the case of Evergreen State College, the search process was unsuccessful and had to be begun again a year later, with a consultant serving as adviser. One member of the second search committee said that in the previous search they treated candidates as if they were seeking junior assistant professors, with the exception that in assistant professor searches they were much less stringent in the academic background they demanded. In their second search, they learned from their earlier errors and proceeded differently and more successfully.[3]

If what a search committee wants is not large numbers of "candidates" but a small number of outstanding prospects, the members of the committee must go courting, rather than sit back and wait for eager supplicants. Recognizing this need to court desirable prospects, Ruth Weintraub has warned that a search committee should "never ask people why they want the job. The good candidates often are not sure they do."[4] One president of a well-known liberal arts college was approached by the chairman of a search committee about being considered for another presidency. Finally, after much persuasion, she agreed to meet with the entire search committee, although she was not at all sure she was interested in leaving her present post, or in moving to that institution. After her meeting with the search committee, she told us of her negative experience. There are two purposes that need to be understood in a situation such as she was in,

[3] One example we have seen of asking the candidate to do the work of the search committee was provided by the search for a chancellor for West Valley Joint Community College District. The search committee sent a brochure to prospective candidates describing the qualifications sought in a chancellor and outlining the application, nomination, screening, and selection process. In addition to a personal letter of application and a "personally prepared resumé of educational, community and professional experience," applicants were asked to complete a "Supplemental Questionnaire." The supplemental questionnaire included eight questions (e.g., one question asked the candidate to "Describe successes you have had in advancing the concept of the comprehensive community college and in advancing the needs of diverse constituencies;" question number two asked for a description of "your experience dealing with strategic planning, goal setting and needs assessment and evaluation;" question three asked about "experience with personnel issues such as affirmative action and collective bargaining;" etc.). The candidate was instructed to answer these eight questions "in narrative style employing only one page per question."

[4] Ruth Weintraub, *AAHE Bulletin*, April 1984.

she explained. The search committee needs to persuade the "non-candidate" that the job is worth considering, and the "non-candidate," if he or she wants to keep the prospect alive until making a decision to pursue or not to pursue it, needs to persuade the search committee that he or she can do the job they want filled. The attitude this president encountered, however, when she met with the search committee was, "Tell us why you are here." She thought that a more productive and less alienating approach would have been, "We understand that you have had some experiences that are relevant to our concerns and we would like to explore them further." Additionally, this president thought that the search committee should have learned more about the people with whom they were meeting prior to the actual interview. This was especially true for people like herself whom they had gone out of their way to recruit.

Many candidates shared with us their surprise at the meagerness or virtual absence of consideration for their welfare at all stages of interviewing. They arrive at the airport in a city where they know no one, and there is no one to meet them. They are expected to find their own way to their hotel and to spend the night alone before the interview with the search committee, with no one checking on them. The next day, they make their way to the place where the interview will be held, and then sit outside this room, waiting to be called in at an hour that may be later than the designated time. It can be awkward, although sometimes amusing and revivifying, when they encounter other candidates in the same hotel or even sitting outside the meeting room waiting their turn. Later, the search committee wonders why these same candidates seem unenthusiastic about the presidency of their institution!

EDUCATING CANDIDATES

Throughout these chapters, we have repeatedly discussed the illusions people at an institution can have about their college or university. They may think their place is so grand that people should be eager to preside over it; the position is persuasion enough, and anyone not persuaded must be a fool or fearful. Not infrequently, however, as a search process continues without producing the outstanding national figures people had thought it would, this mood of almost belligerent buoyancy gives way to despair.

298

Places at the ecological margin of success often begin in this latter mode. In the public sector, this may lead to a search for a native son who is not likely to leave the state, the assumption being that anyone from "outside" wouldn't stay for long. It is not too surprising, perhaps, that citizens of such an impoverished and economically depressed state as West Virginia might harbor such feelings, coupled with resentful pride. But such attitudes turn up in many other places as well. The northern sector of New Jersey is increasingly attractive both for residents and for corporations; yet it continues to regard itself as ancillary to New York City. Hence, when Ramapo College of New Jersey, a state college only a few miles south of the New York state border, went in search of a successor to its founding president, George Potter (Potter is an Englishman, educated at Oxford), the governor, Thomas Kean, playing to localist sentiment, remarked that he hoped that the search committee would not go out of state, but would find someone from New Jersey.

Sometimes the regional imperative is coupled with an ethnic one, as when New Mexico's former governor, Tony Anaya, loudly insisted that the next president of the University of New Mexico should be a chicano or a chicana (in the latter case with someone specific in mind). Localism in such cases combines patronage politics with a certain degree of defeatism. In Massachusetts, such patronage politics took the form of the General Court setting the salary of the chancellor of the board of regents of higher education at $66,000. This salary is considerably below not only that of the presidents of institutions within the system, but also the salaries of chancellors of comparable systems in competitive, wealthy states (although about twice the pay of state legislators, many of whom are lawyers and most of whom hold other jobs). The low salary was seen not only as a means of preventing the possibility of luring a major contender from outside of Massachusetts, but also, in the most recent chancellor's search, of giving an advantage to one candidate, James Collins, a member of the Massachusetts House of Representatives for whom the low salary would not be an obstacle.[5] Many institutions, private as well as public, may be tempted to seek a "local" who will want to stay in the area, for which of course there can be no guarantee, in contrast to working to make things so attractive that a good person from near or far will want to stay.

[5] See Hogarty, "Search for a Massachusetts Chancellor."

On the other hand, it is no favor to the institution or to a prospective incumbent to make things more attractive than they realistically are. We have seen how, at Rice University, members of the search committee acted as suitors to court George Rupp. But capable courtship depends on minimizing the gap between reality and wishful thinking—and legitimating one's veracity. This is all the more imperative since candidates' ambitions and those of their spouses can get the better of their judgment. We have been astonished by the number of serious candidates who become finalists on the basis of the skimpiest information about the institution. They meet with the search committee without having studied the catalogue, read the last annual report, examined the budget, or asked knowledgeable persons in higher education about the institution. Such individuals may mistake the search committee for the institution the committee members both represent and disguise. One acquaintance of ours who was extremely eager to be the president of a good liberal arts college was invited to an interview with the search committee of such an institution, but he had never looked at the college's catalogue, let alone at its chronicled history. He is a person of intelligence and charisma, with impressive academic and professional credentials, and he had apparently assumed that his personal strengths and resumé would make him an obvious choice. After the interview, he was eliminated from further consideration, the chair of the search committee later told us, on grounds of a basic lack of curiosity.

Other candidates, as we have learned from our interviews, decide that it is time for them to become a president. They enter several searches, become semifinalists and learn how to make a good impression on a search committee. Meanwhile, as deans or vice-presidents, they are busy on their home campuses, with little time to explore what a move to a new locale would actually mean in personal as well as professional terms. One of the most common examples is failure to anticipate, when one has lived in cosmopolitan or metropolitan locales, what it would be like to be the president of a college which is the only or the major "industry" of a very small town in a rural area. One candidate who was living in St. Louis was offered the presidency of a state college in a small Pennsylvania town. As he and his wife drove to the town for what was to be the final meeting with the board of trustees, he had misgivings about what life would be like. He later reported to us that he had suppressed these in the full tide of his ambition, while his wife, who also had such misgivings, kept quiet for fear of threatening his hopes and dreams. The president-elect had been an academic vice-president; even so, he did not anticipate the degree to which, once in the presidency, he and his family would be in the spotlight in the small community, with discomforts for school-aged children coming in as visible and locally criticized outsiders. A go-between in the search, such as a search consultant, or indeed any wise confidant, might have reminded the prospective candidate to take seriously the cultural differences that accompany geographical mobility—although most of us are aware of larger orbits of prejudice, such as Yankees hesitant to go South, and Southerners' awareness of Yankee snobberies. Candidates coming out of academia may overestimate their knowledge of other places on the basis of academic gossip or visibility in big-time sports, and they may not appreciate the degree to which the legend of an institution can be belied by its present reality.

Internal candidates are not likely to be confused about the locale, but they may not fully appreciate the difference between the presidency and even an academic vice-presidency. We have been struck by the number of internal candidates who have told us that they never fully appreciated how their college or university looked from the vantage point of the presidency until they themselves occupied that seat. Hardly anyone who comes to the presidency, whether from outside or inside the institution, is exempt from surprises, and of course small changes in the composition of a board of trustees can mean major realignments on the board and eventually in the institution as a whole. Stated starkly, no one ever knows enough to be president. The best transitions help the new incumbent begin the process of self-education and mutual accommodation, in the hope of avoiding fatal errors (although there is never any guarantee of this) during the "freshman orientation" to the presidency.[6]

GATHERING INFORMATION ABOUT CANDIDATES

As we have studied searches, we have been struck repeatedly by how little many search committees know about the prospects who become the final-

[6] For more on this, see Estela Mara Bensimon, Marian L. Gade, and Joseph F. Kauffman, *On Assuming a College or University Presidency: Lessons and Advice from the Field* (Washington, D.C.: AAHE, 1989).

ists for the presidency, and among whom the choice of a new president will be made. Many search committees reduce their pool of prospective candidates to a small number of "semifinalists" based only on these candidates' vitae and the letters of recommendation the candidates have provided the search committee. Members of search committees often do not telephone the writers of letters of recommendation to try to learn how well the recommender really knows the candidate and to what extent the recommender can visualize the candidate at the particular institution in question. On the basis of what often seems perfunctory information, the committee as a whole or in subgroups interviews the group of semifinalists, frequently at a hotel near an airport. Typically eight to twelve people will be seen over the course of several days, with each candidate being interviewed for one or two hours. Since only a few minutes are generally set aside between interviews for note-taking or discussing impressions of the person just seen, the multiple candidates can blur together in the minds of search committee members, with the order in which they have been seen sometimes making a difference in the clarity of recollection. Based on these uneven, foggy impressions of candidates, search committees commonly select a smaller number of finalists for more extensive interviews. Even at this point, with these finalists about to come to campus to meet with large numbers of campus constituents, there may not have been intensive inquiries concerning them, such as might provide the search committee with a better sense of both the potentialities and the perplexities suggested by the careers of these individuals.

Search committee members, like Americans in all aspects of social life, seem to have undue confidence in their judgments of others and to place great faith on the interview to reveal to them the "true nature" of a person. One member of a search committee told us that she knew after two minutes with each candidate whom she liked and didn't like. She saw no reason for lengthy interviews or reference checking. Of course some people have better judgment than others and are more skilled and practiced in making quick decisions. Yet no one is immune to mistakes. And much of the literature on personnel recruitment declares that interviews are not valid in the selection process as predictors of job performance. Interviews, as we discuss later, play an important role in the search for a president in giving the search committee an impression of a candidate's poise and public presence, allowing candidates a glimpse of the college or university, and providing the first opportunity for committee members and a prospective president to establish a working relationship. But, obviously, much more information is needed for search committee members to reach a sound judgment about who should be president. In their excellent book on searches, Ted Marchese and Jane Lawrence recommend that the search committee collect substantial quantities of information about candidates prior to meeting any prospect in person.[7] Moreover, when the search chair, consultant, or search committee members meet with the candidate, they need to have thought carefully about what they want the interview to accomplish. Robert Hahn, academic vice-president at Trinity College of Vermont, has written that the underlying problem of many interviews may be "the lack of appropriate preparation for the interviews, the absence of a pre-planned strategy, and the absence of articulated outcomes. Instead, questioners often come with their own agendas and points to make, and they take turns making them." Hahn reminds search committees that they need to think ahead of time about what they hope to know about a candidate once the session has ended, and then develop questions that will elicit this kind of information.[8] The size of the committee and the mode of its selection, as we have indicated earlier, contribute to the committee's capacity to make optimal use of an interview. We are reminded of one search committee on which almost every conceivable interest group at the institution was included on the search committee, including the gay and lesbian association and the wildlife association. Throughout the search, the members of the search committee fought continuously. When they reached the stage of interviewing candidates, one member of the committee would ask a candidate a question, and someone else on the committee would yell out, "That's a damn stupid question!" Then the representatives would wrangle among themselves. Not surprisingly, many candidates left the interviews and quickly withdrew their names from further consideration.

Executive search consultant John Isaacson of Isaacson, Miller, Gilvar, and Boulware recommends an historical approach to interviewing. Whereas, according to Isaacson, "ninety-eight percent of interviewers employ

[7] *Search Committee Handbook.*
[8] From correspondence of April 16, 1987.

the Future-Oriented/Evaluative School," wherein the interviewer quizzes the candidate about how he or she would handle hypothetical situations, Isaacson says that all that this tells the employer is "how glib the candidate is, whether the candidate has ever had a job very similar to this one, and how cool he is in an unnatural and uncomfortable situation." The historical approach to interviewing, what Isaacson calls "a cross between a psychiatric interview and a police investigation," asks the candidate to talk about his or her past, "the real facts of his career . . . all the gory details, the petty triumphs and the setbacks, the good and the bad," on the assumption that people are consistent and their past patterns of behavior will suggest what their behavior will likely be in the future.[9]

We spoke earlier in this chapter about the mistake of asking candidates to provide reams of material in support of their candidacy. Not only does this request for lengthy applications seriously limit the candidate pool, it often does not contribute much to the learning of the search committee. The search committee has no way of knowing for certain that the applicant or nominee has written his or her own statement personally, and is probably mistaken if committee members believe the statement rather than viewing it as potentially useful propaganda. It is in fact propaganda which is asked for in many announcements in the *Chronicle of Higher Education* or the *New York York Times*, which specify too many criteria, each one either eliminating a potentially worthwhile prospect or simply inviting the expression of a prevailing piety. Whether it is a request to write something, or a criterion not essential in initial recruitment, such procedures seem to be efforts by the search committee to force the candidates to do the work of the search committee.

One of the qualities most difficult to detect for search committees is the extent of courage that a candidate might be able to m   ter when an unpopular stand is in the long-run interests of the institution. Presidents may maintain their popularity for quite a long time by becoming pliable and conciliatory. They leave to their successors, if not undermaintained buildings, certainly overtenured and entrenched faculties.[10] Presidents

[9] John M. Isaacson, "In Search of an Affable Beast. The Care and Recruitment of the Public's Commissioners." A paper presented to the Conference for Newly Elected Mayors at the Institute for Politics of the John F. Kennedy School of Government, November 20, 1981.

[10] Presidents in academia are not the only Americans who choose short-run praise and peace over long-run institutional goals. Contemporary corporate managers are often forced by the fear of takeovers to attend to the daily price of their companies' shares rather than the long-term investment of

304

need the courage to transfer, or, where feasible, to dismiss subordinates who are not working out, and to deny tenure to faculty members. Most of us are not sadistic or ruthless, and it is hard for us to let anyone go. This is especially difficult in small residential institutions where everyone knows the person's family, and connections between the campus and the local community may be strong.[11]

It does not follow that colleges and universities should be attracted to moralistic and self-righteous candidates who, in their prideful resistance to the prevalent pieties, are eager to assure the search committee and the board of their iconoclastic views. Conciliation is not evil per se. It is possible for an institution to be damaged in the long run as well as in the short run as a result of a peripheral crusade.[12]

One question that search committees well might ask of candidates, and about candidates when the time has come to check references, could be whether they have ever taken positions which exposed them to severe attack from people about whose good opinion they cared. For just as one would not want to recruit someone who is simply a crusader, so one also might hesitate to select someone who has never taken a stand, and who is unproven on his or her ability to make dismissals. At the same time, a search committee should have second thoughts about someone who can fire individuals without any pang, or glory in unpopular positions out of vanity.

---

human capital that can insure stability and growth. For many politicians there is only the short run, although today most politicians elected to Congress or a state legislature have safer seats than the average college or university president.

[11] Dismissal has become more difficult as litigation, in this as in other areas of American life, has become a common way to try to intimidate an institution. See, e.g., for some of the costs, "Lawsuits in Academe: Nobody Wins," by George R. LaNoue and Barbara A. Lee, in *AGB Reports*, Vol. 29, no. 1 (January–February 1987), pp. 38–42. Also, George R. LaNoue and Barbara A. Lee, *Academics in Court: The Consequence of Faculty Discrimination Litigation* (Ann Arbor: University of Michigan Press, 1987).

[12] We recognize that a whole library could be written on what is and is not peripheral. For a historic case, consider the famous controversy at Berkeley over the regulation requiring professors to take an oath that they were not members of the Communist Party. Some dedicated faculty members (among them Erik Erikson and Nevitt Sanford) left the university rather than comply, whereas Clark Kerr, then professor of industrial relations, urged faculty who were not themselves Communists to take the oath as a way of taking political pressure off the regents—a position that the non-signers took as too compromising. Similar issues arise today for presidents as to whether or not they will hang onto a small amount of stock in companies doing business in South Africa at the cost of seeing the campus plagued with protests on the issue, not only from activist students, but also from activist faculty. Ethical buying as well as ethical investment; recruiting by the CIA or, perhaps in the future, by defense contractors for SDI and other weapons—all these can become issues crowding out everything else.

There is no sure-fire way to evaluate candidates, either their professional capabilities or their personal qualities. Neither is there a certain way of knowing how candidates would perform in the presidency of a particular institution. In the case of candidates who are sitting presidents, a full-scale inquiry into their work as president can be conducted. Still, even there, the things that are easily measured—student recruitment, success with endowment, institutional visibility and reputation, good maintenance—may be the fruits primarily of a predecessor's efforts or of the president's subordinates. The fact that the president selected, or retained, capable subordinates should not be discounted, however. Still, what wants to be explored (but seldom is) is the capacity of the candidate for continuing to learn about an institution and to help members of the institution to learn more about it and about themselves. This capacity to make adult learning a priority for oneself and for one's subordinates is emphasized by many contemporary students of leadership, notably by Michael Maccoby in *Why Work: Leading the New Generation*. Two-thirds of the candidates, however, have not been presidents hitherto. They have not lived and worked in that isolated position.

In a typical search, an individual named by a candidate as a reference will be telephoned by a member of the search committee and asked about this person and this person alone. The person so telephoned may have limited knowledge of the institution, let alone its current leadership requirements. He or she will be speaking in a kind of vacuum. To the broad question, "How capable is this person of presidential leadership?" the answer one wants to give is, "compared to whom?" Only in extreme cases can one give a generic answer with any confidence. Leadership is always contextual.

In the Rice University search, the members of the search committee asked resource people their judgment of a number of individuals extremely visible in the worlds of higher education—mainly deans, provosts, and presidents at eminent places. This was a way, among other things, of assessing a respondent's level of knowledge as well as quality of judgment, as measured against the responses of others and the accumulated wisdom being garnered by the search committee. None of these names was mentioned as a specific candidate, although conceivable candidates were scattered among the list. This seemed a useful way to test the

306

field, to gain a sense of what was realistically "out there," and to pin down the names of those who should be consulted as resource persons, if not necessarily as prospects. (When we are telephoned about a candidate, we are rarely asked for the names of others whom search committee members might call to give additional perspective to their assessment of the candidate.)

A question search committees commonly ask, both in letters of inquiry and in telephone exchanges, concerns the person's management "style," a question which in the absence of specific context is often vacuous. Questions about style, admittedly, are commonly efforts to get at what Edward Hall called the "silent language" of particular individuals and cultures.[13] The term "style" may accordingly be used as a synonym for "presence" or appearing presidential. Or, sometimes when faculty members ask about style, they want to assure themselves about the candidate's appropriate deference to the faculty and willingness to consult with the faculty. Almost never asked are questions about the ability of the person as coach, mentor, guide, and critic to develop an administrative team or cohort whose joint efforts are more than the sum of the individual parts.[14]

In Chapter IX, we note that search consultants are generally much more skilled than search committee members at the "art of asking questions." Search committee members usually vary greatly among themselves in their skill in this regard. Some search committees fail to recognize this— or at least to act upon this recognition, and in a democratic fashion will ask each committee member to telephone a certain number of the individuals whose names have been given as references. When we have been called in this capacity, we have found an extraordinary range of quality in the sorts of questions and follow-up questions put to us. Some are so shallow as to produce almost no information of substance for the search committee, while others are penetrating and thoughtful. Students can on occasion ask cogent questions, but the person being questioned by a student may wonder about the effectiveness with which the student will carry the information back to the search committee. Of course on this axis faculty members and trustees can also vary greatly. A search committee chair

---

[13] *The Silent Language* (Garden City, New York: Doubleday, 1959).

[14] For illustrations of this theme, see *Presidents Make a Difference*, and John W. White, Jr., "Putting Together a Winning Presidential Team," *AGB Reports*, Vol. 28, no. 4 (July–August 1986), pp. 29–31.

could in principle assign only the most competent interviewers and then try to arrange to have the appropriate questioner call the appropriate referee, but such rationality at the cost of democracy rarely occurs.

When it comes to questioning the candidates, consultants may feel freer to ask questions deemed intrusive or aggressive than would be the case with most trustees or faculty members. Administrator members of search committees and some faculty members may be quite diffident about offending a prospective incumbent, and the candidates may be more shy in responding to people with whom they will have to deal face-to-face on becoming an incumbent.

One area of questioning that search committees are often reluctant to enter directly is a candidate's health. Indeed, one consultant told us that she has been criticized for asking such questions, as if they were somehow discriminatory. She has also been criticized, especially when working with public systems, for writing down the ages of candidates on her master list of prospects. The consultant says, however, that she almost always learns these things indirectly, for they come up in conversations with referees.

In the case of both age and health, this information seems to us to be important data for the search committee. The college presidency requires a person to be energetic, capable of responding to emergencies, and able to maintain schedules which would tax quite a few normally healthy undergraduates. We are surprised that when we are asked about candidates we are not asked about possible addictions, either to drugs or to alcohol (we refer here to severe addiction, rather than occasional recreational use). Yet our work has turned up several instances where a search has come about because the retiring president had been hired with no knowledge of the alcoholism which beset him at his prior place of employment, and which his references kept hidden, whether out of pity or to get free of the impaired individual. Here again, a consultant might be able to ask "tactless" questions more readily than a member of the search committee or a member of the board of trustees of the inquiring institution.

THE ROLE OF THE FAMILY

One area where there has been an ideologically motivated effort to restrict questioning concerns whether or not the candidate is married and has chil-

308

dren. Women's movements have sought to bar such questioning, advancing the argument that the *person* is being hired and not his or her family (or lack thereof). Almost universally today, women's colleges prefer and even expect a female president, married or not, so that a women's college with a male president is now a rarity. Moreover, in state systems, the system chancellor and the overall board may want to show their lack of bias by making sure that at least one campus in the system is headed by a woman. These situations aside, however, female candidates, single or married, may be at a disadvantage in comparison with married men also under consideration, because they do not have husbands who will work gratis for the college or university as the traditional wife of a male president has done (and many still to do). Some feminists—and others on the search committee wanting to be sensitive to these concerns—conclude, therefore, that even though the spouse may serve as a partner in the presidential tasks, no questions should be asked male or female candidates about their families and their expectations about the presidency.

Sometimes there are conflicts over ideologies among the different generations or different constituencies on the search committee concerning such questions as whether one should court the female spouse, or fervently refuse to do so. Does the search committee invite the spouse along on the campus visit and make provisions for her (or him) to attend meetings with the candidate and/or have separate activities (such as touring the community, visiting schools, etc.), or does the search committee act as if the candidate is an isolate, with no one other than himself or herself to consider in the move? In what may be an increasing number of cases, no provision is made for the spouse's visit to the campus. In one search with which we are familiar, the wife of the candidate asked to accompany her husband on the campus visit and was told that there were no funds to permit this. She could rent a car and come on her own. In financially hard-pressed states, the search committee may be anxious not to appear spendthrift, but in other cases where fear of appearing extravagant is not a major factor, there may be a combination of traditional stag insensitivity on the part of a predominantly male board of trustees and of intimidation by a presumed feminist mandate that husband and wife are totally separate individuals and that to ask anything of the wife is to violate her complete autonomy. Yet when the husband or wife is a candidate, the spouse will

309

play an important part in the candidate's decision as to whether or not to come, and if the decision is to come, whether the presidential family will want to stay for a reasonable term of office.

In the whole country until recently, and in many parts of it still, it has been assumed that presidents will be male, that they will be married, and that their wives will act as sociable, but in academic and intellectual matters, silent partners, officiating at receptions, engaging in good works in the community, bringing up children who are not too badly behaved,[15] and attending church regularly, even when their husbands head a secular rather than a church-related institution. On a residential campus with a presidential house provided by the college, the presidential family is often viewed as a useful "role model" for students. In smaller communities, the president may also be a symbolic presence for the local population.

Today, thanks to changed attitudes among many women and some men, such assumptions concerning presidential spouses no longer automatically hold. They may still color expectations, however, giving rise to misunderstanding and conflict. Similarly, only in limited circles—evangelical or Catholic—is divorce seen as a stigma for either a man or a woman candidate. Instead, more significant questions arise about the kinds of arrangements that will be inviting for a presidential couple, for a single president, or for a presidential family. It is an unrealistic bow to ideology to treat husband and wife as if they were solipsistic individuals, even though it is also unrealistic to follow the earlier assumption that husband and wife are one, and that he is the one!

One problem single presidents (and, increasingly, married presidents) often face is that their male predecessor's spouse had served as social hostess, not only planning menus and deciding seating plans, ordering flowers and so on, but also remembering everyone's name and role and helping people to feel comfortable. Many of these things were done without trustees ever really noticing. They were simply taken for granted. Hence, trustees have never thought about making other provisions for the president without a spouse willing to perform these functions. We know of

---

[15] See the amusing account by Polly Davis, wife of the former president of the University of New Mexico, about the way her two boys scandalized the campus, in Joan E. Clodius and Diane Skomars Magrath, eds., *The President's Spouse: Volunteer or Volunteered?* (Washington, D.C.: National Association of State Universities and Land Grant Colleges, 1984), pp. 87–93.

310

presidents who, consequently, have found themselves in effect having to play both roles, host and hostess.[16] Increasingly, boards are realizing that a social coordinator can be employed to take charge of the necessary details of the president's entertaining. Such a staff member is important not only for single presidents but, more and more, for married presidents also, whose spouses, male or female, have their own careers. While they will be present at major functions, they are not available to take on the organization and planning of these and the multitude of other smaller affairs. An example is provided by Judith Sturnick, a single woman who, when she became president of the University of Maine at Farmington, recruited a full-time manager for the president's house to take charge of arrangements for entertaining. Now president of Keene State, she has recognized that it is helpful to have someone at one's side during the actual event itself; hence, she invites individuals and couples from the college and the local community to serve as co-hosts or escorts for social events.[17]

If Judith Sturnick represents the future, there are still plenty of representatives of a more traditional past to be found. Penn State's search for a new president in 1983 provides an illustration. When the trustees settled upon Bryce Jordan as the university's next president, Jordan was familiar with Penn State but his wife had never been there. Jordan had worked in the University of Texas system for many years, serving as the system's chief academic operating officer, executive vice-chancellor for academic affairs, and the founding president of the University of Texas at Dallas. The Penn State search committee had not brought any candidates to the campus because of their desire to maintain confidentiality throughout the entire search process. Mrs. Jordan was asked by the local paper how she thought she would like living in the small college town of State College, Pennsylvania, after having lived in a metropolis. She responded by saying, in effect, that wherever her husband went, she would be content. The reply will surely not have delighted feminists of either sex on the campus, but it was probably candid. There are many careers, whether in the mili-

---

[16] For further discussion, see Roberta Ostar, ed., *The Partnership Model, A Family Perspective on the College Presidency* (Washington, D.C.: AASCU, 1986), and Madeleine F. Green, *The American College President: A Contemporary Profile* (Washington, D.C.: American Council on Education, 1988).

[17] Sturnick, "Partnership in the Presidency: Past, Present, and Future Possibilities," in Ostar, *Partnership Model*, pp. 56–61.

311

tary, the diplomatic service, or international business, where until recently upwardly mobile couples accepted geographical moves as the price for continuing increases in status, and where one did not think twice about being hauled off to an isolated locale when the status and financial benefits were obvious.

As more and more presidential partnerships involve the separate careers of the partners, invention of opportunity and experience with novel patterns will accumulate. In academia and more generally in the professions, recruiters are more and more having to deal with two-career couples and finding that, if they are to compete, they must modify traditional nepotism rules.[18] When the University of Hartford was recruiting Humphrey Tonkin for its presidency, he was president of the State University of New York at Potsdam, and his wife, Jane Edwards, was teaching there. During the University of Hartford's courtship of Tonkin, arrangements were made for Jane Edwards to teach English at the University of Hartford. When James O. Freedman was recruited from the University of Iowa to the presidency of Dartmouth, he made a faculty position for his wife Bathsheba part of the terms under which he would accept the Dartmouth post. These situations are not always easy for the spouse and for the latter's departmental colleagues, but they have the enormous benefit of giving the presidential partners more sense of the common enterprise than either could acquire alone. When Nannerl Keohane became president of Wellesley College, her husband Robert, who had been chairman of the political science department at Stanford, came East to the political science department at Brandeis, and then moved to Harvard after a few years. More complicated were the arrangements made to attract Mary Maples Dunn to the presidency of Smith College. Mary Maples Dunn had been deputy to the president and dean at Bryn Mawr College and her husband, Richard Dunn, was professor of history at the University of Pennsylvania. Smith College provided Richard Dunn with computer facilities in the president's house, so that he could continue working in Northampton on whatever

[18] Judith Martin ("Miss Manners") and Gunther Stent, a Berkeley professor, in an "op ed" column in the *New York Times*, have observed that two-career couples who wish to avoid a commuting marriage are among the most seriously disadvantaged contenders, and that a version of affirmative action on their behalf is warranted, recognizing that in most cases disparities in levels of ability between the two partners are not likely to be extreme. "Practice Nepotism, but Affirmatively," *New York Times*, May 19, 1988, p. A-31.

312

he had been working on at Penn, and the couple was assured that Richard Dunn could readily be shuttled to and from the Hartford-Springfield airport to Northampton on weekends.

When Stephen Lewis assumed the presidency of Carleton College, his wife Gayle quit her full-time job as administrative assistant to the chair of the Williams College Center for Development Economics, to make the move with her husband. During the Carleton search, she indicated that she hoped to be actively involved at Carleton. In early 1989, when Stephen Lewis had been a little over a year in the presidency, the board announced that a new position had been created for Gayle Lewis, that of "associate of the president." Although this is an unpaid position, the appointment entitles Gayle Lewis to some of the job benefits available to other staff members at the college, including access to college facilities, reimbursement for college-related expenses, use of a college-owned vehicle, insurance coverage while on official business, and workman's compensation. She also has been given office space and a telephone to allow her to conduct college business. Board chairman George Dixon noted that "The title gives Gayle a presence on and beyond the Carleton campus, and it will be helpful to her in the fulfillment of all the activities in which she's been involved."[19] This arrangement is similar to one that has been worked out in the University of California system, whereby the wife of the system president and the spouses of the chancellors, when these are significantly involved in university activities, will be granted the title of associate and thereby will receive various benefits, including library cards and the not negligible provision of parking spaces and insurance.

Many presidents have told us how important it is to them to have the company and support of their knowledgeable spouses. The loneliness of the presidency is a continual theme in memoirs and contemporary commentaries. Presidents have no peers at their institutions, no persons with whom they can speak entirely candidly about their personal aspirations and frustrations, their desires and their heartaches. Even when a person comes to the presidency from the faculty of the same institution, the incumbent soon discovers that former colleagues are no longer either colleagues or peers. In due course some presidents find friends outside aca-

[19] Quoted in *Carleton Voice*, Vol. 54, no. 2 (Winter–Spring 1989), p. 21.

demia altogether, and many come to depend on their friendships with other presidents, particularly so if the latter are not direct competitors.[20] The isolation and loneliness of the president is not a new theme, of course. But the contemporary president seems more at risk, reflecting the more volatile situation of leadership, the scrutiny of the media, and the amplified voices of constituents.

COURTING THE PRESIDENTIAL FAMILY

When members of the Rice University search committee went to call on George Rupp, they met him and his wife Nancy at their institutionally provided home on the Harvard Divinity School campus (in some respects, the home is a better place to assess a prospect than an institutionally provided office). Telling both Nancy and George Rupp about Rice's opportunities and needs was the first step in an energetic courtship.

The courtship extended to the Rupp children as well. George and Nancy Rupp's older daughter was taking her junior year in high school abroad in Germany, while their younger daughter was studying in a private high school in Cambridge. Discovering that the younger daughter was crazy about horses, Ralph O'Connor courted her by suggesting that if the family moved to Houston, she could have a horse of her own. This promise helped take the sting away from the thought of her having to leave her Cambridge friends. In the previous chapter, we saw that George Rupp told the chairman of the Rice board of trustees that he would not accept the presidency until he had spoken with his older daughter, who had not been brought into the family councils about the move up to that point.[21] The

[20] Within the large group of liberal arts colleges and universities that make up the Association of American Colleges is a continuing subgroup of a dozen who term themselves "The Learned Colleagues" and who schedule meetings consonant with the AAC general meetings. In recent years, the Learned Colleagues have elected to their membership the presidents of Swarthmore, Oberlin, Carleton, Reed, Occidental, Whitman, Bryn Mawr, and Williams. When the leadership of these institutions changes hands, the new person is not automatically made a member of the Learned Colleagues. Several former presidents have told us that what they most miss when they are no longer presidents is the connection with other presidents, particularly the Learned Colleagues. Similarly, a man who left the presidency of a Big Ten institution to head another university has told us that, despite the athletic rivalries of the Big Ten, what he most missed in his new post was the companionship of some of his fellow presidents in a group noted for its camaraderie.

[21] Many young people find moving to a new school for the final high school year especially troubling. When John Kuykendall was named president of Davidson College, the Kuykendalls' younger son was about to enter the senior year in the Auburn, Alabama, high school, but the opportunity to

314

Rupps had already explored the high school situation in Houston and discovered both a magnet public high school and a good private school to which their daughter could transfer. In all likelihood, the parents were confident that their daughter would not stand in the way of the family's move, but on such matters there is always a certain degree of risk, which the Rice trustees—who had no fallback candidates had Rupp unexpectedly declined—were required graciously to accept.

George Rupp's career makes apparent both his venturesomeness and his ambition. To win his interest in Rice University as against other conceivable chances for a position of even greater prestige (for instance, the presidency of Princeton, his alma mater, where William G. Bowen's retirement was anticipated), he had to be persuaded that Rice, despite its small size and largely regional drawing power for undergraduates, could quickly become a much more nationally visible institution, thanks to the distinction it had already achieved and the financial resources at its present and prospective command. For the truly ambitious, it is not always the most eminent institution which is attractive, but rather, one slightly less known with greater potential, what in market terms would be seen as a "growth stock." In the crucial telephone conversation Bill Martin had with George Rupp when the latter had just about given up thinking about Rice, these points were driven home and Rupp's enthusiasm rekindled. Martin's own enthusiasm, first kept in check when he thought Rupp an altogether implausible prospect, proved contagious. The episode illustrates the fact that courtship is not exclusively the work of the chair of the search committee or of the board of trustees, but can enlist the help of others who may have some closer connection with the candidate.

A similar team effort went into the courting of Geoffrey Bannister to become executive vice-president of Butler University with the altogether likely prospect that he would shortly assume the presidency, as he did the next year, in 1989. When Geoffrey and Margaret Bannister visited Butler in Indianapolis, the wife of the city's mayor, a real estate broker, gave Margaret Bannister a tour of the city and showed her possible houses the Bannisters might consider. The Bannisters' daughter Kate, then entering ninth grade, had been invited to Butler along with her parents, and mem-

---

participate in the soccer program in the new locale made him quite resilient about the move to the tiny college town of Davidson, North Carolina.

bers of the Butler board arranged for a girl Kate's age to show Kate the school she would attend if the family moved to Indianapolis and to take her to a party so that she could meet more young people. When the Bannisters returned to Boston, where Geoffrey Bannister was dean of Arts and Sciences at Boston University and Margaret Bannister was director of Boston University's international study programs, they debated for three weeks as to whether Geoff Bannister should accept the offer from Butler. Not one day passed when they were not telephoned by someone from Indianapolis—a trustee, the incumbent president, a member of the faculty or of the administration, the mayor—someone who stressed how strong was the hope that the Bannisters would come to Butler.

VISITS TO THE CAMPUS

Like the search itself, the campus visit has two sides. For the campus, it is a chance to become informed about the candidates being considered for the presidency and to make comparative judgments among these people. For candidates (and spouses), it is an opportunity to get some sense of the campus. Especially for those who are unfamiliar with the campus, such a visit can substitute reality for fantasy. But there is a certain amount of unreality in the way many campus visits are staged. Two-day schedules may begin with an early breakfast with student leaders and continue to a late evening dinner with the trustees, followed by another full day of rushing from one visitation to another. In the 1989 Western Washington University presidential search, for example, three finalists took part in two-day visitations to the campus. During one twenty-five hour period of each candidate's visit, the finalist made eight major speeches to between eight hundred and nine hundred people, and then answered questions from the audience.

In defense of such schedules, it is said that, after all, presidents lead lives under similar stress and exposure, and marathon-style campus visits are a good way to screen people for their capacity to remain unflustered under pressure. Indeed, it may test the political savvy of candidates to see how they respond when asked to say what they would do concerning an issue about which the questionner has strong and obvious sentiments. Some candidates will make promises which appear expedient in view of the de-

316

mands being voiced, but are later to be regretted when it becomes apparent that the vocal people on campus may be neither influential nor knowledgeable. But those candidates who wisely choose not to answer in concrete terms may be faulted by their audiences for their lack of specificity. Not appreciated is the fact that capable presidents do not handle problems entirely on their own without consultation or delegation. Some candidates may be energetic but also more deliberate when opportunity offers, and are not prepared to treat each question as if it were an emergency about which there could not be consultation and deliberation. Moreover, overcrowded "show and tell" campus visits are apt to put at a disadvantage candidates who have come from a distance, especially if their schedule did not allow them to come a day or so ahead of time to cope with jet lag.[22]

What is most depressing about the blur of campus visits is that the candidate hears few new questions and gives few new answers. Temporary issues become exigent. Students may want to know the candidate's view of the fraternity system, or may ask about the prospects for a new student center. Faculty members may have a plethora of concerns, almost always including their own role in governance, including the curriculum and retention and promotion of faculty. They may also want to know about leave policy, or retirement policy; and some may be hostile to fraternities. Administrators, who may meet with candidates individually or collectively, will have their joint and particular concerns. In the more visible institutions, questions are regularly asked about affirmative action. Here the issues may include recruitment at the undergraduate level, increase of representation on the faculty, a women's studies major or ensuring that attention to "diversity" becomes part of the curriculum. In these evocations there will be echoes from the past and evidence, difficult for the visitor or even the residents to assess, of the dilemmas of the present.

Questions that seem hardly ever to get asked and which, in any case, are difficult to respond to in large meetings, concern how a new president might protect the institution's future against the legacies of the past and the pressures and polemics of the present. Nor is a candidate likely to be

---

[22] Among the campus visitors to "Southern State University" was a man who had come directly out of the hospital because the university's schedule required him to come for those particular two days when he was still ailing. Understandably, he did not show the exuberant vigor of competitor candidates, including the successful finalist, who as dean of the law school was already on campus.

asked, to take one example of many, how he or she proposes to react to what Jerome Bruner has referred to as "the revolution in cognitive psychology." It is possible that a question might be raised about requiring "computer literacy," and a candidate asked what prior experience, if any, the candidate has had with this issue. The questions which might test the range of academic exposure and the breadth of reading of a prospective president are no more likely to be asked than they would be in a political campaign, and at their frequent worst, campus visits degenerate into "photo opportunities" and fugitive political campaigning. At times, candidates for the college and university presidency behave almost as if they were candidates for public office, with political platforms and prepared statements, making promises about what they will do if selected, with these promises based on very little information about the peculiarities of the institution or the complexity of its problems.

Again and again, candidates who have become presidents have expressed their astonishment at the discovery that, once installed, nobody on the faculty or the student body seems interested in their intellectual judgments or ideas about anything whatsoever. They are hired as visionaries and on arrival treated as mere managers. Their efforts with faculty members to raise the level of intellectual discourse make the faculty anxious, especially when the president turns out to have read books in the faculty member's field which the faculty member has not yet gotten around to. It is as if the campus visits were a dream which never really occurred.

Search committee members do not plan to be inconsiderate of candidates visiting the campus, and may be unaware that their treatment is seen in this way. What is often lacking for candidates is adequate hosting. No one person takes charge of the visit or makes certain that the concerns of the candidates are addressed. Several candidates have told us that they were handed a xeroxed schedule for their day or days on campus and then sent on their own to the meetings. If no one from the search committee is with the candidate for the day or days on campus, there is a double loss. The search committee does not learn first-hand how the candidate deals with multiple and varied situations, and the candidate has no one around to intervene if a session gets out of hand or to interpret questions that might hint of problems on campus that the search committee has not pre-

318

viously mentioned. We are not suggesting that the candidate needs to be chaperoned, but rather that, as in other human settings, situations need hosts to bring order, to translate, and where need be, to intervene.

Many campus visits are designed in ways that are invitational to candidates rather than organized as though they were obstacle courses. They are given time to themselves to evaluate, perhaps to make notes about what they have heard, although always with someone from the search committee (or the search consultant) nearby to be of assistance. In the best cases, they are asked about whom they would like to meet in addition to various leaders of the faculty and administration on their schedule. Wise candidates may ask to meet with the head of buildings and grounds, often a good source from whom to learn about under-maintenance or over-use of buildings and to get a sense of the morale of what might be called the ship's crew of a college or university. Librarians are apt to have much more knowledge than power, and the same is true of registrars, and any candidate who is not interested in talking with someone in the admissions office would probably not be a good bet, even for the presidency of a mammoth state university such as the University of Texas at Austin, Ohio State, or Minnesota. Time in the schedule will be left for a meeting with someone the candidate may realize can help provide a better understanding of the locale.

One question candidates and search committees face in planning the campus visit is whether to have the finalists meet with the departing president. Readers may recall that when the four finalists in the University of Florida search came to campus, one of their ports of call was on the departing president, Dr. Robert Marston. For some candidates these are mere courtesy calls; in other searches, these meetings allow candidates to learn a great deal about the institution and the presidency that is helpful to them in making their decision as to whether to accept the position if offered. However, a number of candidates have reported to us their dissatisfaction with what they regarded as meager information ventured in answer to their queries. On such crucial issues as relations of board members with one another, or contacts between the board and the legislature or with the system chancellor's office, some candidates have found departing presidents singularly uninformative. Some departing presidents may well be resentful, even bitter, while others are diffident about volunteering

319

comments. Moreover, some departing presidents, in seeking to avoid the impropriety of influencing the choice of their successor, may in fact be less helpful than would be optimal.

After Humphrey Tonkin had been chosen to succeed Stephen J. Trachtenberg as president of the University of Hartford, Trachtenberg took Tonkin on a verbal "guided tour" of the institution and its people, the campus, and the surrounding area. Although Trachtenberg wanted to be careful not to bias his successor vis-à-vis particular individuals, he was able to convey to Tonkin his own sense of the demographic and ecological setting of the university and some of its history. Some new presidents hesitate to ask their predecessor anything, for fear of seeming ignorant, and others fear to ask for fear of eliciting biased judgments—a self-protective posture that seems to assume that there is some magical way to discover unbiased judgments.

In reflecting on these matters, it is important to remember that search committees differ widely in the degree to which their membership can help candidates get a sense of the institution or, in contrast, constitute human "Potemkin villages" disguising the nature of the institution. Some of the people a candidate might want to meet, such as the departing president's executive secretary or indeed the departing president's spouse, are unlikely to be made formally available to a visitor.

As we noted earlier, Carleton College, in its 1986–1987 presidential search, brought three finalists to campus, none of them a sitting president. We spoke after the search had concluded with Stephen Lewis, the candidate chosen president, and with his wife Gayle. Of course, a candidate's feeling about a search process may be colored by having been the choice of the search committee, the campus, and board. In the case of Carleton, we also heard high praise for the careful manner in which the campus visit was managed from another one of the finalists, a provost at a leading independent university. Both the Lewises and this unsuccessful contender and his wife were enthusiastic about the reception they had been given at Carleton. They spoke of the midwestern friendliness of students, faculty, and administrators; the care taken to see that the candidate and his wife were made comfortable on campus, even in the midst of long days filled to overflowing with appointments; the interest shown in the candidate's spouse, with effort taken to answer her questions and to involve her with

320

people on campus and in the community who shared similar interests; and the thoughtful hosting by board chairman George Dixon of the meeting with trustees. Dixon arranged for the candidate and his wife to sit at different tables (tables were small enough for easy conversation) and to change tables at various points during the course of the evening so that they had a chance to talk with all people present.

From the point of view of the successful candidate, Stephen Lewis, and his wife Gayle, the campus visit was desirable to help them come to a firm decision whether they wanted to make the move from Williams College (where Lewis had been provost for several tours of duty). They were not strangers to the Carleton campus. Lewis is a development economist specializing on Africa, and had first met Carleton president Robert Edwards when Edwards was on the African and Middle Eastern desk at the Ford Foundation. The Lewises' daughter had just graduated from Carleton, and they had come to know the college from the perspective of parents. Yet they wanted to get a better idea of what it would really be like to be there, to be in charge there. Coming to the campus visit at Carleton from the University of Sussex, where Lewis was on a leave of absence from Williams, arriving in the evening and starting two days of the characteristically uninterrupted round of conversations early the following morning, the two of them met, they calculated, at least a hundred people, including administrators, faculty members, students, union officials, and non-academic staff. They were accompanied everywhere by a member of the search committee. Far from being asked why he wanted to be president of Carleton, or why he thought he would make a good one, Lewis was drawn into discussions of current issues without being pressed to make a political commitment to please his audience. The Lewises were both buyers and sellers; and so was Carleton College. Despite jet lag and the grueling round of conversations, both the Lewises were attracted by the spiritedness they encountered, even while appreciating the difficult challenges ahead. That they had met the former president, Robert Edwards, was also helpful to them in understanding the problems facing the college and in considering what the role of the spouse might be. In this case the campus visit was at once part of the courtship and a running start on the incumbency.

For another example we quote from the letter of a sitting president who

321

had turned down many inquiries to head other colleges, but was persuaded to become a finalist at a Midwestern college of the same denominational affiliation as that of his own institution.

> The campus visit included scheduled meetings with the search committee and other trustees, two faculty groups, two student groups, the vice-presidents, another staff group, and then an open meeting to which anyone on campus who was interested was invited. They put me through my paces, but I enjoyed it. The quality of the questions was excellent and so was the quality of the people. The level of commitment to [the college] and of dedication to their work was very high. Among the most interesting questions were these: Would I be prejudiced against persons who were not Christians since I am a minister? Would I have difficulty adjusting to a different culture? Is my success in fund raising a function of my location or is it transferable to the Midwest? Do I think that faculty have to be published to be tenurable? Do I like to be with students? How do I relate to trustees? Why am I interested in [the college] since it has less endowment than [my own college]?[23]

Our correspondent was also impressed with the chair of the board, who chaired the search committee, and after the stimulation of the campus visit, agreed to allow a delegation from the search committee (two trustees and one faculty member) to visit the candidate on his home ground—a risk the latter regarded by that time to be worth running.

NEGOTIATION AND INSTALLATION

The search process is not fully over until the new president and the board of trustees reach agreement on the terms of the presidency. When terms cannot be agreed upon and the "first choice" candidate pulls out, search committees sometimes find they have no other candidate to whom they can turn and the entire process must begin all over again. In other searches, even though there is another finalist whom the board likes very much, since the name of the first person with whom the board was nego-

---

[23] From private correspondence.

tiating is widely known, this next person offered the presidency is seen as "second choice" and, hence, "second best," no matter how well qualified.

Negotiations between the prospective president and the board are critical because they determine what life will be like for the incumbent after installation. Yet many search committees and boards are so captivated by a candidate that they have not thought beyond the raptures of love at first sight. Similarly, candidates may be equally enamored, or blinded by their own ambitions, or less commonly the ambitions of their spouse, that they remain misled by the false advertising (perhaps half-believed) of the search committee. Or the prospective president and spouse may not know what items they should make sure to discuss in their negotiations, and rely, mistakenly in our judgment, on the good faith of the chair of the board to "take care" of them as needed.

Search consultant Raymond Klemmer believes that negotiation of terms should occur long before an offer is officially made, so that there are not altogether unrealistic expectations on the part of any serious candidate. Each finalist should understand the range of the salary, the expectations regarding the presidential residence, etc. We mentioned previously the need to discuss prior to the campus visit, if there will be one, what arrangements might be needed for the president's spouse. It makes no sense to bring a candidate to the campus on false pretenses, as in one search we referred to earlier, when the candidate had been led to believe that there would be a suitable position found on campus for his wife but, when the presidency was actually offered, discovered that no such job for his spouse would be possible.

In another search, at a state college, a press release announcing the selection of the new president was sent out before the details of this appointment were confirmed to the satisfaction of the prospective president. During his candidacy, assurances had been given by the institution's board of trustees concerning such matters as moving expenses, as well as arrangements about the president's house. However, when he met with the chancellor of the board of regents to make sure of the exact terms of his contract, the chancellor had to inform him that some of the trustees' promises could not be met. The negotiations fell apart; the prospective president withdrew his candidacy; the announcement of the presidential appointment, made one week in the *Chronicle of Higher Education*, had to be "corrected" a few weeks later.

Something similar apparently happened in 1988 when the trustees of the City University of New York gave their approval to appoint S. Allen Counter, Jr., to the presidency of Medgar Evers College. Counter, a neurophysiologist at Harvard University and director of the Harvard Foundation, is internationally known for his locating in 1986 the eighty-year-old sons of Robert Peary and Matthew Henson, the first two men ever to reach the North Pole. The announcement of the appointment made headlines in the *New York Times* and elsewhere, and the Medgar Evers faculty was jubilant that someone of Counter's stature would agree to assume the presidency of the small and troubled community college in Brooklyn. The problem was that, according to Counter, he had not made such an agreement. When the board announcement was made, the press release stated that "Dr. Counter of Harvard University was offered and accepted the position of president of Medgar Evers College of the City University of New York. . . . Dr. Counter is discussing with CUNY the terms and conditions of employment for the position."[24] But somewhere in the process of these discussions, talks broke down. Counter has given one story, the CUNY board another. The outcome was that Counter declined the offer of the presidency and did so expressing doubt about "the continued existence and viability of Medgar Evers College as an independent institution." The CUNY board was forced to reopen its search in the midst of bad feelings and bad publicity.

Contract Considerations

In many localities, the president of the local college or university is not only the most significant person in the area, but the salary and perquisites of the position are either a matter of public record or are widely known and commented upon. The press will report that so-and-so landed a "$95,000 job," probably mentioning in the news story that follows that the president is also receiving a "free" house and the use of a college- or university-owned car. It is often noted, too, that the salary of the president is more money than the governor receives, or the mayor, although

[24] Quoted in Teresa A. Mullin, "Counter, Medgar Evers Spar Over Job," *Harvard Crimson*, Vol. 188, no. 96 (August 2, 1988), p. 3.

no comparison is made to other top salaries within the institution (it may be somewhat less than one has to pay in today's desperate efforts to find a dean for the medical school, let alone to the chief executive officers of private enterprises of similar size). Antagonism toward salaries which appear out of line can most readily be mobilized when it is "taxpayers' money" that is involved, but in the independent sector of higher education students may express resentment in terms of objections to rising tuitions, while faculty members and staff complain in terms of their own rates of pay.[25]

When the regents of the University of California chose David Gardner as president, they offered him over $100,000 to lure him from the presidency of the University of Utah to the costlier soil of Berkeley. There were fierce attacks in the press and from faculty members and students—an altogether common experience for presidents in the public sector. The easily aroused resentment over the pay of public officials was harnessed behind an amendment to the California state constitution in November 1986, dubbed the "fair pay" amendment, which would have limited the salary of any official, including university professors and officials, to eighty percent of the Governor's salary, which is pegged at $80,000. Because the amendment would also have eliminated vacation leave-time not taken, there was great opposition in the lower ranks of the state civil service and it was defeated; otherwise, it might well have passed.

Salary is important for its own sake and also as a symbol. As a symbol, it cuts both ways: if it appears egregiously high, as in the instances just referred to, or if it is low in relation to other comparable positions in the not-for-profit sector, it appears to derogate the position itself.[26]

The duration of the prospective president's contract is almost always

---

[25] Such resentment is virtually absent toward athletic or rock stars, who are commonly people of more than ordinary talent from actually or allegedly ordinary backgrounds. Resentment of the fact that corporate executives in the United States are compensated by their boards of directors in a lavish way not conceivable in Japan or Western Europe, with salaries a hundred times that of the lowest-paid worker, rather than only ten or twenty times greater, is beginning only at the margin, as in the Chrysler-UAW wage settlement in the spring of 1988, declaring that there will be no bonuses for top executives unless profits are such as to provide bonuses for workers as well.

[26] See two companion stories in the *Chronicle of Higher Education*, one on presidents' compensation by Scott Heller and another on political backlash by Carolyn J. Mooney, in Vol. 33, no. 35 (May 13, 1987), pp. 1, 18–23. The University of Maine system used the Presidential Search Consultation Service to recruit a system chancellor, Jack E. Freeman, who had been vice-president of the University of Pittsburgh and who stayed two weeks ". . . because his $114,000 salary as chancellor of the University of Maine system caused a public outcry," as Mooney reports. Fortunately, Freeman could return to his Pittsburgh position.

explored at the outset, although in reality there can never be a guarantee, other than in financial terms, since presidents serve "at the pleasure of the board." Less commonly explored at the outset is how the president's pay is to be adjusted in future years, whether annually or, where these occur, when evaluations take place, or in some other fashion, for example, a standard percentage raise plus inflation. For the president-elect to explore topics such as these at the outset would suggest either insecurity or greed or both.

In our experience, disputes between a prospective candidate and trustees over the amount of presidential pay are the exception. Conflicts over the presidential residence are much more common. In a number of cases, inexperienced candidates have allowed the question of presidential residence to remain unresolved, proceeding on the assumption that the board of trustees will do "the right thing." In one case, a search consultant left the process after the group of finalists had been chosen, and the new incumbent assumed that, at the very least, the board of trustees would assist him in finding a place to live (the locale is a private metropolitan commuter university) and would help find mortgage money. But the board, many of whose members were still wedded to the departing president, did nothing of the sort, and the incumbency began on a sour note.

Approximately half of American college and university presidents live in an institution-owned presidential mansion. Whether the institution is public or private, this dwelling is usually regarded as luxurious, and its public rooms enjoyed (and its inner rooms often invaded) by envious faculty and staff and local and distant community people. There seems to be no commoner or quicker way for a president to get into difficulties than to ask for changes in the presidential mansion, even when these changes are designed to facilitate official entertainment by the president, and certainly if the changes are regarded as decorative luxuries. When Robert A. Scott was chosen as president of Ramapo College, the board hoped that the Scott family would live in an eighteenth-century home which the college had refurbished. It turned out that Robert Scott, although not of basketball stature, is taller than were his eighteenth-century counterparts, and eighteenth-century lintels would decapitate him! Although it has sought for the flair of a private college, Ramapo is part of the state college system of New Jersey, and in that political context it turned out to be difficult to find and then to fund another domicile for the president. Even-

326

tually, the board chairman and the president-elect were able to reach a modus vivendi.

In another search at a private denominational college which had no home for its president, the president-elect asked the chairman of the board to find a home for him, while the incumbent-to-be finished his teaching schedule on his home campus, in whose neighborhood he and his wife had just bought a new home for themselves. He was told that a home had been found for him, and later learned that some of the members of the board, local influentials, were planning a real estate development practically next door to this home. He concluded that he had been treated with disingenuousness, since he had not been told of this plan, whose implementation might well lower the value of his new property. He protested, and reported to us that another house was grudgingly provided to him—hardly an ideal way to begin his incumbency.

At "Southern State University" the new president and his wife knew that the presidential mansion, though imposing from the outside, was dreadfully inadequate for the immense amounts of entertaining that goes with the presidency of a major state university proud of its football team. It is typical of the diurnal round of university presidents that 3,000 or 4,000 individuals, or more, will pass through the doors of their "home" in the course of a year. The kitchen facilities were woefully behind the times; the upstairs accommodations for the family left much to be desired. Yet Southern State is a poor state, and the new presidential partners, chosen over others in the locally politicized search we have described, concluded that major renovations to the house would bring immediate reprisal in a flare-up of populist resentment. They refrained—and endured.

Understandably, members of the board of trustees see the president's house on, so to speak, its best behavior. The presidential tasks require sanguinity, not grumpiness, and a querulous wife complaining about the handicaps of the kitchen would strike an inappropriate note at a post-game party. During the period of student-faculty turbulence, and still today on some politically alert campuses, the presidential family, living on campus, becomes an easy target. The telephone may bring threats; the house may be surrounded by agitated students. During Kenneth Keller's term as president of the University of Minnesota, when he became unpopular in part because of his proposed "Commitment to Focus," and in part because of the extensive publicity over the renovations to the president's house and office, he and his family had to put up with garbage dumped in their front yard and profane heckling from motorists passing by the president's home. The president's house, sometimes located near fraternity row, may be fair game for pranksters. At one prestigious college, the wife of the president was awakened in the middle of the night by a knock on the front door of the presidential mansion, and when she went to the door (her husband was out of town on a fund-raising trip), she was greeted by drunk students who "flashed" at her. In recent years a number of presidents (including Harvard's) have preferred not to live on campus, despite recognition of the value of their own accessibility. Some have made the availability of a housing allowance or a home near but not on campus a condition of their accepting the presidency. This preference is accentuated in the recent period of rising real estate prices, which has meant that selling one's previous home and moving into the president's house will leave the family with no equity in a home of its own when it becomes time to depart. Some presidents have asked for institutional help to buy their own home, for even though they might not want to stay in the location after they have left the presidency, it will be a hedge against inflation. Other presidents scout about for a vacation home neither too accessible nor too inaccessible from the campus, good for all weathers, including a possible season of underemployment.

Rare, however, is the president who has much time for vacations.[27] Few presidents possess "the leisure of the theory class."[28] In recent years, several presidents whom we know have planned ahead for a significant break from their diurnal duties by arranging for a semester or full year away from the presidency. When Nannerl Keohane was named president of Wellesley College, she was an associate professor of political science at Stanford with only very minimal prior experience in academic administration. But she had the almost uncanny wisdom to ask for something few presidents anticipate wanting, namely, a full-year sabbatical, in regular academic style, to be taken after six years in the presidency. So far as we know, no other president-elect has asked for this faculty-style opportunity, which by implication includes a promise to stay not only for the term

[27] See Dave Dyson and Ralph Kirkman, "Presidential Priorities," *AGB Reports*, Vol. 31, no. 2 (March–April 1989), pp. 6–11.

[28] We owe this phrase to Daniel Bell, who applied it to the Center for Advanced Study in the Behavioral Sciences at Stanford.

prior to the sabbatical but for a reasonable though unspecified period thereafter. President Keohane took her sabbatical during the 1987–1988 academic year, spending the year at the Center for Advanced Study at Stanford, and leaving Wellesley College in the very capable hands of Wellesley's dean, Dale Marshall, who served as acting president. For the entire year, Nannerl Keohane was available by telephone only for occasional discussion of important policy issues which would have significance beyond the sabbatical year, and only in conversations with three or four people at the institution who were authorized to breach the peace of the sabbatical. In the first semester, she did no alumnae or development work, but in the second semester she made a few fund-raising calls. In the winter of 1987, Derek Bok and Sissela Bok went on a three-month sabbatical to India, Israel, and Spain, leaving Henry Rosovsky, former dean of the Faculty of Arts and Sciences, and current member of the Harvard Corporation, to serve in his place. After serving as president of Arkansas College for nine years, Dan West took a year's sabbatical to pursue doctoral study at the Harvard Graduate School of Education, completing in that year the course work toward his second doctorate (his first degree is a doctorate in divinity). In the year 1981–1982 Paul Bragdon, who had then been president of Reed College for ten years, took a year's sabbatical in Cambridge, making use of a visitor's office at the Harvard Business School, where he had received his M.B.A. many years earlier. He later concluded that a year was too long to be away from so feisty and unruly a place as Reed, and that a half-year would have been more suitable. He returned to spend six more years at Reed, seeing it through difficult financial times. If one wants to lengthen the all-too-brief stints of contemporary presidents, appropriately spaced sabbaticals would help to facilitate presidential renewal. Presidents-on-leave might find such renewal in the process of conducting research, writing, or reading in their academic discipline, or at such places as the Center for the Study of Higher Education in Berkeley or in the Washington, D.C., headquarters of one of the educational associations. For the work-driven individuals who become presidents, the object is personal and professional growth, as well as a respite from the exhaustion of always being "on call" and the redundancy of perennially raised issues and "causes."

One of the most contentious topics arising at the outset of a presidency is how the president's performance will be evaluated. Despite contractual

329

rights which may provide, if not for a golden parachute, then a silver-plated one, all presidents serve at the pleasure of the board. Mindful presidents are eager to understand how they are being received, and most would like to know how they can do their jobs better. The best presidents want people around them who will help them learn. Formal evaluation—sometimes conducted after two years but more commonly after three or five years—proceeds however, from altogether different premises. A relatively recent invention, formal evaluation is often premised on an egalitarian argument: since everyone else on campus is evaluated, it is only fair to evaluate the president also. This contention does not account for the fact that faculty members are evaluated by their peers, and after sufficient time they get tenure, a job security few presidents have (presidents can negotiate for tenure in their academic field, but there is no such thing—nor should there be—as tenure in the presidency). Formal evaluation is in many situations more like a recall in a state political system, allowing constituents on campus if not to force out a president who has offended a substantial segment, at least to hold the president hostage while the evaluation is under way. We believe that formal evaluations conducted at stated intervals and involving large segments of the campus are more apt to be destructive than helpful. Yet there have been cases where evaluation has helped legitimate a president, demonstrating more support for him than had seemed evident in the face of criticism from faculty members, administrators, and students. There have also been cases where presidents have learned from their evaluation certain things about how they have been perceived that they might not have picked up on their own.[29] But, more often in our experience, formal evaluation diminishes the power of the board and handicaps the power of the presidency.

It is most unlikely that a required evaluation will turn a candidate away from a presidency thought otherwise desirable. Anyone prepared to be a president would have more sanguinity. But candidates who have observed the effects of evaluation elsewhere might like to have clarity about the issue before assuming a presidency. Had they read *Presidents Make a Dif-*

[29] Such instances, as well as an excellent discussion of the more general problems of evaluation, are set forth in detail in Diana B. Beaudoin's doctoral dissertation, "Formal Procedures and Informal Influences: Assessing a College President's Performance," Harvard Graduate School of Education, 1986.

ference, they might find attractive Clark Kerr's idea that an informal evaluation of the president by the board is best done after several years to encourage the board and the president to assess how the situation now looks, with enough time elapsed for the incumbent to be quietly assessed and then, if the verdict is a positive one, not assessed again at least for another half-dozen years.[30] By the time of this initial assessment, the president will have passed the frequent but not invariable "honeymoon" stage, but may not yet in the ordinary case have piled up the layer upon layer of faculty and also staff people who have been disappointed by presidential action or inaction.

The president-elect might also want to suggest that the evaluation be done by a consultant mutually acceptable to the president and the board. The consultant might quietly talk with some faculty leaders and with others in the president's financial, legislative, or other environments to get a sense of how things are going and what steps might be taken by the president, the board, or both together so that they would go better, not necessarily more amicably.

A Go-between During Negotiations

In the preceding discussion we have only touched upon a few of the items that the president-elect should discuss with the chairman of the board during the negotiations about the presidential position.[31] Those candidates who have been in a presidency elsewhere will have a good idea of the large and small matters that deserve mention. These include the level of support that will be provided for entertaining, the arrangements for the president to have tenure in an appropriate academic department, the financial provisions for the presidential spouse to travel with the president to academic conventions and fund-raising events, and the arrangements to be made if the president should no longer meet the "pleasure of the board." First-time presidents and their spouses, however, are unlikely to know what it is that they will need. And even those who solicit advice (and copies of actual presidential contracts) from friends who are presidents will find it

[30] Page 57.

[31] For a detailed listing of items for discussion regarding the president's conditions of employment, see the pamphlet by James B. Appleberry, *Guidelines on the Appointment of a President*, distributed by the American Association of State Colleges and Universities (Washington, D.C., 1987).

awkward to quibble over seeming details with the person who has just offered a presidency. Moreover, all presidents-elect want to develop a good working relationship with the chairman of the board and may avoid raising issues that they fear could put them at odds from the very outset.

In 1984, writing about the use of search consultants in *Change*, we recommended their use as go-between in the process of easing the transition and negotiating the terms of the presidential position. Since then, our experience has only confirmed our judgment that consultants may be optimal persons to take on this role. The consultant has already been serving, in effect, as a go-between in the course of the search, and may uniquely have the confidence of both the chairman of the board and the president-elect. Even if a consultant has not been used for the search, one can be employed at this last stage of the process for the sole purpose of helping with the negotiations.

In one search with which we are familiar, the chairman of the board was a lawyer with many years of experience serving as a labor negotiator and felt himself eminently well qualified to handle the negotiations of the presidential contract. Yet these negotiations broke down because agreement could not be reached on an item of crucial importance to the prospective president but considered almost inconsequential by the board chairman. Only several months later did the candidate's spouse suggest to us a compromise that might have been proposed, one that probably would have been satisfactory to both parties, but that she did not think of at the time of the negotiations. Perhaps a go-between would have been able to do what the successful lawyer-negotiator could not do in this situation because he had been one of the negotiating parties rather than the go-between: keeping simultaneously in mind the interests of both parties and thinking creatively about ways to fashion agreements acceptable to both.

The question of evaluation and other questions relating to the president's security and that of a spouse would seem best raised on behalf of the president by such a go-between, a third party. Someone in the midst of finishing up at a current location, often in a rushed fashion, and just starting out on a new assignment, has other matters to think about than remote personal contingencies. In particular, there is likely to be a plateful of issues to be discussed between the new president and a board chairman who may also be new, priorities concerning the institution itself rather than the entry-level perplexities and anxieties of the presidential family. Thus, there frequently is a capital campaign to be discussed. There commonly is curricular reform to be discussed. There may be questions of a delicate nature concerning the predecessor who is still around. There will surely be questions about the competence and degrees of indispensability of senior administrative staff. The institutional agenda is endless, perhaps perilous. If such a go-between makes demands which seem to the board excessive, the principal can always call off the agent and moderate the latter's terms without seeming to be either greedy or unduly anxious.

A consultant with considerable experience, who has seen presidents assume office with buoyancy and depart it in sadness or despair, can counsel both the board and the new president about the kinds of insurance necessary to protect the president and also—in our observation, quite as important—to make it easier for the board to dismiss a president when that is appropriate, rather than out of pity and sentimentality to keep a person on too long. In the course of a search, and in some cases on the basis of prior searches, the consultant will have come to know the chairman of the search committee and the person about to be installed, and will have learned something about the institution as well. Hence, the consultant can serve as a matchmaker whose chief stake in the outcome is that it go well and reflect well on the choice.[32]

Go-betweens During the Incumbency

None of this suggests that others who have become acquainted with the new president in the course of the search should not also try to be helpful. It sometimes happens that a newly installed president, perhaps especially one who starts at the beginning of summer when the campus is relatively empty, will feel isolated, not yet having established collegial relations with anyone. All too soon, the new president will feel almost a surfeit of people, of invitations, of opportunities to make and to lose friends. A consultant

[32] One corporate recruiter told us of a case where a candidate for c.e.o. had assumed that a chauffeured car went with the position. He had such a car and driver at his present location. However, the corporate culture of the institution to which he was moving—at an increased salary—did not offer such a fringe benefit, and in fact frowned upon it. The consultant told the candidate that if the latter insisted, and indeed for the candidate it seemed a question of status rather than of actual need, he would disqualify himself from the position. The candidate reconsidered and, having not lost face directly with the board to which he would be reporting, agreed to the new arrangement.

or third party can help to alert the sensibilities of the trustees to the whole *Gestalt* of the neophyte, who in many cases hesitates to raise questions with the board or with experienced inherited subordinates whose answers the president-elect may feel will be seen as obvious.

The search committee is likely to disband with relief once the person chosen has accepted. But the efforts that went into the search should not disappear without trace.[33] They need to be mobilized during the period in which the new president discovers the institution and in the best cases builds a team to whom authority is delegated and with whom issues and concerns are shared.

As a result of our earlier work on these matters, we developed the tentative notion that the search committee should stay together for the first weeks or perhaps months of the term of office of a president who comes from outside to help assuage the isolation of and smooth the difficulties attendant on installation. In fact, members of the search committee do sometimes informally serve as switchboards to the campus, as one can easily imagine the three faculty search committee members at Rice University doing. However, further reflection led us to conclude that too-close ties between the new president and members of the search committee would look like a payoff for being chosen, except in cases where the search committee members had such exceptional trust and respect from the campus that there would be no suspicion that they were being rewarded for helping to choose the incumbent. For a new president, there are ever so many traps for the unwary,[34] and one has to think of many avenues for facilitating the ability of the newcomer to "case the joint"—if possible, before the first serious conflict or emergency strikes.

[33] Many search committees try to keep a record of their confidential work available to the board at the time another search may become necessary. Newton Minow, chairman of Northwestern University's presidential search, kept a meticulous record of every conversation, every search committee meeting, everything that could be put down on paper, all of which he packaged and sealed until the next occasion when it might come in handy.

[34] Edward Lewis, when he came from an associate deanship at Cornell to be president of St. Mary's College of Maryland, which prides itself on its handsome campus, was distressed to find cars parked not in the nearby parking lots, but in the driveway in front of the administration building. At one of his first presidential staff meetings, he said that he would like the campus police to see to it that such cars were removed. After the meeting, his executive assistant told him that the dean had parked his car in that driveway for many years, and would resent having to move it. The assistant suggested that it would be prudent of Lewis to rescind the order, something Lewis gratefully did.

334

CHAPTER XII

The Multiple Meanings of Searches

THROUGHOUT THIS BOOK, we have chosen to tell the stories of searches and to discuss their various aspects in chronological order. We describe the search from the beginnings of the process: the selection of the membership of the search committee, the discussions about criteria for selection, and the decisions about confidentiality and disclosure. And we follow the search through its final stages: the selection of finalists, the choice of a new president and the negotiations with the person who is chosen. This, after all, is the way the participants experience it, as the search moves along over the course of months or occasionally years. But the reflexivity of human affairs is not captured in a linear sequence. No one aspect of the search fits nicely into one category nor, as is apparent from our references back to earlier chapters or ahead to later ones, into one location in our volume. The search process for a college and university president is an intricate tapestry of human dramas, political struggles, and moral dilemmas. It is both a structured, rational series of events that can be planned and plotted, and it is also, as in the movie *Rashomon*, a process that carries different meanings for its various participants and observers.

Hence, in this last chapter we want to consider the topic of searches for college and university presidents with a somewhat different approach. In their book, *Modern Approaches to Understanding and Managing Organizations*, Lee Bolman and Terry Deal argue that organizations can best be understood when viewed through various "lenses" or "frames," that is, by using differing conceptual schema or theories.[1] They group the array of organizational theories into four frames—structural, political, human

[1] San Francisco, Jossey-Bass, 1984.

resources, and symbolic—which constitute four distinct ways of under-standing organizations and organizational processes. In these concluding remarks, we view the search process through these four "lenses," adding to them a fifth moral "frame." Using these five perspectives on the search allows us to highlight important aspects of the search process and to understand more fully its multiple dimensions and implications.

According to Bolman and Deal, the structural approach to organizations is predicated on a "belief in rationality and a faith that the right structure can minimize organizational problems."[2] In the search process, this is evident in the oft-expressed desire to identify the "best" procedures to follow, the structure most likely to produce success. In the "Abbott College" search, search chairman Martin Sloan took marker in hand at the first meeting of the search committee and drew a chart of the course he wanted the search process to follow. He referred members of the search committee to John Nason's *Presidential Search*, calling it a guide to how to proceed. Similarly, the faculty members of the search committee asked Susan Levin, the college's affirmative action officer, to investigate how other colleges had organized their searches when they felt uneasy about certain aspects of the search—most notably, steps taken to ensure that women and minority candidates were included in the pool, and involvement of faculty members not on the search committee in the last stages of the search. Based on Levin's research, the faculty members of the search committee wrote a letter to chairman Sloan suggesting a "plan of operation." This plan, which Sloan accepted, represented a structural solution to the issues with which the faculty members were concerned. Another structural proposal put forward by one faculty member on the search committee, to add a black trustee to the committee, was not followed. At the close of the search, faculty members again discussed the structure of the process, writing to the chair of the Abbott board about the time-line of the search. They thought that too much time had passed prior to the actual start of the search process, and too little time had been devoted to the task of evaluating candidates in the last stages of the search process.

In the "Southern State University" search, several faculty members not on the search committee expressed their displeasure with the pool of fi-

[2] *Understanding and Managing Organizations*, p. 33.

336

nalists by proposing to re-open the search process. A similar request was made, of course, in the final stages of the Winthrop College search. In both instances, faculty members hoped that a new search would produce a different set of candidates, believing that more extensive advertising of the position or more calls to prospective nominators would result in more desirable choices for the presidency.

Throughout this book we have discussed questions about the search process which are structural in nature, including how members of the search committee are chosen, what committee size is most desirable, what procedures help prevent breaches of confidentiality, how search committees go about choosing a consultant and evaluating candidates. Believing that there is no one best procedure universally appropriate, we have avoided giving definitive answers to questions such as these, while recognizing the pertinence of such structural matters and believing that careful consideration of structure can, at the margin, improve the processes of presidential selection.

Along with James G. March, Robert Birnbaum, and other students of academic organizations, however, we recognize the limitations of structural solutions, markedly so when the problems for which structural solutions are proposed are primarily political. An illustration is the Abbott faculty member's suggestion that a black trustee be named to the search committee. The faculty member thought this would show positive and virtuous intent to recruit minority candidates and to give them serious consideration, a matter of some concern to the faculty and student members of the search committee. But her colleagues on the faculty, aware of the political hazard of the suggestion, were relieved when the trustee chair of the search committee rejected the proposal, for they saw the addition of a trustee of whatever color as shifting the balance of power to the trustees. The committee was composed of five faculty members, two students, and seven trustees, or, as one faculty member put it, seven trustees and seven nontrustees. One more trustee gave the trustee "side" the majority. The Abbott faculty members on the search committee acted throughout as if the search process were a political contest of "us" versus "them." Before each meeting of the search committee the faculty representatives caucused to discuss the intentions of the trustees, decide their own political agendas, and determine strategies. When the choice of president came down to two

337

finalists, William Patterson and Michael Knight, the faculty members organized a petition-signing and a letter-writing campaign, to make their numbers stand as a political show of force to the trustees.

Politics were an important aspect of the "Southern State University" search as well. Law dean Dwight Stanton had powerful people supporting his candidacy. Chief among them were several leading lawyers in the state and a close friend and advisor of the governor. As his wife, Suzanne Stanton, recalled, "People had used their trump cards, thrown in their chits. We were no longer operating on our own." Observers of the 1983 University of Florida search have also interpreted the outcome of that search in exclusively political terms. The choice of Marshall Criser was "political" in the common populist sense of "politics" as something to be deplored. Moreover, there was a political legacy: chancellor Barbara Newell had become identified as a DiBiaggio supporter, and was viewed by many as part of the losing political coalition.

Whereas the emphasis in Bolman and Deal's political frame is on power and conflict, the central focus in their human resource frame is on the needs and the relationships of the people who make up organizations. In any analysis of the search process, this perspective provides a useful reminder that the process of presidential selection touches upon many people's lives in important ways. It touches, often invisibly, on the lives of top administrators who report to the president, with whom they may seek to establish new affective ties (assuming, of course, that the person chosen comes from elsewhere). Serious candidates, especially finalists who were not chosen, have to cope with their defeat, even in instances where they were ambivalent about the position to begin with. Not invariably, but commonly, members of the search committee experience great emotional "highs" and "lows" as they find their time overcommitted, and struggle with one another and with the immensity of their responsibility. The reader will recall that Bill Martin, a faculty member of the Rice University search committee, developed a chronic stomachache near the end of that search process, and his wife joked that she did not think he worried as much over his choice of spouse as he did over the selection of the president. Much of Ralph O'Connor's skill as chairman of the Rice search committee was due to his attentiveness to the feelings of individual members and to the group dynamics within the search committee. The retreat at

338

the outset of the Rice search, and the resource visits which followed, allowed individuals on the committee to become well acquainted, and to develop respect for each other's judgments. At one point in the search, when O'Connor thought that a trustee member of the committee was dominating discussions and thereby alienating others, he spoke privately to the trustee to ask him to defer more often to others. It was also this awareness of the feelings of others that made possible George Rupp's candidacy and eventual selection. The members of the Rice search committee were attentive to George Rupp's professional and family situations. They appreciated the reasons for his initial refusal to be a candidate, but returned to him when some of these reasons were no longer salient; honored his need for confidentiality during the search; captured his interest in the presidential position by presenting it as an extraordinary professional opportunity, "the chance of a lifetime;" and understood, finally, that Rupp's decision to accept the presidency would depend on the wishes of his family as well as his own personal preferences.

Bolman and Deal's fourth approach to understanding organizations, the symbolic frame, is one to which the readers of this volume will already have become attuned. Bolman and Deal declare that the symbolic approach "assumes that organizations are full of questions that cannot be answered, problems that cannot be solved, and events that cannot be understood or managed. Whenever that is so, humans will create and use symbols to bring meaning out of chaos, clarity out of confusion, and predictability out of mystery."[3] Early in the search process, the symbolic frame helps locate the behavior of many search committees in developing the advertisement for and job description of the new president. Although this effort of the search committee often requires a substantial outlay of time, and, in some instances, is the result of extensive political bargaining and negotiation, not atypically the document or documents that are developed are rarely looked at again. Their purpose, it appears, has been largely symbolic. The experience of putting together the list of qualifications has helped search committee members to position themselves vis-à-vis one another while pursuing an important institutional ritual, and it is not surprising that the list itself may describe the institution and the presidential

[3] *Understanding and Managing Organizations*, p. 152.

position more as people would like to imagine them than as they are. Similarly, campus visits often serve largely as institutional rituals, desired because they seem to the campus community to suggest their participation in the important matter of selecting the president, even though the actual turn-out of campus constituents may be minimal and the solicitation by trustees or members of the search committee of their reactions to the finalists virtually nonexistent. A rationalistic or technocratic analysis of the situation would suggest that the campus visit is of little benefit in the many cases where it provides minimal participation and feedback; it may nevertheless give the search process an aura of legitimacy through the symbolism of access it provides.

The symbolic frame can be useful not only in examining the processes by which presidents are chosen, but also by considering the person chosen as a symbol. As we noted early in this book, institutions have their own "sagas"[4] which help explain the way the constituents of the institution view themselves and the way the institution is viewed by outsiders. Presidents, too, develop sagas; that is, their credentials and backgrounds, their gender, race, ethnicity, physical appearance, and dress, the stories they tell about themselves or others tell about them, convey a powerful image. In the "Abbott College" search, faculty and student members of the search committee played with the notion of choosing a black president because of the statement this would make about their institution. They could envisage the discomfiture such a choice—perhaps especially a black woman for a college which had only in the last several decades become coeducational—would cause many trustees and alumni, and could recognize the banner of revolution such a choice would raise, even while being reasonably confident in their political "lens" that the trustees, put on the spot, would never consent to such a choice. In the Winthrop College search, the actual choice of a woman, Martha Piper, was a disappointment to many faculty members and also some trustees, not because they thought that, as a woman, she would not be competent to do the job, but because a woman president might represent, inaccurately, that Winthrop was still a women's college. That she did not come from a prestigious institution was also a negative bit of symbolism. To offset these concerns, the Winthrop

[4] See Clark, *The Distinctive College.*

340

board of trustees made Martha Piper's gender into a public relations advantage, garnering publicity throughout the two Carolinas from the fact that she was the first woman president of a public coeducational institution.

The "frames" of Bolman and Deal are hardly needed to remind us that all human actions carry symbolic freight, of course carried in language but also in the anthropologist Edward T. Hall's "silent language," of gesture and stance. It is as much a mistake to refer to some procedures of a search committee as "merely" symbolic as it is to refer to it as "merely" political or procedural. We think it adds to the Bolman-Deal lenses to view the search process also through a moral frame, as an occasion during which passionate ethical convictions and ideological ones are in contention. One observer of the "Abbott College" search characterized the process as a tug-of-war between trustees and faculty members, regarding it, as in Bolman and Deal's political frame, as a contest over which "side" would mobilize the most power in deciding who would become president. But the issues of confidentiality which arose in that search as faculty members debated whether or not to leak to the press a memorandum they thought would harm the chances of the acting president, illustrated a different sort of contest over what was the moral, the "right" way to proceed. In the conflicts in the University of Florida search between privacy and publicity, the issue was debated in part in terms of effectiveness in securing the legitimacy of the choice, but also in terms of Max Weber's ethic of ultimate ends, in terms of the virtue of "open" searches per se, even if less effective than "closed" ones, the latter being favored by those who argued, in Weber's terms, for an ethic of responsibility, that is, an ethic judged in terms of outcomes.

Seymour Martin Lipset has written, "Americans are Utopian moralists who press hard to institutionalize virtue, to destroy evil people and eliminate wicked institutions and practices. They tend to view social and political dramas as morality plays, as battles between God and the devil, so that compromise is virtually unthinkable."[5] In this regard, America is excep-

[5] "American Exceptionalism Reaffirmed," address at Harvard University, November 7, 1988, in *De Tocqueville Review*, Vol. 10 (1989–1990), p. 29. See, to similar effect, Samuel P. Huntington, *American Politics: The Promise of Disharmony* (Cambridge: Belknap Press of Harvard University Press, 1981), especially pages 154 et seq.

tional, he argues. This is not to say that we are unique among the industrial democracies of the world; the "exceptionalism" is a matter of more or less. For example, what struck Tocqueville as exceptional was the extent of religious activity by congregations, and, still today, America remains by far the most religious country in the developed world. More significant for our purposes in this book is the fact that America's congregational religions have taken their cue from the Protestant dissenters, who believed in the perfectibility of men and women and hence of human institutions, with the corresponding tendency to see one's opponents as evil rather than as mistaken.[6] Even in relative decline, moralism stemming in part from religious tradition remains stronger in the United States in the face of the acids of modernity than in our neighbor, Canada, or in Western Europe or Japan. Many American academics and intellectuals needed the reminder of the Moral Majority and the fundamentalist crusades of recent years to rediscover how religious most Americans remain, far beyond the norms of any other industrialized, urbanized society. The spirit of the dissenters affects the non-devout, just as it affects American Catholics, Jews and Protestants.[7]

Correspondingly, what happens in the course of a presidential transition commonly becomes interpreted as a morality play in which good guys triumphed or lost to bad guys, and in which each step in what Michel Crozier has termed America's delirium of due process[8] becomes defined as a question of virtue.

In this framework, the urge to do what is practical and expedient often has to be disguised in order not to be labeled immoral. The process that is deemed the most "fair" or the most "open" may be at odds with the process that is likely to produce the best outcome. In *Morality and Expedi-*

---

[6] Robert N. Bellah and other observers stress the decline of the belief in civic virtue founded in religion. See Bellah, *The Broken Covenant: American Civil Religion in Time of Trial* (New York: Seabury Press, 1975), and the more recent Bellah et al., *Habits of the Heart: Individualism and Commitment in American Life* (Berkeley, Los Angeles, and London: University of California Press, 1985.

[7] The priest-sociologist Andrew M. Greeley terms the orientation stemming from Protestant dissenters the "dialectial imagination," tending to definitions of good versus bad. This differs markedly from the Catholic or state-church orientation in America, Canada, and Europe, which tends toward the "analogical imagination," for example, seeing God in all things, rather than as separate from man. See Greeley, "Protestant and Catholic: Is the Analogical Imagination Extinct?" *American Sociological Review*, Vol. 54 (August 1989), pp. 485–502.

[8] Crozier, *The Trouble with America*, trans. Peter Heinegg (Berkeley: University of California Press, 1984).

342

ency: The Folklore of Academic Politics, Frederick G. Bailey offers a sharply sardonic distillation of his observations of the conflicts between accomplishing something effective and making a moralistic statement.[9] Bailey gives recognition to Americans who are frankly egocentric, neither believing in virtue nor making any pretense of it themselves. He observes also that there are those who are so conciliatory, so sympathetic, that they abdicate their principles. But on the whole, what strikes him as specifically American is the degree to which a moral argument becomes irrefutable, and when countered by another moral argument, the outcome can then become "a tug of war."

Indeed, in our own experience in discussing searches before audiences of faculty members, students, and journalists, the question of confidentiality often becomes the salient moral issue. To almost all journalists, most students, and a sizable cohort of faculty members, candor in the search is everything, and confidentiality must give way to a policy of open records, open letters, and open meetings, even if the result is harm to individuals and possible harm to the search. Everywhere, the effort to close searches is put on the defensive by the belief that anything not put on public display must stink. It is not easy for Americans to believe that if one thing is good, and something else is good, then these "goods" may not be compatible. What is believed to be right in terms of an ethic of ultimate ends should also work out well—an optimistic premise which hides the degree to which one must make choices.

The process of choosing a college president is interesting to those who participate in it, observe it, or study it, because of its multiple meanings. It has significance in and of itself, as a period of leadership selection and transition for a particular institution. It provides a window on larger issues of higher education governance, leadership, and change. And it reflects complicated issues and moral dilemmas in our society.

[9] What is said in this text distills a much more complicated argument.

APPENDIX

W E BEGAN OUR FORMAL STUDY with some hypotheses developed from our informal observations of college and university search processes. Early in our research, we sought to place this knowledge of individual searches into a larger perspective. In 1981 we sent a seven-page questionnaire to sixty-five colleges and universities that had conducted searches in the academic year 1980–1981.[1] Fifty-two questionnaires were completed and returned.

The questionnaire focused on two issues of the search process: the membership of the search committee and the policies and experiences relating to confidentiality and disclosure of information about the candidates and search committee deliberations. We asked about the size and composition of search committees and how committee members were chosen. We asked about sources of information that had been available concerning how to conduct a search, and whether the use of a search consultant was considered. Above all, we inquired concerning the issue of confidentiality. Was confidentiality sought at the outset? If so, what information was to be shared only with members of the search committee, or with the search committee and the board, and what information was to be shared more widely? Finally, we asked about actual experiences with confidentiality. What had remained confidential? What had leaked and to whom and how? What had been the consequences of intended and unintended disclosures, both for candidates and for the search process? The survey was not meant to provide extensive quantitative data, but rather to indicate what was salient in the conduct and outcome of searches. American higher education is so extraordinarily diverse, and the histories of particular institutions are

---

[1] This sample included all institutions in categories 1, 2, and 3 of the Carnegie Commission's *Classification of Institutions of Higher Education* (that is, most four-year colleges and universities) which had placed advertisements for a president in the *Chronicle of Higher Education* during an eight-month period (the eight months with the largest number of presidential job notices during that academic year).

often so cyclical and even erratic, that it seems fair to say that even within the same types of institutions, such as selective private liberal arts colleges, every search is idosyncratic.

The data collected from the questionnaires gave us a snapshot of the range and frequency of various search practices.[2] Next, we sought a more intensive picture of the forces at play during the search process. Whereas the surveys had been answered by only one person connected with a search, our case research involved lengthy interviews with many different people, allowing us to see how the search appeared from a large number of vantage points, thereby giving us the data which made possible a richer and more complete analysis of the course of events and their consequences.

We selected the sites for our case studies by identifying certain aspects of the search that we wanted to examine more closely, for example, struggles over confidentiality and disclosure, the "sunshine search," the use of a consultant, and other strategies, and then identifying a search process where these were present. When we went into the field to do a study, we did not regard ourselves as investigative journalists, although there are some parallels in terms of trying to get a straight story and also in terms of our use, among our other informants, of journalists who had covered a search. But unlike a journalist, we began by asking the new president and the person who served as chairman of the search committee for permission to come to campus for interviews with those who could help us understand what transpired while events were still reasonably fresh in memory. In so doing, we assured them that the identity of their institution could remain confidential if, on seeing a draft of our case study, they so desired. As mentioned earlier, two of the case studies included in this monograph are disguised. We believe strongly that people who have submitted themselves to scholarly research, including agreeing to in-depth interviews and allowing us access to confidential documents, should not suffer because of their willingness to cooperate. Similarly, we believe that institutions, like people, are vulnerable, and it is not our wish to cause them harm.

While the names of the two disguised institutions might well be of interest to our readers, we believe that their identities are not necessary for

[2] The questionnaire results are described in Judith McLaughlin's essay, "From Secrecy to Sunshine."

346

the arguments that we wish to make. The issues of these searches can be presented with the institutions disguised without losing their forcefulness or their substance. Indeed, it might be argued, although this was not our reason for the disguises, that giving these institutions fictitious names makes the issues more generalizable. The reader is not tempted to dismiss the problems of the search as particular only to *that* college or university, but recognizes them as more universal dilemmas.

In the course of our research for the five cases in this book we interviewed, either on campus or away from campus, the chairman of the search committee and committee members; the new president and the president's spouse, where there was one. Whenever possible, we interviewed the former president as well. We interviewed the chairman of the board and other influentials on the board, in the faculty, and in the administration. We also talked with students who had served on the search committee and with those, such as student journalists or student government leaders, who had observed the search from afar. We interviewed individuals who had been candidates and, as in the case of Winthrop and of other searches treated less extensively, many consultants. Occasionally, logistics prevented our meeting the chairman of the board or of the search committee, in which case we arranged long telephone interviews. These were somewhat less satisfactory than on-site interviews, though we should add that we found—as have many search committees and consultants—that people are at times extraordinarily frank on the telephone, certainly compared to what they will say in writing and even, in some instances, compared to what they will say when physically present.

Of course the memories of these people, like those of the authors, are fallible and subject to distortion. In our observations, these limitations were more common than direct concealment. Recognizing these potential sources of bias, we were repeatedly reminded in our ethnographic work of the metaphor of *Rashomon*: We heard a very convincing story from one participant. This story was then confirmed by another and seemed consonant also with the written records we had examined (minutes of search committee meetings, correspondence with candidates, newspaper files, etc.); but, as we continued our round of interviewing, we found that inconsistencies surfaced. Sometimes these inconsistencies, on closer examination, were merely refinements of situations we had already known

347

about, but occasionally, when we pursued them we found that they gave another cast altogether to the story we had been developing. Indeed, although our fieldwork at "Abbott College" and "Southern State University" was completed some time ago, our exchanges with participants have continued, providing us with further assurance that we have come nearer to approximating a reasonably disinterested and nontendentious account.

Yet we know from experience that such assurance is precarious. Unsettling details that do not fit have turned up in several searches from quite circuitous routes. In one instance, an inquiry was directed for another purpose to the home base of someone who had not been a candidate for the presidency in the search we investigated, nor in the preceding search, but a search before that. The story is never done. We simply had to face the fact that our work must stop at some point.

In addition to our questionnaire and our case research, we studied in varying particularity a large number of other searches by means of correspondence or interviews with one or more members of the search committee, trustees, candidates, or search consultants.

In recent years, the social sciences and the lay educated public have become familiar with the discussion of networks, notably the infamous "old boy network," which is suspected of being operative in many presidential searches as in other human enterprises. Study of search procedures highlights another kind of network which has been of considerable interest to sociologists in the last several decades, namely, what has been called "thin" ties, where the connection, albeit peripheral, even accidental, makes very large differences in the outcomes of transactions and careers. This is in contrast to the "thick" ties of kinship or childhood. When a search committee begins reading over several hundred resumés and letters of nomination, a candidacy may be saved from likely elimination by quite thin ties indeed.

We have used our own thin ties to learn something about a great many searches that have occurred since our survey was done. And people connected to us by thin ties have made use of us. We are on the "nominations network," and hence are regularly asked to suggest possible candidates for presidencies. When we are called or written to, we make a nomination whenever possible, and then ask the search committee chair or executive

348

secretary to the search to give us as much information about the search as they can comfortably provide.

In our approximately ten years of joint research, we have thus investigated more than two hundred searches. We have had the privilege of sitting in on a search committee meeting in only a handful of cases; most of our understanding of the group dynamics of search committees has been constructed ex post facto.

Because of the high turnover of presidencies, we have had the opportunity to observe some institutions go through more than one presidential search. One of the problems, indeed, with writing a book about presidents is that, invariably, many of the people in the positions when you study them are no longer in the same positions when your research is published. Our readers may find this to be the case.

We have also obtained perspective on the search process and how it has changed over time by reading college histories and the biographies and autobiographies of former college and university presidents. This literature has illuminated our understanding of the recurring tensions in higher education as well as bringing into sharp focus the new social and political pressures which affect higher education.

In all phases of our research we have found that most search committee members and candidates have been willing to confide in us. When we mailed our questionnnaire to the heads of search committees, we included our phone number, suggesting that people might telephone us with their responses, if this was more convenient for them than submitting them in writing. We received several telephone calls, but these were in addition to written responses, rather than in lieu of them. It is often the case that search committee heads are extremely busy people. Asking them to direct the search might be seen as following the mandate that if one needs something done, one turns to the busiest person around. Yet we found that these very busy people submitted their questionnaires with an unusually high rate of return, taking great care in their responses and volunteering comments in the spaces provided for them. This level of response in the written questionnnaire, coupled with the willingness, even eagerness, with which people talked with us about their search experiences verified for us how salient, and, often, how agonizing, if not traumatic, a search can be.

349

With others connected with the search, as well, we found that the opportunity to share the experience of the search, in confidence, with outsiders who possessed a genuine interest in the course of events that had transpired, was sufficiently desired so as to make it worth these people's time to assist us with our work. The search process can arouse powerful emotions in its participants: apprehension, great hopes, bewilderment, bitterness, exhilaration, disappointment. Serious members of the search committee often feel intensely the responsibility that they shoulder for making what is a critical decision for their institution. But the need to maintain confidentiality means that there are very few people in whom they can confide their fears, frustrations, and often quixotic hopes. Hence, when we approached these people by questionnaire and in confidential interviews, many were pleased to have an opportunity to share their thoughts and feelings. One faculty member of a search committee, in response to Judith McLaughlin's thank-you note to him for taking part in an interview, wrote back to say that he should be the one doing the thanking "for the therapy" that the interview session provided him! The whole body of our work would have been far less fruitful if those who received our questionnaire or our requests for interviews had taken their experiences lightly. We have learned an enormous amount from all of these people. We are most grateful to them for their cooperation with our research.

ABBREVIATIONS

AAHE   American Association for Higher Education
AASCU   American Association of State Colleges and Universities
AAUP   American Association of University Professors
AGB   Association of Governing Boards of Universities and Colleges
ASHE   Association for the Study of Higher Education

BIBLIOGRAPHY

AAUP. "Faculty Participation in Selection, Evaluation, and Retention of Administrators." *Academe* 67, no. 5 (October 1981): 323–324.

Adatto, Kiku. "Sound Bite Democracy: Network Evening News Presidential Campaign Coverage, 1968 and 1988." Research Paper R-2, June 1990. Cambridge, Massachusetts: Joan Shorenstein Baronne Center on the Press, Politics, and Public Policy, Harvard University, 1990.

AGB and American Council on Education. *Deciding Who Shall Lead: Recommendations for Improving Presidential Searches.* Washington, D.C.: AGB, 1986.

Alden, Vernon R. "Corporate Boss, College President." *AGB Reports* 20, no. 3 (May–June 1978): 14–19.

Alexander, Chauncey A. "What Does a Representative Represent?" *Social Work* 21, no. 1 (January 1976): 5–9.

Alton, Bruce T. "Presidential Search: Identifying Candidates." *AGB Reports* 30, no. 1 (January–February 1988): 24–27.

———. "Why Presidents Quit." *AGB Reports* 24, no. 1 (January–February 1982): 47–53.

Appleberry, James B. *Guidelines on the Appointment of a President.* Washington, D.C.: American Association of State Colleges and Universities, 1987.

Ashworth, Kenneth. "Search, Searching, Gone. Will Public Disclosure of Presidential Search Proceedings Drive Candidates Away?" *Change* 14, no. 3 (May–June 1982): 20–23.

Bailey, Frederick G. *Morality and Expediency: The Folklore of Academic Politics.* Chicago: Aldine, 1977.

———. *Stratagems and Spoils: A Social Anthropology of Politics.* Oxford: Basil Blackwell, 1969.

———. *The Tactical Uses of Passion: An Essay on Power, Reason, and Reality.* Ithaca, New York: Cornell University Press, 1983.

Baldridge, J. Victor. *Governing Academic Organizations: New Problems, New Perspectives.* Berkeley, California: McKutcheon, 1977.

———. *Policy Making and Effective Leadership.* San Francisco: Jossey-Bass, 1978.

Barber, Benjamin R. *Strong Democracy: Participatory Politics for a New Age.* Berkeley: University of California Press, 1984.

Barber, James David. *Politics by Humans: Research on American Leadership.* Durham, North Carolina: Duke University Press, 1988.

Bassett, Glenn A. "Strategies of Executive Selection." *Personnel* 43, no. 5 (September–October 1966): 8–15.

Beadle, Muriel. *Where Has All the Ivy Gone? A Memoir of University Life.* Garden City, New York: Doubleday, 1972.

Beaudoin, Diana B. "Assessing a College President's Performance: Formal Procedures and Informal Influences." Ph.D. diss., Harvard Graduate School of Education, 1986.

Bell, Daniel. " 'American Exceptionalism' Revisited: The Role of Civil Society." *The Public Interest*, No. 95 (Spring 1989): 38–56.

Bellah, Robert N. *The Broken Covenant: American Civil Religion in Time of Trial.* New York: Seabury Press, 1975.

Bellah, Robert N., Richard Madsen, William M. Sullivan, Ann Swidler, and Steven M. Tipton. *Habits of the Heart: Individualism and Commitment in American Life.* Berkeley, Los Angeles, and London: University of California Press, 1985.

Bénézet, Louis T., Joseph Katz, and Frances Magnusson. *Style and Substance: Leadership and the College Presidency.* Washington, D.C.: American Council on Education, 1981.

Bennis, Warren G. *The Leaning Ivory Tower.* San Francisco: Jossey-Bass, 1973.

———. *On Becoming a Leader.* Reading, Massachusetts: Addison Wesley, 1989.

———. "Searching for the 'Perfect' University President." *Atlantic*, April 1971.

———. *The Unconscious Conspiracy: Why Leaders Can't Lead.* New York: AMACOM, A Division of the American Management Association, 1976.

———. *Why Leaders Can't Lead. The Unconscious Conspiracy Continues.* San Francisco: Jossey-Bass, 1989.

Bennis, Warren G., and Burt Nanus. *Leaders: The Strategies for Taking Charge.* New York: Harper & Row, 1985.

Bensimon, Estela Mara, Marian L. Gade, and Joseph F. Kauffman. *On Assuming a College or University Presidency: Lessons and Advice from the Field.* Washington, D.C.: AAHE, 1989.

Bensimon, Estela Mara, Anna Neumann, and Robert Birnbaum. *Making Sense of Administrative Leadership: The "L" Word in Higher Education.* Washington, D.C.: ASHE/ERIC Higher Education Report, Association for the Study of Higher Education, 1989.

Berendzen, Richard. *Is My Armor Straight? A Year in the Life of a University President.* Bethesda, Maryland: Adler & Adler, 1986.

Bers, Trudy, and Pat DelRay. *The Independent College Presidency.* Washington, D.C.: Council of Independent Colleges, 1980.

Besse, Ralph. "A Comparison of the University with the Corporation." *AGB Reports* 15, no. 3 (November–December 1972): 2–14.

Birenbaum, William M. *Something for Everybody Is Not Enough: An Educator's Search for His Education.* New York: Random House, 1971.

Birnbaum, Robert. *How Colleges Work. The Cybernetics of Academic Organization and Leadership.* San Francisco: Jossey-Bass, 1988.

———. "Leadership and Learning: The College President as Intuitive Scientist." *Review of Higher Education* 9 (1986): 381–396.

———. "Presidential Searches and the Discovery of Organizational Goals." *Journal of Higher Education* 59, no. 5 (September–October 1988): 489–509.

———. "Presidential Succession: An Interinstitutional Analysis." *Educational Record* 52, no. 2 (Spring 1971): 133–145.

———. "Presidential Succession and Institutional Functioning in Higher Education." *Journal of Higher Education* 60, no. 2 (March–April 1989): 123–135.

Bisesi, Michael. "Presidential Search: 4 Specific Tasks." *AGB Reports* 27, no. 3 (May–June 1985): 22–23.

Bisesi, Michael, and George Huxel. "Hidden Agendas, Credibility, and Search Committees." *AAHE Bulletin* 38, no. 6 (February 1986): 14–15.

Block, Seymour Stanton. *Benjamin Franklin: His Wit, Wisdom and Women.* New York: Hastings House, 1975.

Bloustein, Edward. "Group Privacy: The Right to Huddle." *Rutgers-Camden Law Journal* 8, no. 2 (Winter 1977): 219–283.

Blumberg, Arthur. "Beyond Something Called the Deanship: A Story about a Memorable Academic Leader." *Teachers College Record* 90, no. 1 (Fall 1988): 85–98.

Bok, Sissela. *Lying: Moral Choice in Public and Private Life.* New York: Pantheon Books, 1978.

———. *Secrets: On the Ethics of Concealment and Revelation.* New York: Vintage Books, 1984.

Bolman, Frederick deWolfe. *How College Presidents Are Chosen.* Washington, D.C.: American Council on Education, 1965.

———. "How Will You Find a College President?" *AGB Reports* 12, no. 7 (April 1970): 3–12.

Bolman, Lee G., and Terrence E. Deal. *Modern Approaches to Understanding and Managing Organizations.* San Francisco: Jossey-Bass, 1984.

Bowen, Catherine Drinker. *Miracle at Philadelphia: The Story of the Constitutional Convention, May to September, 1787.* Boston: Little Brown, 1966.

Boyer, Ernest L. *College: The Undergraduate Experience in America.* Carnegie Foundation for the Advancement of Teaching. New York: Harper & Row, 1987.

Brewster, Kingman. "The Politics of Academia." *AGB Reports* 12, no. 3 (November–December 1969): 15–22.

Brissette, Judith A. "A Comparison of the Roles of Male and Female Spouses of Presidents of Selected Four-Year, Private Colleges." Ph.D. diss., University of Toledo, 1982.

Brombert, J. D. "The Role and Effectiveness of Search Committees." *AAHE Bulletin* 26, no. 8 (April 1974): 7–10.

Brown, David G. *The Mobile Professors.* Washington: American Council on Education, 1967.

Brubacher, John L., and Willis Ruby. *Higher Education in Transition: A History of American Colleges and Universities, 1636–1976.* New York: Harper & Row, 1976.

Burnham, John C. "Where Has Greatness Gone?" *Midwest Quarterly* No. 27 (Winter 1986): 129–148.

Burns, James MacGregor. *Leadership.* New York: Harper & Row, 1978.

Caplow, Theodore, and Reece J. McGee. *The Academic Marketplace.* New York: Basic Books, 1958.

Carbone, Robert F. *Presidential Passages: Former College Presidents Reflect on the Splendor and Agony of their Careers.* Washington, D.C.: American Council on Education, 1981.

Carpenter, Don A. "Presidential Search, Utah Style." *AGB Reports* 21, no. 5 (September–October 1979): 13–18.

Chaffee, Ellen E. *After Decline, What? Survival Strategies at Eight Private Colleges.* Boulder, Colorado: National Center for Higher Education Management Systems, 1984.

Chaffee, Ellen E., and William G. Tierney. *Collegiate Culture and Leadership Strategies.* New York: American Council on Education/Macmillan, 1988.

Chait, Richard P., and Andrew T. Ford. *Beyond Traditional Tenure: A Guide to Sound Policies and Practices.* San Francisco: Jossey-Bass, 1982.

Chait, Richard P., and Barbara E. Taylor. "Charting the Territory of Nonprofit Boards." *Harvard Business Review* Special Report No. 89101 (January–February 1989).

Clark, Burton R. *The Distinctive College: Antioch, Reed, and Swarthmore.* Chicago: Aldine, 1970.

Cleveland, Harlan. *The Costs and Benefits of Openness: Sunshine Laws and Higher Education.* Washington, D.C.: AGB, 1985.

Clodius, Joan E., and Diane Skomars Magrath, eds. *The President's Spouse: Volunteer or Volunteered?* Washington, D.C.: National Association of State Universities and Land Grant Colleges, 1984.

Cohen, Michael D., and James G. March. *Leadership and Ambiguity: The American College President.* Second Edition. Boston: Harvard Business School Press, 1986.

Coleman, Jonathan. *Exit the Rainmaker.* New York: Atheneum, 1989.

Commission on Strengthening Presidential Leadership, Clark Kerr, Director. *Presidents Make A Difference: Strengthening Leadership in Colleges and Universities.* Washington, D.C.: AGB, 1984.

Conant, James Bryant. *My Several Lives: Memoirs of a Social Inventor.* New York: Harper & Row, 1970.

Conger, Jay A. *The Charismatic Leader: Behind the Mystique of Exceptional Leadership.* San Francisco: Jossey-Bass, 1989.

Corbally, Marguerite Walker. *The Partners.* Danville: Interstate Printers and Publishers, 1977.

Cote, Lawrence S. "The Relative Importance of Presidential Roles." *Journal of Higher Education* 56, no. 6 (November–December 1985): 664–676.

Cronin, Thomas E. *Direct Democracy: The Politics of Initiative, Referendum, and Recall.* Cambridge: Harvard University Press, 1989.

Crozier, Michel. *The Trouble with America.* Trans. Peter Heinegg. Berkeley: University of California Press, 1984.

Davis-Van Atta, David, Sam S. Carrier, and Frank Frankfort. "Educating America's Scientists: The Role of the Research Colleges." Oberlin College, 1985.

DeCew, Judith Wagner. "The Realm of the Private in Law and Ethics." Paper presented at the Bunting Institute, Cambridge, Massachusetts, September 1988.

Demerath, Nicholas J., Richard W. Stephens, and R. Robb Taylor. *Power, Presidents, and Professors.* New York: Basic Books, 1967.

Dexter, Lewis A. *Elite and Specialized Interviewing.* Evanston, Illinois: Northwestern University Press, 1970.

Dobbins, Charles G., and Thomas M. Stauffer. "Academic Administrators—Born or Made?" *Educational Record* 53, no. 4 (Fall 1972): 293–299.

Dodds, Harold. *The Academic President: Educator or Caretaker?* New York: McGraw-Hill, 1962.

Dresch, Stephen. "On the Nature and Pathologies of Meritocractic Collectivities." Unpublished paper, Michigan Technological University, 1987.

Dyson, Dave, and Ralph Kirkman. "Presidential Priorities." *AGB Reports* 31, no. 2 (March–April 1989): 6–11.

Eissner, Judith. "Reflections on the Skidmore Presidential Search." Draft, 1987.

Elmore, Richard. "Backward Mapping: Implementation Research and Policy Decisions." *Political Science Quarterly* 94, no. 4 (Winter 1979–1980): 601–616.

Fisher, James L. *The Board and the President.* New York: Macmillan, 1990.

———. *Power of the Presidency.* New York: American Council on Education/Macmillan, 1984.

———. "Presidential Assessment: A Better Way." *AGB Reports* 28, no. 5 (September–October 1986): 16–21.

Fiske, Edward B., comp. *Selective Guide to Colleges.* New York: Times Books, 1985.

Fouts, Donald E. "Picking a President the Business Way." *AGB Reports* 19, no. 1 (January–February 1977): 6–10.

Franke, Ann H. "Disclosure of Tenure Evaluation Materials." *Academe* 74, no. 6 (November–December 1988): 36–37.

Friedman, Robert S. "Presidential Selection: Making It Work." *AGB Reports* 25, no. 5 (September–October 1983): 44–46.

Gaines, Francis Pendleton. *Presidents and Deans: A Changing Academic Scene.* Tucson, Arizona: University Associates, 1987.

Gamson, Zelda F., ed. *Liberating Education.* San Francisco: Jossey-Bass, 1984.

Gans, Herbert J. "Bystanders as Opinion Makers: A Bottoms-Up Perspective." *The Gannett Center Journal* 3, no. 2 (Spring 1989): 97–104.

Gardner, John W. *On Leadership.* New York: The Free Press, 1990.

Garrison, Stephen A. *Institutional Search: A Practical Guide to Executive Recruitment in Nonprofit Organizations.* New York: Praeger, 1989.

Gilley, J. Wade, Kenneth A. Fulmer, and Sally J. Reithlingshoefer. *Searching for Academic Excellence: Twenty Colleges and Universities on the Move and Their Leaders.* New York: Macmillan, 1986.

Gilmore, Thomas North. *Making a Leadership Change: How Organizations and Leaders Can Handle Leadership Transitions Successfully.* San Francisco: Jossey-Bass, 1988.

Gilmore, Thomas North, and James Krantz. "The Splitting of Leadership and Management as a Social Defense." *Journal of Human Relations* 43, no. 2 (1990): 183–204.

Goldsmith, James W. "A Study of the Perceptions of College Search Committee Chairs Concerning the Use of Paid Consultants in Presidential Searches." Ph.D. diss., University of Nevada-Las Vegas, 1989.

Grant, Gerald, and David Riesman. *The Perpetual Dream: Reform and Experiment in the American College.* Chicago: University of Chicago Press, 1978.

Grantham, Shelby. "Life After the Presidency." *Dartmouth Alumni Magazine* 77 (November 1984): 27–30.

Greeley, Andrew M. "Protestant and Catholic: Is the Analogical Imagination Extinct?" *American Sociological Review* 54 (August 1984): 485–502.

Green, Madeleine F. *The American College President: A Contemporary Profile.* Washington, D.C.: American Council on Education, 1988.

———. *Leaders for a New Era.* New York: American Council on Education/Macmillan, 1988.

———. "Presidential Leadership: Changes in Style." *AGB Reports* 28, no. 1 (January–February 1986): 18–20.

Greenberg, Milton. "Search and Ye Shall Find?" *Educational Record* 69, nos. 3–4 (Summer–Fall 1988): 48–51.

Greene, Janice S., Arthur Levine, and Associates, eds. *Opportunity in Adversity: How Colleges Can Succeed in Hard Times.* San Francisco: Jossey-Bass, 1985.

Guller, Carol H. "Ph.D. Recipients: Where Did They Go to College?" *Change* 18, no. 6 (November–December 1986): 42–51.

Guskin, Alan. "A Strategy to Rebuild Antioch College, 1987–1992: State of the College Address." *Antioch Notes* 57, no. 1 (Fall 1987): 8.

Hall, Edward T. *The Silent Language.* Garden City, New York: Doubleday, 1959.

Harrington, Mona. *The Dream of Deliverance in American Politics.* New York: Alfred A. Knopf, 1986.

Hesburgh, Theodore M. "The College Presidency: Life Between a Rock and a Hard Place." *Change* 11, no. 4 (May–June 1979): 43–47.

Hirschman, Albert O. *Exit, Voice, and Loyalty: Responses to Decline in Firms, Organizations, and States.* Cambridge: Harvard University Press, 1970.

———. *Rival Views of Market Society and Other Recent Essays.* New York: Viking, 1986.

———. *Shifting Involvements: Private Interest and Public Action.* Princeton, New Jersey: Princeton University Press, 1982.

Hogarty, Richard A. "The Search for a Massachusetts Chancellor: Autonomy and Politics in Higher Education." *New England Journal of Public Policy* 4, no. 2 (Summer–Fall 1988): 7–38.

Holmes, David R. *Stalking the Academic Communist: Intellectual Freedom and the Firing of Alex Novikoff.* Hanover, New Hampshire: Published for University of Vermont by University Press of New England, 1989.

Horowitz, Helen Lefkowitz. *Campus Life: Undergraduate Cultures from the End of the Eighteenth Century to the Present.* New York: Alfred A. Knopf, 1987.

Houle, Cyril O. *Governing Boards.* San Francisco: Jossey-Bass, 1989.

Hughes, Raymond M. *A Manual for Trustees of Colleges and Universities.* Ames, Iowa: The Iowa State College Press, 1943.

Huntington, Samuel P. *American Politics: The Promise of Disharmony.* Cambridge: Belknap Press of Harvard University Press, 1981.

Hyde, Robert. "The Presidential Search: Chore or Opportunity?" *Educational Record* 50, no. 2 (Spring 1969): 186–188.

Ingraham, Mark H. *The Mirror of Brass: The Compensation and Working Conditions of College and University Administrators.* Madison: University of Wisconsin Press, 1968.

Ingram, Richard, and Associates. *Handbook of College and University Trusteeship.* San Francisco: Jossey-Bass, 1980.

Isaacson, John M. "In Search of An Affable Beast. The Care and Recruitment of the Public's Commissioners." A paper presented to the Conference for Newly Elected Mayors at the Institute for Politics of the John F. Kennedy School of Government, Cambridge, Massachusetts, November 20, 1981.

Jencks, Christopher, and David Riesman. *The Academic Revolution.* Garden City, New York: Doubleday, 1968.

Kaffer, Robert E. "Off On the Wrong Foot." Occasional paper. Denver, Colorado: Higher Education Executive Associates, Inc., 1984.

———. "Presidential Search: How to Ruin It." *AGB Reports* 23, no. 5 (September–October 1981): 16–18.

Kaplowitz, Richard. *Selecting Academic Administrators: The Search Committee.* Washington, D.C.: American Council on Education, 1973.

Kauffman, Joseph F. *At the Pleasure of the Board: The Service of the College and University President.* Washington, D.C.: American Council on Education, 1980.

———. "The College Presidency—Yesterday and Today." *Change* 14, no. 3 (May–June 1982): 12–19.

———. "The New College President: Expectations and Realities." *Educational Record* 58, no. 2 (Spring 1977): 146–168.

———. *The Selection of College and University Presidents.* Washington, D.C.: American Association of Colleges, 1974.

Keane, Joseph A. "Why Deans Stay Put: Because of Search Committees." *AAHE Bulletin* 41, no. 1 (September 1988): 8–9.

Keller, George. *Academic Strategy: The Management Revolution in Higher Education.* Baltimore: The Johns Hopkins University Press, 1983.

Kellerman, Barbara, ed. *Political Leadership: A Source Book.* Pittsburgh: University of Pittsburgh Press, 1986.

Kemeny, Jean A. *It's Different At Dartmouth: A Memoir.* Brattleboro, Vermont: Stephen Greene Press, 1979.

360

Kern, Edward. "Quest for a Silver Unicorn." *Life*, June 4, 1971.

[Kerr, Clark.] *Presidents Make a Difference: Strengthening Leadership in Colleges and Universities.* Report of the Commission on Strengthening Presidential Leadership. Washington, D.C.: AGB, 1984.

Kerr, Clark, and Marian L. Gade. *The Guardians: Boards of Trustees of American Colleges and Universities, What They Do and How Well They Do It.* Washington, D.C.: AGB, 1989.

————. *The Many Lives of Academic Presidents: Time, Place and Character.* Washington, D.C.: AGB, 1986.

Kets De Vries, Manfred F.R. "The Dark Side of CEO Succession." *Harvard Business Review* 66, no. 1 (January–February 1988): 56–60.

Kiersh, Edward. "Presidential Searches: Divided We Stand." *Change* 11, no. 6 (September 1979): 29–35.

Killian, James R., Jr. *The Education of a College President: A Memoir.* Cambridge, Massachusetts: MIT Press, 1985.

Knapp, Robert H., and H. B. Goodrich. *Origins of American Scientists.* Chicago: University of Chicago Press for Wesleyan University, 1952.

Knapp, Robert H., and Joseph J. Greenbaum. *The Younger American Scholar: His Collegiate Origins.* Chicago: University of Chicago Press, 1953.

Kolman, Eileen, and Don Hossler. "The Influence of Institutional Culture on Presidential Selection." *The Review of Higher Education* 10, no. 14 (Summer 1987): 319–332.

Ladd, Everett Karll, Jr., and Seymour Martin Lipset. *The Divided Academy: Professors and Politics.* New York: McGraw-Hill, 1975.

LaNoue, George R., and Barbara A. Lee. *Academics in Court: The Consequence of Faculty Discrimination Litigation.* Ann Arbor: University of Michigan Press, 1987.

————. "Lawsuits in Academe: Nobody Wins." *AGB Reports* 29, no. 1, (January–February 1987): 38–42.

Lester, Virginia. "Sunshine Hurts My Eyes." Paper delivered at AGB Annual Meeting, San Francisco, April 1990.

Levi, Edward H. "Address before the Association of the Bar of the City of New York," April 28, 1975.

Linsky, Martin. *How the Press Affects Federal Policymaking: Six Case Studies.* New York: W. W. Norton & Company, 1986.

Lipset, Seymour Martin. "American Exceptionalism Reaffirmed." Address at Harvard University, November 7, 1988; published in *De Tocqueville Review* 10 (1989–1990): 3–36.

Lipset, Seymour Martin, and Everett Karll Ladd, eds. *Culture and Social Character: The Work of David Riesman Reviewed.* Glencoe, Illinois: The Free Press, 1961.

Little, Joseph W., and Thomas Tompkins. "Open Government Laws: An Insider's View." *The North Carolina Law Review* 53, no. 3 (February 1975): 451–489.

Lutz, Frank W. "The Deanship: Search and Screening Process." *Educational Record* 60, no. 3 (Summer 1979): 266–271.

Maccoby, Michael. *Why Work: Leading the New Generation.* New York: Simon & Schuster, 1988.

McFarland, Andrew S. *Common Cause: Lobbying in the Public Interest.* Chatham, New Jersey: Chatham House, 1984.

McGuigan, Patrick B. *The Politics of Direct Democracy in the 1980s: Case Studies in Popular Decision-Making.* Washington, D.C.: Institute for Government and Politics of the Free Congress Research and Education Foundation, 1985.

McKenna, David L. "Recycling College Presidents." *Liberal Education* 57, no. 4 (December 1972): 456–463.

McLaughlin, Judith Block. "Confidentiality and Disclosure in the Presidential Search." Ph.D. diss., Harvard Graduate School of Education, 1983.

———. "From Secrecy to Sunshine: An Overview of Presidential Search Practice." *Research in Higher Education* 22, no. 2 (1985): 195–208.

———. "Plugging Search Committee Leaks." *AGB Reports* 27, no. 3 (May–June 1985): 24–30.

McLaughlin, Judith Block, and David Riesman. "The Shady Side of Sunshine." *Teachers College Record* 87, no. 4 (Summer 1986): 471–494. Reprinted in *Change* 21, no. 1 (January–February 1989): 45–57.

———. "Simplifying the Search: A Primer on the Use of Consultants in Presidential Recruitment." *Change* 16, no. 6 (September 1984): 12–23.

Mansbridge, Jane J. *Beyond Adversary Democracy.* New York: Basic Books, 1980.

March, James G. "How We Talk and How We Act: Administrative Theory and Administrative Life." The Seventh David D. Henry Lecture, University of Illinois, September 1980.

Marchese, Theodore J. "Search from the Candidate's Perspective: An interview with Maria M. Perez." *AAHE Bulletin* 42, no. 4 (December 1989): 3–5, 11–13.

Marchese, Theodore J., and Jane Fiori Lawrence. *The Search Committee Handbook: A Guide to Recruiting Administrators.* Washington, D.C.: AAHE, 1987.

Marchese, Theodore J., and Ruth Weintraub. "Searching for Talent: An Interview with Ruth G. Weintraub." *AAHE Bulletin* 36, no. 8 (April 1984): 3–6.

Meyer, Herbert E. "The Headhunters Come Upon Golden Days." *Fortune*, October 9, 1978.

Moll, Richard. *The Public Ivys: A Guide to America's Best Public Undergraduate Colleges and Universities.* New York: Viking, 1985.

362

Moore, Kathryn. *Women and Minorities, Leaders in Transition: A National Study of Higher Education Administrators.* Washington, D.C.: American Council on Education, 1984.

Moore, Kathryn, Ann M. Sanlimbene, Joyce D. Marlier, and Stephen M. Bragg. "The Structure of Presidents' and Deans' Careers." *Journal of Higher Education* 54, no. 5 (September–October 1983): 500–515.

Morrisett, Lloyd N. "Excellence on the High Wire: Why Oberlin Must Increase its Endowment per Student." *Oberlin Alumni Magazine,* Winter 1989.

Mottram, Richard. "Executive Search Firms as an Alternative to Search Committees." *Educational Record* 64, no. 1 (Winter 1983): 38–40.

Muller, Steven. "Great Men." *Science,* August 14, 1987.

Munitz, Barry, and Charles B. Neff. *The Business of Presidential Search.* Washington, D.C.: AGB Pocket Publication Series, no. 17, 1990.

Nason, John. *Presidential Assessment: A Guide to the Periodic Review of the Performance of Chief Executives.* Washington, D.C.: AGB, 1984.

Nason, John, with Nancy R. Axelrod. *Presidential Search: A Guide to the Process of Selecting and Appointing College and University Presidents,* rev. ed. Washington, D.C.: AGB, 1984.

Ness, Frederic W. *An Uncertain Glory.* San Francisco: Jossey-Bass, 1971.

————. "The Recruitment and Retention of Presidents." *AGB Reports* 13, no. 1 (September 1970): 3–17.

Orlans, Harold. "The Revolution at Gallaudet: Students Provoke Break with Past." *Change* 21, no. 1 (January–February 1989): 8–18.

Orren, Gary R. "Thinking about the Press and Government." In *The Press and Policymaking,* Martin Linsky, ed. New York: W. W. Norton, 1986.

Ostar, Roberta H. *Myths and Realities: 1983 Report on the AASCU Presidential Spouses.* Washington, D.C.: AASCU, 1983.

Ostar, Roberta H., ed. *The Partnership Model: A Family Perspective on College Presidency.* Washington, D.C.: AASCU, 1986.

Padden, Carol, and Tom Humphries. *Deaf in America: Voices from a Culture.* Cambridge, Massachusetts: Harvard University Press, 1988.

Pattillo, Manning M. "How to Choose a College President." *AGB Reports* 15, no. 5 (February 1973): 2–8.

Perlman, Daniel. "Paradoxes of the Presidency." *AAHE Bulletin* 42, no. 2 (October 1989): 3–6.

Phillips, Robert L. "Selecting the Academic Dean." *Educational Record* 50, no. 1 (Winter 1969): 66–70.

Porter, Earl W. "The Presidential Search as the Presidents See It." *AGB Reports* 25, no. 6 (November–December 1983): 43–47.

———. "Presidential Selection at Large State Universities." *AGB Reports* 24, no. 6 (November–December 1982): 40–43.

Rainsford, George N. "Presidential Transition." Unpublished paper, Lynchburg Virginia, May 23, 1984.

Ranslow, Paul Byers, and David Charles Haselkorn. "Bradford College: Curriculum Reform and Institutional Renewal." In *Opportunity in Adversity: How Colleges Can Succeed in Hard Times*, Janice S. Greene and Arthur Levine, eds. San Francisco: Jossey-Bass, 1985.

Rauh, Morton A. *The Trusteeship of Colleges and Universities.* New York: McGraw-Hill, 1969.

Reid, John Y., and Sharon J. Rogers. "Rumors and Reality: A Research Study of the Process of Selecting Provosts and Academic Vice Presidents." Prepared for the National Conference on Higher Education of the American Association of Higher Education, Washington, D.C., March 4–6, 1981.

Reinert, Paul C., S.J. "The Problem with Search Committees." *AGB Reports* 16, no. 7 (April 1974): 10–15.

Riesman, David. "The College Presidency." *Educational Studies* 13, nos. 3–4 (Fall–Winter 1982): 309–335.

———. "Conflicts between Confidentiality and Publicity in the Search Process for College and University Presidents." Talk to National Academy of Education meeting, Cambridge, Massachusetts, May 7, 1983.

———. *Constraint and Variety in American Education.* Lincoln: University of Nebraska Press, 1956.

———. "Epilogue: Refractions and Reflections." In *The President's Spouse: Volunteer or Volunteered?*, Joan E. Clodius and Diane Skomars Magrath, eds. Washington, D.C.: National Association of State Universities and Land Grant Colleges, 1984.

———. Foreword to *Is My Armor Straight? A Year in the Life of a University President*, by Richard Berendzen. Bethesda, Maryland: Adler & Adler, 1986.

———. *On Higher Education: The Academic Enterprise in an Era of Rising Student Consumerism.* San Francisco: Jossey-Bass, 1980.

———. "Orbits of Tolerance, Interviewers, and Elites." *Public Opinion Quarterly* 20 (1956): 49–73.

———. "The Personal Side of the Presidency." *AGB Reports* 24, no. 6 (November–December 1982): 35–39.

———. "The President's Spouse: The University's Added Dimension." In *The Proceedings of the 20th Annual Meeting: Great Expectations.* Washington, D.C.: AASCU, 1981.

————. "Selection Procedures for College and University Presidents: Search and Destroy Missions?" The 4th Reverend Charles F. Donovan, S.J., Lecture, sponsored by the School of Education, Boston College, 1983.

————. "Some Observations on Leadership in the Liberal Arts College." In *The Incarnate Imagination: Essays in Theology, the Arts, and Social Sciences in Honor of Andrew Greeley: A Festschrift*, Ingrid H. Shafer, ed. Bowling Green, Ohio: Bowling Green State University Popular Press, 1988.

————. "Some Personal Thoughts on the Academic Ethic." *Minerva* 21, nos. 2–3 (Summer–Autumn 1983): 265–284. Reprinted as "Academic Colleagueship and Teaching." *Antioch Review* 43, no. 4 (Fall 1985): 401–422.

————. "The Vulnerability of the Private Liberal Arts College." *Liberal Education* 73, no. 1 (January–February 1987): 37–39.

Riesman, David, and Sharon Elliott Fuller. "Leaders: Presidents Who Make a Difference." In *Opportunity in Adversity: How Colleges Can Succeed in Hard Times*, Janice S. Greene and Arthur Levine, eds. San Francisco: Jossey-Bass, 1985.

Riesman, David, Robert Potter, and Jeanne Watson. "Sociability, Permissiveness, and Equality: A Preliminary Formulation." *Psychiatry* 23, no. 4 (November, 1960): 196–225.

————. "The Vanishing Host." *Human Organization* 19, no. 1 (Spring 1960): 17–27.

Ritchie, M.A.F. *The College Presidency: Initiation into the Order of the Turtle*. New York: Philosophical Library, 1970.

Robinson, James A. "Lieutenants to Learning: A Bibliography of Participant-Observation by University Presidents." *Journal of Higher Education* 59, no. 3 (May–June 1988): 327–351.

Rosovsky, Henry. *The University: An Owner's Manual*. New York and London: W. W. Norton, 1990.

Rudolph, Frederick. *The American College and University: A History*. New York: Vintage Books, 1962.

Rupp, George. *Beyond Existentialism and Zen: Religion in a Pluralistic World*. New York: Oxford University Press, 1979.

Sacks, Oliver. *Seeing Voices: A Journey into the World of the Deaf*. Berkeley: University of California Press, 1989.

Sellery, Robert A., Jr. "How to Hire an Executive." *Business Horizons* 19, no. 2 (April 1976): 26–32.

Shaw, Kenneth A. "Presidential Search: What to Look For." *AGB Reports* 23, no. 5 (September–October 1981): 12–15.

Shils, Edward A. *The Torment of Secrecy: The Background and Consequences of American Security Policies*. Glencoe, Illinois: The Free Press, 1956.

Sibbald, John. *The Career Makers: America's Top 100 Executive Recruiters.* New York: Harper Business, 1990.

Sloper, D. W. "The Selection of Vice-Chancellors: The Australian Experience." *Higher Education Quarterly 43,* no. 32 (Summer 1989): 246–265.

Smith, Richard Norton. *The Harvard Century: The Making of a University to a Nation.* New York: Simon & Schuster, 1986.

Snow, C. P. *The Masters.* New York: Charles Scribner's Sons, 1951.

Sonnenfeld, Jeffrey. *The Hero's Welcome: What Happens When CEOs Retire.* New York: Oxford University Press, 1988.

Stadtman, Verne A. *The University of California, 1868–1968.* New York: McGraw-Hill, 1970.

Stauffer, Thomas M. "Selecting Academic Administrators." *Educational Record* 57, no. 3 (1977): 170–175.

Stead, Ronald S. "Presidential Search: Ensuring a Good Start." *AGB Reports* 29, no. 5 (September–October 1987): 14–18.

Stoke, Harold W. *The American College President.* New York: Harper and Brothers, 1959.

Stouffer, Samuel A. *Communism, Conformity, and Civil Liberties: A Cross-Section of the Nation Speaks its Mind.* New York: Doubleday, 1955.

Subcommittee of AAUP Committee A on Academic Freedom and Tenure. "On Open Meetings." *Academe* 72, no. 1 (January–February 1986): 3a–4a.

Taylor, Carol Smith. "Presidential Selection Procedures in Higher Education: Case Studies." Ph.D. diss., School of Education, University of Massachusetts, 1987.

Taylor, Steven J. "Observing Abuse: Professional Ethics and Personal Morality in Field Research." *Qualitative Sociology* 10, no. 3 (Fall 1987): 288–302.

Thernstrom, Abigail N. *Whose Votes Count: Affirmative Action and Minority Voting Rights.* Cambridge, Massachusetts: Harvard University Press, 1987.

Touchton, Judith G. " 'Maybe We Need a Search Firm?' Questions to Ask Yourself and Your Consultant." *AAHE Bulletin* 42, no. 4 (December 1989): 6–9.

Trow, Martin A. "Reorganizing the Biological Sciences at Berkeley." *Change* 15, no. 8 (November–December 1983): 28–53.

———. "The University Presidency: Comparative Reflections on Leadership." Ninth David D. Henry Lecture, University of Illinois at Urbana-Champaign, Urbana, Illinois, 1984.

Van Helden, Albert. "Guidelines for Membership of the Rice University Presidential Search Committee." Internal document, Rice University, 1984.

Van Wylen, Gordon J. *Vision for a Christian College.* Grand Rapids, Michigan: Wm. B. Eerdmans, 1988.

Vaughan, George B. *The Community College Presidency.* New York: American Council on Education/Macmillan Series on Higher Education, 1986.

Vaughan, George B., and Associates. *The Presidential Team: Perspectives on the Role of the Spouse.* Washington, D.C.: American Association of Community and Junior Colleges, 1987.

Veblen, Thorstein. *The Higher Learning in America: A Memorandum on the Conduct of Universities by Business Men.* New York: B. W. Huebsch, 1918. Republished with an introduction by David Riesman, Stanford, California: Academic Reprints, 1954.

Veysey, Laurence. *The Emergence of the American University.* Berkeley: University of California Press, 1965.

Walker, Donald E. *The Effective Administrator.* San Francisco: Jossey-Bass, 1979.

Weintraub, Ruth. "Selecting a President—Paths and Potholes." In *Beyond the Falling Sky*, Thomas M. Stauffer, ed. Washington, D.C.: American Council on Education, 1981.

Wharton, Clifton, Jr. "Autonomy in Academia: The State's Responsibility to Higher Education." Asquith Lecture, Harvard University, April 14, 1986.

White, John W., Jr. "Putting Together a Winning Presidential Team." *AGB Reports* 28, no. 4 (July–August 1986): 29–31.

Wilbur, Denise. "Presidential Transitions: How Important Are They to Administrative Success?" Paper presented at Annual Meeting of the American Educational Research Association, San Francisco, April 1989.

Williams, Glenn D. "The Search for Dr. Perfect." *AGB Reports* 18, no. 4 (July–August 1976): 39–43.

Wood, Gordon S. *The Creation of the American Republic, 1776–1787.* Chapel Hill, North Carolina: Published for the Institute of Early American History and Culture at Williamsburg, Virginia, by the University of North Carolina Press, 1969; reprinted New York: W. W. Norton, 1972.

Wood, Miriam Mason. *Trusteeship in the Private College.* Baltimore, Maryland: The Johns Hopkins University Press, 1985.

Wriston, Henry M. *Academic Procession: Reflections of a College President.* New York: Columbia University Press, 1959.

Young, Christine A. "Presidential Search: Setting Priorities." *AGB Reports* 29, no. 6 (November–December 1987): 13–18.

Zinser, Elisabeth. "Reflections on Revolution and Leadership by Surprise." *Educational Record* 69, no. 2 (Spring 1988): 22–25.

INDEX